Charles Carroll

FAITHFUL REVOLUTIONARY

Charles Carroll of Carrollton

FAITHFUL REVOLUTIONARY

Scott McDermott

Copyright © 2018 Scott McDermott

This is an edited and revised reprint of the book *Charles Carroll of Carrollton: Faithful Revolutionary*, originally published in 2002.

Second printing, 2004
Third printing, 2005

This edition, January 2018

The total or partial reproduction of this book is not permitted, nor its informatic treatment, or the transmission of any form or by any means, either electronic, mechanic, photocopy, or other methods without the prior written permission of the owners of the copyright.

Published by Scepter Publishers, Inc.
info@scepterpublishers.org
www.scepterpublishers.org
800-322-8773
New York

All rights reserved.

Library of Congress Cataloging-in-Publication Data

Names: McDermott, Scott, 1968- author.
Title: Charles Carroll of Carrollton : faithful revolutionary / Scott McDermott
Description: New York : Scepter Publishers, 2018. | "Edited and revised reprint of the book Charles Carroll of Carrollton: Faithful Revolutionary, originally published in 2002." | Includes bibliographical references and index.
Identifiers: LCCN 2018002815 (print) | LCCN 2018002919 (ebook) | ISBN 9781594173189 (eBook) | ISBN 9781594173127 (pbk. : alk. paper)
Subjects: LCSH: Carroll, Charles, 1737-1832. | Statesmen--United States--Biography. | Catholics--United States--Biography. | United States. Declaration of Independence--Signers--Biography. | United States--Politics and government--1783-1865. | Maryland--Politics and government--1775-1865.
Classification: LCC E302.6.C3 (ebook) | LCC E302.6.C3 M34 2018 (print) | DDC 973.3092 [B] --dc23
LC record available at https://lccn.loc.gov/2018002815

ISBN: 9781594173127 Paperback
ISBN: 9781594173189 eBook

PRINTED IN THE UNITED STATES OF AMERICA

For Judge William R. Baker, 1932-2013
duc in altum

Contents.

ACKNOWLEDGMENTS. ~ 11
PREFACE. ~ 13

Part I. Exile.

The Origins of the English Reformation ~ 18
Lord Baltimore's Experiment ~ 21
The Plundering Begins ~ 25
The "Glorious Revolution" ~ 27
1715 ~ 30
Building an Empire ~ 33
St. Omers ~ 36
"Aut Caesar Aut Nullus" ~ 39
Suarez and Montesquieu ~ 42
The Persecution Revives ~ 46
France Expels the Jesuits ~ 49
Carrolls and Calverts ~ 51
"We Live in the World" ~ 53
The Common Law ~ 58
Bereavement ~ 60
Marriage Negotiations ~ 63

Part II. First Citizen.

Parliamentary Tyranny ~ 67
The Saxon Myth ~ 69
The Mental Revolution ~ 70
The Republican Empire Stirs ~ 73
The Mercantile System ~ 75
The Spirit of Liberty ~ 78
The Habit of Business ~ 80
Labor, Free and Unfree ~ 83
Marriage ~ 85
The Search for Harmony ~ 89
Deadly Potential ~ 92

The Townshend Acts ~ 94
The Fee Controversy ~ 97
The Challenger Scores ~ 99
The Champion Retaliates ~ 101
The Contest Continues ~ 104
The Tea Act ~ 108
The First Continental Congress ~ 110
The Peggy Stewart ~ 112

Part III. Revolutionary.

The Provisional Government of Maryland ~ 115
The Council of Safety ~ 117
Sense and Sensibility ~ 120
North Meets South ~ 122
"CX" ~ 125
The Quebec Act ~ 126
The Canadian Campaign ~ 128
The Canadian Commission ~ 131
The Journey to Canada ~ 133
The Commissioners Take Charge ~ 136
Maryland Declares Independence ~ 140
Carroll the Signer ~ 143
The Maryland Line ~ 146
Planters vs. Populists ~ 148
The Maryland Constitution ~ 150
The New Government Begins ~ 154
The Tender Law ~ 157
The Irish Presence ~ 159
Saratoga ~ 161
Valley Forge ~ 163
The French Alliance ~ 166

Part IV. Senator.

The Depreciation of Congress ~ 169
Interest: Private vs. Public ~ 171
The Articles of Confederation ~ 173

Domestic Crisis ~ 174
Tory Confiscations ~ 176
The March 1780 Assembly ~ 179
The Army Struggles ~ 180
The Arnold Treason ~ 182
Greene Takes Over ~ 183
The War Comes to Maryland ~ 185
The Dog in the Manger ~ 187
Yorktown ~ 188
Peace ~ 190
Rapprochement with Great Britain ~ 194
The Constitutional Convention ~ 196
The Maryland Ratifying Convention ~ 201
The First United States Senate ~ 203
Freedom of Religion ~ 206
The Private Sector ~ 209
The Slavery Question ~ 212
Foreign Entanglements ~ 213
The Adams Administration ~ 214
The Jeffersonian Revolution ~ 216

Part V. Patriarch.

Religious Seeking ~ 219
Homewood House ~ 221
The American Narcissus ~ 223
The Education of Women ~ 226
Burr ~ 228
Embargo ~ 230
Families Divided ~ 232
The War of 1812 ~ 235
Decline of the Heir ~ 237
The Three Graces ~ 240
Two Grandsons ~ 243
Slavery Questions ~ 244
Manifest Destiny ~ 246
Family Tragedy and Triumph ~ 248
John H. B. Latrobe ~ 252

Rehabilitation ~ 254
August 2, 1826 ~ 256
Democracy in America ~ 258
Last of the Romans ~ 260

NOTES ~ 263
WORKS CITED ~ 333
INDEX ~ 343

Acknowledgments.

Thanks, first of all, to my coworkers at the Walker Management Library, especially Sylvia Graham and Carol McCrary. They covered for me while I was away doing research and supported my project throughout. Thanks also to my current colleagues at the Vanderbilt Divinity Library for their support and encouragement.

My colleagues in the Interlibrary Loan Department of the Jean and Alexander Heard Library of Vanderbilt University, including Jim Toplon, Merry Balthrop, and Marilyn Pilley, obtained invaluable materials for me. So did my friends at Vanderbilt's Annex Library, especially Peggy Earheart and Joe Collins.

I would also like to thank the Heard Library Administration for keeping so many excellent and obscure sources in their print collection. The presence of the *Archives of Maryland* and other resources on the Vanderbilt campus saved me several trips to Baltimore.

Judith Proffitt at Homewood House graciously arranged a tour of the house and provided copies of letters from the Chew Family Papers; I am grateful. Thanks to Dani Diehlman, who gave up her Sunday afternoon to show me the Charles Carroll House in Annapolis. I appreciate the staff of the Maryland Historical Society for reference assistance, especially Francis O'Neill and Robert Bartram.

Thanks to Ann Van Devanter Townsend for her pioneering work in Carroll studies and for her gracious assistance in tracking down Carroll family portraits. Thanks also to Charles Carroll Carter and Rosemary Carter for their enthusiasm, encouragement, hospitality, and helpful suggestions.

Many people helped in the process of gathering photographs for the book, including Catherine Arthur at Homewood House; Joyce Edmonston at the Carroll House in Annapolis; Nancy Press and S. Revak at the Baltimore Museum of Art; Tom Evans at the National Graphic Center; Dr. Barbara A. Wolanin, Curator for the Architect of the Capitol; the Hon. Alan M. Hantman, Architect of the Capitol; Betty Cohen in the United States Senate Historical Office; Clare Colgrove and Jamie Arbolino in the United States Office of Senate Curator; Suzanne Warner, Melissa Gold, and Susan Brady of Yale University; Dr. Edward Papenfuse, Dr. R. J. Rockefeller, Michelle Kloss, and Dr. Mark Tacyn of the Maryland State Archives; Marico Iida of the Frick Art Reference Library; James Kilvington at the National Portrait Gallery, United Kingdom; Lucile Walker, David Alan, and Nicholas Scheetz of Georgetown University; the Sisters of the Good Shepherd; Mrs. Eleanor Schapiro; John Hawk, Fr. Michael Kotlanger, and Courtney Conley of the Gleeson Library at the University of San Francisco; seemingly the entire staff of the Maryland Historical Society, including Mary Markey, Mary Herbert, Jennifer Bryan, Paul Rubenson, Donna Williams, David Prencipe, Donald Renaud, Mimi Calver, and Ruth Mitchell; and Philip Carroll.

Sally Mason and Ronald Hoffman courteously replied to my queries. I highly recommend their work of many years to all students of the Carrolls.

The staff of the Manuscript Division Reading Room at the Library of Congress and the Manuscripts and Archives Division of the New York Public Library were helpful. So were my former colleagues at Olin Library of Cornell University.

I would also like to compliment the staff of the Mt. Vernon Hotel in Baltimore.

Thanks to Steve Walsh and Rev. John Sims Baker for reading chapters of the work. I was sustained in the project by my friends, associates, and family, in the United States and in France, who asked questions and offered encouragement. You know who you are; I sincerely thank you.

I owe special thanks to John Powers of Scepter Press. Perhaps he will make me a writer yet.

And, of course, Judge Bill Baker made this book possible. It is dedicated to him.

Preface.

I am grateful to Scepter Publishers for making *Charles Carroll of Carrollton* available once again in a paperback edition. Never has Carroll's political wisdom been more sorely needed, as the American political landscape has changed since the book first appeared in 2002.

Then, the unity that prevailed in the wake of the 9/11 terrorist attacks had only just begun to unravel. Sixteen years later, we see evidence that Americans are more polarized than ever before, as evidenced by the deadly violence that erupted in Charlottesville, Virginia, in August 2017.

What would Carroll have thought of such events? They had parallels in his time. A riot in 1812 between Federalists and Jeffersonian Democrats in his own city of Baltimore led to a mob attack on Revolutionary war veterans. The targets were not shielded by their Revolutionary credentials. The mob broke into a house where they had sought protection together, killed an aged war hero, and injured a former Revolutionary general. That general was the father of a five-year-old boy, Robert E. Lee.

Carroll feared that the liberty earned by the Revolution and then enshrined in the Constitution could eventually turn into license. "A government of laws and not of men" proclaimed by John Adams could be replaced by the politics of the will, a kind of majority of the moment. But it could also turn back to what its Founders had intended.

Is it much different today? Would people think the country was about to dissolve if the vice president of the United States shot the leader of the opposition party? And this took place only sixteen years after the country began. The Republic has seen numerous examples of outrageous behavior, yet it still carries on. And those who think there can be no recovery from the legal protection given to same-sex marriage and abortion should remember that the government managed to end more than two hundred years of the violation of natural rights in the form of human slavery.

In pre-Revolutionary Maryland, Carroll could not vote or hold public office. But he boldly stepped into the independence movement at a time when others were afraid to take a stand. As a consequence, he became one of the most influential leaders of the movement. In 1827, at age ninety, he recalled that "to obtain religious as well as civil liberty, I entered zealously into the Revolution." With that step, he was elected to the Continental Congress and became the only Catholic signer of the Declaration of Independence. The end of his life set another record: he was the last signer to survive, dying at age nintey-five in 1832.

Carroll's life in politics us shows that history is not the inexorable process of superhuman forces. Leaders always make a difference. Along with Washington, Adams, and others who worked in the common cause of independence, Carroll played his part. In his case, it was the wealthy heir who risked fortune and life to protect the two most important freedoms we have, religious and political. His life provides ample lessons to inspire modern-day men and women of faith to risk themselves in the public square.

Scott McDermott, Assistant Professor of History
Albany State University, Albany, Georgia

Life was given us—to live.

Charles Carroll of Carrollton
*urging James McHenry to come out of retirement and
put his talents to work for the common good*

PART I.

Exile.

CHARLES CARROLL of Carrollton came into the world doubly stigmatized. He was born on September 19, 1737, to Charles Carroll of Annapolis and Elizabeth Brooke. The elder Carroll was one of the two richest men in Maryland, and a Roman Catholic. Carroll for many years refused to marry Elizabeth Brooke legally. He feared that if he were to die first, Elizabeth would take the Carroll fortune into another man's family. And he wanted to test his son before granting him the inheritance.

Thus, not only did Carroll of Carrollton's religion place him within one of the most persecuted groups in the British Empire but his contemporaries saw him as a bastard, in the literal meaning of that term. A Frenchman who visited Annapolis in 1765 noted that the elder Carroll "has no family, only a b. [bastard] son who he intends to make his sole heir." Fifty years later, a Maryland society matron, Rosalie Stier Calvert, wrote that "Carroll is an illegitimate son."

Carroll was born in his father's imposing house in Annapolis. This tall, plain structure still holds a commanding view of the Spa Creek harbor. From the house, the water looks very close, but from the creek the mansion appears to be set well back, surrounded by a huge expanse of lawn. The Carrolls, clever and ambitious, planned it that way.

At some point, though, the patriarch sent Elizabeth and their son into exile at Doughoregan Manor, near Elk Ridge. This manor now stands in the Baltimore suburbs, not far from Baltimore/Washington International Airport, but then it was remote. Carroll would later remember "those happy days spent at Elk Ridge in her sweet company, our lonely retreat and mutual fondness." Carroll was isolated from other boys of his age and class. A small army of slaves, who no doubt pampered him, were his companions. It is not surprising that the boy grew inordinately attached to his mother. Elizabeth Brooke's portrait and her surviving letters reveal a beautiful, feminine, gentle woman. In her solitude, she doted on her only son.

Carroll of Annapolis was also a loner. According to the French visitor, his contemporaries viewed him as "the most moneyed man in Maryland but at the same time the most avaricious." Carroll's outspoken Catholicism, too, made him disagreeable to the Protestant gentry of Maryland. The elder Carroll was deeply bitter about his family's treatment at the hands of the Protestant majority. Maryland had been founded by a Catholic as a refuge for people of all religions. But in one of the great ironies of American history, militant Protestants, who had come to the colony for asylum, usurped the government and deprived Catholics of their rights.

The Origins of the English Reformation

The Carrolls were Irish noblemen, descended from the O'Carrolls, chiefs of Ely. In 1552, Teige O'Carroll was named Lord Baron of Ely by King Edward VI.

They remained faithful to the great tradition of Irish Catholicism. The mind of the Church had always emphasized that the object of politics is the common good. Christianity substituted the *ius naturale*, natural law, for the Imperial Roman, Stoic emphasis on the prerogatives of individuals. The *ius* was an objective, right ordering of society. During the Catholic era, the great monasteries in Great Britain and Ireland supported the poor. The Church also checked the power of the Crown, providing the beginnings of a mixed constitution. It declared that any law that conflicted with the natural law was null and void. "A law has as much force as it has justice," wrote St. Thomas Aquinas. "If, however, in some point it conflicts with the law of nature it will no longer be law but rather a perversion of law."

Toward the end of the Middle Ages, some Catholic thinkers began taking Catholic thought in a more individualistic direction. William of Ockham argued that only the individual has a real existence. His ideas, and those of John Duns Scotus, tended to revive the Stoic politics of will. Thus, when Henry VIII became infatuated with Anne Boleyn, these ideas were at hand to justify his actions. When the Pope refused to grant him a divorce, Henry, substituting his own will for divine law, declared himself the supreme head of the Church in England.

William Tyndale supplied the theory behind this move by inventing the divine right of kings. This concept is often mistakenly associated with Catholicism, because its most strident advocate was the Catholic King James II. In fact, the divine right of kings goes against the entire Catholic tradition. The Church has always taught that sovereignty is delegated by God with the consent of the people. The people bestow sovereignty when a new political system comes into being, and they have the power to revoke their grant of sovereignty if their rulers behave tyrannically. A tyrant deserves to be deposed, wrote St. Thomas: "Since he had not acted faithfully in discharging the royal office, so the covenant made by his subjects might likewise not be kept." But Tyndale held that the King's mandate comes directly from God, without any mediation through the pope or the people.

Henry VIII seized the lands and treasures of the Church. By distributing this booty among the nobility, he was able to create a class of people who were financially interested in the Reformation. These men, in turn, brought the Protestant Elizabeth to power. Elizabeth's reign was the heyday of the persecution of Catholics. She encouraged those professional informers, the *pursuivants*, whom David Hume defined as "a kind of harpies." The *pursuivants* became rich by betraying their neighbors for offenses against the state religion.

The Tudors also invented the policy of "surrender and regrant," which brought the great Irish estates under English control. The landlords had to surrender their lands to the monarch, who returned them on feudal terms, making the landlords royal vassals. King James I seized the O'Carroll family lands under this policy in 1615. When the O'Carrolls joined a 1641 rebellion, Charles I degraded them further, to tenants at pleasure. Under "surrender and regrant," Irish Catholic landholdings fell from fifty-nine percent in 1641 to twenty-two percent in 1688, and to fourteen percent in 1703. When the Declaration of Independence was signed, only five percent of Irish land remained in Catholic hands.

Pope Pius V excommunicated Elizabeth in 1570. His bull *Regnans in Excelsis* absolved all Englishmen of allegiance to her and could even be construed as supporting her assassination. Thus, all Catholics were seen as potential traitors. Anyone being reconciled to the Catholic Church, or reconciling others, was subject to the horrifying penalties of high treason. English students in continental seminaries were also attainted of treason. By 1593, convicted Catholics could travel no more than five miles from their homes, at the risk of losing all goods, lands, and annuities for life. Nor could they own a horse worth more than five pounds. The Mass was prohibited. On one occasion, Parliament came near to requiring that all Catholic children be taken from their parents at age seven and raised by Protestants.

There were other acts as well. But the rigor of their execution was softened by the fact that Elizabeth's successor, James I, became financially dependent on recusancy fines, the penalties Catholics had to pay for not attending Anglican services. To eliminate the Catholic community entirely would have killed the goose that was laying the golden eggs. Nevertheless, periodic outbreaks of anti-Catholic hysteria resulted in new hangings, drawings, and quarterings until the public rage was satisfied.

Responding to divine-right theory, the Jesuit St. Robert Bellarmine clarified the position of the Church. Bellarmine insisted that sovereignty could be established only by the consent of the people. On the other hand, all law, as "a participation of the eternal law," binds on pain of sin. But when a human law conflicts with divine law, it ceases to be law and ceases to bind. This does not mean that law should be based upon public opinion; to the contrary, human law is the application of the natural law to particular cases. But when the arbitrary will of a ruler—whether an individual or a group of men—creates tyranny, the covenant between ruler and ruled ceases to exist. Divine grace cannot be the only title to power. Because grace is inscrutable, "no claim to such power would be certain."

Part I: Exile

The Stuarts, however, made divine-right theory their own. King James I called Bellarmine's defense of popular sovereignty "an excellent ground in divinity for all rebels and rebellious people." Interestingly, this placed Catholics and Puritans in a temporary alliance during the seventeenth century. They routinely quoted each other's political writings. "Jesuits are nothing but Puritan-Papists," declared James I.

Sometimes diplomatic pressures from the continent of Europe would improve the lot of English Catholics. King James freed more than four thousand Catholics from prison while trying to win the hand of a Spanish princess for his son. A key figure in these negotiations was Sir George Calvert, a member of the King's Privy Council. As a secret Catholic, Calvert must have rejoiced when James promised the Spaniards that he would stop enforcing the penal laws. But the negotiations failed. When James placed Calvert on a commission to punish recusant Catholics, Sir George announced his Catholicism publicly. Accepting Calvert's resignation, James elevated him to the Irish peerage as Lord Baltimore.

Lord Baltimore's Experiment

In spite of this magnanimous gesture, Baltimore knew that his sovereign could not be trusted. James later told the French that he would stop enforcing the penal laws if they would marry Princess Henrietta Maria to his son Charles. But as soon as the deal was closed, James repudiated his offer of amnesty for Catholics. Soon after his reception into the Church, around 1625, Lord Baltimore began planning a colony for English Catholic refugees.

Baltimore decided to plant his colony, which he called "Avalon," on Newfoundland. King James gave him very generous terms. The Avalon charter granted Baltimore a palatinate, a state within a state. As proprietor, Baltimore had extensive vice-regal powers. But the most significant feature of the charter was its promise to uphold "God's Holy and True Religion," without mentioning the Church of England. What this phrase meant was open to multiple interpretations.

In practice, it meant religious toleration of a sort enjoyed nowhere in the Western world. Baltimore brought both Protestant and Catholic clergy to Avalon, where they celebrated their separate rites under the same roof. This Arcadian situation was soon disrupted. A Puritan minister notified Plymouth Colony magistrates that there were "Popish doings" at Avalon. Baltimore resolved to try again farther south. He obtained a charter from the new King, Charles I, for a colony on the Chesapeake. He named it Maryland after Queen Henrietta Maria. The Avalon colony continued; it paid tribute to Maryland until just before the American Revolution.

Like Moses, Baltimore never saw his promised land. He died in 1632 and was buried, according to the law, in an Anglican church. The new Lord Baltimore, Cecil Calvert, maintained his father's Catholicism and his religious tolerance. The second Baltimore commanded Catholics "to be silent upon all occasions of discourse concerning matters of religion" during the voyage to Maryland. Their religious devotions were to take place privately. Baltimore had to be careful about offending Virginia, which claimed the land that he was about to occupy. He was also convinced that the essence of Christianity was God's commandment "to love one another."

Baltimore asked all Maryland governors to swear that they would never "trouble, molest or discountenance" any Christian for religious reasons. Public office should be awarded based on moral virtue and not religious profession. The governors also had to promise to promote "public unity." If anyone should trouble any other person on account of religion, they were to defend the victim and punish his persecutor. The elected assembly of Maryland upheld these provisions in its 1649 Religious Toleration Act.

Religious tolerance was vigorously enforced. In 1638, a group of Protestant servants sued their Catholic overseer, William Lewis. Lewis had objected forcefully when a Protestant preacher called the pope and the Jesuits the Antichrist. After a Jesuit, Fr. Copley, took the Protestants' side, Lewis was fined five hundred pounds of tobacco. The same fine was levelled against Thomas Gerard in 1642 for locking up a Protestant chapel and hiding the key. A 1649 law imposed triple damages on anyone who wronged another on account of religion. It was forbidden to call anyone: heretic, schismatic, Idolator, puritan, Independent, Presbyterian, popish priest, Jesuit, Jesuited papist, Lutheran, Calvinist, Anabaptist, Brownist, Antinomian, Barrowist, Roundhead, Separatist, or any other name or term in a reproachful manner relating to matter of religion."

Nearly all the Maryland priests were Jesuits. Lord Baltimore could not openly assist them, because the Society of Jesus was demonized in England, so the priests had to support themselves through agriculture. The Maryland Jesuits ran their own plantations and, as a matter of course, held slaves. This arrangement suited the fathers, who had little interest in parish ministry. Most were attracted to Maryland by the opportunity to evangelize Native Americans. Others served as domestic chaplains to the gentry.

One of the first actions of the Maryland Assembly, however, was to require the Jesuits to serve as pastors to the general public. Gradually, the fathers grew to like this ministry. Their unique devotional practices, which cultivated fervor without emotionalism, deeds rather than words, took root in the colony. This was in keeping with the new Catholic outlook in England, which emphasized personal conversion over public militancy.

The Maryland charter contained several striking features that proved important in later political crises. Unlike the Avalon charter, it provided that the "ecclesiastical laws of England" would be upheld. This was inserted to throw militant Protestants off the scent of Catholic activities in Maryland. Under English law, however, written technicalities were not very important, and the proprietor had wide latitude in enforcing the charter. Marylanders were granted all the rights of freeborn Englishmen, as "natives and liege-men" of the Crown. Their laws would require the assent of the proprietor rather than the King. In a last striking concession, the English government promised never to impose any "importation, custom or other taxation, rate or contribution, whatsoever."

In theory, then, the proprietor enjoyed an almost unlimited authority. But Lord Baltimore stipulated that he would only use his power of legislation "of and with the advice, consent and approbation of the freemen" in the assembly. This backfired on Baltimore when the legislature rejected his first slate of laws, in 1637. The assembly demanded the right to initiate all legislation. Baltimore gave in, but he retained extensive powers. He could propose legislation through his council, exercise a veto, control the elections, and dissolve the assembly. The proprietor could also make ordinances on any matter that did not affect property rights, as long as his laws were "consonant to reason."

As the legal head of the Church in Maryland, Baltimore was entitled to collect "patronages and advowsons," but he declined to do so. With the religious issue off limits, the assembly found little need for lawmaking. Early Maryland legislation barely mentions religion, in contrast to the voluminous law codes compiled in Massachusetts Bay. Because Lord Baltimore did not require assemblymen to swear oaths, Quakers could take an active political role. Other sects, such as the Hussites, were also welcomed. A Jew, Dr. Jacob Lumbrozo, exercised the rights of a citizen, even sitting on a jury in the 1660s.

Maryland's separation of church and state went well beyond what William Penn advocated in Pennsylvania. And Rhode Island's much-vaunted religious tolerance specifically excluded Catholics. A 1664 act that denied Catholics the vote was finally repealed when the French navy arrived in Newport during the American Revolution. Papists and Quakers, said Rhode Island founder Roger Williams, "are both spitting and belching out fire from one fire of Hell."

Baltimore's tolerance and his open-door policy to Protestants were criticized, even by his own clergy. Fr. Andrew White, the "Apostle of Maryland," noted with some disgust in 1641 that three-quarters of the settlers were heretics. Baltimore's tolerance created the potential for religious conflict in Maryland. But under the circumstances, his neutral approach to religion was the only way to preserve any rights at all for the Catholic Church.

Part I: Exile

The Plundering Begins

Before long, Lord Baltimore's universal tolerance allowed the serpent to spoil his ecumenical paradise.

During the English Civil War, Puritans in Parliament cited the natural law against Charles I's divine-right theory. When war broke out in 1642, Maryland found itself caught between Puritans in Massachusetts Bay and royalist Cavaliers in Virginia. After Massachusetts refused to trade with Maryland, Lord Baltimore invited all religious dissenters in Massachusetts to take refuge in his colony. Similarly, in 1648, four to six hundred Virginia dissenters accepted Baltimore's offer of asylum.

Baltimore's policy of luring settlers away did not endear him to his powerful southern neighbor. A Virginia Cavalier, Captain Claiborne, had mounted an unsuccessful naval assault against Maryland in 1634. Claiborne resented losing Kent Island, where he had established a trading post, to the new colony. Now, in 1644, Claiborne joined forces with a Puritan, Richard Ingle, and invaded Maryland, seizing control. The Claiborne occupation became known as the "plundering time." Driven out, Claiborne returned again in 1655, deposing the governor and depriving Catholics of the vote. But Oliver Cromwell, the English Lord Protector, restored the proprietor and commanded Claiborne's party "not to busy themselves about religion."

Lord Baltimore, characteristically, pardoned the insurgents. One of Cecil Calvert's last acts as proprietor was to renew the Toleration Act in 1674. He left a potentially explosive situation for his son, Charles Calvert, the third Lord Baltimore, to deal with. Protestants had acquired an electoral majority in the colony. They controlled the council and the governor's office by 1649. Puritans, as well as numerous freed servants and men without property, enjoyed the franchise. In 1650, Governor William Stone and his colleagues penned a "Protestant Declaration," which attested that they enjoyed full freedom.

Charles II's restoration in 1661 did nothing to relieve English Catholics; if anything, the situation worsened. The fabricated "popish plot" of Titus Oates created another temporary reign of terror. As a result, the Catholic interest in Maryland retrenched. Catholic relatives of the proprietor held a majority in the council after 1669. In the same year, the lower house of the assembly, the House of Delegates, complained that the proprietor and the council were removing laws from the statute book, imposing excessive taxation, and abusing the veto power. (The proprietor could exercise a pocket veto by refusing to assent to acts of assembly.) The council responded defensively, creating new offices for Calvert kin and restricting the electoral franchise.

The third Lord Baltimore offended the assembly in 1676 when he appointed Cecilius Calvert, a minor, as governor. Although that year's assembly affirmed the historic religious toleration of Maryland, proprietary mismanagement continued to do damage. In England, a cabal of peers was conspiring to exclude Charles II's Catholic brother, the Duke of York, from the succession. The proprietary party in Maryland responded by adopting more and more the divine-right language of the Stuarts. They indulged themselves in Restoration grandeur, being carried by liveried lackeys through the streets of Annapolis in sedan chairs.

Jealousy among Protestant gentry and poor whites increased. In 1677, a discontented Anglican, Rev. Yeo, started a movement to strengthen the Church of England in the colony. There were only three Anglican ministers in Maryland at that time, and all were notoriously lax. Lord Baltimore expressed support for an increased Anglican presence, but he balked at establishing the Church of England as the state religion, on the very reasonable grounds that most Maryland Protestants were dissenters. The citizens would not support ministers of other persuasions with their taxes. Baltimore also refused to appoint a commission to inquire into the religious practices of Marylanders, fearing it would disturb the peace.

The Anglicans began agitating for direct royal rule. They wanted to impose the oaths of allegiance and supremacy, which Catholics could not take in good conscience, upon all officeholders. The Puritans, for their part, developed scruples about tolerating the Mass in the colony. They worried that allowing

Popish worship would saddle them with the "guilt of permission." This anxiety produced the anti-Catholic document known as the "Complaint from Heaven with a Hue and Cry."

THE "GLORIOUS REVOLUTION"

This was the hornet's nest onto which the first Charles Carroll, known as Charles Carroll the Settler, stumbled. Carroll the Settler was a lawyer, having studied at London's Inner Temple. According to family tradition, the Settler had high hopes for Catholic emancipation when the Duke of York obtained his throne as James II. But Lord Powis, the Settler's mentor, warned him that "affairs are going on very badly; the king is very ill-advised." Powis, who had spent six years in the Tower after the Titus Oates hoax, spoke to Lord Baltimore on Carroll's behalf. On July 18, 1688, the Settler was appointed attorney-general of Maryland.

During his voyage, Carroll changed his family's motto. It had been *In fide et in bello forte*—"Strong in faith and in war." Henceforward the Carroll motto would be *Ubicumque cum libertate*: "Anywhere so long as there be freedom."

Unfortunately, as Carroll of Carrollton later recalled, "My grandfather was destined to experience, even in the asylum he had selected, the evils of that religious persecution from which he had so recently fled." The Settler presented his credentials in Maryland on October 13, 1688; two weeks later, James II was deposed in the Glorious Revolution.

During this crisis, Parliament invoked the principles of natural law, as they had in 1642. But by this time, secular thinkers had pushed the concept of natural law further and further in the direction of self-interest and individual will. The Dutch jurist Hugo Grotius said that "the first principle of the natural order...is the love whose primary force and action are toward oneself." Grotius claimed that "by nature it is our right to do all things that are not evil in themselves." Samuel von Pufendorf associated natural law so closely with self-preservation that it seemed to collapse into the desires of the individual. The concept of popular sovereignty, too, was being used to support the politics of will, by such men as Roger Williams. As David Hume insisted in his *History of England*, the revolutionaries of 1688 simply made a new constitution out of public opinion.

The Glorious Revolution also threatened the English mixed constitution. As long as Parliament, which desired sovereignty, was pitted against an absolutist king, there was some balance in the government. But Charles I had already admitted that "the King in Parliament" had supreme power. After the 1688 Parliament awarded the throne to William and Mary, mixed government became a nostalgic fiction. King and Parliament were welded together as a unitary sovereign. From that point forward, the monarchy could influence Parliament only through corruption.

When hostilities began, in 1688, the Maryland Council showed how out of touch it had become by congratulating Baltimore on raising a troop of horse for King James. In fact, Lord Baltimore saw which way the wind was blowing. He dispatched a messenger to proclaim William and Mary in his colony, but the emissary died en route. Meanwhile, Protestant dissidents whipped up opposition to the proprietor. They spread rumors that Maryland Catholics were conspiring with the Native Americans against Protestants. Boatloads of Irish were said to be on the way over, to cut Protestant throats. After drawing up an indictment against Baltimore, the Protestants seized power, on the pretext that the proprietor refused to acknowledge the new King and Queen. The revolutionaries soon moved the government from St. Mary's City to Annapolis.

The Glorious Revolution crushed all the aspirations of the English Catholic community. A few embittered noblemen joined the pro-Stuart Jacobite opposition. In Maryland, Carroll the Settler was deprived of his new office. So were all Roman Catholics, and even, the Settler claimed, all "honest" Protestants "that refuse to join with them in their irregularities." He was not the sort of man to take this lying down, and his resistance earned him physical punishment, "a hard seasoning of which I am now, thank God, almost recovered." The Settler was in and out of jail between 1691 and 1694 for various "high misdemeanors" against the new regime.

Part I: Exile

Carroll was far from destitute, however. Lord Baltimore, deprived of his public role, still maintained a considerable private establishment in the colony. The Settler retained his status as chief attorney in this private organization. He also received huge tracts of land in the colony. The ex-proprietor insisted that Carroll live near his estate in order to keep him company. The Settler had a guaranteed income of fifty pounds a year, more than the average planter, as well as numerous perquisites from his legal activities.

Carroll the Settler was certainly better off than the rest of his family. His grandfather Anthony Carroll had been killed fighting for the Stuarts in Europe during the 1650s. The Settler's brother Thomas died at the Battle of the Boyne on July 12, 1690. Another brother and a nephew were also involved in the Jacobite resistance, finally surrendering to the authorities. Almost all of the Settler's near relatives eventually found their way to America; by 1750, only three remained in Ireland.

The Settler always kept his Irish identity and made it his project to bring as many Irish to Maryland as possible, in spite of taxes designed to discourage Irish immigration. He demanded that his son, Carroll of Annapolis, style himself "Marylando-Hibernus" while studying in France. Carroll of Annapolis, in turn, lectured his own son about "the duty all Irishmen owe to the glory and honour of their country." The third Charles Carroll, however, chafed at his father's Irish victim consciousness. Declining to visit Ireland, Carrollton mused, "how unavailing to remember what we cannot revenge! How melancholy to behold ancient, noble, and once flourishing families reduced to beggary!"

The Protestant Revolution, as it was called in Maryland, finally brought the colony a religious establishment. Despite being a small minority, the Church of England became the state religion, bringing with it a tax of forty pounds of tobacco per capita. The assembly failed, however, in its attempt to make attendance at Anglican services compulsory. King William, not wishing to grant all the rights of Englishmen to the colonists, twice vetoed an act of assembly that declared all English laws to be in force in Maryland. But Maryland had become just as addicted to meddling with religion as the other colonial governments. Only in 1693, 1703, 1711, and 1716 were no laws concerning religion passed under the Protestant establishment.

Governor Lionel Copley congratulated the state on having escaped the "arbitrary will and pleasure of a tyrannical Popish government." Now the Protestant government sought to impose its will and pleasure on Catholics in the form of penal laws. The 1704 "Act to Prevent the Growth of Popery" levied fines of £250 sterling, or six months in prison, for converting Protestants or celebrating Mass in public. Catholic schoolmasters were liable to banishment. Parents who sent their children to European seminaries were fined and deprived of their right to purchase or inherit land. Catholics managed to salvage their right to hear Mass in private homes. The assembly agreed to permit private Masses for eighteen months, until the new Queen, Anne, expressed her pleasure. Anne's "Suspending Act" confirmed this privilege.

Aside from the heavy tithes, the Protestant Marylanders were disappointed in royal rule. All acts now required the Crown's approval, and for the first time the assembly was officially subject to Parliament. English administrations turned a deaf ear to the colonists' attempts to invoke their charter rights. As the eighteenth century progressed, therefore, the assembly increasingly cited not just the charter, but also natural law theory. "It is we that are the people's representatives," they asserted in 1725, "for whom all laws are made and human government established." The legislators also quoted the Bill of Rights produced during the Glorious Revolution. After George I came to the throne in 1715, the assembly generally managed to circumvent the process of royal approval.

1715

Lord Baltimore's beautiful experiment had been destroyed. The Church was driven underground. But Charles Carroll the Settler was undaunted. Catholics still possessed a few privileges, most notably voting. In 1715, the Settler decided to fight his way back into power.

He had been carefully positioning himself for a number of years. In 1689, he married a rich widow. When she died, he managed to repeat the coup, winning the hand of Mary Darnall, a Catholic heiress. Mary's father, Henry, was agent and receiver general for Lord Baltimore, keeper of his lordship's seal, and register of his land office. Henry Darnall died in 1711, and the Settler picked up these offices. He was still the proprietor's Attorney General. Though his practice was limited to Chancery and Prerogative Courts, the Settler was described in 1714 as "Attorney in fact for diverse merchants and others in Great Britain." As the land registrar, Carroll amassed 47,777 acres before his death, with an option for 20,000 more. He also owned a store in Annapolis and had begun to lend money at interest.

The year 1715 was an explosive moment in Maryland politics. Two crucial events followed the succession of George I: a Jacobite rebellion in England, which became known as the '15, and the restoration of the proprietary family to power. Charles Calvert's son Benedict was a divorcé with huge expenses for maintaining his ex-wife. In hopes of regaining the proprietorship, Benedict Calvert embraced the Church of England. Lord Baltimore stopped his son's allowance, but soon died. The new Lord Baltimore, as an Anglican, was poised to resume the proprietorship. But before he could enjoy it, he too died, on April 16, 1715.

The fifth Lord Baltimore was Benedict Calvert's son Charles, a former student at the Jesuit academy of St. Omers in Flanders. This Charles Calvert had once sworn that he would rather "lose his estate than his [Catholic] religion." Now reconciled to the Church of England, the young lord assumed the full proprietorship on December 15, 1715. This meant that the Settler lost the attorney-generalship, because the proprietor's private estate once again became part of the public sector, and Catholics were barred from public office. Carroll the Settler at once embarked for England, to lobby for the return of Catholics to public posts.

In so doing, he incurred the wrath of the only other Marylander who was a match for him, Governor John Hart. Hart, a Protestant Irishman, believed that Carroll had promised never to seek the restoration of Catholics to office. When the Settler returned, triumphantly waving a commission that authorized him to resume the attorney-generalship, Hart railroaded through the assembly an act requiring all public officials to swear the oaths of supremacy and abjuration.

Carroll, refusing to take the oaths, blithely continued to exercise his official duties. But then the Settler's hopes were dashed by a member of his own family. William Fitzredmond, his nephew, toasted the Stuart Pretender's birthday, June 10, 1716, and denigrated King George I. The Settler was now trapped. If he wanted to save his political career, he would have to repudiate his nephew, letting Fitzredmond languish in jail. On July 10, Carroll intervened on behalf of his nephew, sealing his own political fate. Gov. Hart protested to the proprietor. Lord Baltimore had no choice. If he continued to favor the Settler, he would be perceived as a "Papist in Masquerade." Carroll's commission was revoked.

Carroll's defeat by the Protestant establishment was more than a personal setback. His ambition cost Maryland Catholics their privilege of voting. The assembly disenfranchised all Catholics on April 29, 1718, a prohibition that would last right up to 1776. The Settler's responsibility for this debacle lent greater urgency to the struggles of the next two Charles Carrolls. They would atone for the Settler's fault and vindicate his memory by fighting for Catholic civil liberties. The fortunes of Catholic Marylanders throughout the eighteenth century were inseparably bound to the triumphs and disasters of the Carrolls.

In the aftermath of 1715, numerous Maryland Catholics conformed to the Church of England. Those who remained Catholic, it has been claimed, were forbidden to walk in front of the state house, presumably for fear of a second Gunpowder Plot. Annapolis tradition holds that Catholics had to wear swords to guarantee their safety.

As the century progressed, social stratification increased.

Tidewater whites sank into peonage, as wealthy families increasingly monopolized the available land. Catholics as well as Protestants joined the scramble for wealth, which went unchecked by any strong religious impulse.

That Maryland never founded a Harvard, a Yale, or a William and Mary has been blamed on religious tensions within the colony. Members of rival communions refused to support schools run by other denominations. The English government provided no help in this matter. According to Benjamin Franklin, a Virginia minister went to London to lobby for a state college, pleading "that the people of Virginia had souls to be saved." "Souls!" replied William III's attorney-general. "Damn your souls, make tobacco!"

Building an Empire

The impoverished state of Maryland education made the gentry more inclined to send their children abroad to school. This gave Maryland a more cosmopolitan outlook than most other colonies. Catholic education, of course, was totally unavailable in Maryland. So Carroll the Settler defied the penal laws by sending his sons to school at St. Omers, in a part of Flanders that was then controlled by France (it is now part of Belgium).

While Carroll of Annapolis, the second of three sons, was preparing to defend his thesis in philosophy, the Settler sent word that his oldest son had died at sea. He demanded that his surviving sons "take much the same steps your brother did, especially in your dedication to me." The Settler promised that the young men "shall not be behindhand in my esteem, with your [late] brother," but this was "provided I hear you do well." He advised Carroll of Annapolis to make his thesis defense only if his professors thought he could "go through it with applause." Otherwise, "it is better let alone, for a dunce in a pulpit makes but a very awkward appearance."

The death of the heir entirely changed Carroll of Annapolis' life. He had wanted, it seems, to be a priest, but this was now inconsistent with his father's requirements. And when the Settler died in 1720, the new heir had to sacrifice his legal education in England. Carroll of Annapolis returned to Maryland to manage the family's affairs. He would never let the rest of his family, especially his own son, forget what he had given up for their sake. As the new head of the clan, he exacted his pound of flesh in return. The deaths of other heirs enabled Carroll to consolidate his patrimony, and he charged his relatives a five-percent commission on all transactions he performed as executor.

Carroll of Annapolis pursued wealth with a vengeance. In so doing he was typical of Catholic gentry both in England and Maryland. The laws left them little else to do besides make money and spend it. The first Marquis of Halifax commented that penal laws made Catholics into "men of pleasure, by excluding them from public business." And their business thrived. The Settler's estate was worth about thirty thousand pounds sterling. The new "Squire Carroll" dominated the economic life of Annapolis from his house on Spa Creek and owned one-fourth of the land in that city. Two-thirds of its residents, it is believed, were his debtors. By 1762, Carroll had 23,230 pounds sterling nine shillings sevenpence out on loan. His annual income amounted to some eighteen hundred pounds sterling.

The Squire's abrasive personality and acquisitiveness put people off. Still, he had admirable qualities. Carroll of Carrollton would later praise his father's "activity, thought, perseverance, and economy," but he was capable of generosity. He tried to help Acadians whom the English deported from Nova Scotia in 1755. The anonymous French visitor, already mentioned, remarked that "I was never genteeler received by any person than I was by him." The Squire also involved himself in public projects, such as the 1729 creation of Baltimore City. His temperance distinguished him from fellow planters in Maryland and Virginia, who were known for "immorality, drunkenness, rudeness, and immoderate swearing." In spite of his faults, Carroll of Annapolis was the natural leader of the Catholic faction in Maryland.

There was widespread resentment between Protestants with political power and Catholics with economic clout. The strange history of the Baltimore Iron Works shows how this conflict was expressed, even within the Carroll family. The Iron Works was organized in 1731 by Carroll of Annapolis, with his cousin, also named Charles Carroll, and Daniel Dulany the Elder. The cousin, known as "Charles Carroll the Surgeon," made a fortune by switching from medicine to commerce. He abandoned his Catholic faith along the way. Dulany, a Protestant, rose from indentured servitude to claim the Settler's old office of attorney-general.

This was not exactly a recipe for harmonious partnership. Indeed, the trio, while enjoying a profitable business relationship, lost no opportunity to attack and sue one another over the next quarter-century. First, Dulany had Carroll of Annapolis arrested in 1739 for nonpayment of quitrents, which the great planters owed the proprietor. Then, in 1748, Squire Carroll alleged that the Surgeon had been selling goods to the Iron Works at inflated prices. The Surgeon vehemently denied this charge, but Carroll of Annapolis insisted that all the partners must consent to such transactions in the future.

Carroll the Surgeon would exact a highly public revenge for this humiliation. He and the Squire were named co-executors for their Catholic kinsman James Carroll, who had made his will before the Surgeon left the Catholic Church. Now, the Protestant Carroll developed scruples about enforcing the will, since one of the beneficiaries was a Catholic priest. This took place while the Surgeon was a member of the House of Delegates. Carroll of Annapolis, according to Governor Horatio Sharpe, wrote an advertisement "which reflected much on the conduct and character" of the Surgeon. In his choleric fashion, the Squire marched up Duke of Gloucester Street to the state house and nailed his advertisement to the door.

Once again, the Carrolls brought down negative repercussions upon the entire Catholic community. The House of Delegates resolved "that the papists were bad members of the community, and unworthy of the protection and indulgence which had been given them." The delegates placed Carroll under house arrest for libelling one of their members. The Squire escaped being thrown into the public jail by a vote of only twenty-eight to twenty-two. It is interesting, in view of later events, that Daniel Dulany, Jr., voted against arresting Carroll.

The libel incident blew over, in spite of the Surgeon's efforts to have all Masses forbidden. But Carroll of Annapolis continued to fall afoul of the law. He once served jail time for challenging another delegate, James Hollyday, to a duel. Remarkably, though, the Iron Works flourished. It has been called "one of the largest and most successful industrial organizations in eighteenth-century America," foreshadowing later industrial innovations. Part of its success is owing to the fifth Lord Baltimore, who, defying mercantilist ideology, made land grants to iron producers.

The Baltimore Iron Works was an "iron plantation," worked primarily by slaves. In addition to performing menial tasks, slaves were trained as smiths, carpenters, founders, and refiners. They were routinely rewarded with cash or goods for extra work. The partners prized slave labor as far superior to the work of white indentured servants. The poor whites were generally so drunk that they could not take care of themselves without the assistance of the company commissary. Daniel Dulany, Jr., told Carroll of Carrollton that "white servants seldom turn out well in Maryland, that they disagree with the negroes and will not eat with them." Built on slave labor, the Iron Works produced more than twenty percent of the total iron exports of the colonies between 1734 and 1737. It helped make the American colonies the world's third largest raw iron producer by 1775.

St. Omers

In 1747, the ten-year-old Carroll of Carrollton was sent, in strictest secrecy, to the underground Jesuit academy of Bohemia Manor. The school, at the head of Chesapeake Bay on the eastern shore of Maryland, was intentionally remote from Annapolis. If Carroll's attendance had become known, the family could have suffered severe consequences.

Part I: Exile

The records of the clandestine school have survived. It had a more practical bent than similar schools in Europe, offering bookkeeping, surveying, and navigation, in addition to the classics. Maryland's leading Catholic families took the risk of sending their sons: there were Roziers, Youngs, Darnalls, Brookes, Neales, Brents, Sewalls. The most promising student was probably John Carroll, the Settler's nephew by marriage. This Carroll, destined to become the first archbishop of Baltimore, registered at Bohemia in 1745. John's brother Daniel would later serve in the federal Constitutional Convention.

In 1748, Charles and John Carroll, who were second cousins once removed, left for Flanders to continue their education at St. Omers. Run by exiled English Jesuits, St. Omers had been founded in 1592 by Fr. Robert Persons, companion of the martyred Edmund Campion. Its purpose was conveyed in the inscription over the college doors: "*Iesu, Iesu, converte Angliam, fiat, fiat*"—"Jesus, Jesus, convert England, may it be, may it be." Boys were smuggled into the college from England, described in code as "packs of merchandise." Despite the danger, the school generally operated at full capacity, peaking in 1685 with one hundred eighty boys. Lack of space was frequently the only obstacle to expansion.

Many graduates of St. Omers joined the Society of Jesus, and some suffered martyrdom. Fr. Andrew White, the chaplain accompanying the first Maryland settlers in 1642, was an early alumnus. Three great-nephews of the Settler, Anthony, James, and Henry Carroll, also became Jesuits. It was clear from an early age that John Carroll would follow. Carrollton reported in March 1750 that "Jacky" was "mightily beloved in the house." By 1753, Carroll of Annapolis supposed that John "is gone up the hill," St. Omers slang for entering the Jesuit novitiate. Several other colonial Americans were doing their novitiates at that time.

But St. Omers was more than a conduit of vocations to the Society. It became an intellectual center of opposition to the Reformation, from whence pamphlets, such as Bellarmine's reply to James I on the power of the pope to depose kings, were smuggled into England. St. Omers also sought to train secular leaders. For this reason, the Jesuits insisted on calling it a college rather than a seminary. Students were guaranteed a free choice of their way of life. The emphasis was on the formation of Christian gentlemen. Nonclerical activities, such as riding horses for sport, were allowed for many years.

To be sure, some aspects of St. Omers discipline were unsuited for the encouragement of lay vocations. Nearly continuous surveillance by prefects gave rise to excessive scruples. Carrollton had such practices in mind when he told his father, years later, that "that education is only fit for Priests." Nearly all conversation was in Latin, and dinner table "recreation" featured translations between Latin and Greek.

But there was much in the St. Omers program to benefit an aspiring civic leader. The Jesuit *ratio studiorum* included humane letters and philosophy in addition to theological studies. The focus was on *ratio et oratio*: reason and speech, to cultivate the whole man in preparation for moral, political, and intellectual leadership. The boys vented their competitive instincts in the academic sphere as well as the physical; the students were trained to dispute with each other and with their masters.

The Jesuits, unlike most pedagogues of the day, never punished the boys for falling short academically. They took a less rigid approach than other educators. Ignatius Loyola asked that Jesuit teachers consider "circumstances of time, place, persons, and other such factors, according to what seems best in our Lord." Accordingly, the boys' emotions found an outlet in drama, though it was generally in Latin. Students could spend their free time studying history and geography, as well as English prose and poetry.

The routine was strict, but not cruel. Carrollton rose at five A.M. On Sundays and feast days, he was allowed a "long sleep," until 5:30! He meditated for a quarter hour before daily Mass and took Communion probably once a month and on major feast days. Though study consumed most days, Tuesday and Thursday were half holidays, with walking, games, and a special supper. In addition, Carroll enjoyed a mid-afternoon meal called "Bread and Beer."

The Jesuits strove to give an example of Christian fellowship, so that Carroll of Annapolis referred to the teaching staff as "the family." They led the older boys through the spiritual exercises of St. Ignatius. Carrollton was strongly marked by this experience, which he received under the guidance of Fr. Levinas Browne. In later life, when asked how "he could rise so early, and kneel so long," Carroll gave credit, "with his high tone of cheerfulness," to the Jesuits at St. Omers.

"Aut Caesar Aut Nullus"

Most of the records of the English College of St. Omers were destroyed in the Sack of Louvain during World War I. Thus, the correspondence of Carroll and his father is an important source of information on the college. The boy's first surviving letter is dated September 4, 1749. He proclaims that "I cannot be better satisfied," and hopes to rank first or second in his Latin class. He apologizes for not writing more, pleading that he had fallen and injured his arm.

This artless letter summarizes all of Carroll's anxieties at school. His father demanded affectionate letters and high academic performance. "Aut Caesar aut nullus," Carroll of Annapolis urged: either Caesar or nothing. Being third in school was not good enough. The Squire announced that he was keeping copies of all his letters to his son, to testify to his paternal care, and as a reproach should Carrollton not live up to his expectations. In those days, parental love was not unconditional. Good progress reports, wrote Carroll of Annapolis, would "increase the love I have for you."

For any child, the Squire's demands would have been daunting. For young Carroll, as an illegitimate son, they were overwhelming. The boy knew that he was guaranteed nothing, that if he disappointed his father, disinheritance would probably result. Carrollton struggled to conform. "I hope to be always amongst the first, at least I promise you my endeavours shall not be wanting." He claimed that "I can easily see the great affection you have for me by sending me here."

Inwardly, though, there was resentment, which sometimes spilled out. He was assigned a personal tutor, his Jesuit cousin Anthony, to make up for the deficiencies in his earlier education. Anthony Carroll was Carroll of Annapolis' watchdog, sending the Squire frequent reports on the boy's standing in class. Sometimes the tutor pushed too hard. Carrollton's letter home of March 23, 1751, reads in full: "Cousin Anthony forced me to write to you. I have very little to tell you only that I am very well. I am your most dutiful & obedient son."

Anthony Carroll also complained that his pupil was "giddy. This will perhaps seem odd to you." It does indeed, given Carroll's later shyness and soberness. But a 1757 letter of John Carroll to Carrollton backs up the tutor's criticism. "I believe you will mind very little what I say to you," wrote John, "if I say it in a serious way."

Carroll of Annapolis would continue to nag his son about writing letters until he was well into his twenties. The boy was supposed to write three times a year, and later, six. At one point, the Squire demanded that his son spend half an hour every day writing a journal, to use as a source for his letters home. When Carrollton's letters were too short, his father remonstrated. If the length was adequate, then he found fault with the handwriting.

Perhaps the Squire was right to be worried. His son's refusal to write was more than mere boyish thoughtlessness. Silence was Carrollton's only rebellion, his way of expressing anger at his overbearing father's demands. Carroll of Annapolis had good intentions. He wanted his son to use his wealth and gifts for the general good, in contrast to the wasted lives of many other planters. He never neglected to praise his son's progress.

But Carroll's desire to test his heir scarred the boy. He held the reward of legitimacy over his son's head until Carrollton proved himself worthy of a father's love. A 1757 letter from Onorio Razolini alludes to the Squire's strategy. Razolini congratulated the elder Carroll for deciding to marry Elizabeth Brooke. "If you remember," recalled Razolini, "I told you that your son would answer all your expectations."

Eventually, Carroll of Carrollton won this hollow victory.

Part I: Exile

His teacher Mr. John Jenison (English priests were not yet called Father) described the teenage Carroll's "universal good character." Admired by his peers, Carrollton's popularity never made him "degenerate into the mean character of a favorite which he always justly despised." All in all, Carroll's behavior "gave me the greatest satisfaction without the very least alloy of displeasure." Of course, being universally admired does not imply being loved. Charles Carroll left St. Omers as a young man of impeccable character and excellent manners, without the gift of making friends. His one lasting, intimate relationship would be with his father.

Now Carroll of Annapolis moved to reward his son for his performance. Elizabeth Brooke hinted in 1756 that her husband might at last marry her. "For what may I not expect from your Papa's tenderness & affection, which I have hitherto been happy enough to preserve." The middle-aged couple were legally married by a Jesuit priest on February 15, 1757, when their son was nineteen. Both took the legal status of their marriage quite seriously. Witnessing a will in 1754, Elizabeth gave her last name as Brooke. When the will was probated in 1759, she signed "Elizabeth Carroll, late Elizabeth Brooke." After the marriage, Carroll of Annapolis began signing his letters to Charles "your most affectionate father." Previously, the boy had had to settle for "most affectionately yours, Charles Carroll."

It is hard to reconcile the Squire's religiosity with his delayed marriage. The scandal he gave is evident in the comment of a proprietary official in 1743. "Is he [Carroll of Annapolis] in great esteem among you," John Gibson asked, "because the contrary is asserted here, but perhaps his admired cousin is now his wife, and then all's well."

Perhaps the Squire managed to convince himself that his liaison was a "clandestine marriage." These unions were considered acceptable by the Church for many years, though they were not solemnized by a priest. The Council of Trent required a priest and witnesses to make a marriage valid, but Trent's decree *Tametsi* had not been officially promulgated in Maryland.

Ronald Hoffman and Sally Mason's book *Princes of Ireland, Planters of Maryland* is the definitive account of the Carrolls' domestic history. Hoffman and Mason argue that if a clandestine marriage had been contracted by the consent of both parties, the 1757 wedding could not have been solemnized by a priest. The Carroll union would already have been valid in the eyes of the Church.

The only other explanation is that the Carrolls confessed their sin and lived chastely for years after Carrollton's birth. This, too, seems farfetched. Unless further research uncovers a missing piece of the puzzle, the conclusion that Carroll and Brooke flouted the laws of the Church until 1757 is inescapable.

Suarez and Montesquieu

Not all of Carrollton's endeavors were directed toward pleasing his father. Becoming passionately interested in history and political theory, Carroll absorbed ideas that, in later life, informed his actions as a political leader.

Carrollton's teachers undoubtedly exposed him to the political writings of the great Spanish Jesuit Francisco Suarez. Like most Spanish scholastics, Suarez followed St. Thomas rather than Ockham in his emphasis on the common good. The Spanish doctor, however, had to cope with the emergence of a monolithic and powerful state. The new national states that replaced the Holy Roman Empire often claimed for themselves the privileges of the Church, such as appointing bishops. Sometimes, as in England, the state suppressed the true religion entirely. Suarez, therefore, emphasized individual rights and privileges more than Thomas had, in order to balance state power.

Unlike most Protestant thinkers, however, Suarez is careful to locate these individual prerogatives firmly within the common good and the natural law. True individual rights are implied by the common good and make sense only within the context of the natural law. For example, "Thou shalt not kill"—a precept of natural law—implies the right to life. In our day, however, secularism has given rise to numerous new "rights," such as the "right" to an abortion, a divorce, or contraception, which are destructive of the common good and contrary to natural law. Suarez avoids this excessive individualism, never losing sight of the natural law. Like Bellarmine, he insists on obedience to legitimate authority. And, like Bellarmine, Suarez allows the people to depose tyrants.

After St. Omers, Carroll went to Rheims, where he was allowed to study poetry, history, geography, and heraldry. Then he attended the College of Louis-le-Grand in Paris. Here Carroll was exposed to Enlightenment thinkers. It would be a mistake to say that the Jesuits were Carroll's primary influence. Both Carrolls, father and son, were men of the Enlightenment. Carroll of Annapolis owned Voltaire's *Universal History*, although Voltaire was still on the Index of Forbidden Books. Carrollton also expressed eagerness to buy Voltaire's works. His library in later years would include volumes of Rousseau, Gibbon, Godwin, Rapin, and Hume.

Carrollton was less enthusiastic about Locke than most of his contemporaries, perhaps because Locke opposed religious toleration for Catholics, arguing that the claims of the Church were incompatible with the English constitution. Carroll informed his father in 1757 that "you need not buy Mr. Locke's work, it will be of no great service to me." The seminal influence on Carroll was Montesquieu, whom he quoted often throughout his career.

Montesquieu, who died in the Catholic faith, started from the Catholic principle of popular sovereignty. He made it clear that a body politic may choose to create a monarchy, a republic, or even a despotism. The government that is most conformable to nature is the one that agrees with the humor of its people.

Because Montesquieu used this language of "diversity," he is sometimes deemed "relevant" in our day. But the Baron did not prize diversity for its own sake. The laws of nature remained his master concept. These laws play out differently in concrete situations. But, Montesquieu insisted, "each diversity is *unifor-*

mity, each change is *constancy*." States that ignore natural law will soon find themselves at the mercy of "events that incessantly arise from the nature of things."

Like Suarez, Montesquieu reacted against the power of the new state. The example of the Puritan government in England showed that even holy doctrines can have disastrous consequences. Thus, Montesquieu argued, a well-ordered state regulates even virtue, when it is taken to excess. Power must check power.

Montesquieu was the great theorist of mixed government. He called a mixed constitution of checks and balances "a master-piece of legislation, rarely produced by hazard, and seldom attained by prudence." The degradation of the nobility and the Church had left a political void; there was no one to challenge the power of the state. Montesquieu wanted to restore the rival estates. "Abolish the privileges of the lords, of the clergy, and of the cities in a monarchy, and you will soon have a popular state, or else an arbitrary government." The Church must be left alone in its area of competence, which includes marriage and the family.

Thus, Montesquieu expressed what we now call the principle of subsidiarity. We must recognize, though, that subsidiarity requires hierarchy, even in a republic. It is true that Montesquieu praised "mediocrity"—a general equality of fortune—as a means to promote republican virtue. But Montesquieu distinguishes this "mediocrity" from what he calls the "spirit of extreme equality." A good republic does not try to level all distinctions among persons. "Such is the difference between a well and an ill policied democracy," Montesquieu observed, "that in the former men are equal only as citizens, but in the latter they are equal also as magistrates, senators, judges, fathers, husbands, masters." Montesquieu is part of the great Catholic tradition, from Thomas to Bellarmine, who pointed out that men are equal in essence but not in "wisdom or in grace," to Leo XIII, who called it "most repugnant to reason to endeavor to confine all within the same measure, and to extend complete equality to the institutions of civil life."

But who would safeguard the principles of subsidiarity and

hierarchy in Montesquieu's mixed government? Evidently not the judiciary, which the Baron called "next to nothing" in his scheme. A judge must rule according to the "exact letter of the law," rather than enforcing his "private opinion." Instead, Montesquieu gave the constitution to a "Senate" for safekeeping. This Senate would be a legislative body of the nobility, who would have the power to veto unconstitutional acts of the popular branch of the legislature. They would also serve as a tribunal of impeachment in cases of executive misconduct. Montesquieu wanted the executive branch to be strong enough to prevent legislative gridlock. But his senators would be the primary guardians of public virtue and the constitution.

Montesquieu even found a place for federalism in his plan for mixed government. Republics cannot function unless they are small, a condition that leaves them vulnerable to conquest. The only solution for republics is to confederate. Book IX of *The Spirit of Laws* provided a blueprint for the *Federalist Papers*. The confederated government must be strong enough to guarantee each citizen "a certain subsistence." It should accomplish this primarily by promoting the spirit of industry and commerce.

The state must not overstep its bounds. There is a danger, Montesquieu warned, that republics will impose higher taxes than monarchies do, because the citizen thinks that "he is paying himself." But the "real wants of the people" must not "give way to the imaginary wants of the State." If taxes are too high, the citizen only appears to be free: "the power of the people has been confounded with their liberty."

And what is liberty? "In societies directed by laws," Montesquieu wrote, "liberty can consist only in the power of doing what we ought to will, and in not being constrained to do what we ought not to will." This definition, steeped in natural law, is Catholic through and through. Carroll's reading of Montesquieu gave him the inspiration for the Senate and the electoral college. Of all the founding fathers, with the possible exception of John Adams, Carroll did the most to implement Montesquieu's vision of mixed government.

The Persecution Revives

Carroll of Carrollton successfully defended his thesis in universal philosophy on July 8, 1757. He received a certificate with an engraving of John the Baptist. The caption read: "preparing the way of the Lord." He was about to turn twenty.

His father was en route to Paris, but he did not arrive in time to witness the defense. Carroll of Annapolis had other business. He hoped to persuade King Louis XV to grant him part of Louisiana, in what is now southwestern Arkansas, as a refuge for Maryland Catholics. Carroll went to such a great effort because he saw the threat of disaster looming over his family's fortunes in Protestant America.

The outbreak of the French and Indian War had placed Catholics in an uncomfortable position. The rumor mill generated stories of a conspiracy between Catholics and Native Americans in Maryland. Rev. Thomas Chase, father of Samuel Chase, who would later figure prominently in Carrollton's life, announced from the pulpit that Catholics were preparing to massacre Protestants. The black people were supposedly involved as well. A priest had been seen in a French officer's dress. Rev. James Sterling called on all "sons of the Reformation" to "guard your holy Religion from Papal persecution, idolatry, gunpowder treasons, and worse than Smithfield fires!"

Driven by this mass hysteria, the assembly in May 1756 attempted to impose stricter penal laws in Maryland. Priests would have to register their names and post bond for their good behavior. Those who proselytized would be attainted of treason. Anyone educated at a foreign seminary would be disqualified from inheriting money or holding lands. According to Gov. Sharpe, "many other restraints" were proposed as well. Fortunately for the Catholics, the two houses of assembly could not agree on how to use the funds that the new penal laws would raise. The measure was tabled.

Gov. Sharpe disliked the persecution. He asked the local justices to report on the behavior of Catholics. Forwarding the results to the proprietor, Sharpe attested that "if I was asked whether the conduct of the protestants or the papists in this province hath been most unexceptionable since I have had the honour to serve your lordship, I should not hesitate to give answer in favour of the latter."

There is no doubt that Catholic Marylanders saw themselves as Englishmen and hoped for a British victory. Even Carroll of Annapolis, the proud Irishman, looked forward to the day when "all French America...must be our own." His son praised "our late glorious success at sea." But the assembly, continuing to fear a Catholic fifth column within Maryland, barred Catholics from militia duty. This, in turn, was used as a pretext for a double tax on land owned by Catholics.

The double tax infuriated the Squire. He and "sundry Roman Catholics" fired off a petition to the governor. They reminded Sharpe of the "equality of freedom & favour & liberty of conscience" provided by the Charter. The petitioners expressed their pent-up anger that the 1649 Toleration Act, "so often & so solemnly confirmed" at the request of Protestants, had been revoked. By the penal laws, they argued, Catholics "are almost reduced to a level with our Negroes, not having even the privilege of voting."

Lamely, the governor replied that the Catholics should have protested at the time the law was passed. This enraged Carroll of Annapolis. The governor had not bothered to inform the Catholic planters of the double tax until the day it was voted on in the assembly, when it was already too late. Deciding to emigrate, Carroll set out for Europe on June 2, 1757. It was immediately bruited about that the Squire was going to betray state secrets to the enemy. Gov. Sharpe gave no credence to such slanders, although he noted that "if [Carroll] is inclined to give the enemy any intelligence about our American affairs, none is more capable."

Carrollton had not seen his father for ten years. They apparently got along well during the Squire's French visit. The son later wrote that "I think of you very often in the day and the agreeable time we spent together in Paris." The recent marriage of the elder Carroll no doubt helped the cordiality between father and son. The French King thought Carroll's proposal too grand, but nonetheless offered him a sizeable tract of land. Carroll of Annapolis also received aid from the vicar general of Louisiana, the Abbé de l'Isle-Dieu, whom Carrollton called "the only Frenchman I ever knew susceptible of friendship." The Squire seemed determined to throw in his lot with France.

After the grief he experienced at parting from his father that winter, Carroll of Carrollton took a "slow, dull, and melancholy" journey to Bourges, where he was to study Roman and French civil law. Provincial society did nothing to lift Carrollton's spirits. "I may really call my present manner of living a true solitude." He refused to go out more than twice a week, since "there is no instruction to be reaped in those companies when they do nothing but play at cards." Carroll also felt awkward with young ladies. Totally ignorant of the local dances, he was a "perfect stranger" at balls.

Carrollton did what was most natural to him: retreated into his books. "I find no [other] conversation than that of a Horace, a Vergil, a Racine, &c. Their company is instructive and at the same time agreeable." Sometimes, he wrote, he abandoned the poetic muses for "the profitable and faithful lessons of History; here I learn to be wise at the expence of others, and to attain to true glory by the example of the Great, Good, & Just." As for the law, Carroll found it "very dry and tedious. It requires a good memory and common sense." But he was able to master Justinian's *Institutes* during the first six months of 1758.

Soon, however, Carrollton had had enough of Bourges. In January 1759, he escaped Bourges and returned to Paris, presenting his father with a *fait accompli*. Perhaps he felt emboldened by his new legal status as heir, or maybe his one disastrous romantic adventure compelled him to retreat. Carrollton had taken up with the "young, pretty, witty daughter" of an English buttonmaker, Mr. Alcock. The manufacturer invited Carroll and a friend, Mr. Willoughby, to stay overnight. Willoughby drank too much. Roused from sleep by the call of nature, Willoughby stumbled into a room, thinking it was a water closet, and began to relieve himself. Unfortunately, he was soaking the bed of a maid, who happened to be in it. Her shrieks awakened the household. Carroll delicately related this story to his father in French. Back at Louis-le-Grand, Carrollton claimed that "no desire of ease & pleasure determined me to this change; the only reason is my advantage & advancement in the law." Friends had advised him that Bourges was an "improper place" for legal studies.

As the younger Carroll prepared to move to London to study English law, the Squire persisted in his emigration plan. He promised not to sell the Annapolis estate, the slaves, or the Iron Works, in case Carrollton decided to live in Maryland. "But I doubt not you will think as I do," wrote the Squire, "if you should ever know our people."

Carrollton had mixed feelings about the project, but he had to tread carefully around his temperamental father's moods. He sympathized with the Squire about the "injustice and ungratefulness" of Marylanders. "What have we done to deserve such treatment from them? Their complaints, as well as their reasons, I am convinced are entirely groundless." But when Lord Baltimore, in June 1759, asked that the persecutions cease, Carroll wrote hopefully to his father, "I suppose you will lay aside all thoughts of leaving Maryland." Although the Marylanders were an "uncultivated insolent rabble," perhaps they would "become milder & tractable when they begin to grow more civilised."

But Carrollton's first impression of England, in the autumn of 1759, swayed him toward emigration. "I can't conceive how any Roman Catholic, especially an Irish Roman Catholic, can consent to live in England or any [of] the British dominions," he wrote. Although most of the penal laws were not enforced, they remained on the books, ready to be executed whenever Parliament demanded it. "Now where is the man of spirit," the young man wondered, "that can behold the rod lifted up, tremble, and kiss the hand of him that holds it?"

France Expels the Jesuits

But time and reflection convinced Carroll of the advantages of the English system, compared to the French. At least in

England, there was some security for "property, liberty, and safety," from "power and its natural ally, injustice." There the laws, however defective, applied to all men equally. The doom hanging over the Society of Jesus strongly influenced Carrollton's political thought. The Jesuits were hounded out of France by a congeries of special interests, among them Jansenists, Gallicans, *philosophes*, and Freemasons, led by the King's mistress, Madame de Pompadour.

In 1759, Portuguese Jesuits were accused of plotting to assassinate their king. The popular image of Jesuits as Machiavellian politicians, and the writings of Suarez and Mariana on the right of resistance to tyranny, fed the calumny. Carroll of Annapolis followed the controversy eagerly. He blamed the anti-Jesuit furor on envy. "They are not only too virtuous, but too wise to engage in assassinations."

Carrollton was not quite so sure. He admitted that most of the stories going around were "destitute of common sense." But when the Jesuit constitutions were published, the younger Carroll was shocked by their emphasis on obedience, as opposed to reason. He charged the Jesuits with "a blind impetuosity of will & eagerness to obey without the least enquiry or examination." Although "I revere the virtue, I esteem the learning" of the Jesuits, their constitutions were "contrary to the true spirit & discipline of the Catholic church." The Squire replied that Jesuit obedience extended only to "things innocent, indifferent, and just. Have they murdered, burnt or destroyed in virtue of their obedience?"

The attack on the Society was taken up by the French *parlements*. These were independent legislative bodies, which were in theory subordinate to the King. However, structures of accountability were lacking, so that the *parlements* frequently acted as if they were sovereign. Louis XV's technically "boundless" power was insufficient to control these assemblies. The *parlements* forbade the Jesuits to publish anything in their own defense, even while they authorized scurrilous anti-Jesuit pamphlets.

Carrollton, still much influenced by the Enlightenment, predicted that Jesuit educators would be replaced by "men of republican principles who will not fail to inspire the youth with the love of liberty." But he was not too blind to notice that the *parlements* were in fact void of republican virtue. When the legislatures expelled the Jesuits from France on August 6, 1762, Carroll deplored "the injustice, violence, & precipitancy in their proceedings." "The name of liberty," concluded the disappointed idealist, "as well as of religion, has often covered the worst designs." Carroll had arrived at the conviction upon which John Adams later insisted, that legislative assemblies could also become tyrannical. "The decisions & proceedings of most assemblies, when once passion or interest prevails, are more tyrannical & oppressive than the sportive cruelty of a lawless tyrant."

The woes of the Jesuits mounted. Flanders followed France's lead, expelling the Society. This meant the end of St. Omers. At the English College, John Carroll and two other priests were arrested but managed to smuggle the boys out. When replacement priests arrived in October 1762, they found an empty house. After many adventures, the school found a new home at Stonyhurst in England.

The Bourbons, supported by the exiled Stuarts, continued to agitate for the total suppression of the Society of Jesus. The Jesuits' fate was sealed when Empress Marie-Thérèse abandoned them for the sake of her daughter Marie-Antoinette, who married the French dauphin. Pope Clement XIV dissolved the Society on August 16, 1773.

Carrolls and Calverts

Of course, Carroll of Annapolis already had reason to mistrust legislative assemblies, given his experience with the House of Delegates. By 1760, the Squire had given up trying to influence that body and was concentrating on the executive branch. Having mended fences with Gov. Sharpe, the senior Carroll instructed his son to lobby the proprietary family in England on behalf of the Catholic colonists. Carrollton was to remind the proprietor that the Settler had been dismissed from his position "to gratify a faction whose aim was to divest the [Calvert] family of the government." In return for Lord Baltimore's favor, young Carroll would offer "to promote the interests of the proprietary family where you can do it in honor and justice." But, mindful of past injustices, he should always put the family's and Maryland's interests above the Calverts'.

Carrollton met Cecilius Calvert, the proprietor's uncle, in April 1760. Calvert claimed that "he was much offended at those laws," meaning the double tax, and "at the violence of our assembly & some Protestants." The testimony of the justices of the peace, which Sharpe had forwarded, was for Calvert "a convincing proof of [Catholic] innocence." In other words, Carrollton wrote, "the Proprietary being convinced of our innocence permitted that very innocence to groan under oppression."

The younger Carroll was so flabbergasted at this admission that he was speechless. Later, he regretted not pursuing the point, and his father gently chided him for his diffidence. "What you said to Mr. Calvert was very proper," wrote the Squire, "and what you omitted to say would still have been more proper." "It is necessary on some occasions to be firm [and] resolute & to show a proper resentment," the elder Carroll counseled.

Carrollton met the Calverts again in February 1761 to recommend a cousin, Henry Darnall III, for public office. Carroll of Annapolis coached his son on how to bring up Catholic grievances. "Should [Calvert] show the least resentment either by word or by his behaviour, ask him who has most reason to be offended," the proprietor or the unjustly persecuted Maryland Catholics. This time, when Carrollton brought up the double tax, Cecilius Calvert protested feebly that Lord Baltimore "was advised to it." Again, the young man was amazed at the Calverts' "injustice & pusillanimity." Carroll of Annapolis gave up. "I do not care to mortify Mr. Calvert who can urge nothing to excuse his family's ingratitude to the Roman Catholics, and therefore I drop this subject."

In spite of this setback, Carroll of Carrollton by now strongly preferred to live under English rule. The destruction of the

Jesuits had taught him that even Catholic countries could undermine the rights of the Church, in the absence of good government. "I know of no Catholic country," Carrollton argued, "where that greatest blessing, civil liberty, is enjoyed." He urged his father to be patient with his fellow Marylanders. "True happiness on earth is not to be met with," he wrote, this side of heaven. "If you repair to France, there you will only exchange religious for civil tyranny...of the two, the greatest evil. Civil oppression has nothing to console us, religious persecutions are always attended with this consolation at least, of not going unrewarded."

Carrollton advised his father to continue cultivating the governor. With a sympathetic governor, "one not to be awed or overruled by the clamors of a mob, we may laugh at and despise its insolence: its giddy fury will turn to its own shame." In addition, the Calverts had promised not to approve any more penal laws, "if the Roman Catholics did not give occasion to them by their disaffected behaviour."

The Squire did not fully abandon his emigration plan until England defeated France in 1763. Peace reduced tensions between Maryland Catholics and Protestants. In any case, after the war, French America no longer existed. But just before the fall of Quebec, General Montcalm made a prophecy: England, he said, would find a tomb in victory.

"We Live in the World"

After the sheltered, contemplative life of school and college, Carrollton found English society daunting. A candid self-evaluation resulted. "I am naturally timid & bashful," he wrote his father. He looked forward to a life of "rural amusements... united to Philosophy." Since he would be excluded from politics, "I must endeavour then to be esteemed in private life." This he found challenging. "I am too stiff & reserved. I can only be free and open with an intimate friend." But two years after his arrival in England, Carroll was still "intimate with nobody."

To some extent, Carroll of Annapolis was to blame. He had warned his son to be "very circumspect," since London was "an open and wide ocean of danger." Late eighteenth-century England was notorious for lax morals. Extramarital affairs, prostitution, drug and alcohol abuse, all were common. Only later, in the Victorian era, would English society acquire its reputation for prudery. "In your situation," the Squire counseled, "the greatest resolution will be necessary to withstand the many temptations you will be exposed to: so abandoned will you find most men as to be ashamed of ever appearing virtuous." The young man should "be reserved" even with his fellow Marylanders, and under no circumstances should he pursue "intimacy or familiarity with the fair sex." "I often wish it was possible for me to inspect & direct your conduct," worried the senior Carroll.

This advice was inappropriate for the shy, scholarly Carrollton. The Squire began to realize this when he learned that his son had declined an invitation from former Maryland governor Thomas Bladen. Since Bladen had been civil to the family, Carrollton's refusal amounted to a deliberate snub. The younger Carroll pleaded that Bladen's circle played cards for high stakes, "to which I am very averse: as I have no great inclination for cards & am unlucky." He also feared entrapment by Bladen's "remarkably handsome" daughter. "A too great intimacy in a family where there are young [women] may give room to idle reports & familiarity with the sex is immediately construed into love." In spite of his great wealth, Carroll shunned the English gentry, preferring to travel with his old schoolmaster, Mr. Jenison. "The frequenting of company in high life would be attended with great expence & loss of time, & other inconveniences; without any other advantage than the knowledge of such persons, their follies, vices & extravagances."

This attitude was hardly suitable for someone in Carroll's state of life. Faced with the prospect of a hermit son, Carroll of Annapolis did an about-face. "A man can hardly be too reserved," he wrote, "but a prudent reserve should be always hid by a well dissembled show of candor, affability, openness, and unreserve. Would you not wish that all men would act with candor, affability, openness and unreserve towards you?" The way to be loved and esteemed was to sacrifice one's own preferences in nonessential matters. "We live in the world, and ought to know it," insisted the father. "That knowledge gives us weight in it, and makes us agreeable in company and conversation." The only way to know the world was to go into it. "A knowledge of it in theory you will find very defective."

Carroll suggested that his son attend the Newmarket races to socialize. He also urged Carrollton to go to coffeehouses and other places where politics were discussed. "Should you for example be asked, on your return, what sort of man is Mr. Pitt...and you should say 'I never saw him and know nothing of the matter,' after a stay of four years in London, might you not be looked upon as incurious? As if you could not give an account of Westminster Bridge or St. Paul's?" To facilitate Carroll's entry into society, his father impishly forwarded his comments on Bladen's daughter to the ex-governor. "A man can lose nothing by a little complaisance of that sort, & custom has made it all most necessary."

Carrollton declared his willingness to be more agreeable. He seized the opportunity to ask for more money, so that he could go out "in a proper genteel handsome way." The thrifty Squire complied, even sending funds for a riding master. Carrollton hoped that riding would give him "an easy and genteel carriage, which I am sensible, I stand in need of." Too much studying had caused him to slouch. His father agreed, provided that "this carriage, this manner must be quite easy and natural; any affectation is disgusting." Fine gentlemen should be emulated, not "fops."

The heir made rapid progress in society. Soon he asked to buy a horse for "some excursions & jaunts of pleasure." Dutifully, Carrollton attended the House of Commons and wrote a description of Pitt's mannerisms. He is also said to have dined with Edmund Burke. By 1761, a cousin wrote that "Charly is very well and is a fine gentleman," earning "great applause from all his acquaintances that converse with him." Another friend of the family reported on Carroll's "elegant way of living" in London.

The junior Carroll survived smallpox in 1763, without too many scars. As a result, he began wearing a wig. Soon, however, on his father's advice, he let his hair, "thick and flowing" even in his old age, grow back. This was how Sir Joshua Reynolds painted him, with long black hair pulled back from his high forehead. Reynolds, the most celebrated English painter of his day, emphasized Carroll's high brow and piercing, dark gaze. The young man's olive coloring and aquiline nose make him look foreign, from the English point of view; he could pass for a Spanish or an Italian nobleman. His full lips are tightly closed, as if he were holding back some opinion that it would be imprudent to utter. He looks intellectual, self-contained, somewhat haughty. Yet there is neither meanness nor brutality in his refined countenance.

Carroll of Annapolis continued to insist that his son make a constant effort to be virtuous. "*Initium Sapientiae Timor Domini*," he liked to repeat: The fear of the Lord is the beginning of wisdom. But the Squire also tried to introduce his son to the sweetness of true devotion. The reason, intellect, and will should guide, but not stifle, the other faculties of the soul. "Prayer does not consist in a set form of words," he explained. "It is the heart, the will, the attention & intention which accompanies them that carries them like a pure sacrifice to the throne of the Almighty." Carroll discouraged his son from being overly rigid about honor at the expense of fellowship. "A pipe of wine is a pipe of wine," the Squire wrote, "but honor is an empty-sounding thing like an empty pipe."

Carroll of Carrollton willingly accepted his father's doctrine. "A good conscience & a virtuous life are certainly the greatest blessings we can enjoy on earth. I don't aim, nor never did, at canonization; I detest screwed up devotion, distorted faces, & grimace. I equally abhor those, who laugh at all devotion, look upon our religion as a fiction, & its holy mysteries as the greatest absurdities. I observe my religious duties, I trust in the mercy of God, not my own merits, which are none, & hope he will pardon my daily offences." "I love him," Carrollton concluded, "though far less than his infinite goodness deserves & I could wish to do."

Part I: Exile

Carroll never developed much of an affinity for the English Catholic gentry. Politically, they were still mired in the Jacobite resistance, with its emphasis on the divine right of kings. Carrollton, on the other hand, had been exposed to the broader Catholic political tradition on the continent, and his views had advanced considerably beyond High-Toryism. An encounter with a penniless, drunken Jacobite exile in France had done nothing to increase his sympathy for the deposed Stuarts. Jacobitism made the English Catholic gentry into a picturesque holdover from the past. The Catholic Church seemed to most Englishmen like a Gothic ruin, symbolized by the ruined monasteries scattered across the landscape.

But things were different in Maryland, where Catholics sought a rational basis for political action in the Maryland charter. Pragmatic action to secure justice, rather than quixotic loyalty to deposed princes, marked their increasing political maturity. Accordingly, Carrollton sought out his fellow Marylanders, Protestant as well as Catholic, in England. There, he first met his future colleagues William Paca and John Hammond. Numerous Marylanders came to study law at the Middle Temple, including Hammond, Lloyd Dulany, and Richard and Edward Tilghman. They were joined by soon-to-be-prominent figures from other colonies, such as John Dickinson, Thomas McKean, John Laurens, and Arthur Lee.

The most significant connection Carroll made was with Daniel Dulany, Jr. Respect and rivalry marked their relationship from the beginning. Carroll of Annapolis called Dulany "indisputably the best lawyer on this continent," but "vain & proud & designing." Carrollton, still prone to vacillation and awkward in speech, looked on the forceful Dulany with admiration and distaste. "Dulany has an easy, fluent, and persuasive tongue," he observed, "is bold in asserting, positive in his assertions, ready to contradict, impatient of contradictions, imperious, decisive & dogmatical."

The younger Carroll blamed Dulany's lack of social grace on his low birth. He was offended when Dulany sent him a legal packet by way of a Carroll relative, instead of calling in person. "Common civility required a return of the visits I paid him,"

[57]

Carrollton complained. "To be wanting in civility through indolence bespeaks ill breeding; through mere pride or childish vanity implies the want of good sense." Dulany was that lowest of creatures, a "politician," something both Carrolls held in contempt. By 1763, the Squire and Dulany were involved in mutual lawsuits.

The Common Law

Although the cream of the American ruling class was enrolled in the Temple, Carroll had a violent aversion to entering it. Carrollton told his father that his legal studies would be pointless, since as a Catholic he could never be admitted to the bar. He described life at law school in lurid terms. He could "pardon a little obscenity," Carrollton wrote, "provided it be not too barefaced and extended no farther than words." But at the Temple, "wine and jovial company" led inevitably to "bad & criminal actions." "Disgusted with the difficulties and dryness of the study," the young man claimed, "the law books are thrown aside. Dissipation succeeds to study, immorality to virtue; one night plunges them in pain, misery, and disease."

Carroll was homesick. He was out of his depth in the society of Englishmen. His pleas to return to Maryland approached desperation. He begged his father to teach him the family business, instead of forcing him to study law. "What, must I live all my life time separated from you? What crime have I done to deserve perpetual banishment?" Carroll of Annapolis tried to reason with his son. "It is a shame for a Gentleman to be ignorant of the laws of his country and to be dependent on every dirty pettifogger," he wrote. A legal education would enable Carrollton to help his friends and relations, endearing him to them. He might be able to improve the conditions of Catholics. The Squire had more hope of Catholic emancipation than his son. Carrollton would need to know the law, if he "should be called upon to act in any public character."

To be sure, Carroll of Annapolis wanted his son to fulfill his own aspiration to be a lawyer, which he had had to abandon when the Settler died. But he had Carrollton's best interests at heart. Southern planters in the eighteenth century may have been the most litigious group in history. Burke remarked that "in no country perhaps in all the world...is the law so general a study" as in America. "All who read, and most do read, endeavor to obtain some smattering in that science." The Squire knew from experience that systematic legal study would be impossible once Carrollton became involved in the family business. And he was farsighted in his prediction of a public role for his son.

Carroll of Annapolis would have preferred to have his son at home. But he was willing to sacrifice his own happiness, he said, for the sake of Carrollton's future. "Your welfare, interest, and happiness only induce me against my natural fondness and propensity to see you and have you with me," he wrote. "I love you entirely...but no consideration...can influence me to call you from the study of the law.... Let me not suffer so cruel an absence without answering the end for which alone I submit to it."

This argument calmed Carrollton, temporarily. He praised his father's "well regulated love." "Nothing but a sincere love guided by reason, I am persuaded, could have kept me so long from you." Still, the young man was maudlin when he thought of home. "How shall I ever be able to think of you without shedding tears due to the memory of the best, the dearest, tenderest parent?" And Carroll continued to miss his mother. If his reunion with her "depended only on desires, as they are mutual, it would a long time ago have been brought about. I am as yet to undergo three or four years banishment, such is your will and such my inclination, as I know it conformable to yours & beneficial to me."

Carrollton hated English common law, which "disgust[s] a liberal mind." Roman and civil law, which were more systematic, the young man found "agreeable." But the common law was "a mere chaos," full of "jargon" and "barbarous language." Carrollton developed at this time an interest in mathematics, which stood in stark contrast to the irrationality of common law. He found pleasure in "the strictness of geometrical demonstrations for the thorough conviction of their truth: would there were the same certainty, the same fixed principles in the law!" Nor did the law satisfy Carroll's interest in "mankind's experience." He had become "passionately fond" of works of history. Without historical knowledge and interest in humanity, a lawyer was just "an insignificant pettifogger grovelling... in the mean but gainful application to all the little arts of chicane."

In July 1762, Carrollton once again begged to return home. Carroll of Annapolis was unmoved. "This is in my own hand," he wrote, "because I do not care my clerk should know that you still persist...to desire to come in next Spring. Were I to consent to it, would not that consent make us ridiculous in the eyes of thinking men?...Is a year to be higgled for by a man of your sense & age...are six years of your life to be flung away? If that should be the case, I have done my duty. You will too late repent your not corresponding with my will & intention."

In spite of all his father's entreaties and warnings, Carrollton could never bring himself to enroll in the Temple as a regular student. He remained a "lay resident in the precincts of the Temple." The young man devised his own educational program, weighted toward mathematics, bookkeeping, and surveying. Finally, in January 1763, he notified his father that "my reading the law will be somewhat interrupted, at least for some while," by the demands of his other studies. "My health will not permit me to apply as closely and as long as I could wish: and I am persuaded you would not have me upon any account endanger my constitution which, though pretty good, is none of the stoutest, and will not bear much fatigue."

Bereavement

This time, Carroll of Annapolis gave in. It was the death of Elizabeth Carroll that finally wore down his resistance.

Carrollton's future had always depended on how well he pleased his unpredictable father. In his unusual situation, Carroll relied on his mother's reassurance. Only "a very long letter from Mama," he wrote, can "make me amends" for his misery in England. "Your Papa's love for you is so great," she had written in 1754, "and he is so well pleased with your diligence, improvement, & good dispositions [that] he is inclined to do everything for your satisfaction." After the Squire's journey to France, Elizabeth Carroll reported that "no parent can have a greater tenderness for his child than yours has for you."

Her own feelings for her son bordered on idolatry. Carrollton's letters, "so full of tenderness & affection," brought her to tears. "You [were] always an affectionate, tender, good child... you are still the same." The dependence between mother and son was mutual. When Carrollton wrote in 1760 to express his "great uneasiness" about Mrs. Carroll's health, his concern made her recall "what you used to tell me, when a little boy lolling & fondling about me, that you loved me dearly & always should have the same fondness & affection for me, during life." The Squire had withheld his full, unconditional love from Elizabeth by refusing to marry her for many years. Perhaps the boy was trying to make up for his father's lack of commitment through his own total devotion.

On March 31, 1761, Carrollton wrote a long, confidential letter to his mother. He complained of frequent colds, "attended with a dizziness & swimming of the head." He predicted that his mother would be disappointed with him when he returned to Maryland. Good reports from his friends were "owing more to their good nature & friendship, than to any... merit of mine," the young man wrote. "What I say is not dictated by an affected modesty, worse than pride; 'tis the sentiment of my mind: I detest dissimulation and dissemblers." Carrollton chattered blithely about the "wiles, the winning arts of women." But he was "frightened at the clinking of matrimonial chains; those are never to be broken."

Then Carroll returned to his central preoccupation. "My expressions of love and tenderness for you when a boy," he wrote, "were the language of native simplicity: the dictates of a heart that could not then, nor will now dissemble its real sentiments: these are unalterably the same: my love, my affection, my tender concern for my parents are not diminished by length of time and place: they are only strengthened and confirmed by reason, which teaches me to acknowledge and be grateful for the greatest obligations from the best of parents."

His mother was already dead. Carroll of Annapolis' letter did not arrive until early June. He recommended that his son turn to religion, "the only solid comforter of the afflicted," in his grief.

Carrollton was devastated. "I loved my Mama most tenderly: how strong, how cogent were the motives of my love! How affectionate, how tender, how loving a mother was she to me! What fond, delusive hopes have I entertained of seeing her again! I was too credulous: all my imaginary joys are vanished in an instant: they are succeeded by the bitter, cruel thoughts of never seeing more my loved lost mother. The greatest blessing I wished for in this life was to see, to enjoy my parents after so long a separation, to comfort, to support them in an advanced age: one is for ever snatched from me!"

He wanted to know whether his mother spoke of him during her illness. "Did she not so much as say, remember me to my absent son? How little does he now think of his dying mother! What grief, what affliction will my death give him!" He reproached his father for keeping him away from his mother. "Had I been here in her last moments to take a last farewell, that had been some sad relief: even this was denied me." He wished to return to Maryland with the next fleet. By November, Carroll was more resigned. "The loss of my dear mother still sits heavy on my heart: but as my grief is unavailing and prejudicial to myself, I endeavour to get the better of it."

"Your mention of your Mama to me and your letter to her softened me," admitted the Squire. "Time will give us more fortitude." He reassured Carrollton that his mother had thought of him while dying, but he refused to supply any more information. "I could not say less as you desired to be informed as to these particulars, I cannot say more the subject being too moving.... In the future let us mention her as seldom as possible, we can never cease to think of her & pray for her." Elizabeth Carroll once told her son that she and her husband had agreed not to speak of Carrollton, to reduce their sadness at his absence. Now the Squire adopted the same stoic policy after his wife's death.

Part I: Exile

In his emotional detachment, the elder Carroll differed from many men of his era, who cultivated sensibility and sentimentality. Neither the sentimental mode, which Carrollton indulged, nor his father's stoicism quite did justice to the grief that both men felt. As a result, emotion gave way to anxiety. Carroll of Carrollton developed an obsessive fear that his father, too, would die. "Pray do not talk of leaving me," the young man wrote. "There is nothing after your displeasure I so much dread as your death."

Carroll's proclamations of love and devotion for his father grew more and more effusive. "You have been to me the best, the kindest father: my constant effort will be to make a suitable return to please you.... I love you most tenderly. My daily prayers are that we may long live happy together." Part of this was pragmatic. Carrollton was panicked at the prospect of having to take on the family business before he was ready, "surrounded with enemies, engaged in hereditary quarrels, bewildered [by] the labyrinths of law." "Take care of your health if you love me," he begged.

The Squire tried to restore his son's peace of mind. "Dear Charley," he wrote, "I am convinced you would be sincerely concerned for my death, I know in that case you would sustain a great loss, but not nigh so great as you present it to yourself." He refused to let his son return home yet. "You see things in so partial a light, you have it so much at heart to return, that your reasoning is unbecoming your good sense." Instead, he set out to reassure his son in a typically eighteenth-century manner: he made his will, and left Carrollton everything. It helped. "The sending a copy of your will," the younger Carroll wrote, "proves how much you love me." Relieved, the heir promised that "if I survive, you may depend on a due & entire exaction of all you recommend or order to be done."

Marriage Negotiations

Carrollton's character was still in formation. His fear of being left alone caused him to regress after his mother's death. For the next ten years, Carroll's actions were mostly reactions to his father's wishes. They changed as those wishes changed. After his father cautioned him not to marry hastily and without parental consent, Carrollton assured the Squire that he would seek his consent before marrying. When Carroll of Annapolis urged his son "on no consideration, to marry a Protestant," Carrollton echoed that "no consideration whatever shall prevail upon me to marry a protestant."

The senior Carroll warned that unless "your wife be virtuous, sensible, good natured, complaisant, complying & of a cheerful disposition, you will not find the married state a happy one. Next to these, family & fortune come under consideration." Carrollton took his father's advice seriously, to the point of doubting that he would ever meet a suitable bride. No Englishwoman of gentle birth would "follow me to a barbarous uncivilised country." He had never met any Catholic women to suit him. "I have never been in love," Carrollton said, "& hope I never shall be."

Again, Carroll of Annapolis had to change course. "What, not one cheerful, sensible, virtuous, good-natured woman in ten thousand? Pray, how many cheerful, sensible, virtuous, good-natured men do you reckon in a like number. To do the sex justice," the Squire observed, "I believe they outnumber us in good qualities." Carroll's personal merit and huge fortune made him probably the most eligible Catholic bachelor in the British Empire. Carroll of Annapolis promised not to pressure his son into marrying. "But many men talk as you do until they are far advanced in years, some until they are past their grand climacteric, & then become fond doting husbands."[1]

This letter was written on July 22, 1763. We do not know when it was received, but by October, Carrollton had executed an about-face. He wrote his father that he was going to Paris to court Miss Louisa Baker, to whom he had been introduced by a Jesuit friend, Alexander Crookshanks. "Her youth & inexperience will, I hope, smooth the path of victory.... Her genuine candor & simplicity will unfold her true character, all her

---

[1] According to Hoffman and Mason (163), "climacterics" were periods of special vulnerability to crisis. They were believed to occur every seven or nine years in a person's life. The "grand climacteric" took place at age sixty-three.

virtues, & her imperfections." The elder Carroll had recommended that his son seek a wife "bred in a monastery," and indeed, Louisa was now living in an Ursuline convent.

Carrollton's willingness to postpone his return home was even more startling than his sudden conversion to the idea of marriage. If Louisa encouraged him, he would have to put off his departure for a year. However, Carrollton ruled out the possibility of remaining in England permanently, although his father offered to send him his fortune. "The situation of our affairs absolutely require[s] my residence in Maryland," the heir wrote, "and I cannot sacrifice the future aggrandisement of our family to a woman." Carroll's growing sense of America's future greatness also made him unwilling to be an absentee landlord in England. Casually, he made a prediction that put him well ahead of most colonials. "America is a growing country," he declared. "In time it will & must be independent."

Now it was the Squire's turn to become impatient. "A thing of so much importance as matrimony is not to be precipitated. But as you took it into your head last October, I hope if you proceed you may finish it so as to be with me next summer, or at farthest, in the fall." Carroll of Annapolis helped his son's cause by giving him the ten-thousand-acre manor of Carrollton. Fearing that Louisa's father might marry again and produce heirs, he urged his son to "get the [Baker] estate settled on the lady." The Squire also had to guard against the possibility of his son's early death, "which is not improbable," Carrollton admitted, "as I am of a weak constitution." Carroll of Annapolis did not want Louisa to inherit the Carroll estate if his son were to die young. Instead, he offered her a cash payment of eighteen hundred pounds a year if she were to become a widow. In return for this jointure, Carrollton was to receive a large cash dowry from the Bakers.

Carrollton's suit ran into trouble, however. In January of 1764, under the stress of the marriage negotiations, the young man suffered a clinical depression. On his doctor's orders, he went to take the waters at Bath. "I think I feel myself benefited by them," Carrollton wrote. "For this some time past, I have felt a gradual decay of strength and wasting of flesh, attended with unusual low spirits: my nerves are weak, and my whole frame very delicate." At Bath, Carroll met Louisa's mother and sisters, much to his disgust. "If the daughter's temper resembles the mother's," he wrote his father, "I shall leave England next May or June." Louisa's older sister instantly disliked Carroll. This low opinion she "was pleased to form of me behind my back, from little inadvertencies." Her sister's reaction influenced Louisa, for whose good opinion Carroll "would have given the world."

Alarmed, the Squire hoped that his son's illness sprang only from "the anxiety your passion for Miss Baker gives you." He offered to give his son the Annapolis house, and retire to Elk Ridge with Louisa's father, if that would "promote your happiness." Evidently, though, Mr. Baker found this proposal less than appealing. Nor was he pleased at the prospect of his teenage daughter crossing the Atlantic. When Baker suggested that Carrollton stay in England, the suitor took offense at "so unnatural a proposal." "You know little of me, Sir," Carrollton wrote, "and do me injustice to imagine that I can be prevailed on to live absent from a father, whom I most tenderly love, to whose company & conversation I would willingly sacrifice every other enjoyment." Carroll made sure his father got the point. "I choose rather to forego my own happiness than make a parent miserable." This statement sums up Carrollton's life before the American Revolution.

As his marriage prospects grew more and more remote, Carroll's health improved. "I find myself much mended…& in better spirits." When Baker asked Carrollton to return to Maryland and resume his courtship in three or four years, the matter was dropped. His disappointment had not soured the young man on marriage, however. If he met with a Maryland lady to his liking, Carrollton wrote, "I should choose to settle without loss of time: the sooner, the better, for then I might live to bring up my children: if I stay till I attain the age of 36, the chances of my living so long are against me as I am of a thin & puny habit of body."

Carrollton set out for home around the time of his twenty-seventh birthday. After his long exile, he could never again bring himself to leave America.

PART II.

First Citizen.

It seemed as if malign powers were conspiring to keep Charles Carroll from the home for which he longed. He set sail on September 19, 1764, but the ship met unfavorable winds. It "tossed about the whole month of November," he wrote, "in so much we scarce made 100 leagues on our way in 30 days." Finally arriving in Virginia, Carrollton notified his father on December 20 that he would be home shortly. But harsh weather stranded Carroll on Maryland's eastern shore, where he took refuge with the Tilghman family. He reached Annapolis on Tuesday, February 12, 1765.

Elizabeth Carroll, in her last letter to her son, had reminded him of his promise to give a ball for the people of Annapolis when he returned. It is not known whether this took place, but Carrollton's return was an event of some importance. The *Maryland Gazette* reported the news on February 14. Another significant event coincided with Carroll's homecoming. King George III assented to the Stamp Act on March 22, 1765.

Parliamentary Tyranny

The English revolutionaries of 1642 and 1688 had frequently cited natural law in their opposition to the divine right of kings. In reality, both revolutions turned into a power play by Parliament, which proved itself sufficiently tyrannical in its own right. The mixed constitution was replaced by a unitary sovereign called the "King in Parliament." As time went on, Parliament became omnipotent and unassailable. Elections were held less frequently in the eighteenth century, every seven years instead of every three, and few were eligible to vote.

David Hume was the most acute observer of English life in the aftermath of the Glorious Revolution. He saw clearly that Parliament had become "uncontrollable." Royal influence was exercised only through corruption. There was no longer any "middle power, or independent powerful nobility" to protect the constitution. And yet the people believed that the Glorious Revolution had set them free. This belief lulled them into complacency, so that "the people, though guarded by multiplied laws, are totally naked, defenceless, and disarmed." The apparent liberty of England, paradoxically, made the government more absolute, since it inspired blind trust. Hume pointed out that Parliament had granted more monies during the first two months of the Seven Years' War than it had during Elizabeth's entire forty-five-year reign.

Dissident thinkers looked for a way to confront the power of the unitary state. They tried to make the English common law the ultimate arbiter of justice. The common law became "metaphysically endowed with the attributes of natural law with which it was fully identified." The problem was that the common law, though it contained much that was in accord with natural reason, could not bear this construction under the circumstances. The judges who interpreted the common law had become passive functionaries in a Leviathan state.

Nor did English judges see the common law as a vehicle for natural law. It is true that the jurist Sir Edward Coke, reporting the famous case of Dr. Bonham, declared that "when an act of Parliament is against common right and reason, or repugnant, or impossible to be performed, the common law will control it, and adjudge such act to be void." Sir William Blackstone, too, asserted that "no human laws should be suffered to contradict" the natural law. Coke and Blackstone were constantly cited by English and American activists, all to no avail. Most justices did not recognize that natural law could invalidate an unjust statute. Nor was Magna Carta considered the point of reference for all law, as the United States Constitution is.

The problem was that, with the destruction of the Catholic Church, England was severed from its roots in Christian political thought. Even Coke and Blackstone, who paid lip service to the natural law, sought the origins of the English constitution in the misty Teutonic past, rather than in the Christian dispensation. Coke saw Magna Carta as merely an affirmation of the Saxon polity, "no new declaration." Blackstone argued that English liberty derived from "that ancient constitution, of which our ancestors had been defrauded by the art and finesse of the Norman lawyers."

The Saxon Myth

According to the Saxon myth, the English constitution was born among the Gothic tribes described by Tacitus. These Germanic tribesmen had supposedly elected their kings, as well as a *witenagemot*, or parliament. They also enjoyed trial by jury. Their public virtue enabled the Goths to defeat the degenerate Roman Empire, and later, to take their system to England. Political leaders such as William Petyt and Algernon Sidney had developed the myth after the Restoration; Sidney lost his head for it. The story was then taken up by the influential historian Paul de Rapin.

It is not difficult to see the anti-Catholicism of this narrative. Just as the Goths defeated the first Rome, the Reformation was a Saxon revival against Norman power and the Roman Church. The Saxon myth also fed into racial ideologies that were used to justify the oppression of the Irish, among others. Modern historians portray Saxon society as a primitive feudalism, not a nascent republic. In fact, warrior chieftains lived off the labor of peasants. Constitutional government originated in Christendom, not among the pre-Christian Goths.

The most influential exponent of the Saxon myth in America was Thomas Jefferson, who called Tacitus "the first writer in the world." Jefferson always preferred Rapin's history to Hume's.

John Adams, on the other hand, had no time for Saxon reveries. It is true that he could never bring himself to accept dogmatic Christianity. "An incarnate God!!!" he once exclaimed. "An eternal, self-existent, omnipotent, omniscient author of this stupendous universe, suffering on a cross!!! My soul starts with horror at this idea, and it has stupefied the Christian world." But Adams saw clearly that the basis of politics had to be the natural law. English liberties were nothing other than these "rights of nature" which were "antecedent to all earthly government." These rights were etched "on the frame of human nature, rooted in the constitution of the intellectual and moral world" by the "Great Legislator of the Universe."

The Mental Revolution

Adams wrote Jefferson in 1815 that "the Revolution was in the minds of the people, and this was effected, from 1760 to 1775." The mental revolution that Adams described was an increasing loss of trust in the English constitution and the common law, and a movement toward the natural law. Concurrently, there was born the concept of a written constitution, which would embody the natural law concretely. English rights became identified with natural rights, so that the colonists gradually stopped claiming their common-law rights as Englishmen and started asserting their natural rights as human beings.

Essentially, the revolutionaries were rediscovering the Catholic political tradition, based in natural law, with its emphasis on the common good, corporatism, hierarchy, subsidiarity, and popular sovereignty. Because most of the founding fathers came from unorthodox religious backgrounds, they distorted the concept of natural law, generally in the direction of individualism. Americans still live with the consequences of these distortions. Nevertheless, the American reinvention of Catholic political thought—for such it was—is a great achievement. The United States created the first government in the history of the world that is explicitly based in natural law. We must diagnose the founders' misunderstanding of that law, as we attempt to understand their vision of a just republic.

St. Thomas proclaimed that "the end of law is the common good." Later Catholic thinkers developed a theory of the *corpus mysticum reipublicae*, the mystical body of the commonwealth. This political mystical body was a facsimile of the mystical body of Christ, the Church. The Church was united to its head, the pope, and the commonwealth was united to its sovereign. The analogy was taken further. Nicholas of Cusa argued that the state was born of the body of the people by their free consent, just as Christ had been born by Mary's *fiat*. In other words, the people delegated sovereignty, and the people could resume sovereignty if the ruler broke his covenant with them. In practice, a *maior et sanior pars* of the people, the most responsible members of the community, could act on behalf of the whole society to establish good government.

These ideas found their way into English political life early on, beginning with Magna Carta. When Edward I renewed the promises contained in that document, he pledged never to impose taxes "but by the common consent of the realm and for the common profit thereof." By the fourteenth century, Parliament was believed to represent "the body of the whole realm." This tradition was abandoned when Henry VIII claimed a direct divine mandate. In response, St. Thomas More insisted that "the consent of the people both bestows and withdraws sovereignty." This original consent is a natural right pertaining to the political body of a nation, as is the right of resistance to tyranny.

When Carroll returned to America in 1765, few men in the colonies were ready to speak of natural rights. Richard Bland in Virginia and Jonathan Mayhew in Massachusetts were the first to rediscover the Catholic tradition. Mayhew, however, altered the tradition by applying his New Light theology to the natural law. The "New Lights" were a Calvinist, or post-Calvinist, branch of the Congregational Church. They emphasized the sacredness of conscience, proposing that each soul had direct access to God, unmediated by ecclesial structures. The conscience, the "moral sense," was the natural law of God written on the heart. New Light theology's sacralization of individual prerogatives had an explosive impact on colonial society. It was the divine right of kings again, with the proviso that every man was a king.

Mayhew's "Unlimited Submission" sermon, John Adams wrote, "was incorporated into my nature and indelibly engraved on my memory." Fortunately, Adams was enough of a realist not to get carried away in Mayhew's excesses. Like Carroll, and following Montesquieu, he favored a mixed and limited government that would check the passions of individuals. In order to create a mixed government, sovereignty had to be removed entirely from the government. This would keep any one branch of government from claiming an ultimate sovereignty, as Parliament had in England. In the new American governments, sovereignty would be returned to the people. As James Wilson described it, the people would then delegate sovereignty "to such bodies, on such terms, and under such limitations as they think proper."

Thus, the United States ended up with multiple, overlapping sovereignties, and a mixed government. This federal structure, in its pristine form, embodied the principles of hierarchy and subsidiarity. It was reminiscent of St. Thomas' ideal state, where "one is set in authority on account of his virtue, to rule over all; and under him are others ruling on account of their virtue; and nevertheless such government belongs to all, both because the rulers can be chosen from all and because they are chosen by all." The flip side of hierarchy is subsidiarity. Legislation, wrote the Angelic Doctor, "should take account of many things, as to persons, as to occupations, and as to times, because the political community is composed of many citizens and its good is procured by many actions."

The American system also resembled the hierarchical government established by Moses, so much so that both Jefferson and Franklin based their designs for the Great Seal of the United States on the Exodus. And, of course, the American structure of government bears a resemblance to the Catholic Church, with its monarchical pope, its senatorial cardinals, and its bishops united with the laity. All these estates, taken together, make up a complete body.

Although the republic was rooted in Catholic thinking, most of its members still associated Catholicism with Stuart tyranny until the Revolution. One of Mayhew's sermons was published in a book called *The Pillars of Priestcraft and Orthodoxy Shaken*. James Otis, a disciple of Mayhew in Massachusetts politics, described Newport, Rhode Island, in 1765 as the haunt of

"Turks, Jews, and other infidels with a few renegade Christians and Catholics."

The Republican Empire Stirs

Because of the popular prejudice, Catholics had to be cautious. Political discussion had become the colonists' obsessive pastime, but our anonymous French traveler reported in 1765 that Catholics did not join so freely in the debate.

Things were changing, however, especially in the South, where revolutionary sentiment was already well advanced in 1765. Historians have been misled by the Founding Fathers in this regard. John Jay claimed in 1821 that he never heard any American speak in favor of independence before 1775. Even as hostilities were beginning, Franklin told Lord Chatham that, in all his extensive travels, "I never had heard in any conversation, from any person, drunk or sober, the least expression of a wish for a separation."

As we have seen, however, Charles Carroll already believed in 1764 that America "must and will be independent." The French traveler confirms that Carroll was not alone. "No nation whatsoever seems better calculated for independency," the Frenchman minuted, "and the inhabitants are already entirely disposed thereto and talk of nothing more than it." When the Stamp Act came up in conversation, planters would lay aside their petty quarrels, swearing that they would be damned before they would pay it. Startlingly, the French diarist claimed that the Virginians were ready to turn to Catholic France for help, if it became necessary to defend Patrick Henry. The traveler predicted that Protestant Americans would "lay aside their religion, when their interest requires it, as well as the English can, and always have done."

Americans were beginning to feel their power. Carrollton estimated that there were 2,500,000 colonists, and predicted that twenty years would double that number. "The power of this continent is growing daily," Carroll wrote an English friend, "and in time will be as unbounded as our dominions are extensive. The rapid increase of manufactures surpasses the expectations of the most sanguine American. Even the arts and sciences commence to flourish, and in these, as in arms, the day, I hope, will come when America shall be superior to all the world." "I do not believe the universe can show a finer country," Carrollton bragged, "producing within itself not only all the necessaries, but even most of the superfluities of life."

English society was based primarily on the concept of honor. It was necessary for those in government to keep up appearances in society, so financial corruption was tolerated. However, the ruling class were expected to use their wealth for the benefit of those beneath them, supporting the lower classes with lavish spending. William Graves, an English acquaintance of Carrollton, urged the heir to practice the code of *noblesse oblige*. Graves wrote Carroll of Annapolis that "the only matter I used to caution your son against was too much economy." "I should wish your son to spend the whole of his present income among his tenants, manufacturers, & neighbors, by doing principally what none but a man of affluence can do."

Carrollton was having none of it. "I do not intend, as you advise, to spend my annual income," he told Graves. "The gentlemen of this province were never fond of expense and less now than ever; in these times of necessity and oppression it is a duty every man of fortune owes his country to set an example of frugality and industry to the common people." This was a totally new concept of gentility. Following Montesquieu and Hume, Carroll saw work and industry as virtues, luxury and idleness as vices. "The mistaken policy of England," he predicted, "will force us to be industrious."

When the Marylander set out to lobby his English correspondents against the Stamp Act, he often invoked the natural law. But Carrollton was not ashamed to argue from pragmatism and self-interest. American petitions against the Stamp Act were useless; an embargo on British goods was necessary, "to make the oppressors feel it." He preferred "an argument rather levelled at their pockets than understandings, which may indeed greatly contribute by emptying of those to open these."

Carrollton could not understand why the House of Commons continued to cling to "an empty point of honor...a thing so unsubstantial." As for the English merchants, "their own interest, if not the interest of their employers, which I am sorry to say, seem to be two very distinct and separate interests, should have induced them" to petition against the Stamp Act. Carroll seemed unaware that honor was still the master principle of English society. His appeals to interest fell on deaf ears.

Cathy Matson and Peter Onuf have argued that the key ideological shift in the years before the Revolution was the identification of self-interest with public virtue. Carrollton epitomizes this shift, which made possible the creation of a "Republican Empire." Thrift and temperance, which benefited individuals, would also promote the common good. It was necessary, Carroll wrote, to reduce the number of "great and lucrative posts" in the British administration. The public debt should be discharged. The "venality, avarice and profusion of all orders of men" should be "restrained by wholesome laws and the universal depravity of their manners reformed. These vices in all states have ever been destructive to public liberty."

America would be the new empire of liberty. But it would not last forever, Carrollton warned. "Liberty will maintain her empire, till a dissoluteness of morals, luxury and venality shall have prepared the degenerate sons of some future age, to prefer their own mean lucre, the bribes, and the smiles of corruption and arbitrary ministers, to patriotism, to glory, and to the public weal." "A period is already set to the reign of American freedom," Carroll wrote, "but that fatal time seems to be at a great distance." In 1765, Americans were still "not yet corrupt enough to undervalue Liberty, they are truly sensible of its blessings."

The Mercantile System

Mercantilism, which restricted colonial manufactures and limited American trade with other countries, was bound up with the English politics of honor. The colonists were supposed to be loyal to the mother country, at the expense of their self-interest. When Pitt defended the right of Parliament to restrain American industry, Carrollton scoffed at his abstract reasoning. "An argument that proves too much proves nothing." Mercantilism, Carroll argued, violated the first principles of the English constitution. "If I could make a coat of my own wool, much cheaper and better than what I could have from England, would it not be the highest injustice to force me to forego such an advantage: would it not be raising a very heavy tax upon my property without my consent?"

Twentieth-century historians have developed a critique of colonialism in Africa and Asia. Their analysis is not generally applied to the American colonists. The white American settlers were no doubt better off than modern victims of colonialism, since they were not a conquered people. However, the Americans labored under many of the disabilities common to colonial structures. The deeper origin of the Stamp Act crisis may be found in the injustice of the mercantile system.

There was little protest against the mother country before 1765, because the British maintained a very relaxed grip on the colonies. The colonies did not mind being restricted to producing raw materials, so long as smugglers gave them access to cheap finished goods from foreign countries. The British pretended not to notice the smuggling, which violated the mercantilist ideology. Nor did they bother to collect the tax placed on molasses in the 1730s.

This strange *laissez-faire* version of mercantilism began to change after the French and Indian War. Since the colonists had done almost nothing to help the war effort, the British acquired a mountain of debt with their new empire. English resentment strengthened the administration's will to enforce mercantilist principles. The Sugar Act of 1764 reduced the Molasses Act tax, but guaranteed that it would actually be collected. While the colonists were still recovering from this indignity, the Stamp Act was imposed.

Even if the colonists had been inclined to accept the new duty on printed materials, it would have been impossible for them to pay it. Benedict Calvert noted that there was not enough money

Part II: First Citizen

in the colonies to pay the tax. Even while the new taxes were being laid, a Currency Act had forbidden emissions of paper money in the colonies. And importation of specie—gold and silver—from England had long been prohibited.

In any case, little specie would have found its way to the colonies, because of the unfavorable balance of trade. Restrictions on American lumber and iron production meant that imports from England far outweighed exports to the mother country. Not only did the trade imbalance drive money out of Maryland, the planters' indebtedness inflated what little was left. One hundred fifty pounds in Maryland currency was worth one hundred pounds sterling in 1753. Bills of exchange could be bought from planters with good credit in England, but the exchange rate was even worse than that for Maryland currency. Interest rates were exorbitant: Charles Carroll the Barrister once paid £52 annually on a debt of £217.

Even Gov. Sharpe regretted that Parliament had forbidden emissions of paper money. Carroll of Carrollton realized that the scarcity of money was at the heart of the colony's financial woes. To circumvent the provisions of the Currency Act, the assembly decided to print money without making it a legal tender. However, this bill was held up by a dispute over the salary of a clerk of the council. At last, in 1766, a compromise was reached. In paper dollars, $173,733 at 4s. 6d. to the dollar were emitted, about £39,090 sterling. "A medium of trade is absolutely necessary to a trading people," commented Carrollton. "Such has been found the want of it in this province, that even the resentment and spirit of party itself has given way to so useful a measure."

The problem of debt remained. Carrollton spoke for many planters when he blamed corrupt English merchants, or factors, for the crushing colonial debt. "Our factors are closely combined," he complained. "Tho' hating and hated by each other they confederate to oppress us." The Stamp Act provided a pretext to cut down on English imports, redress the balance of trade, and reduce colonial debt. Carroll made sure his English correspondents were informed about the non-importation movement. When New York and Philadelphia merchants resolved to boycott British goods, Carrollton told an English friend to "draw from it what inference you please. The inferences I have drawn are these—the Americans are jealous of their privileges, and resolved to maintain them."

A word that would become emblematic of Carroll's political thought makes its first appearance in these letters on the Stamp Act. Unlike the Irish, he wrote, the Americans will never let themselves become "slaves and beasts of burden": they have too much "spirit." "To judge from the number of the colonists, and the spirit they have already shown, and which I hope to God will not fail them on the day of trial, twenty thousand men would find it difficult to enforce the [Stamp Act]; or more properly speaking, to ram it down our throats."

The Spirit of Liberty

As the ships containing stamped paper approached Maryland, Carrollton envisioned an army of "harpies, *id est* stamp men, excise men, ministerial men etc. etc." draining the vitality out of the body politic. The result would be "political death." Perhaps these imperial "harpies" reminded Carroll of those earlier civil servants, the pursuivants. This would account for the pleasure Carrollton took in the activities of the Sons of Liberty, in spite of his mistrust of the mob.

In Baltimore, a Sons of Liberty chapter developed out of a "mechanical company," that is, a combination police force, fire department, and militia. The leader of the Sons in Annapolis was Samuel Chase, whom a contemporary described as "a busy, restless incendiary, a ringleader of mobs, a foul-mouthed and inflaming son of discord." Chase had been denied membership to the Homony Club, a prestigious gentlemen's society. He was in chronic financial trouble.

Carrollton approved when Chase's mob hanged and buried in effigy Zachariah Hood, the Maryland stamp agent. Hood "is hated & despised by every one," Carroll reported. "He has been whip-pilloried & hung in effigy in this place, Baltimore town & at the landing." "This place" is Annapolis; "the landing" is Elk

Ridge, the scene of Carroll's lonely youth. The Hood effigy was allowed to make a "last dying speech," offering "a succinct account of his birth & parentage & education." The effigy confessed that it had been apprenticed to "Old Nick" (Satan).

The strategy of the Sons of Liberty was to force government offices to reopen and conduct business without the stamped paper. At first, Carrollton and other gentlemen approved. But as the Sons grew bolder, Carroll became apprehensive about "the clamorous public." At an Annapolis meeting, "some expressions were very unguarded, to say no more." The idea of opening the offices "seemed to the most thinking men of the town, improper at that juncture."

Soon, however, the Baltimore Sons of Liberty descended on the capital, at the invitation of Chase and William Paca. The Sons demanded that the offices be opened, and it was agreed that public business would resume on April 1, 1766. According to Carrollton, this "satisfied the Sons of Liberty, who were on this occasion more satisfied than they usually are." After Zachariah Hood fled Maryland in disgrace, Gov. Sharpe feared the triumphant mob. "They begin to think they can by the same way of proceeding accomplish anything their leaders may tell them they ought to do," wrote the governor.

Carrollton had not forgotten the lessons of the Jesuit expulsion. He saw the Sons as "men of little note." "The clamour of the People out of doors proceeds from their ignorance, prejudice and passion: it is very difficult to get the better of these by reasoning." Carroll's strategy, anticipating Hamilton's approach, was to channel the passions of the people toward public virtue. This could be done by appealing to their enlightened self-interest. The mob should be guided by elite statesmen, who would treat them in a "condescending" manner. In 1765, this term had positive connotations of unselfishness and open-mindedness.

Like Montesquieu, Carroll feared legislative tyranny more than executive. "England can never be enslaved but by a corrupt Parliament," he wrote. "No stretch of the prerogative for the general good will ever endanger our constitution." The common good required a mixed constitution, in which neither the legislature nor the executive could dominate. "The genuine principles of either Whigism or Toryism are equally dangerous to our constitution!" Carroll declared. "The power of the King and Lords would be annihilated by the former; by the latter the liberty of the subject would be taken away and despotism established in its stead."

Carrollton had already advanced well beyond the prevailing political ideas in England. His efforts to lobby his trading partners against the Stamp Act were unsuccessful. One desultory riot in London was dispersed by troops. Although the Stamp Act was repealed, the British government refused to concede the point of honor at stake. They passed a law that declared that Parliament had the right to tax the colonies when it chose. The Declaratory Act "does not in the least damp our joy," Carroll wrote. "It will not hurt us much to resolve or pass an Act that the Parliament has a right to tax America, if they never put it in practice."

The Stamp Act repeal partially restored Carroll's confidence in the English system. He hoped that "this act of justice and condescension" would calm the colonists' passions. "The minds of men were estranged; a spirit of resentment roused by oppression had diffused itself thro' all ranks." But things would never really be the same, since the force of popular will had been unleashed.

The colonial legislatures also rediscovered their charter rights during the Stamp Act crisis. Citing Lord Baltimore's original charter, a Maryland judge held the Act unconstitutional. Other colonies, including Massachusetts, Connecticut, and Rhode Island, claimed the right of home rule from their charters. Carrollton insisted that the colonies had "a competent legislature within themselves to raise taxes."

THE HABIT OF BUSINESS

Carroll was, of course, barred from that legislature. Nor could he vote. As an attorney, he could only give advice and arrange pleadings by other lawyers.

Part II: First Citizen

Carrollton claimed not to mind that "Providence" had disqualified him from public life. "Among all the disadvantages a Roman Catholic labours under, there is still this advantage: he may be honourable, honest, independent." Carroll rejected the system of public honors: "Posts of dignity & profit are almost incompatible with virtue." Placemen, state employees dependent on the government payroll, were merely "slaves, more worthy of hatred than envy." Thus, Carrollton was willing to accept a permanent exclusion of Catholics from public office, the House of Delegates excepted. "My views reach not beyond the narrow limits of this province," he declared. "So little is my ambition, and my bent to retirement so strong, that I am determined, leaving all ambitious pursuits, to confine myself to the improvement...of my paternal acres."

He was serious. For Carroll, liberated from his hated legal studies, had discovered the God-given cure for his anxieties: work. "My poor little thin carcass keeps its own," he wrote, "& my spirits are kept up...by a variety of employments, business, exercise & study. In short, I never allow myself time to be idle, or the spleen to prey upon me, and to this perpetual occupation I ascribe the nearly equal flow of spirits, which I cannot say is constitutional, being naturally rather of a melancholy & contemplative cast."

It was a great deal of work that faced Carrollton, hardly a "retirement." By 1774, the Carrolls were paying quitrents on 58,621 acres. To be in the wealthiest one percent of the population for that year required at least £2,272 sterling. The Carrolls were worth £100,000 sterling. They acquired land holdings in New York and Pennsylvania and became interested in land and transportation companies. In 1772, Carrollton subscribed £1,000 to the Potomac Company, which sought to improve navigation of that river.

One hundred thousand pounds sterling may not seem like the stuff of legend to us, but in that time and place it was an unthinkable sum. With the Stamp Act and then the Townshend duties, the British administration hoped to raise a total of £40,000 sterling per year. When the

Maryland Assembly set out to provide the colony with a circulating medium, it emitted the equivalent of £39,090 sterling in paper money. The Carrolls easily outstripped the financiers of Boston and Philadelphia, ranking near the greatest merchants of London and Glasgow in terms of wealth.

The younger Carroll never actually lived at Carrollton. He made his home in Annapolis, and his father ruled Doughoregan Manor, which still stands near Ellicott City, Maryland. This arrangement no doubt helped maintain family harmony. Carrollton described the "perfect understanding between my Father and me." There were "no transactions which we keep secret from each other." Carroll of Annapolis still enjoyed "the spirits of youth and the understanding of a man of forty," his son testified. "He is the greatest comfort of my life, & I do all in my power to render him happy & easy."

Indeed, his father had become Carrollton's emotional mainstay. The heir corrected a rumor that the Squire had awarded his son £40,000 sterling. "Not only 40,000 pounds but the whole of my Father's estate is at my disposal. We are, and are likely to continue on the best of terms: never Father and son were [on] better." Carrollton's stridency on the subject of imperial relations alienated his English friends, and distance took its toll. His English correspondents gradually dropped away and were not replaced by close friends in the colonies. By the time of the Revolution, Carroll revealed himself only in letters to his father.

Under his father's tutelage, Carrollton became a businessman of renowned shrewdness. At first, he hated the more tedious aspects of his work. "I have been poring these two or three days past over all old accounts of near thirty years standing that are now become the subject of a chancery suit," Carroll lamented in 1765. "I am quite weak with the fatigue." His father regretted that "you cannot without fatigue go through the business you must transact." "Never do anything in a hurry," he counseled his son. "Thought & reflection ought to accompany the most trifling transactions, when they are omitted, it is an indication that application & business is very disagreeable." Carroll of Annapolis offered some excellent advice to relieve his son's stress. "The way to do it with ease is to do only one thing at a time & to do it so & so deliberately as if you had nothing else to do."

At times, the Squire's legal vendettas caused him to lay heavy burdens on Carrollton. On one occasion, he insisted that his son personally look through all the rent rolls of Baltimore and Anne Arundel Counties. The elder Carroll refused to let his clerks do this work: "They are too lazy & indolent & careless." While the father could be demanding, we must remember that Carrollton had begged to return home so that the Squire might form him in the way of business. Carroll of Annapolis taught his heir to be frugal, without becoming "penny wise & pound foolish." He showed his meek son how to hold his own in the marketplace. Carrollton should watch the markets, say nothing, and hold on to his tobacco until the buyers came up to his price.

Labor, Free and Unfree

Most disagreements between father and son were over plantation management. Carrollton once criticized his father for not feeding his field slaves well enough. "It is true they do not live so well as our house negroes," the Squire protested, "but full as well as any plantation negroes, & [I] think I can safely say no man in Maryland can show in proportion to our number, such likely well-looking slaves." Carroll of Annapolis, in turn, implied that his son's slave "family" was a den of thieves. "There are some light-fingered people in your family," he charged. "I lost a pair of thread stockings when last with you, pray inquire for them. Nanny is not the only thief in your house, I think to give Molly & Henry a severe whipping when I go down if my stockings are not found."

The question of corporal punishment was a delicate subject between the two men. Carroll of Annapolis believed that his son neglected to discipline his servants. Whipping was a fact of life, not only for slaves, but for white indentured servants like one Harry. "It is with great reluctance I part with Browne," the

Squire sniped. "He is a willing & diligent man. You will spoil him. The best servants must be minded, indifferent & lazy ones corrected: Harry shall have a good flogging & a collar this evening." (Iron collars were commonly inflicted on refractory servants.)

As if to prove that he could be a disciplinarian, Carrollton told his father in 1769 that some slaves "have been well whipped, & Will shall have a severe whipping tomorrow." Conversely, the elder Carroll would sometimes defer to his son's scruples on the subject. Squiers, an indentured servant, "was not whipped," the patriarch assured Carrollton in 1770. "He wears a collar...but I think to take it off soon."

The white indentured servants, mostly Irish, enjoyed more legal protection than slaves. But the same terminology was used for both groups. Clement Brooke, an associate in the Baltimore Iron Works, mentions that the company has decided "to purchase 5 negroes & 5 white servants." Brooke reported that "I have already bought 5 convicts for labourers & a shoemaker." Carrollton also spoke of buying a Scot to be his father's gardener.

The Carrolls regarded the slaves as their "people." Carroll of Annapolis interested himself in Magdalen's struggle against excessive drinking, and hoped that doctors would find a cure for the worms that had killed one Antony. When Grace died, the junior Carroll expressed a wish for her salvation: "Poor old creature, I hope she is happy." When Carrollton complained that some stallions were looking starved, the Squire refused "to pamper my horses & pinch my slaves...imitate me."

The younger Carroll took over his father's position in the Iron Works during the 1760s. He proved less litigious than the Squire, but did employ strong-arm tactics when necessary. Some partners were overcharging the company for supplies, so Carrollton proposed that their iron sales be stopped. When the partners refused, Carroll threatened to withdraw from the Iron Works unless all the company accounts were immediately settled.

Carroll's business education helped solidify his politics of "interest" and "spirit." Carrollton's policy was "to carry on the

Works with vigour & spirit." He proposed improvements that would be in "our interest." Gradually, the young businessman let go of antiquated business and political concepts. His conversion to the idea of compound interest is an example.

Compound interest results when unpaid interest is added to principal, and further interest is charged on the total amount. Medieval ethics considered compound interest usurious and illegal. While a law student, Carroll warned his father that the practice was still prohibited in common law. "The regulating of interest is undoubtedly as much the object & proper concern of the law as any one thing besides."

Carroll of Annapolis proclaimed his right to charge compound interest "in conscience, justice, & reason." In the new capitalist economy, money could be used to make money through investment. Thus, a creditor who was deprived of the use of his money became entitled to charge compound interest. The Squire's more modern outlook eventually persuaded his son. A 1798 List of Assets makes it clear that Carrollton routinely took compound interest.

Marriage

Since the Louisa Baker disaster, Carrollton's view of marriage had changed. While in England, beauty was his major criterion for female attractiveness. "The most beautiful are always the most powerful, at least with me. I would defy an ugly woman endowed with all the sagacity of a sphinx ever to entrap me." Since then, his youthful passions had cooled, he told a friend. "A man of common sense...is well convinced, or ought to be, of the emptiness of that passion (which exists nowhere but in romance). If he marries, he will marry from affection, from esteem, and from a sense of merit in his wife."

Beautiful, shallow women now left Carrollton cold. "Their charms...have but a few years to last, and in the eyes of a husband, but a few months; and good sense, good nature, improved by reflection, by reading, are the only means to hold the affection of a husband, and to perpetuate that empire which beauty first established. What more dreadful, what more irksome, than to be linked for life to a dull, insipid companion, whose whole conversation is confined to the color and fashion of her dress—the empty chit-chat of the tea table?" "Domestic cares, and charge of a family" would "do honor to a lady in the highest station of life."

This conception of womanhood was admirable, if somewhat severe and ideal. Still, Carrollton had become more adept in dealing with the generality of women. He praised a kinswoman's "obliging temper, and...pleasing fancy. These amiable endowments...endear you to all who have had the pleasure of your acquaintance." Soon after his return to Maryland, Carroll was made a benedict. He found Rachel Cooke "no ways inferior to Louisa." Her "sweetness of temper, and other amiable qualities have contributed to efface an impression which similar qualities had made on a heart too susceptible...& on a mind not sufficiently strengthened by Philosophy."

After the couple, who were cousins, obtained a dispensation of consanguinity, the wedding was scheduled for July 8, 1766. But once again, the prospect of marriage brought Carrollton to the brink of nervous collapse. The nuptials had to be postponed due to Carroll's "fever." He had been in a "declining way" before contracting the fever. Carrollton recognized the link between matrimony and his illnesses: "If I do not recover my health & strength I shall drop all thoughts of entering into that state [marriage]." Perhaps, given his mother's emotional dominance of his childhood, he subconsciously feared that all women would be equally needy.

The wedding was rescheduled for November. By then, Rachel Cooke had herself fallen ill. With her fiancé at her bedside, she died on November 25. "I loved her most sincerely," Carrollton wrote, "& had all the reason to believe I was as sincerely loved. Judge of my loss & by it of what I now feel." He forced himself to "drop this melancholy subject." Two years later, Carroll had become philosophical. Introducing William Cooke to an English friend, he explained, "It was this gentleman's sister I was to have espoused. *Sed Dis aliter visam* [but to the gods it seemed otherwise]."

It is not surprising that the woman whom Carrollton married came from his father's house. When he was in England, Carroll had spoken to the Calverts on behalf of Henry Darnall III, a relative who was seeking public office. Lord Baltimore apparently warned Carrollton that Darnall was not to be trusted. Darnall III was eventually convicted of embezzlement, and Carroll of Annapolis lost a £1,000 deposit he had put up to guarantee Darnall's good behavior.

Darnall's son, Henry Darnall IV, married Rachel Brooke, a niece of the Squire. Darnall IV was a "worthless good for nothing body," according to Elizabeth Carroll. The Darnall-Brooke union was such a disaster that Mrs. Carroll cautioned her son against "engaging in that state of life yet awhile." The couple had one child, Mary Darnall, known as Molly. When Darnall IV absconded, the Squire invited his wife and daughter to live permanently at Doughoregan. In September of 1772, the family learned that Henry Darnall IV had been executed. The news, Carroll of Annapolis reported, made Molly "low spirited."

When Carrollton and Molly were engaged in the winter of 1767–68, a dispensation was once again necessary. They were related on both sides. There was a further obstacle. At age eighteen, Molly was too young to execute the "Indenture," or prenuptial agreement, that the Carrolls required. Barring an act of the assembly, Carrollton would have to wait two years to marry. The impatient suitor spoke of "how disagreeable such a delay must be to one in my situation."

Still, the heir could not think of marrying without the indenture. "Riches are not always bestowed upon the deserving," he wrote. "I mention not this circumstance as an objection to the lady (I prefer [her] to all the women I have ever seen, even to Louisa...) but only as a reason inducing the necessity of a settlement." "I am willing & desirous that all my future actions should stand the test of those two severe Judges, Reason & Justice," Carroll added.

Daniel Dulany, Jr., opposed the enabling act. When Carroll and Dulany crossed swords in the newspapers in 1773, the marriage controversy inspired the following piece of whimsy. The poem's speaker is Carrollton.

> When your letter I read my heart leap'd for joy
> That I an occasion so apt might employ
> My rancour, and venom innate to let fly
> At a man I abhor—and I'll tell you why
> I could not be married (you've heard of the fact)
> Before I got an enabling act,
> For a man you'll allow, would cut a poor figure
> Tho' big as myself, or perhaps somewhat bigger,
> Who to any fair virgin his honor shou'd plight
> Without being enabled to do—what is right
> In this he opposed me.

But Dulany's attempt to delay the marriage failed. The *Maryland Gazette* of June 9, 1768, reported that "on Sunday evening was married at his father's house in this city [Annapolis], Charles Carroll Jr. Esq., to Miss Mary Darnall, an agreeable young lady endowed with every accomplishment necessary to render the connubial state happy."

Molly possessed a surprising vivacity, given the tragic circumstances of her youth. She liked traveling, much to the Squire's disgust. The patriarch carped when the young couple took a trip in the summer of 1770, and again when they visited Philadelphia in fall 1771. "You cannot be well spared from Annapolis," he wrote on the latter occasion, "& it will be very hurtful to our interest here [at Doughoregan] for me to be so long absent at this season." Carroll of Annapolis also criticized Molly's extravagance. "Can fine furniture, clothes, &c. be put in competition, with a provision for children[?] Pride & Vanity are not to be indulged at their expense, nor are you to be fools because many are so. What is decent & convenient, you ought to have, there is no end to a desire for finery of any sort."

These were not the words of a disapproving in-law. For all practical purposes, the Squire was Molly's father, and their relationship was as intense as that of any father and daughter. When Molly begrudged him his new granddaughter's presence on his birthday, Carroll of Annapolis complained. But he hoped Molly would nurse her son, because "a child's temper & disposition is said to be influenced more or less by its nurse. I would not desire the boy to have a better than its Mama's."

Molly was brought up by her mother, whose life was ruined by a bad marriage, and by the overprotective Squire. It is hardly astonishing, then, that when Molly Carroll encountered suffering, she turned to laudanum. This opium derivative was commonly prescribed and readily available at the time. She became addicted, with profound consequences for the family.

The Search for Harmony

For a few years after the 1765 Stamp Act, life in the colony remained superficially tranquil. Annapolis society experienced its "golden age." At the center of social activity was the Carroll mansion on Spa Creek, with its famous gardens. Molly's outgoing nature no doubt helped Carroll overcome his shyness with his Annapolis neighbors. On one occasion, it was reported, Carroll made one of a "merry set of gentlemen who erected a commodious tent on the ice, where they diverted themselves with dancing reels on skates, serving good dinners and diverse other amusements."

Carrollton's election to the Homony Club was the ultimate sign of his acceptance into the local elite. Prominent Maryland clubs had never before admitted Catholics. The new governor, Robert Eden, was a member. Others included William Eddis, the colonial secretary, Rev. Jonathan Boucher, William Paca, Lloyd Dulany, and, at last, Samuel Chase. Politics was a forbidden subject at the Homony Club, though most of the colony's political leaders joined. Instead, debates centered on philosophy, aesthetics, and science. The club sought to raise the level of culture in the colony. Carrollton subscribed to a fund to send Charles Willson Peale to London for artistic training in 1767.

It was fortunate that Carroll found this social outlet, for his English friends one by one dropped him. Carroll's one-sided transatlantic correspondence makes melancholy reading. The Marylander constantly reproached his friends for their neglect, and pleaded with them for the favor of a letter. "I long to hear from you," he wrote William Graves. Carroll asked Edmund Jennings "why friends should not write to each other twice or thrice a year." To Christopher Bird, his best English friend, Carrollton was reduced to beginning a letter "Dear Sir": "the last ship expected from London is arrived, and no letters from you: what am I to think of your silence, or what can I impute it to? I hope no disaster has happened in your family or to yourself."

Carroll's abandonment by his friends was partly the result of his increasing stridency on colonial matters. In a letter to Graves, Carroll crossed out the comment that a seat in Parliament might prove "as fatal to private friendships; as dangerous to public liberty." But what Carroll did say was unlikely to please Graves. "I am determined to force you to keep up a correspondence," Carroll wrote. "A short letter once a year will satisfy me; am I unreasonable? What vast employments should hinder you from gratifying a friend's request, so easily complied with? Have you as yet worked yourself into an administration or into the good graces of the ministers? Or are you one of those very uncommon personages who prefer an honest & patriotic conduct to the smiles of a court?"

It is rather painful to watch Carroll, with all his gifts, lowering himself to beg for friendship. Yet his letters are absolutely assertive and uncompromising on the issue of imperial relations. When Graves finally wrote Carroll, asking him whether he meant to visit England, the patriot retorted "no, unless I should be transported under the obsolete act of Henry the 8th to be hanged in England for being a true American." Carrollton seemed to realize that his opinions would damage his friendships. "Honest & well-meaning men generally entertain the same sentiments of public measures....because none but honest men can be sincere friends, and none but honest men will think alike."

Religious differences took their toll as well. One gets the impression that either Carrollton's Catholicism or his political ideas might have been acceptable, but not both. He tried to joke about it, as when he scheduled his wedding to Rachel on

Guy Fawkes' Day. "It happens to be gunpowder plot [day]—but no wonder that a bloody-minded Papist should choose for feasting and merriment a day which had like (if you believe the story) to have proved so fatal to a Protestant King and Parliament."

Graves urged Carrollton to conform to the Church of England for practical reasons. "Well, I see, you want to make a convert out of me, not out of religious zeal," Carroll replied. "But all modes of Religion being in your estimation indifferent to our Creator, I may as well embrace that which my countrymen have embraced. What if they have embraced an absurd one? Yes, certainly, because the one I have been brought up in is still more absurd. Granted, for argument's sake; what, then, do you advise me to quit a false religion & adopt one equally false, & this merely to humor the prejudices of fools, or to be on a footing with knaves?" At this stage, Carroll's motivation for remaining Catholic was not primarily religious. "I have too much sincerity and too much pride" to apostatize, he wrote, "even if my filial love did not restrain me."

Carrollton described himself as a "warm friend to toleration. I execrate the intolerating spirit of the Church of Rome, and of other Churches, for she is not singular in that." Attempts to impose religious orthodoxy "have not reformed the morals of men. They have indeed answered the purposes of ambition, they have abetted the revenge of an enraged party, and sometimes too they have served the cravings of lust." Nor was persecution effectual in obtaining conversions. "Those against whom it is employed are apt to conclude that their opinions can not be confuted by other arguments."

Carroll met his father's assertions of dogma with indifference. Although the Squire encouraged his son to read apologetic works, Carrollton declared in 1766 that "I read no controversy." During Lent, the elder Carroll would send a priest down from Doughoregan, reminding Carrollton to make his Easter confession and Communion. Lacking a regular system of government, the Church in Maryland was dominated by the lay gentry. When it was rumored that a bishop was coming to the colony in 1765, the gentry protested. Eight years later, even the Jesuits joined in a similar complaint. Carrollton was unimpressed with his Catholic preceptors, but he also ignored the writings of Deists and other unorthodox Christians that were popular at the time.

Deadly Potential

The quarrel between the Carrolls and the Dulanys was about to explode into public life. All of Maryland would be affected by the conflict between the country gentry, epitomized by the Carrolls, and the placemen of the proprietary party, led by the Dulanys. Grave consequences would ensue for the governing class in the colony. The fate of Catholics, in particular, depended on the outcome of the conflict between the two warring clans.

On September 29, 1769, an ominous letter reached Carroll of Annapolis from William Deards, an employee of the family. Lloyd Dulany, brother of the younger Daniel Dulany, had made statements defaming both Carrolls. "Mr. Carroll thinks, and I believe anyone of common spirit would think so too, that they are not to be put up with—& has determined to give L[loyd] D[ulany] the opportunity of meeting him tomorrow morning."

Lloyd Dulany's initial letter does not survive. Carrollton replied that "your language & your character are alike contemptible; I heartily despise both: your bravadoes do not intimidate me in the least." Carroll blamed Dulany, Jr. for the calumny. "Too dastardly to appear in defence of his own character," Daniel was using Lloyd as a screen. Carrollton told Lloyd that he would ride out the next morning, as usual. "I shall then be prepared to give you a proper reception if you come in my way, as I shall be provided with pistols."

This invitation did not exactly conform to the laws of honor, but Carroll would not let the Dulanys maneuver him into making a formal challenge. "I did not know what a jury might judge of that matter," Carrollton told his father, "for as our common people have not very nice notions of honour, they might think

Part II: First Citizen

the challenger, however great the provocation, the aggressor." He planned to "take no further notice of Lloyd: but shall go prepared to blow out his brains, if he should offer any insult to my person."

Carrollton had a pair of pistols belonging to Molly's father. Perhaps because of their negative associations, he asked his father to send him another set. The Squire sent a pair of shoes and a stretcher, as well.

Meanwhile, Lloyd Dulany penned another letter, full of bluster. Dulany called Carroll of Annapolis "the deep stain of the times...the laws have long scandalously slept, in not dragging him forth, as a sacrifice to public justice." He threatened to publish "an authenticated copy of a record of one of his precious deeds." He accused Carrollton of concealing "violent struggles in your breast...betwixt your unparalleled & dastardly fears & your highly attenuated venom. Tell me prithee, whither shall I fly to kiss your hands in a *private place*....you silly little puppy." "As for your hint of my acting for another, it is a lie, spick & span from your jesuitical forge," Dulany concluded.

Carroll rode out, with Deards at his side as a witness. But Dulany did not appear. "Molly is but indifferent," Carrollton wrote his father. "Her anxiety at the issue, & apprehensions of some future meeting have greatly discomposed her spirits." He confessed that "I am not very well myself." "The uneasiness I have felt on yours & her account for some days...in case of an accident to me, has hurt my rest."

By October 1 the affair had ended, and Carroll could reflect on his encounter with the *code duello*. The more he thought about it, the more absurd the code of honor seemed. The law, and not private individuals, should punish libelers. "If the grossest insinuations are permitted to be thrown about against a gentleman's character with impunity, there is an end of civil society. Every sturdy insolent fellow, confiding in his strength, might insult a worthy honest man who might be weaker." If Carroll had been slain, "what dear connections should I have left behind me! & who would have grieved at Lloyd's death? I do not believe a single tear would have been shed on the occasion." Carrollton was outraged that he had nearly fallen martyr to the "silly pride" of the Dulanys. "They would, & yet with all their assurance they cannot deny their father was an indentured servant."

The abortive Carroll-Dulany duel was an episode in the gradual death of the gentlemen's code of honor in the United States, which was consummated when Aaron Burr slew Alexander Hamilton in 1804, provoking public outrage.

The Townshend Acts

The British administration was still concerned about its own honor after the Stamp Act debacle. To save face, as well as to raise revenue, Chancellor of the Exchequer Charles Townshend proposed duties on British exports to America. The items taxed included glass, paper, tea, and lead. Townshend's timing was perfect. The opening of a new market for colonial wheat in Southern Europe had improved the balance of trade dramatically. The Townshend Acts took effect in the summer of 1767 and met with little opposition at first. "I do not as yet hear," Carrollton wrote, "that the late duties imposed by act of Parliament on paper & other articles imported have occasion[ed] any great disgust."

There was a new nonimportation movement, which Carroll supported, but it was slow getting started. The colonial intelligentsia, allied with the lower classes, had to coerce merchants into nonimportation. Fear of the mob brought Boston and New York into the boycott in 1768, followed by Philadelphia a year later. Baltimore's boycott included only those items that could easily be obtained from smugglers. Only two Baltimoreans were tried for violating nonimportation, and both were acquitted.

Prosperity set radical leaders and merchants at odds. Colonial tradesmen would not act on principle if it damaged their business. The planters were sinking back into their morass of debt. By 1775, John Adams noted that "half of the nation if not more are debtors." Franklin remarked drily that if Americans would save their money instead of wasting it, they could bribe the whole English government.

Fortunately for the radicals, economic conditions took a steep plunge. Beginning in 1769, the trade imbalance began to widen. The tobacco market also fell into crisis. When a cartel of factors conspired to fix tobacco prices, planters united in 1770 to demand no less than a guinea (slightly more than one pound sterling) per hundredweight. Some planters began to do business with factors in the colonies, to avoid the extra taxes on crops shipped to England. In addition, Carrollton complained, tobacco exported to the mother country mysteriously lost weight en route.

Then, in 1772, the European tobacco market collapsed. The currency shortage exacerbated the problem. Scottish factors, failing right and left, could no longer back bills of exchange. The disappearance of these bills from the money supply made it harder for planters to pay their debts, and thus drove tobacco prices down even further. "Such a conflagration there has never been in the memory of man," wrote the merchant Joshua Johnson, a Maryland native. "I should not be surprised at a general revolution of the mercantile world."

The economic disaster revitalized the nonimportation movement. Charles Carroll the Barrister, the Surgeon's son, had become a leader in the Annapolis boycott. The Barrister had caused a sensation in 1768 by refusing a seat on the Governor's Council, thus serving notice that the patriots could not be bribed with offices. He signed a letter of May 1769, announcing the formation of a nonimportation association. In October 1770, this association publicly advocated colonial self-taxation. In spite of their family history, Carroll the Barrister became Carrollton's first political confidant and ally. "The society of a few choice friends," Carrollton wrote his Protestant cousin, "is worth all the pomp & emptiness of a court, where friendship never approaches."

Another ally joined the Carrolls in the person of Joshua Johnson's older brother Thomas Johnson. A Carroll kinsman, Ignatius Digges, sued the Squire for his wife's inheritance. As executor, Carroll had invested the money on behalf of Mary Digges. Thomas Johnson defended Carroll of Annapolis in the suit. Apparently, Johnson was so moved by Carroll's uprightness and innocence, or by his own performance, that he broke down in tears during his closing argument, and was unable to proceed. "Many in court could not refrain from tears," Carrollton wrote. Not all were convinced: Gov. Eden was heard to say "that he supposed the old gentleman [Carroll of Annapolis] would be on the high ropes." Digges won £1,500 in the suit. The Squire made sure that Johnson received £50 for his trouble.

The elder Carroll got a boost out of the sympathy that the lawsuit generated. During the early 1770s he was more active in politics than his son. The Squire carried on an epistolary debate with Daniel Dulany and attended a nonimportation meeting near Elk Ridge in 1771. "Had I not seen it," he commented, "I could not have believed the people here to be so indifferent about a matter which so much concerns them." Carrollton still held back, probably because the burning issue of the moment in Maryland had to do with Anglican clergy salaries. Throughout his career, the younger Carroll avoided all public disputes concerning religion. This did not stop the council from accusing the patriot party of being led astray by a Papist on the clergy issue.

Carrollton was biding his time, watching from the sidelines. "This is dead time with us," he wrote the Barrister in August 1771. "Politics are scarce talked of. The scene of action will soon be opened, and I doubt not we shall have a hot campaign this fall." Carrollton continued to sketch out his vision of an empire of liberty. He cited Tacitus' description of the Emperor Trajan, who "joined two things previously incompatible, empire and liberty." It would be better, he wrote, "to see all the powers of the state resolved into one" than to surrender to the corrupt Parliamentary oligarchy.

Around this time, Carrollton cultivated the friendship of the man who was destined to become the first monarch of the empire of liberty. George Washington dined at the Carroll house in Annapolis in September 1771 and October 1772.

Part II: First Citizen

THE FEE CONTROVERSY

When the moment came, Carrollton struck. Gov. Eden handed the patriots an issue that brought the feud between the Carrolls and the Dulanys to a head. In the process, the patriots formed a coherent party, all classes mobilized against the administration, and Carroll of Carrollton rose from political oblivion to lead the reform movement.

The House of Delegates passed a bill in 1770 regulating officers' fees and prohibiting sale of offices. Historically, the assembly had fixed officers' fees, but now the governor was unable to agree with the delegates on a fee scale. Late that year, Gov. Eden set the officers' fees by proclamation at the level that the assembly had approved in 1763. The opposition members of the House of Delegates immediately attacked the proclamation as another British assault on American liberty, predicting terrible consequences if government became financially independent of the electorate. By a 31 to 3 vote, the delegates called the new fees "robbery."

"Could you imagine the right of fixing officers' fees by proclamation would be claimed at this time of day?" Carrollton wrote the Barrister. But he could not conceal his delight that the battle was finally joined. "War is now declared between Government and the People, or rather between a few placemen, the real enemies to Government, and all the inhabitants of this Province." When Carroll said "placemen," he meant "Dulanys." Aside from Carrollton's scorn for the Dulanys, "placemen" was a particularly inflammatory term in Maryland, where the power of the governor's court surpassed that in any other colony. Even Walter Dulany once ran for office with Samuel Chase using the slogan "No Placemen," but the unlikely pair fell out when Dulany accepted a place as a naval officer.

In the fall of 1772, Chase joined with William Paca and Thomas Johnson, over the signature "Independent Whigs," to attack Gov. Eden in the *Maryland Gazette*. Thenceforward, the opposition would be known as the Independent Whigs, or, as the Squire preferred, the Popular Party. In many respects, the

Popular Party was quite conservative, though it consistently upheld the concept of republican virtue over the traditional bonds of honor and loyalty that characterized the court party. Nor did the Popular Party see itself as a party. Except for Chase, its leadership belonged to the propertied classes.

Chase was able to draw planters back into the radical movement by presenting the opposition to fees as a tax revolt. Furthermore, the tobacco inspection system had ground to a halt as a result of the legislative deadlock. Tobacco prices immediately dropped, not only because of the lack of quality control, but also because the inspectors' certificates had served as a form of currency. The planters had to get involved in the controversy because of the urgent need to resume the inspections. But Chase's chronic indebtedness and his brash personality, which earned him the nickname "Bacon Face," made him an unsuitable ally for the planters. Chase needed a leader who would unite the gentry with the Baltimore merchants. He found one in Charles Carroll, businessman and planter.

Carrollton may have been more eager for the fight than Chase. In 1827, during Carroll's lifetime, the *Truth Teller* printed an anecdote believed to have been written by Dr. Richard Steuart, who knew Carroll. John H. B. Latrobe, a Carroll employee, repeated the story. Chase supposedly said to Carroll in the early 1770s that "we have the better of our opponents, we have completely written them down."

"And do you think," Carrollton asked, "that writing will settle the question between us?"

"To be sure," Chase replied. "What else can we resort to?"

"The bayonet," Carroll said. "Our arguments will only raise the feelings of the people to that pitch, when open war will be looked to as the arbiter of the dispute."

Whatever Carrollton's private feelings were, the public image of the Popular Party was moderate. Proprietary official William Eddis observed that their debates were characterized by "great power of eloquence and force of reason; and the utmost regularity and propriety distinguished the whole of their proceedings." This would remain true as long as Carroll and the gentry kept a firm grip on party leadership.

Part II: First Citizen

Carrollton and Daniel Dulany, Jr., were now on a collision course. The Squire made sure that his son did not try to avoid confrontation. "Act with the Governor & visit him as usual," the father commanded. "You may resolve to live in a desert if you will not generally associate with foolish, fickle, mean-spirited men." Carroll was sure to encounter Dulany at the governor's mansion. At one Eden soirée, Dulany earned notoriety when he wrestled with a Mr. DeButte. The governor's wife was reportedly so shocked that she suffered a miscarriage.

The younger Carroll never underestimated Dulany. In 1765, he strongly recommended Dulany's pamphlet "Considerations on the Propriety of Imposing Taxes in the British Colonies." John H. B. Latrobe later heard Carroll praise his opponent's "rare talent" and "distinguished abilities." Dulany was in an ambiguous position: financially dependent on the British administration, he nevertheless tried to play a patriotic role in the imperial dispute. Josiah Quincy captured this tension when he described Dulany as "a diamond of the first water, a gem that may grace the cap of a patriot or the turban of a sultan!" As a descendant of Catholics, Dulany was moderate in his Protestantism. "Persecution is so horrible that human nature starts at it," he wrote.

The Challenger Scores

Dulany's descent began on January 7, 1773, when the *Maryland Gazette* published his letter over the signature "Antilon." Dulany was the most powerful man in Maryland politics, at the top of his profession. But as a result of this letter, his political career would be destroyed within two years. Charles Carroll of Carrollton, who emerged to challenge Dulany in the *Gazette*, would assume Dulany's power and preeminence.

An "antilon" is a stinging plaster that draws out infection, in this case, an infection in the body politic. Antilon's first letter presents a dialogue between "First Citizen" and "Second Citizen." First Citizen is an Independent Whig; Second Citizen is loyal to the administration. Dulany's First Citizen is a caricature of a democratic politician. Dulany portrays the Whigs as unrealistic in their belief in republican virtue and naïve for trusting the general public with political power. According to Dulany, the Independent Whigs are trying to replace stable government and established religion with the "publication of the opinionist."

Second Citizen, on the other hand, is a realist. He follows the old code of honor, or "personal attachment" in government. He adheres to the traditions of the Church of England, rather than republican virtue, as the basis of morality. Instead of natural law, the Second Citizen emphasizes the common law, which grew up in concrete situations, the practical give-and-take of English political life. Second Citizen ridicules First Citizen for "pronouncing, that certain bodies of men have peculiar and indubitable rights, at the very time he is moving heaven and earth to destroy the only Law, which is the foundation of those rights."

For Dulany, only the English church and state can guarantee the "blessings of order" and prevent the "horrors of anarchy." Dulany's argument is that of a good conservative, within the assumption that the English constitution was ordained by God. When Charles Carroll of Carrollton replied to Antilon in the *Gazette* of February 4, 1773, he adopted a different kind of conservative strategy. Carroll appealed to the natural law underlying the English constitution, while presenting republican virtue in a more pragmatic, less theoretical light.

Carrollton, adopting the persona of Dulany's First Citizen, complains that Dulany offered a "lame, mutilated, and imperfect" version of his remarks. The First Citizen defends the power and prerogatives of government against the "awful tribunal" of public opinion. He quotes Tacitus on the need to reconcile empire and liberty and even defends the British Crown, citing the maxim that "the King can do no wrong."

Exempting the governor, as the King's representative, from all blame for the fee proclamation, Carroll attacks the governor's advisors, the placemen. He compares the "present ministers of this province" to "those, who influenced Charles the First, and brought him to the block." Citing Dulany's "Considerations," First Citizen wonders how the patriot of 1765 turned into the fawning minister of 1773. After Dulany was admitted to power, he became loyal to the administration and sought to make "all power...center in one family. Is all your patriotism come to this?" In his "meanness" and "insolence," Dulany "would wish to be the first slave of a sultan, to lord it over all the rest."

Carrollton's point is that government can no longer be based on patronage. "Men under the bias of self-interest, and under personal obligations to Government, cannot act with a freedom and independency becoming a representative of the people." Instead, the standard of political justice must be the common good, and the people must be led by men of independent means. Carroll had refined his ideas about self-interest in politics. "Power, Sir, power is apt to pervert the best of natures." In order for personal interest to be compatible with the public good, it must be channeled through a limited and mixed government.

First Citizen's letter caused a sensation. Chase and Paca praised Carroll on February 11 for the "honest freedom" of his writing. "We had for a long time impatiently waited for a man of abilities to step forth, and tell our darling ministers in a nervous style the evils they have brought upon the community." In the eighteenth century, "nervous" meant forceful, stimulating. Carrollton had thrown off his childish sycophancy and diffidence, taking his proper place as a leader of men.

The Champion Retaliates

Dulany fired back in the *Gazette* on February 18. Citizens offended by the fee proclamation, Antilon argues, could take their case to court. The goal of the proclamation was to prevent "extortion and oppression" by keeping officers from charging exorbitant fees. Dulany condemns the House of Delegates for rejecting a fee schedule that would have allowed planters to pay the fees in tobacco, substantially reducing their costs. He asks drily whether the "general welfare of this province would have been sacrificed" if the delegates had approved this proposal.

Antilon then ridicules Carroll's use of the maxim that "the King can do no wrong." He points out that First Citizen, by defending the prerogatives of the Crown, looks more like a Tory than a Whig. Dulany seizes the opportunity to smear Carroll by accusing him of loyalty to the Stuarts and the divine right of kings. He attacks "St. Omers...the best seminary in the universe of the champions for civil and religious liberty."

Gloves off, Dulany launches an *ad hominem* attack. He first takes on Carroll of Annapolis. During the 1750s, the Squire had "nearly ruined the party, of whom the importance and powers of superior wealth, and superior talents, placed him at the head." Now, "to what black passion shall we charge his dislike? Age must have cooled the ardor of ambition; but malignity will not cease" until the old man's death.

Antilon then directs the full fury of his assault at Carrollton, who is "anxiously looking forward to the event, most devoutly wished for, when he may shake off his fetters, and dazzle the world with the splendour of his talents." Carroll's physique resembles that of a monkey, inspiring pity and laughter. But "when we behold the animal with the torch, or firebrand, bent on mischief, we should dread its fury, if not out of the reach of it."

Something must be said about the monkey comparison. Dulany was not alone in considering Carroll to be disfigured. Another newspaper columnist described Carrollton as "curtail'd of fair proportion." The late 1700s were the heyday of "physiognomy," a pseudo-science that sought to link character with physical appearance. A physiognomist would immediately have noticed that Carroll's arms and legs were large in proportion to his torso. The Thomas Sully portrait of Carrollton makes a virtue out of this shaming defect. The large hands recall the important documents Carroll wrote, and his prominent legs give the Signer stability, strength, and majesty.

Dulany's vulgar insults give us an idea of the suffering of Catholics under the old regime in Maryland. But Carrollton's vindication had begun. The public was eager to see First Citizen's reply to Antilon's abuse. When Carroll's second letter appeared on March 11, the Squire reported that "all the strangers in town retired to their lodgings, many to private places (to avoid interruption) to read it." The next morning, "every mouth was open in praise of the First Citizen."

Carrollton's second letter in every way deserves the applause it received. First Citizen attacks monolithic state sovereignty, arguing for a mixed government. He quotes Montesquieu: "There is no liberty if the power of judging be not separated from the legislative, and executive powers." The executive branch, headed by the governor, may not encroach upon the prerogatives of the other branches. The fundamental issue is not the abuse of royal prerogative, but the necessity of checks and balances. Even if English judges have settled fees without legislative approval, First Citizen argues, they have not settled their own fees. State power is necessary, but no branch of government may become independent.

Carroll presses this point. "Have not the officers who advised the Proclamation, and the governor who issued it...set their own rates, and made their own demands? Answer this question, Antilon?" Carroll recommends that the public follow the lead of the delegates in condemning the fee proclamation, but he does not claim that the lower house holds sovereignty. He recommends, instead, that the upper house of the legislature be strengthened. Meanwhile, taxation without representation is intolerable. "In a land of freedom, this arbitrary exertion of prerogative will not, must not, be endured."

The First Citizen turns Antilon's slanders against him. When officials resort to "virulent invective, and illiberal abuse, we may fairly presume, that arguments are either wanting, or that ignorance and incapacity know not how to apply them." Carroll scoffs at the idea of a "confederacy" between the Carrolls and the Independent Whigs to overthrow the government. "Why do you suppose this confederacy? From a similitude of sentiments with respect to your conduct, and proclamation? If so, then indeed are nine-tenths of the people of this province confederated with the First Citizen."

Carrollton takes offense at Dulany's remark about his eagerness to "shake off his fetters." He interprets this to mean that he hopes for the death of Carroll of Annapolis. "What behaviour, what incident, what passage of his life, warrant this your opinion of the son, supposing it to be real? That they have always lived in the most perfect harmony, united by nature's strongest ties, parental love, filial tenderness, and duty, envy itself must own." As for his resemblance to a monkey, Carroll "would not exchange the infirmities of his puny frame, were it, on that condition, to be animated by a soul like thine."

When Carrollton made a court appearance after his second letter was published, his father heard that "every eye was fixed on you with evident marks of pleasure & approbation." As for the Squire, he wished "that you may with good health live to see a son think as you do & express his thoughts with your force, elegance, and ease. Should that happen, you will be sensible of the pleasure I feel." Carrollton had finally won his father's unqualified approval. Carroll of Annapolis wanted to hear any comments on his son's public performance: "let me have them all, the merest trifle is interesting."

The younger Carroll also began to receive signs of interest from the political elite of the colony, including Major Daniel of St. Thomas Jenifer. With his uncanny knack for playing both sides of an issue, until he could determine which would prevail, Jenifer would have a long life in Maryland politics. "I suppose Antilon will be totally eclipsed, by the shield of the man with the long name," Jenifer wrote the Squire. "Your son is a most flaming Patriot, and a red hot Politician: he and I have frequent skirmishes in the field of Politics, each retiring victor, and of consequence always ready to renew the attack." Carrollton did not trust Jenifer, but his father cultivated the major as a link to the governor.

The Contest Continues

On April 3, Carrollton rode out and encountered Daniel Dulany, Sr. "He looks hearty & well," Carroll reported. "I believe he is glad the controversy is dropped." But the younger Dulany was nursing a grudge and avoiding social engagements

Part II: First Citizen

on the excuse of illness. Dulany was composing his third Antilon letter, which appeared on April 8.

Antilon's third effort is even more bilious than its predecessor. He continues to label Carrollton as a Jacobite. Carroll followed Hume in arguing that the Glorious Revolution preceded, rather than followed, the abdication of James II. Calling Hume a Stuart apologist, Dulany claims that Carroll saw the Glorious Revolution as "rather an act of violence, than of justice." It does not occur to Antilon that Carroll approved of the 1688 Revolution on the basis of Catholic political tradition. James' abdication was irrelevant, since he had already forfeited his authority, returning sovereignty to the people, who established a new contract of government. Although Carroll's conclusions are debatable here, he is arguing from Catholic political premises.

Dulany obstinately portrays Carrollton as an advocate of government by public opinion. He reminds the First Citizen of the occasion in 1754 when Dulany voted in the minority against arresting Carroll of Annapolis. "The Citizen need not go far to have the matter explained, and, I imagine, he may be inclined to think resolves ought not always to fix men's opinions, since sometimes, they may be dictated by passion." Now, Dulany makes it clear that his tolerance of Catholics does not extend to offering them political rights. Carrollton has been disenfranchised "on account of his principles, which are distrusted" by the English constitution.

Nor does Dulany scruple to compare Carrollton once again to a monkey. He doubts that "the worship of a monkey" will bring about "the demolition of our religious establishment." Dulany's abuse fired up the Squire, who was now egging Carrollton on. He sent his son notes to help him compose a response. "The prepossession is so strong & great in your favour," he assured Carrollton, "that it is not to be removed by [Dulany's] scurrility."

But Dulany's relentless accusation of Jacobitism forced Carrollton onto the defensive. As a result, First Citizen's third letter, published on May 6, 1773, is his weakest in terms of political argument. Dulany argued that governmental power "ought to be active, when the reason of it calls for exertion." The fee proclamation promoted the general welfare, and hence was lawful. Carroll actually agreed with Dulany on the need for an energetic government. But admitting this would have damaged his case against the fee proclamation.

The problem in Maryland was not an excess of power in the government as a whole. The issue was that the various powers of government were monopolized by the same officers. Carroll realized this, but he was not yet ready to advocate the replacement of the English system by a truly mixed government. So First Citizen falls back on the trite arguments of parliamentary supremacy, lamely arguing that "the power of the parliament ...is, and must be supreme." Such a position is uncharacteristic of Carroll's thought, taken as a whole. It is true, however, that the legislative branch historically set fees in Maryland.

What makes his third letter memorable is Carrollton's eloquent defense of Catholic civil rights. "Who is this Citizen?" Carroll asks. "A man, Antilon, of an independent fortune, one deeply interested in the prosperity of his country: a friend to liberty, a settled enemy to lawless prerogative." As for the persecution of Catholics, *Meminimus, et ignoscimus*—"We remember, and forgive."

First Citizen's May 6 letter represents a watershed in the political fortunes of American Catholics. From that day, it was inevitable that political rights would be restored to Catholics in Maryland. This third letter produced an avalanche of popular support. The fee proclamation received a mock funeral in Annapolis, where newly-elected delegates offered "their thanks to the First Citizen, for his spirited, eloquent and patriotic opposition to the proclamation while alive." William Paca and Matthias Hammond published a letter calling Carrollton "a distinguished advocate for the rights of your country." Even Rev. Jonathan Boucher, who was sharpening his quill to reply to the First Citizen, said that Carroll "was an author with whom it was an honor to contend."

With Carrollton so clearly in possession of the field, Dulany had to make one final assault. The last Antilon letter, printed on June 3, is the most cogently argued of the four. As if he were finally taking Carroll seriously, Dulany abandons personal abuse and sets forth his arguments systematically. Within the framework of the British constitution, what Antilon says makes a great deal of sense. Even Coke permits judges to set fees; legislative provisions accounted for only a small portion of officers' fees existing in England. Dulany returns to his charge that the Whigs are trying to undermine all established authority. They "would, like Archimedes, undertake to turn the world, which way they please."

Now Carrollton could return to the offensive. Carroll's fourth and last letter of July 1, 1773, expands on the brilliant analysis of his second letter. He anticipates Cardinal Newman's argument that, in the absence of correct theology, other intellectual disciplines begin to theologize. In this case, it is the common law that Dulany elevates into the realm of theological truth. Carroll criticizes "the legal subtleties and metaphysical reasoning of my adversary." Rhetorically turning Dulany's anti-Catholicism against him, he asks Dulany to respond "without equivocation." It is Dulany, not Carroll, who would "make a most excellent inquisitor."

Carrollton was not trying to overthrow the concept of authority in favor of public opinion. But in this fourth letter, to borrow Dulany's metaphor, he uses the natural law as a lever to overturn the English constitution, which had been corrupt ever since the Reformation. It is the English state, and not the Catholic Church, that is a Gothic ruin. "A perfect symmetry, and correspondence of parts is wanting; in some places, the pile appears to be deficient in strength, in others the rude and unpolished taste of our Gothic ancestors is discoverable."

For English chaos, Carrollton wishes to substitute the clarity of natural law. He privileges the "clear and fundamental" maxims of the constitution. Insisting on the rule of law, and not of men, Carroll looks ahead to written constitutionalism. Law must be concrete, and its "true spirit and original intent" should be honored.

Carrollton saw clearly that the future belonged to written constitutions and mixed government. But he was in the same position as the Massachusetts Assembly. "They are obliged to drop hints only, where a full display of arguments is necessary; but such a deduction of consequences from their political principles would discover [reveal] what they now think will soon happen." Carroll knew what was coming: a complete rupture with England and the creation of a new social contract in America. His strikingly original fourth letter made that clear, for those who had ears to hear.

As for Antilon, nothing more would be heard from him. Carrollton stepped forth as the man of the hour, while Dulany drifted into irrelevance. He later became a Loyalist. "The union of all America has swallowed him up in the great vortex," Carroll wrote of Dulany. "He follows its motion, but not daring to be the first mover, nor possessing a temper sufficiently intrepid to guide its course. He is carried away with the whirlwind, he does not ride on it, nor directs the storm." The First Citizen, on the other hand, now moved into the center of Maryland politics. For the next twenty-five years, Carroll would direct the political storm in Maryland.

The Tea Act

An early twentieth-century biographer of Carrollton, Lewis Leonard, remarked that in order to become influential, the Catholic Carroll had to make himself indispensable. He had now accomplished this. If Maryland continued in its anti-Catholic prejudice, Carroll vowed, "I will serve them in a private capacity notwithstanding—nay, I have done it."

Carroll of Annapolis was also emboldened by his son's success. In fact, he was starting to sound like a Son of Liberty. Pro-administration protests might "give offence to the County & its representatives, & be attended with consequences not agreeable to the protesters." The assembly should declare those who paid the fees "enemies to their Country." He now recommended that Carrollton avoid the governor, that "very silly idle dissipated man." If Gov. Eden should request British troops for Maryland, the Squire predicted, "he may perhaps meet with greater mortifications than the burning of his proclamation."

As a sign that Carrollton was a force to be reckoned with, he was now routinely attacked in the press. "Broomstick and Quoad" authored a poem:

> The pains you've been at and the things you have wrote,
> To tell us our Governor lies in his throat,
> To prove all his Council by Loyola's rules
> (Some one who's a knave) a Cluster of fools,
> Entitle you, Sir, to the thrice honor'd name
> Of Maryland patriot—huzza to the fame!

"Consistent Protestant" doubted that Carroll was a good Catholic, since he did not support the confessional state. Another writer claimed that First Citizen wanted "a Protestant people to me bend the knee." Carrollton had his defenders, as well. "Protestant Planter" regretted that Carroll's opponents had portrayed him as a "political parricide, as the worst of evils, as a man attempting to subvert both church and state."

As further testimony of Carroll's importance, the Independent Whigs began to adopt his position on certain issues. Johnson, Paca, and Chase argued that proclamations were permissible, but only for the general good. "Voter" advocated strengthening the upper house of the assembly, so that the councillors would be the "guardians of the people."

But in spite of gaining the political momentum, the Whigs mismanaged the fee controversy. The delegates lost their leverage against the fee proclamation by passing a tobacco inspection bill. Then, in 1774, the Independent Whigs lost face when their leaders compromised with Eden on the fee scale. The rank-and-file delegates rebelled against the party leadership.

By then, however, the issue of British taxation had eclipsed the fee controversy. The Tea Act of May 1773 tried once again to make taxation palatable to the colonists. The East India Company was allowed to bypass English middlemen, lowering the price of their tea. Though taxed, tea now cost less than before, and less than smuggled Dutch tea. The concealed duty caused an immediate uproar. The Maryland Assembly resolved against unconstitutional taxation in July 1773. A Maryland Committee of Correspondence was appointed on October 15. The Boston Tea Party took place two months later.

The tea crisis caused a complete realignment of Maryland politics. The Homony Club dissolved in rancor. The proprietary party disappeared as a political force. Further, as Thomas Jennings reported, "there is a schism among the Patriots." Carroll, Chase, Thomas Johnson, and Paca led the conservative wing. A democratic opposition surfaced, led by Matthias Hammond and John Hall. Hammond's enmity toward Carrollton was fueled by a property dispute: a resurvey gave the Carrolls five hundred acres of Hammond land.

At a May 25, 1774, meeting of Anne Arundel County citizens, the two factions went head to head. Chase, Paca, and Carrollton tried to assume leadership of the meeting, but were opposed by Hammond and Hall. Finally, a compromise was reached. Both sets of leaders were included on the county's committee of correspondence. The meeting also agreed on a motion instructing lawyers not to sue on behalf of British creditors, unless the Boston Port Act, a harsh response to the Tea Party, was repealed.

Carrollton resumed his strategy of cultivating allies among his English correspondents. In August 1774, he warned Wallace and Company that the First Continental Congress would meet on September 5 to debate nonimportation. Carroll predicted "a general scheme of Union...for the Government of all the Provinces," resulting in "a total stoppage of trade between the mother Country and the Colonies." A "total redress of all grievances" would be necessary before trade could resume.

The First Continental Congress

Carroll of Annapolis had high hopes for the First Continental Congress. "I hope the Colonies will be unanimous & resolute, for their freedom depends upon their being so."

Though not an official delegate, Carrollton went to Philadelphia as an observer. "This congress is really composed of sensible & spirited men," he reported. "There are in all 49 deputies, and not one weak man among them. Several of great abilities." Carroll was well received at the Congress, dining out almost every night with delegates. He discussed literature and "a little on politics" with John Dickinson. Perhaps he prayed at night before the crucifix, a foot tall, with which he traveled. This reminder of Carroll's piety is now displayed at Homewood House on the campus of the Johns Hopkins University.

The prevailing mood was still conciliatory. Maryland instructed its delegates to work for a "happy reconciliation." The 1774 Congress was dominated by conservatives Joseph Galloway and John Dickinson, who longed for a reunion with the mother country. The metaphor of parent and child was constantly employed. The colonies were like sons who had grown to maturity but were punished for asserting their adult prerogatives.

Out of this metaphor a new concept of government emerged, which we now call "dominion" status. The King, without Parliament, was urged to assume personal sovereignty over the colonies, which would perform the legislative function themselves. Carrollton accepted the idea of dominion, which existed nowhere but in theory. By now, the King could not be separated from Parliament. When the British Empire did finally implement dominion theory, the monarch's sovereignty over the dominions quickly became meaningless.

Americans' continuing loyalty to George III was embodied in Joseph Galloway's Plan of Union, which he submitted to Congress on September 28, 1774. Galloway proposed an American legislature, whose president-general would be appointed by the King. All laws affecting the colonies would require the assent of both the American and British legislatures, with the American body "inferiour." Thus, Galloway's plan leaves sovereignty firmly in the hands of Parliament. The English constitution was still the colonists' frame of reference in 1774. Although the Galloway plan was based more on sentimental attachment to the Crown than on political reality, it was defeated by only one vote.

Carrollton was more realistic than most of the delegates. "I still think this controversy will at last be decided by arms," he declared. This statement seemed prophetic when a rumor of hostilities reached the Congress. "Boston, it is said, has been cannonaded," Carrollton minuted. The bombardment supposedly took place after a raid on American stores of ammunition. Though false, the story's details were eerily prescient of the events of April 18, 1775. Carroll knew that "the smallest incident may bring matters" to a crisis.

The First Continental Congress called for nonimportation from Great Britain, beginning on December 1, 1774. The tobacco states got nonexportation postponed for a year. The delegates dispersed, after a banquet of five hundred plates, thirty-two formal toasts, and a cannon salute. Strangely, one of the toasts praised Daniel Dulany, Jr.

The *Peggy Stewart*

While Carrollton attended Congress, Major Jenifer suffered persecution within the administration. "It has been represented that he is too intimate with the Carrolls & the Pacas," Carroll reported. "Did you ever meet with an instance of greater meanness?" Soon, however, the Anne Arundel Committee of Correspondence would adopt an even more inquisitorial position than the governor.

On October 15, 1774, the brig *Peggy Stewart* arrived at Annapolis, bearing tea. Anthony Stewart, its owner, paid the tea tax. He pleaded that he paid the duty only in order to get fifty-three passengers off the ship after their three-month voyage. But Stewart had already incurred the radicals' wrath by opposing the measure to stop collections by British creditors.

The Anne Arundel Committee demanded that Stewart sign their prepared statement, worthy of a twentieth-century communist reeducation program. The document apologized for his "daring insult, an act of the most pernicious tendency to the liberties of America." Stewart agreed to sign. He promised to destroy "the detestable article which has been the cause of this our misconduct...to show our desire of living in amity with the friends of America."

But Stewart's promise to dispose of the tea was not enough for the democratic faction. Charles Ridgely, a Baltimore activist, told Stewart that his family would be in danger unless he set fire to the ship itself. Ridgely promised protection if Stewart complied. Carroll the Barrister and Chase objected to this ultimatum.

According to Annapolis lore, Carrollton's intervention was decisive. We know from one of the Squire's letters that Carrollton favored "moderate measures." But after the democrats grew threatening, Carrollton recommended that Stewart destroy his ship. "It will not be in my power to protect him," Carroll is quoted as saying, "unless he consents to pursue a more decisive course of conduct. My advice is, that he set fire to the vessel, and burn her, together with the tea that she contains, to the water's edge." This account was published three times during Carroll's life, and it is very likely that Carroll saw at least one of the texts, written by his associate Latrobe.

Anthony Stewart's daughter, "the fair Scotch Peggy," is said to have watched as her father burned the ship he had named for her. So, presumably, did Carroll watch the *Peggy Stewart* burn. Whatever misgivings he may have felt, however distasteful he found his radical allies, he was now a part of the new American body politic. Having made his commitment, Carroll's mind would never change.

PART III.

Revolutionary.

Now Carrollton had to try to save the Revolution from its radical friends. But first, there was a brief comic interlude. Annapolis legend has it that Lloyd Dulany gave a dinner shortly after the burning of the *Peggy Stewart*. He served untaxed tea from a bowl that had arrived on the destroyed vessel. Dulany hastened to apologize, claiming that the bowl was a personal gift and not a part of the ship's cargo. The captain had delivered it in person. "We accept your explanation," Carrollton replied, "provided the bowl is used to draw always this same kind of tea."

Meanwhile, Carroll of Annapolis received a visit from one of the religious enthusiasts who were becoming more numerous in the colony. George Shipley came to claim one thousand acres of Carroll land and four slaves. He had received a vision, notifying him that Carroll would sell him the property for £3,000. Shipley asked Carroll whether he had received any signs to confirm the vision. "I assured him I had not, & that I should require undoubted ones before I complied, but on such I would certainly conform to the will of the Lord." The Squire listened "patiently & with a very grave countenance, but at last told him he must certainly be either a madman or a knave."

The Provisional Government of Maryland

The Maryland Convention, a patriot shadow government, had been meeting in Annapolis since June 1774. Carrollton served as a delegate from Anne Arundel County. The convention maintained a permanent presence through standing committees of correspondence and of observation. Carrollton joined the correspondence committee in December 1774, and in January 1775, he was chosen for the committee of observation. This was a significant appointment, since the committee of observation selected the delegates to the convention.

Carroll and the other Whig leaders sought to defuse faction. They urged in December 1774 that "all former differences about religion or politics and all private animosities and quarrels of every kind, from henceforth cease and be forever buried in oblivion." But the observation committee rejected the democratic faction's attempt to stop debt collections. The moderate Whigs, including Carroll, were aided in their consolidation of power by a backlash against the *Peggy Stewart* incendiaries.

With a clear mandate, Carroll and his clique focused on pressing problems. They tried to keep merchants from raising prices during nonimportation. The committee of observation encouraged home manufactures, in violation of British mercantile policy. They also developed a policy for dealing with violators of nonimportation. Before February 1, 1775, British goods were auctioned off, and their owners were reimbursed. After that date, all contraband shipments were sent back to England. A day of public fasting and humiliation was proclaimed for May 11, 1775, three weeks after the war began.

The proprietary administration was hanging on, barely. Carrollton and four other patriots signed a letter attacking the government for filling offices with men of "courtly principles." But the revolutionary committees were assuming more and more power. The vacuum of established authority encouraged vigilantes and mobs. Carrollton's group took action to stop mob violence. They drafted a document called the "Association of the Freemen of Maryland," which the convention adopted on July 26, 1775. The "Association" promised to "prevent any punishment from being inflicted on any offenders, other than such, as shall be adjudged by the civil magistrate, continental congress, our convention, council of safety, or committees of observation."

In this attempt to end vigilante justice, the Convention unwittingly gave the radicals a weapon to use in their reign of terror. Those who refused to subscribe to the Association of

Freemen, called "non-associators," were marked as traitors to the revolutionary state. Non-associators began to receive warnings with ominous signatures like "Legion." When Baltimore County Sheriff Robert Christie called the revolutionaries "rebels," the Baltimore Whig Club told him that if he stayed in Maryland, "your life will be sacrificed by an injured people."

The revolutionary committees were blamed for the radicals' excesses. A citizen of Annapolis called the committees the "truest though absurdest tyrants that any country ever had cause to complain of." Claiming that the patriot leaders had made escape almost impossible, he nevertheless believed that thousands were "anxious for a defection." A merchant asked, "What think you of this land of liberty, where a man's property is at the mercy of anyone that will lead the mob?" Such ironies abounded. Carrollton had joked about being prosecuted by the British under an act of Henry VIII, but now the convention resurrected a statute of Edward III that made any correspondence with the enemy treasonable.

Strangely enough, the main Tory enclave in Maryland was the militia, especially on the Eastern Shore. In April 1775, Gov. Eden armed the militia who were loyal to him. He began promoting Loyalists to be justices of the peace and created a private militia of his own, which grew to nearly two thousand men. Eden was becoming increasingly alarmed. Just after Lexington and Concord, he had praised the convention's "great temper and moderation." But a few months later, he charged that "all power is getting fast into the hands of the very lowest people."

The Council of Safety

What soured Eden on the patriots was probably the defection of Major Jenifer, who became president of the revolutionary Council of Safety in August 1775. Carrollton also sat on the council, which took command of the Maryland war effort on August 29. The Council of Safety immediately took action to secure war material, offering "liberal encouragement" to armaments suppliers in a September 1 advertisement. On

September 10, Carrollton wrote Jenifer to obtain gunpowder, although the council was not sitting. "As the exigency seems pressing, we must not stand so much on form," Carrollton told the Major.

The public terror of slave rebellion created the first major crisis for the Council of Safety. The council feared that Eden would imitate the strategy of Virginia's Governor Dunmore. Dunmore had caused a panic by offering to free slaves who volunteered for his militia. Patriots who captured these runaways cut off their hands before hanging, drawing, and quartering them. Those who reached British lines also suffered a grim fate. Dunmore later sold them into West Indian slavery.

The Council of Safety took no action against Eden, until Richard Henry Lee began agitating in Congress for the governor's arrest. On May 15, 1776, Congress urged the expulsion of the Maryland proprietary government. But Samuel Purviance of the Baltimore Committee of Observation had already taken matters into his own hands by arresting the governor.

Instead of making Eden an example, the Council of Safety turned against the radicals. They remonstrated with Purviance: "the assumption of power entrusted to another body was a high handed and dangerous offence." Carrollton and the council demanded that Eden be allowed to leave the colony unmolested. They told John Hancock that the governor's arrest threatened the colony with "immediate anarchy and convulsion."

Jenifer later claimed that the council was "highly applauded" for its "spirited conduct" against Purviance. But it seems that Jenifer actually knew about Eden's kidnapping beforehand. He was employing a "good cop, bad cop" strategy, using the Whig Club to terrorize dissenters, even while the council publicly denounced the club's excesses. The convention later censured Purviance mildly, while praising his "active zeal in the common Cause."

Eden took refuge on a British ship. In June 1776, he was rumored to have welcomed runaway slaves on board. The council confronted Eden, who denied the charge but vowed to receive all Loyalists on the ship, including indentured servants.

Part III: Revolutionary

"So scandalous a transaction," Carrollton commented, "has opened the eyes of the Convention & has inspired them with some warmth & spirit." The Maryland Convention was under criticism for its moderation. General Charles Lee called the Marylanders "the namby pambys of the senatorial part of the continent."

Lee's choice of words is interesting. Carrollton would later reinvent the concept of a Senate and deploy it in Maryland to correct the politics of popular will. Montesquieu inspired Carroll's small and aristocratic Senate, chosen by an electoral college. There has been much debate about whether the American Revolution was essentially radical or conservative. In fact, there were two revolutions, a radical and a moderate. The states that harnessed the radicals' energy for the moderates' goals functioned best. No state accomplished this better than Maryland, under Carrollton's leadership.

Carrollton was a pivotal member of the Council of Safety. In early 1776, William Neill applied to him directly with a plan to raid the Caribbean for munitions. So did Purviance, who wanted to recapture an American ship. When the British ship *Otter* appeared off Baltimore in March 1776, Carroll commanded Thomas Dorsey to march his men to defend the city, "unless you have express directions from the Council of Safety to go with your battalion to some other place. They will confirm this order of mine."

As one of the few men in the colonies with industrial experience, Carroll played a vital role in producing munitions. His subcommittee for the manufacture of saltpeter proposed in December 1775 to create saltpeter mills in each county, as well as a general refinery and powder mill. Carroll also invested in a Philadelphia saltpeter mill. He expanded the Baltimore Iron Works. Carrollton later wrote to Franklin of the new salt mines, iron works, and distilleries that sprang up in Maryland to serve the Revolution.

Nor was Carroll averse to making a profit, when this could be done without hampering the war effort. After Lexington and Concord, Carrollton expected his factors to get a high price for his tobacco, "as certainly that intelligence would give a start to the market." He told Wallace & Company to "regulate your conduct...principally by the probability or improbability of a continuance of this Civil War." Carroll had given up lobbying his English correspondents, believing that peace was unlikely and that "we shall prove victorious."

His father, on the other hand, was still trying to convince William Graves. On the fourteenth cramped page of a letter to Graves, the patriarch apologized that "my hand is far from being so steady as formerly. I now write very slowly." The old man would soon have to resume management of family business during his son's frequent absences. By February 1777, Carrollton had surrendered the Iron Works papers to his father. The Carrolls transferred their custom to the house of Joshua Johnson, who established himself in France during the Revolution. Joshua Johnson later became a public servant; his daughter, Louisa Catherine, married John Quincy Adams.

Sense and Sensibility

Molly Carroll, too, took a greater role in plantation management during the war. She had a growing family. The couple's first surviving daughter, Mary, was born in 1770. A second, who died young, was named Louisa Rachel, after Carroll's former loves. In August 1774, Carrollton wrote Graves that Molly "is now big with a son and heir—at least so the old gentleman wishes. I believe he will lose all patience should it turn to a girl."

The Squire's hopes were fulfilled when another Charles Carroll was born on March 2, 1775. He claimed that he had no partiality for the boy, as opposed to "my dear little" Mary. But he worried over Molly's milk supply, and criticized her for venturing out in the snow to socialize. "Are such risks to be ran by a rational creature for a little pleasure or gratification?"

Charles Willson Peale portrayed Molly holding Locke's *Treatise on Education*. But the Carroll children's upbringing was hardly a model of rational rearing. Their father was frequently absent. They were supervised by their opium-addicted mother, their doting grandfather, and a corps of slaves. It should come as no surprise that the next generation of Carrolls lacked discipline and emotional balance. They were not alone in this. The children of the war displayed a romantic narcissism in contrast to, and reaction against, their fathers' self-sacrifice. Among the Carrolls, the boy Charles, later known as Charles Carroll of Homewood, was most strongly dominated by his passions.

But the Founding Fathers, for all their surface stoicism, were also much influenced by the passions. John Locke has often been portrayed as the guiding spirit of the Founders. But Locke's rationalism and rejection of religious certainty were foreign to the American mind. Eighteenth-century skeptics like Locke disturbed the traditional conception of the universe. American thinkers desired to reestablish moral certainty, without restoring the lost city of Christendom, with all its demands on belief and on behavior.

The answer to their dilemma came out of Scotland. Common Sense theory was a combination of medical and moral ideas that made the individual person the locus of morality. As the name implies, Common Sense thinkers valued not only the higher powers of man, but his sensible nature. Lord Shaftesbury was perhaps the first to emphasize the role of passion and sensibility in moral decision-making. The Scottish thinkers took this one step further, positing a "moral sense" that served as an infallible guide to behavior. The moral sense superseded older concepts of natural law and informed conscience.

American colleges were profoundly affected by the new ideas coming out of the Scottish universities. Moral sense ideas were also spread by such organizations as the American Society for Promoting and Propagating Useful Knowledge, founded in Philadelphia in 1766. They were popularized in Laurence Sterne's sentimental fiction. Thomas Jefferson called Sterne's work "the best course of morality that ever was written." All the Founders were influenced by moral-sense thought. We call the sage of Philadelphia "Dr. Franklin" because of his honorary degree from St. Andrew's University in Sotland. And, of course, Thomas Paine's "Common Sense" was the most influential piece of revolutionary propaganda.

Carrollton was part of a different tradition, and he usually spoke of "spirit" rather than "sense." For example, he asked whether the British ministers "expect to escape the vengeance of an insulted, a spirited and powerful people." But even Carroll used the moral-sense vocabulary. British leniency, he said, would promote "attachment and affection," as well as great "advantage."

The documents produced by the Congress are also full of moral-sense language. John Dickinson of Pennsylvania cited natural rights against British oppression. But as a man of sensibility, Dickinson dreaded separation from England. "Torn from the body, to which we are united by religion, liberty, laws, affections, relation, language and commerce, we must bleed at every vein." Yet "our attachment to no nation upon the earth should supplant our attachment to liberty."

By 1776, there was no hope of reconciliation. The English constitution had changed beyond recognition since 1688. It no longer had room for such anomalies as colonial charters, palatinates, or multiple levels of sovereignty. The tide of rationalization left nothing but the King in Parliament as the foundation of the state. Franklin understood as early as 1768 that "Parliament has a right to make all laws for us, or...no laws for us." It would be left to the Americans to reinvent a divided and tiered sovereignty in the form of federalism.

North Meets South

Carrollton was delighted when George Washington assumed command of the Continental Army, camped at Cambridge, Massachusetts. He wrote Washington, praising him as "the man singled out by the unanimous voice of his country, for his love & attachment to it, and great abilities." But though Carroll knew war was inevitable, it made him uneasy. "When I reflect that men are oftener actuated & governed by their passions, than by their interests, I expect nothing but civil war, in which

Part III: Revolutionary

the victory will be almost as fatal to the victors, as defeat." His father was more sanguine and accurately predicted Washington's cautious strategy. "It is certainly our interest to protract the war, never to engage but with manifest advantage," the Squire wrote.

There were many in the colonies, and especially in the North, who did not see the wisdom of this approach. They believed that the republican militia, which John Adams eulogized as "an illustrious school of military virtue," would soon drive the British out by sheer moral force. But Washington knew that citizen-soldiers would never win the war. The twelve-month enlistments in Massachusetts Bay spelled chaos. The general complained that men were constantly coming in and out of camp, drawing provisions without giving "one hour's service."

Nor was Washington impressed with the New Englanders' vaunted morality. "Notwithstanding all the public virtue which is ascribed to these people," he wrote, "there is no nation under the sun that pays more adoration to money than they do." The Yankees "suffer nothing to go by them that they can lay hands on." Stephen Moylan, Washington's Catholic aide-de-camp, shared his general's astonishment. "The deficiency of public spirit in this country," Moylan wrote of Massachusetts, "is much more than I could possibly have an idea of."

The New England egalitarian ethic made military discipline impossible. An exasperated Moylan confided that an officer "must shake every man by the hand, & desire, beg & pray, do brother, do my friend, do such a thing, whereas a few hearty damns from a person who did not care a damn for them would have a much better effect." The New Englanders elected their own officers. As a result, Washington noted, the officers' main concern was "to curry favour" with their men.

The commander in chief knew that discipline was "next under providence" as a factor in military success. He lobbied Congress to increase the maximum number of lashes from one hundred to five hundred. In this regard, too, the Southern commanders poured scorn on their Northern counterparts. William Smallwood, Maryland's most celebrated officer, claimed that Northern generals "have introduced a new system for conducting this war." "Instead of instructing their troops in the principles of military discipline...they train them to run away."

In public, Washington held his tongue. He did his best to eliminate "the unhappy and pernicious distinctions and jealousies between the troops of different governments." The general also defended his Catholic soldiers from Protestant antagonism. He forbade the customary burning of the Pope's effigy on Guy Fawkes' Day, calling it a "ridiculous and childish custom." Foreseeing the need of French Canadian help, Washington declared his surprise "that there should be officers and soldiers in this army so void of common sense as not to see the impropriety of such a step at this juncture."

The war was already setting a new standard of cruelty. The British were angered by the Americans' frequent breach of military etiquette, which probably owed more to ignorance than calculation. The British high command retaliated by sending smallpox-infested prostitutes and slaves into the Cambridge camp. When the British burned Falmouth, Maine, in October 1775, Moylan declared that "there is not the least remains of virtue, wisdom, or humanity in the British court." Casualties, too, were beyond all expectation. Bunker Hill was the deadliest battle in history up to that time, in terms of the percentage of bullets finding their mark.

Washington faced shortages of supplies that would have crippled a less resourceful general. The patriot army maintained its siege of Boston for several months, in spite of an almost total lack of gunpowder. British General Gage heard of the powder shortage, but he did not attack. The story was so incredible that Gage assumed Washington had fabricated it to deceive him.

Under these circumstances, it was a miracle that the British evacuated themselves from Boston. Gage embarked his troops for Canada, and Washington entered Boston on St. Patrick's Day, 1776. "No man, perhaps," Washington reflected, "since the first institution of armies, ever commanded one under more difficult circumstances than I have done."

"CX"

The new body politic was advancing rapidly. "That which was esteemed moderate, six or eight months ago," wrote "Countryman," "is now by the alteration of circumstances and things, become spiritless, cold, and inimical to America."

On March 26 and April 2, 1776, Carrollton published articles in *Dunlap's Maryland Gazette*, a new Baltimore paper, using the pseudonym "CX." The "X" stands for the Greek letter *chi*, so that Carroll was identifying himself: Carroll, Charles. He was able to be far more candid about his ideas on government in these pieces than the "First Citizen."

Boldly, Carroll started his first CX essay with a quotation from Hume. While stable government was much to be desired, CX wrote, and "changes in the constitution ought not to be lightly made," the English government was now irredeemably corrupt. In any case, he asserted, Great Britain possessed but a "limited sovereignty" over the colonies, where "legislative powers have been granted by compact, and long enjoyed by common consent."

It was time to declare independence and create new governments in the colonies. The new states must not follow the example of the Glorious Revolution by making the legislature "a part of that very administration, they were by the original institution intended to control." Instead, CX insisted on a rigorous separation of legislative, executive, and judicial powers.

The second CX paper offered a blueprint for the new government. Offices should become less lucrative. Judges ought to hold office for life during good behavior. The assembly would reelect the governor and council every year.

The legislature must consist of two houses, Carrollton wrote. The upper house should be strengthened considerably. "To give to that branch of the legislature more weight, it should be composed of gentlemen of the first fortune and abilities in the Province; and they should hold their seats for life. An Upper House thus constituted, would form some counterpoise to the democratical part of the legislature, although it is confessed, that even then the democracy would be the preponderating weight in the scales of this government."

The lower house should truly represent the people. Carroll wanted to do away with voting by counties in the assembly, and apportion seats in the lower house according to population. The "welfare...of the whole province" should take precedence over the special interests of the individual counties. The upper house, in turn, would make sure that this popular representation did not lead to mob rule.

THE QUEBEC ACT

The colonists could not yet appreciate the symbolism of the St. Patrick's Day conquest of Boston. Indeed, a major *casus belli* was the Quebec Act of June 13, 1774. The Quebec Act established the Catholic Church in Canada, enabling it to collect tithes from its members. Church attendance was not compulsory, of course, but Canadian Catholics could worship without restraint. Catholics were also allowed to sit on the council that governed the province under the Act.

None of this seems outrageous, given that there were some 150,000 Roman Catholics in Quebec and only 360 Anglicans. But the other colonies were immediately thrown into a frenzy. William Lee called the Quebec Act "absolutely a dissolution of this government, the compact between the King and the people is totally done away with." Isaac Low went so far as to label the King a "Roman Catholic, nay a Roman Catholic tyrant." In England, Lord George Gordon compared George III to James II before a crowd of forty thousand. A hissing mob greeted the monarch with shouts of "Remember James II" as he went to sign the Act.

Aside from anti-popery, there were rational grounds for the public fury. All of the English territory west of the Appalachians and north of the Ohio River became part of Quebec. Since the Quebec Act provided for no popular assembly, only a governor and council, this was convenient for the Crown. The Quebec Act guaranteed neither habeas corpus nor trial by jury. The annexation of the Northwest to Canada meant the cancel-

Part III: Revolutionary

lation of land claims by colonies, land companies, and individuals. Concerned about the decline of the English population relative to that of the colonies, Parliament discouraged emigration to Canada by preserving its French seigneurial system of land tenure.

The colonists saw the Quebec Act, with some justification, as a prelude to the establishment of centralized, arbitrary government over the other thirteen colonies. To the Continental Congress, it was "clear beyond a doubt, that a resolution is formed and is now carrying into execution to extinguish the freedom of these colonies by subjecting them to a despotic government." Similar language about the Quebec Act eventually found its way into the Declaration of Independence.

But in addition to constitutional concerns, the American response to the Quebec Act reveals a deep, visceral reaction to Catholicism, especially French Catholics. "False Frenchmen" were the snake in the American paradise. After the Quebec Act, "Virginius" expected the Inquisition to be reestablished in Canada. In the minds of the colonists, the Inquisition was linked with Native American atrocities. Protestant settlers lived in terror of torture at the hands of Native Americans and Roman Catholics. A French resurgence in Canada, and the Spanish presence in Louisiana, "threatened this Continent with slavery."

Still, Congress knew that Canadian support would vastly improve their chances of winning the war. Canada provided the British with a staging ground for a potentially devastating attack down the Hudson-Champlain waterway. The strategic importance of Canada led the colonists into blatant hypocrisy. On the one hand, Samuel Adams warned the Mohawk people of the Catholic menace. "We much fear some of your children may be induced," Adams wrote, "instead of worshipping the only true God, to pray his dues to images made by their own hands." Meanwhile, the Massachusetts Convention promised to obtain a priest for the devoutly Catholic western Abenaki of Maine, then known in New England as the St. François tribe. in return for their support.

Congress itself made the worst blunder in this regard. In late 1774, John Dickinson penned an address to the Canadians that promised toleration of the Catholic Church, should Canada join the confederacy. But John Jay's address to the British people condemned Catholicism in the strongest terms. "Nor can we suppress our astonishment," wrote Jay, "that a British Parliament should ever consent to establish in that country a religion that has deluged your island in blood, and dispersed impiety, bigotry, persecution, murder and rebellion through every part of the world." Astonishingly, the First Continental Congress opted to send both messages in October 1774.

A letter from Montreal summed up the results, in an exaggerated fashion. "The decent manner in which the religious matters were touched" in the message to the Canadians, and "the encomiums on the French nation, flattered a people fond of compliments. They begged the translator, as he had succeeded so well, to try his hand on that address to the people of Great Britain." But when the residents of Montreal heard Jay's "picture of the Catholic religion and the Canadian manners, they could not contain their resentment, nor express it but in unbroken curses."

John Adams later recalled that he had been "so shallow a politician" that these compositions "all appeared to me...like children's play at marbles or push-pin." However lightly the Congress took their verbal pyrotechnics, the fiasco of the October 1774 messages mobilized the Canadian Church against the Americans, creating a powerful obstacle to the Congress' plans in Canada. When the 1774 Congress took up the Suffolk Resolves, which also condemned the Quebec Act in bigoted terms, Carrollton simply returned to Maryland.

The Canadian Campaign

The congressional paranoia about Canada increased during 1775. "We have received certain intelligence," Congress declared that July, "that General Carleton, the Governor of Canada, is instigating the people of that province and the Indians to fall upon us." A French alliance was still unthinkable to Protestant America in 1775. But Canadian support for the Revolution was seen as a necessary substitute.

Part III: Revolutionary

Fear of Canadian invasion was used to justify the seizure of Fort Ticonderoga by Benedict Arnold and Ethan Allen. Now Arnold pressed his plan to invade Canada upon the Congress. George Washington agreed. "The safety and welfare of the whole continent may depend" on Arnold's scheme, the general wrote.

Washington penned his own letter to the Canadians, a jewel of moral-sense rhetoric. He looked forward to the day when all "the Inhabitants of America shall have one sentiment." Washington played down the fact that the Americans were invading Canada. He promised that Arnold would "act as in the Country of his patrons and best friends." Privately, the commander in chief asked Arnold to "look with compassion on their [Catholic] errors without insulting them."

The invasion was two pronged. General Schuyler was to strike up Lake Champlain, reduce Montreal, and proceed to Quebec City. Arnold would lead his force up the Kennebec River, which runs through the Maine wilderness, to Quebec. But Schuyler dragged his feet, keeping his force at Ticonderoga until August 30. This gave the impetuous Ethan Allen time to forge ahead and attack Montreal. Allen's looting of the city was a public-relations disaster.

Arnold, meanwhile, ran into trouble. His unreliable maps showed Quebec as one hundred eighty miles from the mouth of the Kennebec, when in fact it was twice that far. En route, a division of New Englanders abandoned Arnold and returned to Cambridge. Among those who stayed with the expedition was Aaron Burr, whose father, a New Light Presbyterian, founded Princeton University. Burr was accompanied by his Native American mistress, known as "Golden Thighs." There were no religious trappings on this mission. An American minister in Canada complained that the army had observed no days of thanksgiving or prayer.

To the French Catholic hierarchy, it seemed that the heathen *Bostonnais* had come to destroy their Church. Bishop Jean Olivier Briand did his best to mobilize Catholic Canadians to defend their newly restored privileges. Briand ordered his priests to withhold the sacraments from anyone who fraternized with the Americans. In this he was implicitly supported by the Vatican. When King George allowed Catholics to serve as officers in his army, Pope Pius VI called him the "best of sovereigns," "full of mildness to Catholics."

Although the Church supported British rule, many of the French *habitants* were dissatisfied. Montreal merchants shared the Americans' resentment of mercantile restrictions. Carleton had to threaten the merchants to keep them in line. The tenant farmers hated the feudal land-tenure, which the Quebec Act had retained. Canadians were also subject to British impressment for forced labor.

Thus, when Arnold finally arrived at Saint-Marie on November 3, 1775, the French Canadians willingly fed his starving army. Arnold's journey has been justly compared with Hannibal's crossing of the Alps. Unfortunately for the Americans, Quebec was reinforced on November 12, and its inhabitants were recruited, cajoled, and forced to join in its defense. "Had I been ten days sooner," lamented Arnold, "Quebec must inevitably have fallen into our hands." Arnold began a siege and waited for the other wing of the American force, which on November 13 occupied Montreal. The charismatic Richard Montgomery had assumed command from the ailing Schuyler.

Time favored the British. More reinforcements would surely come in spring, when the frozen St. Lawrence River melted. In addition, most American enlistments expired on January 1. An attack would have to be made soon. "Relying on that Providence" which so far had favored America, Montgomery chose December 31, 1775, for the storming of Quebec. The British easily repulsed the attempt, killing Montgomery and wounding Arnold in the leg.

Arnold managed to maintain the siege, partly by keeping Montgomery's death a secret from his French Canadian admirers. As the news inevitably became known, the Canadians began to defect. The Americans had run out of specie but continued to requisition food, paying with promissory notes. Worse, an anti-Catholic bigot, General David Wooster, commanded the Montreal garrison. Wooster, who considered the French

Part III: Revolutionary

Canadians "enemies and rascals," offended Catholics by abusing the clergy.

The Carrolls were deeply interested in Canadian events. Squire Carroll hoped that "possessing Canada would quite confound" the King's "hellish schemes." Carrollton collected hard money for the besiegers of Quebec in Anne Arundel, offering continental paper in exchange. He managed to gather about £120 sterling.

The Canadian Commission

Soon, Carrollton would find himself at the center of the Canadian conflict. The army begged Congress to send a commission to Canada, with enough cash to overcome the impression of American bankruptcy. On February 15, 1776, Congress named Benjamin Franklin, Samuel Chase, and Carroll of Carrollton to the commission. Even more remarkable than Carrollton's appointment was Congress' request that he "prevail on Mr. John Carroll to accompany the committee to Canada." In addition to the priest, the commission was to take £800 sterling and eight tons of powder.

The New Englanders accepted this unusual embassy with composure. John Adams minuted that Carrollton was "a Roman Catholic but an ardent patriot." But Adams cautioned a correspondent "to communicate the circumstances of the Priest, the Jesuit, and the Romish religion, only to such persons as can judge of the measures upon large and generous principles."

Rev. John Carroll had returned to Maryland after the suppression of the Jesuit order. His presence on the mission would allay the scruples of Canadian Catholics, who risked losing the sacraments if they supported America. But Fr. Carroll was dubious about Congress' appeal to the Canadians. "They have not the same motives for taking up arms against England which renders the resistance of the other colonies so justifiable," he declared. "Or if they find themselves oppressed, they have not yet tried the success of petitions and remonstrances all which ought, as I apprehend, to be ineffectual before it can be lawful to have recourse to arms and change of government."

Still, John Carroll consented to go. He must have found it impossible to decline an honor that would raise the standing of American Catholics. Carrollton, too, obeyed the summons, arriving in Philadelphia on March 2, 1776. He began studying military strategy. But Carroll soon became disgusted with the politics surrounding the Canadian embassy, as Dickinson and Jay fought to weaken the commission. "These public honors set very heavy on me," he wrote his father. "I think I am fitter for private station."

The society of Benjamin Franklin somewhat compensated Carroll for congressional headaches. He was "quite charmed" with Franklin's wit and wisdom. "What a man!" Carrollton later recalled. "Nothing is serious enough to suppress the humor that bubbles up in Franklin." Behind Franklin's charm lay the canny and opportunistic politician. His 1746 pamphlet "Plain Truth" raised the specter of Catholic disloyalty and Popish domination. Now that the wind was blowing a different way, Franklin hobnobbed with the Catholic Carrolls. Poor Richard's ability to change with the times, and get away with anything, would become instrumental for the American war effort.

Carrollton's trip to Canada may be seen as a delayed adolescence. It was his first serious attempt to break out of the Squire's paternal domination and become a man in his own right. Nevertheless, Carroll still looked to his father for approval and support. He wrote to Carroll of Annapolis at every opportunity and complained when no letters reached him in return.

Furthermore, Carroll expected Molly to share the letters he sent his father. Although he rarely wrote to her separately, Carrollton wanted Molly to write him "long letters," because she "has little to do." His letters to his wife were dry and stilted; those to the Squire, deep, newsy and engrossing. In one, Carroll reported on his fascination with the women of Philadelphia. As if to make up for his tactlessness, he sent Molly six pairs of shoes.

After the British evacuation of Boston, the patriots enjoyed a wave of optimism. Canada became the center of attention, since most observers, including Carrollton, thought the British would not attack New York City. If the Americans took Quebec, Carrollton believed, "it will not be very difficult to draw the Canadians into the union on certain terms: I am sure it is their interest to unite with us." The colonists must consider the Canadians "as countrymen & friends" in order "to render the latter attached to us."

The instructions that Congress approved for the commissioners on March 20 used similar moral-sense language, combined with veiled threats. The commissioners should "urge the necessity the People are under of immediately taking some decisive step to put themselves under the protection of the United Colonies." This first attempt at American diplomacy was already a part of the great tradition of U.S. foreign policy, which Theodore Roosevelt immortalized in his injunction to "speak softly, and carry a big stick." The commissioners were also to set up a "free press" in order to spread revolutionary propaganda.

Congress repeated their promise of religious toleration for Canadian Catholics. The commissioners were given extraordinary powers to settle disputes between the army and civilians, to reform abuses in the army, even to suspend officers pending congressional hearings. They were empowered to open trade with the Native Americans and to bargain for their neutrality. All officers were required to support the commissioners in their tasks.

As the hour of departure for the dangerous journey approached, Carrollton grew pensive. He feared "the application I must give to business…it will be extensive, intricate, & troublesome." And "what if we should not please?" Carroll worried. Nevertheless, he knew that "neither interest nor inclination will lead us to our former dependence." Carrollton was talking about the Empire, but he could have been referring to his relationship with the Squire, in spite of his old anxiety to please. "I believe we shall have no peace," he predicted, "but what we can obtain at the point of the sword."

The Journey to Canada

The commissioners departed Philadelphia on March 26, 1776. Arriving in New York City three days later, they found a martial spirit. "Gentlemen of the first, and men of all ranks" were working together on fortifications. "I was told by a gentleman, that some gentlemen not used to work with a spade, worked so long, to set an example, that the blood gushed out of their fingers." While this spirit continued, Carrollton concluded, America would be "unconquerable."

The party took ship on April 2 for Albany, which they reached five days later. I will not recreate the commissioners' journey in detail, since Richard Ketchum has admirably done so in his book *Saratoga*. Our main source for the trip is Charles Carroll's journal and his letters home. They reveal Carroll's urbanity, his great sense of history, and his determination in the face of adversity.

Carrollton's writings as a commissioner also show a hard-headed businessman who saw opportunities for profit wherever he went. On the Hudson, Carroll remarked that "this river seems intended by nature to open a communication between Canada and the province of N. York by water." His host in Albany, Philip Schuyler, estimated that £50,000 sterling would perfect the water route between New York and Quebec. Later, at Crown Point, Carrollton realized that the abandoned barracks could make "a fine manufactory." And he had plans for Canada, as well. Once that country "enjoys a good government," Carroll hoped, the land along the Richelieu River would be turned into pasture.

Carrollton found a kindred spirit in Schuyler, whose fabulous landholdings dwarfed even the Carrolls'. But in spite of Schuyler's hospitality, the trip's prospects rapidly worsened. Delayed by ice on Lake George, the commissioners received dispatches from Canada of such a discouraging nature that Franklin told Hancock "I am afraid we shall be able to effect but little there." The goals of the mission were revised downward. Canadian neutrality was now the best the Americans could hope for.

Carrollton began to meditate on the Hudson-Champlain passage in a more ominous light. If the British regained Canada, they could strike down the waterway toward New York City, cutting New England off from the rest of the colonies. Carroll began to devise defensive works that might slow the

British passage: a fort at the falls of the Richelieu, pickets in the lake at Isle aux Noix, and a flotilla of armed vessels. Perhaps, Carroll reasoned, "we may defy the enemy on Lake Champlain for this summer and fall at least, even should we unfortunately be driven out of Canada."

Diminishing expectations did not spoil the commissioners' good fellowship in their slow journey up Lake George, which the French had called Lac du Saint Sacrement. Franklin facetiously wrote Josiah Quincy to bid him farewell, since he expected the trip to finish him off. But the sage was lively enough to compose a satire on the British retreat after Lexington and Concord. The Earl of Sandwich had said that "the Yankees would not face us." In Franklin's poem, a British soldier says:

> If they could not get before us, how could they look us in the face?
> We took care they should not by scamp'ring away apace.
> That they had not much to brag of, is a very plain case,
> For if they beat us in the fight, we beat them in the race.

Carrollton contented himself with making fun of Chase's appetite. "Mr. Chase and I landed to examine a beautiful fall of water. Mr. Chase very apprehensive of the leg of mutton being boiled too much, impatient to get on board." The Marylander lacked Chase's cast-iron stomach. He became violently sick while traveling in the commissioners' square-sailed, single-masted gunboat, thirty-six feet long and eight feet wide. But he was eager for the adventure. One night he and Chase went ashore to sleep beneath a tent made of bushes, although there were beds on the boat. Carroll dubbed the spot "Commissioners' Point."

Carrollton was generally matter-of-fact about the natural beauty of the wilderness. Of a chain of mountains, he observed that "the snow's not dissolving in their latitude at the end of April is a proof of their altitude." But on the Hudson, he was overwhelmed by the "amazing steep & rocky hills" which appeared to crowd in on the boat by moonlight. "The different shades [and] reflections of light presented alternately the most pleasing & horrifying prospects." A waterfall, "swollen with the melting of the snows and rain," offered "a sublime but terrifying spectacle."

Carrollton's sense of history is also striking, especially his familiarity with the campaigns of the French and Indian War. At Ticonderoga, Carroll described the remains of a French *abatis*, a defensive work made of sharpened tree branches. These ghostly reminders of the previous conflict were still a hazard for the commissioners, whose boats struck against pickets the French had driven into the riverbed twenty years earlier. The Americans had occupied the forts along the waterway, and Carroll was alarmed at their ruined condition.

On April 27, the commissioners reached St. John (Quebec), and proceeded to Montreal on the 29th. Benedict Arnold, who had relinquished his Quebec command to Wooster, welcomed them in great style. Carroll regretted the loss of Montgomery, who had won "the affections of the Canadians." But he was impressed with Arnold's "good taste and politeness: an officer bred up at Versailles could not have behaved with more delicacy, ease, and good breeding." If Arnold survived, Carroll predicted, he would become a "great man." Carrollton did not realize that Arnold's loyalty to the old code of honor would, paradoxically, lead him into dishonor.

Carroll enjoyed the good life in Montreal, reveling in the "ease and softness" of the French ladies. He made an excursion to the fort at Chamblay, shooting the rapids of the Sorel River. On May 6, Carrollton paused to reflect. "If the Congress had any opinion of my abilities they were certainly mistaken," he wrote. "My abilities are not above the common level, but I have integrity, a sincere love for my country, a detestation of tyranny, I have perseverance, and the habit of business, and I therefore hope to be of some service."

The Commissioners Take Charge

One major problem was the increasing alienation of the inhabitants. Arnold's proclamation that private property was sacred to Americans had become something of a joke. The commissioners reported that the army's commanders "have recourse to violences in providing the army with carriages, and other conveniences, which indispose and irritate the minds of the people." The American credit was nonexistent. "Not the most trifling service can be procured without an assurance of instant pay in silver or gold," the commissioners wrote. A ferryman detained their messenger "till a friend passing changed a dollar for him into silver."

Then there was the crisis of manpower. When Arnold left Quebec for Montreal, he reported that 786 of his 2,505 men were sick. Smallpox was the main scourge; the British had once again sent infected women into the camp. In addition, fifteen hundred enlistments expired on April 15. John Hancock notified the commissioners on April 26 that Congress had added six fresh battalions to the four already en route to Quebec. But five days later, when General Thomas assumed command at Quebec from Wooster, only one thousand of nineteen hundred men were fit for duty. Ominously, Thomas had never been infected with smallpox.

The Americans decided to move their sick soldiers downriver. While this was taking place, on May 5, British ships appeared at Quebec. "We were employed at this time in carrying the sick, artillery, &c., on board the bateaux," Thomas noted drily, "the enemy, in landing their troops, and, as the event shows, in preparing to make a sally." The Americans fled, leaving their cannon, five hundred muskets, and a boatload of gunpowder. Two hundred wounded men were also captured. Otherwise, "we have lost but few men it is thought in our retreat," Carrollton wrote on May 10. "Indeed it was made too hastily for the enemy to kill or take many of them."

The commissioners knew that their situation was hopeless. "We are afraid it will not be in our power to render our Country any farther services in this Colony." On May 11, Franklin left, accompanied by John Carroll. Chase and Carrollton chose to remain until the retreat was completed. In the meantime, their responsibilities increased. They were forced to "become generals, commissaries, justices of the peace, in short to act in twenty different capacities."

The financial situation was now desperate. Carroll tried to borrow hard money on his own credit, by selling bills of exchange, without success. It would be better to withdraw the army, he told Congress, than to leave it unprovided. But a few days after the Quebec rout, another brigade arrived from the colonies, carrying only ten days' provisions. Apparently the Americans thought Providence would take care of their needs. "For God's sake send pork and powder," Carrollton and Chase begged Schuyler. "If further reinforcements are sent without pork to victual the whole army, our soldiers must perish, or feed on each other."

The commissioners had grown thoroughly disillusioned with the revolutionary army, which lacked those high ideals bandied about in Philadelphia. They took out their frustrations on General Thomas, who had come down with smallpox. "The officers are not sufficiently active," they told Thomas, "nor do they seem activated by those disinterested principles and generous sentiments which might be expected from men fighting in so just and glorious a Cause." The *habitants*, too, were just out to make a buck. Far from being oppressed, the tenant farmers were actually richer than the *seigneurs*.

Carrollton and Chase realized that it was impossible to maintain an army on republican virtue. "It is very difficult to keep soldiers under proper discipline without paying them regularly." They admitted the need to seize goods in exchange for promissory notes. This was "a violent remedy, which nothing can justify but the most urgent necessity." But without confiscations, "our soldiers will soon be reduced to the dreadful alternative of starving, or plundering the inhabitants."

While Carrollton and Chase were willing to stand up to the military commanders, they admitted to having "neither abilities nor inclination" to be generals. On May 11, the commissioners wrote Franklin that they had urged Arnold to abandon Deschambault, which was exposed to attack from Quebec, and retreat to the fort at St. John. Four days later, they advised Thomas of the "great importance" of Deschambault, beseeching him to hold it. They pestered the dying Thomas to inoculate the troops—although at that time a smallpox inoculation could produce serious illness and required a quarantine.

But Carrollton reserved his sharpest darts for Wooster, who "is, in our opinion, unfit, totally unfit, to command your Army, and conduct the War." By May 17, Wooster "is now shamefully flying out" of Canada. "I wish he was gone," Carroll commented. "One Nicholson...was made town major by Wooster: this low life scoundrel has done nothing but pillage & commit outrages on the inhabitants of this city during the whole winter." When Nicholson too fled, the commissioners ordered his arrest. Like Thomas, Wooster did not have long to live. He perished in the British raid on Danbury, Connecticut, in 1777.

The generals, for their part, compared the commissioners to the smallpox. They called the ambassadors "Apostles of Confusion." When Chase and Carrollton finally joined the retreat, on May 31, Arnold said that the commissioners were departing, like good fortune.

Carrollton's "uneasiness" in Canada, he told his father, surpassed any anxiety he had previously known. Nevertheless, his ardor for the revolutionary cause increased. Native Americans had caused the death of several American prisoners by exposure, leaving them nearly naked on a stormy night. Carroll called Britain, which refused to control its Native American allies, "that detestable government execrated from my soul." He parted contemptuously from the Canadians, who "must receive a government from their masters; they are not fit to choose one for themselves."

The retreating Northern army, six thousand in number, was in wretched condition. Half were sick. A hospital was set up at Fort George on Lake George. The able-bodied set about fortifying Ticonderoga. The French Catholic hierarchy gloated over the American reversal. Bishop Briand ordered a thanksgiving Mass for the first anniversary of the New Year's Eve defeat. Briand called the American loss "a singular dispensation of Divine Providence." God "delivered them into our hands... that God of goodness, against whom neither science, nor wisdom, nor strength, nor craft, nor knavery can prevail."

But the Canadian expedition benefited the Americans in the

long term. As a preemptive strike, it prevented the British from advancing down the Hudson-Champlain waterway for a crucial two years. Schuyler and Horatio Gates adopted Carroll's advice about defensive measures. Carrollton recommended "entrenching, making abbaties [sic], breaking up the roads, harassing the enemy on their march." This strategy of attrition would spell disaster for the British when they came south in 1777.

There was another result of the Canadian commission, which must remain speculative. On their long journey, Carroll surely discussed the prospects of a French alliance with Franklin. Soon, the sage was sent as ambassador to the court of Louis XVI. "Doctor Franklin is gone you know where," Carroll informed his father in November 1776.

The Canadian commission undoubtedly prepared the way for the French alliance by softening American attitudes toward Catholics. For the first time since Lord Baltimore's day, an American government promised Catholics the free exercise of their religion. In time, the Americans would come to believe the promise of tolerance they first extended to the Canadians in 1776.

Maryland Declares Independence

Rev. Carroll made a fast friend out of Franklin on their return trip, partly by defending him against their disagreeable traveling companions, Canadian Whigs who criticized the way the mission had been handled. "The lady had the assurance to tell us," wrote John Carroll, "that the Commissioners had advised with and been governed by Tories." The priest later described his time with Franklin as "one of the most fortunate and honourable events of my life."

John Carroll was a keen observer of politics. On May 28, he urged his cousin to get back to Maryland. Conservatives had taken control of the Maryland Convention in the absence of Carrollton and Chase, blocking any move toward independence. Franklin also wrote to tell the two remaining commissioners that Congress had advised each colony to create new governments. This made Carrollton's presence in Maryland even more vital.

Chase and Carroll stopped in New York on their way home, where Carrollton visited with "my old acquaintance and friend" Stephen Moylan, who was now Washington's quartermaster general. The commissioners proceeded to Philadelphia, where they made their official report to Congress on June 11. Maryland delegate Thomas Stone told Major Jenifer that opinion was favorable toward the commissioners, who had "done as much as it was possible for men to do."

On the same day, delegates from undecided states were dismissed to their home colonies in order to consult with their conventions. Both Chase and Carrollton favored independence. Interestingly, Chase promised John Adams to return with Maryland's voice for independence *and* a "foreign alliance." He, too, must have taken part in the conversation between Carrollton and Franklin about France.

Carrollton and Chase faced an uphill battle in the Maryland Convention, which had instructed its congressional delegates that January "to disavow, in the most solemn manner, all design in the colonies of independence." Under Chase's leadership, the Independent Whigs appealed to the local committees. By June 21, Chase told Adams that "county after county is instructing" its convention delegates to vote for independence. Anne Arundel did so the next day. The convention met on June 24th and approved American independence on the 28th.

Carrollton was deputed to write a "Declaration of the Delegates of Maryland" explaining the decision. A draft in his hand survives. It differs in significant ways from the declaration Jefferson was then composing.

Carrollton's declaration hardly mentions the King, referring to the "Legislative & Executive Powers" of England generically. A reference to the "Tyrant" of Britain is crossed out and replaced with "monarch." Jefferson, on the other hand, largely ignores the British administration, concentrating his full rhetorical broadside against George III. "The point," as Owen Dudley Edwards argued, "was to curse the King." The British troops had been commonly called the "ministerial army," since the King could do no wrong. Now Jefferson made George III personally responsible for waging "cruel war against human nature itself."

Carroll and Jefferson also had a different view of popular sovereignty. The central passage of Carrollton's document reads as follows: "We the Delegates ~~of the People~~ [sic] of Maryland in Convention assembled do declare that the King of G.B. has violated his compact with this People, and that they owe no allegiance to him." Carroll upholds popular sovereignty and social compact theory here, while avoiding the politics of popular will. The convention delegates are not "delegates of the people" but "delegates of Maryland." They represent the *maior et sanior pars* of the people. Jefferson, on the other hand, never mentions the social compact. He saw the constitution as something that was continually under revision by public opinion, not a permanent fiduciary obligation, as Carroll believed.

Carroll stays with the traditional natural rights of life, liberty, and property. "Slaves, savages, and foreign mercenaries have been meanly hired to rob a People of their property, liberty & lives, guilty of no other crime than deeming the last of no estimation without the secure enjoyment of the two former." Jefferson, of course, substitutes a right to the "pursuit of happiness" for the right to property. By inventing this new right, Jefferson profoundly distorted the concept of natural law, with dramatic consequences for the rest of American history.

Maryland's Declaration appeals for its truth "to that Almighty Being, who is emphatically styled the Searcher of hearts, & from whose Omniscience nothing is concealed." Jefferson's original draft described the natural law as a "sacred and undeniable" truth. Franklin insisted on suppressing even this vague reference to the divine, and so we have the phrase: "We hold these truths to be self-evident." This was more honest, given the unorthodoxy of the drafting committee, but also more narcissistic and self-affirming. Jefferson's draft avoids philosophical certainty in favor of moral-sense drama. The colonies experience the "last stab of agonizing affection" and "renounce forever these unfeeling brethren."

The American Declaration of Independence did not break

decisively with English constitutionalism or with the Saxon myth. It was first published in book form as part of a volume entitled *The Genuine Principles of the Ancient Saxon, or English Constitution*. However, having the natural law tradition, for the first time, formally stated as the foundation of government, represented an advance for civilization.

The English constitution, which provided for mixed government by different estates, had been finally destroyed by the Glorious Revolution of 1688. This was the culmination of a long process that began with Henry VIII's defiance of the Church. Jefferson's Declaration, however imperfectly, acknowledged that the British Crown had violated its covenant with the people. By destroying the political body of the King, Jefferson created a new body politic. After the Declaration was adopted, mobs symbolically marked this change by vandalizing King George's portraits, including the famous statue on the Bowling Green in lower Manhattan.

Carrollton's Declaration, which was approved by the Maryland Convention with few changes, supplements Jefferson's document, correcting its deficiencies. Its justification for the Revolution remains firmly within the Catholic tradition of natural law. Carroll's ideas point to the real reason the Revolution was legitimate: the King in Parliament had destroyed the English constitution by co-opting the nobility and depriving the Church of its independence.

Carroll the Signer

On July 4, 1776, Charles Carroll of Carrollton was selected by the Maryland Convention as a delegate to Congress. The election of a Catholic to public office was another sign of the change in the body politic. Carroll came to Congress too late to vote for independence, on July 2, or to approve the Declaration, on July 4.

Carroll noted a year later that July 4 "is to be celebrated as the anniversary of Independence." It is an interesting commentary on the American mind that we celebrate our independence on the anniversary of Jefferson's Declaration and not on July 2, the day when independence was approved. Our July 4 observance acknowledges that natural rights are embedded in our political culture. It also indicates the centrality of the written word in America. England had the orators, America the writers. A recent commentator has called the Revolution "the war of the pen against the tongue."

Indeed, only one thing united all the Founding Fathers: they liked to read books. Jefferson lamented his "malady of Bibliomania," while Adams claimed that "I have spent an estate in books." Male literacy, at about sixty percent, was higher in the colonies than in the mother country. The roster of subscribers for Franklin's lending library included twenty tradesmen for every gentleman. This voracious appetite for books naturally found its outlet in writing. Franklin said that the colonists had inverted the rhyme,

> A Man of Words and not of Deeds,
> Is like a Garden full of Weeds

to read

> A Man of Deeds and not of Words
> Is like a Garden full of _____

"I have forgot the rhyme," Franklin quipped, "but remember 'tis something the very reverse of a perfume."

The spoken word had lost much of its impact, while print had the power to immortalize an author. But the Protestant founders did not value writing for its own sake. It was a record of the inner life, or moral sense, of man. The moral sense was the writing of God directly on the soul. It was not an oral communication, from a priest, for example, nor was it purely literary. Hamilton remarked, famously, that "the sacred rights of mankind are not to be rummaged for, among old parchments or musty records. They are written as with a sunbeam in the whole volume of human nature by the Hand of Divinity itself and can never be erased or obscured by mortal power."

Part III: Revolutionary

On July 19, Congress resolved to make a parchment copy of the Declaration of Independence. This document was signed on August 2, as an 1826 letter of John Quincy Adams to Carrollton affirms. Carroll was present, and ready to sign. However flawed, the Declaration affirmed the political reality of a just revolution against an illegitimate English government. By signing, Carrollton did not signal his total agreement with Jefferson's thinking. He simply acknowledged the change that had taken place in the body politic.

The members present on August 2, 1776, joked about the potentially fatal consequences of signing. According to Latrobe, John Hancock addressed Carroll, asking him if he would sign.

"Most willingly," Carrollton replied.

"There go a few millions," commented a bystander.

John Adams praised Carroll for the risk he took that day. "In the cause of American liberty, his zeal, fortitude and perseverance have been so conspicuous that he is said to be marked out for peculiar vengeance by the friends of Administration; but he continues to hazard his all, his immense fortune, the largest in America, and his life." Adams predicted that "this gentleman's character will hereafter make a greater figure in America."

As the years went by, the Jeffersonian distortion of natural law created an unbridled individualism that severely damaged the American commonwealth. But in spite of his increasing alienation from political life, Carrollton never regretted signing the Declaration. He remembered his colleagues fondly. "All who took part in that hazardous and glorious cause are dear to me," he said at the age of ninety. "All acted from principle and all contributed more or less to our Independence."

Religious tolerance had much to do with Carrollton's decision to sign. "Reflecting, as you must, on the disabilities, I may truly say, of the proscription of the Roman Catholics in Maryland, you will not be surprised that I had much at heart this grand design founded on mutual charity, the basis of our holy religion." Religious tolerance did not secure the Church all its rights, such as authority in the area of marriage. But tolerance was certainly preferable to the establishment of Protestant churches in the new states. Such establishments would surely have taken place in the absence of full religious tolerance. The very existence of the true Church would have been threatened.

Carrollton valued tolerance, not only for these practical reasons, but for its own sake. Since charity was "the basis of every virtue" and the center of Christianity, Carroll promoted the Faith through persuasion and good example rather than coercion. In this, he was the true heir of Cecil Calvert.

THE MARYLAND LINE

Having subdued Canada, the British set their sights on New York City in the summer of 1776. General Howe planned to attack from the sea. If successful, his forces could link up with troops from Canada on the Hudson-Champlain waterway, cutting the United States in half.

The Council of Safety mobilized Maryland's entire quota of troops for the defense of New York. The cream of the Maryland Line was General Smallwood's brigade, sporting immaculate scarlet and buff uniforms. The Maryland officers were "distinguished by the most fashionable cut coat, the most *macaroni* cocked hat, and hottest blood in the union." One battalion was known as the "Ladies' Light Infantry" or "Silk Stocking Infantry" for their gallantry toward the female sex. Passing through Philadelphia, Smallwood's brigade impressed John Hancock as "an exceeding fine body of men."

The Maryland Line's first heroics came when the British invaded Long Island. To cover his retreat, General Stirling ordered the Marylanders to attack Lord Cornwallis at the Cortelyou House on August 27, 1776. A nineteenth-century historian of the Battle of Long Island wrote that the Maryland Line, "sons of the best families of Catholic Maryland, had been emulous of the praise of being the best drilled and disciplined of the revolutionary forces." At the Cortelyou House, 256 Marylanders were killed or captured.

After Long Island, Washington called on the Maryland Line for the most dangerous duties. The New England forces had become notoriously unreliable. Tench Tilghman, one of the "Ladies' Light Infantry," described the defense of Harlem Heights. "I don't know whether the New England troops will stand there," he wrote, "but I am sure they will not upon open ground." "The Virginia and Maryland troops bear the palm," Tilghman claimed. "The Eastern [New England] people are plundering everything that comes in their way."

Beaten, Washington was forced to withdraw from New York. Smallwood's brigade covered his retreat. "We shall give them a genteel drubbing," wrote one soldier, "in case the Yankees will fight with as much spirit as the Southern troops. General Washington gave great applause to our Maryland troops for their gallant behavior yesterday." At White Plains, the Marylanders charged downhill into advancing British troops.

The loss of New York gave the Americans a rude awakening. Carroll tried to put a good face on the defeat: "It is not of much consequence, if we can prevent their farther progress." The faith in militia, and the belief that virtuous citizen-soldiers required no drill, disappeared that summer.

The setback also brought the first challenge to Washington's leadership. Against Washington's wishes, Congress and the general staff insisted on holding Fort Washington on Hudson Cliffs, in Upper Manhattan. After Howe captured the fort and three thousand men, General Charles Lee intrigued with Horatio Gates for Washington's deposition. Fortunately, Lee was captured by British cavalry in December.

Alarmed, Hancock wrote the Maryland Convention, falling back on Protestant rhetoric. "Everything is at stake. Our religion, our liberty, the peace and happiness of posterity, are the grand objects in dispute." The convention set about raising eight more battalions. It was by then generally recognized that the outcome of the Revolution would depend on troops from the Southern and middle states. Washington urged Virginia, Maryland, and Pennsylvania "to turn out every man they possibly can."

Maryland responded, raising 15,229 regular soldiers and 5,407 militia during the war. The total of 20,636 men was the highest number, in proportion to population, of any state. This figure does not include Pulaski's Legion, formed in Baltimore in the spring of 1778, or Marylanders enlisted by other states. Governor Joseph Reed of Pennsylvania admitted Maryland's preeminence in 1780. "Maryland excepted," Reed wrote, "this state always had a greater proportion of troops in the field than any State." Since it was spared much destruction, Maryland was also able to contribute more than its share of provisions to the war effort.

Planters vs. Populists

In spite of its evident patriotism, Maryland's government was still suspected of treasonous intent. Major Jenifer remarked, "is it not amazing that...there should be men to be found, who charge the present ruling powers of Maryland, with designs of betraying the rights of America, when it is evident that we have done more for the gen[era]l defense, than any one Colony on the Continent." In fact, Maryland's impressive contribution took place because of its conservative government, not in spite of it. Maryland enjoyed social stability during the war because its elite consolidated power, defending the state from the politicians of popular will.

In August 1776, after signing the Declaration of Independence, Carrollton returned home to fight for sound political principles in the Maryland constitutional convention. His allies were the great planters, the merchants, and the Catholics. Approximately one-twelfth of the population was Catholic, and nearly all of them supported the Revolution. A British officer later recalled that "by far the greatest number of Catholics are on the western shore [of Maryland], and what is very surprising it was also the most violently rebellious and disaffected."

Rev. Boucher ascribed Catholics' patriotism to Carrollton. Motivated "solely by his desire to become a public man for which he was unquestionably well qualified," as Boucher claimed, Carroll supported the Revolution. "This seemed to settle the wavering disposition of the Catholics in Maryland; under so respectable a leader as Mr. Carroll they all soon became good Whigs." It seems likely, though, that most Catholics would have supported the revolution against the monolithic, Protestant state. They had, after all, been formed in the Jesuit tradition of resistance to unlawful authority.

Carrollton probably had more influence on his fellow planters than on his fellow Catholics. Maryland had always been governed by its propertied class. Great planters engrossed more and more of the land after the Glorious Revolution, while white freemen sank into tenantry. Just before the Revolution, the average delegate held almost twenty-five hundred acres, the typical councillor eight thousand acres. Carrollton gave a similarly aristocratic tone to the revolutionary government.

Opposed to the elite were the artisans and mechanics of Annapolis and Baltimore. Although ninety-five percent of Marylanders still lived on farms, Baltimore was growing rapidly and provided a constant source of democratic agitation. Most dissidents, however, were rural poor whites, especially on the eastern shore. Indeed, not only the democrats, but even the Tories, were decidedly plebeian in Maryland. A Tory/democrat leader emerged in the person of Colonel William Fitzhugh, who called Carrollton and Chase "the ring leaders of mischief in this province." Fitzhugh charged that Chase and Carrollton, "a Papist," advocated terrorism against loyalists.

Populist discontent was strongest in the county militias, whether they were loyal to the Crown or to Congress. One such disaffected militiaman was Alexander Magee, who charged that the whole imperial dispute had been concocted "for the purpose of enslaving the poor people." In December 1775, the militia had demanded the right to elect its own officers. When the June 1776 convention asked Thomas Johnson to command the Maryland forces, the democrats passed a resolution forbidding army officers from sitting in the convention. Carrollton denounced the "absurd" measure, but Johnson's commission was revoked.

Encouraged by this success, the Anne Arundel County militia devised its own plan for the new state government. They proposed two houses elected annually by the people. The legislature would choose all judges, as well as the governor, who would have no veto power. Guided by Annapolis demagogues Hammond and Hall, the freemen of Anne Arundel County adopted the militia plan. Hammond and Hall also called for universal manhood suffrage among freemen and the stoppage of debt collections. Other radical groups demanded a plural executive, the abolition of the poll tax, and the vote for all militiamen.

The militia plan resembled the populist constitution of Pennsylvania. Maryland's northern neighbor had a unicameral legislature, an impotent executive, and elected judges. Pennsylvania also had a board of censors, which functioned as a Star Chamber to eliminate dissent. Carrollton referred sarcastically to the "mild mercies of the free government of Pennsylvania." "Feeble beyond conception," in Carroll's words, Pennsylvania added nothing to the war effort until it restructured its government. Meanwhile, it enjoyed such scenes as a pitched battle at James Wilson's house between radicals and moderate Whigs, after Wilson proposed rewriting the state constitution.

Carrollton knew that the new states had the opportunity to establish "the most perfect forms of Government which human frailties will admit of." He feared they would squander it. "The seeds of disunion are sown, and I am much mistaken, if the soil will not be exceedingly productive."

The Maryland Constitution

Property qualifications provided a bulwark against the democratic faction in the election of delegates to the Maryland constitutional convention. Fifty acres or £40 sterling were required to vote in the election of August 1, 1776. Although the standards were somewhat lower in Annapolis, these levels were comparable to the suffrage requirements in the old provincial government. In addition, secret ballots were banned. Voters had to call out their choices *viva voce*, which gave the local gentry a salutary influence over their votes.

Hammond and Hall told their followers to ignore the property qualifications. An electoral revolt resulted. Five counties dismissed the election judges and allowed all arms-bearing taxpayers to vote. Among the casualties was Carrollton, who was not elected from Anne Arundel County. "If they can find a better Representative," Carroll proclaimed, "they have my free [consent] to choose him. I shall never court popular favour, but always endeavour to deserve it." The convention set aside the irregular elections, but new voting returned eighteen of the twenty winners from August 1. Carrollton, however, was elected in Annapolis.

Chase and Carroll the Barrister had won seats in Anne Arundel. But they resigned when the freemen of that county drew up a set of instructions that Carrollton called "weak, impudent & destructive of all government." Fitzhugh was also acting in a "most outrageous" and "very wicked" manner. Another election on September 4 returned Chase to the convention but awarded the Barrister's seat to John Hall.

Carrollton prepared for battle. He appealed to the gentlemen of the state to "exert themselves." Unless the gentry mobilized, "this Province will in a short time be involved in all the horrors of an ungovernable & revengeful Democracy, & will be dyed with the blood of its best citizens." "Selfish men" were pretending to represent the poor in order to gain mastery over the lower classes. But if the elite rose to the occasion, "we shall be able to establish a very good government in this State," better than any other state constitution. He needed his father's moral support. "I long to see you," he told the Squire, "I therefore beg you will come to Annapolis."

Carrollton sat on the drafting committee for the new plan of government. His influence on the "Declaration of Rights" and "Constitution" that emerged is unmistakable. The Declaration of Rights invokes social compact theory, insists on mixed government, and appeals to popular sovereignty, while denying the politics of popular will. Its first article affirms that "government of right originates from the people, is founded in compact only, and instituted solely for the good of the whole."

The Declaration of Rights requires that the three branches of government be "forever separate and distinct from each other." It awards judges life terms during good behavior. But it privileges the assembly, forbidding any "power of suspending laws, or the execution of laws, unless by or derived from the legislature." This provision denies the executive a veto, and also eliminates judicial review.

Who, then, would protect the public liberty from demagogues? The Maryland Constitution entrusted this role to the upper house of the legislature, the Senate. A series of electoral hurdles guaranteed the disinterestedness and excellence of the fifteen senators. Each had to possess at least £1,000 in American currency, about $8,500 today. They were chosen by an electoral college, made up of two delegates from each county. These electors, in turn, had to be worth £500 currency, the same amount required to become a delegate.

Then, too, anyone who wanted to vote for senatorial electors or delegates had to own property. Carrollton must have suffered great anxiety as the convention considered allowing all taxpayers to vote. This measure lost, 29 to 24. The constitution, as adopted, required £30 currency, about $254 today, in order to vote. This was a substantial drop, given the inflation of the currency. Still, the sum was high enough to reduce the risk of bribery. The Lockean connection between liberty and property was intact. The constitution also retained *viva voce* voting. Under the new provisions, the franchise included fifty-five percent of white male freemen, according to a rough estimate.

The drafting committee had suggested seven-year terms for senators and three-year terms for delegates. To Carrollton's distress, the convention reduced the senators' tenure to five years and restricted the delegates' to three. In addition, the governor would be elected annually by the legislature, and would be saddled with a council of five members. "God knows what sort of a government we shall get," Carroll lamented. Although the majority had good intentions, these were insufficient. "A knowledge of history, & insight into the passions of the human heart are likewise necessary." Though such knowledge was rare, "every man thinks himself a judge and an adept in the great & difficult science of legislation."

Carrollton resigned himself to the new government's faults. "If we can not now get a government as perfect as we could wish, time perhaps may disclose its defects & point out the proper remedies if men will be honest & apply them." Carroll had won a number of victories. The militia would not elect their own officers. The Declaration of Rights provided strong protection for life, liberty, and property. A motion to exclude all nonassociators from holding public office in the future was defeated.

Maryland also expanded religious freedom. The convention stopped short of full toleration, but it extended religious liberty to all Christians. The Declaration of Rights restricts public office to Christians by means of an oath. But in other respects, its language on religious freedom is preferable to that in the First Amendment of the United States Constitution. Maryland's founding document speaks of "the duty of every man to worship God in such manner as he thinks most acceptable to him." Unlike the First Amendment, the Maryland Declaration of Rights could not be used to attack religion, but only to protect and encourage it.

Carrollton's most striking contributions to American political life were the Senate and the Electoral College. The inspiration for the Senate came from Montesquieu. A strong and independent Senate, made up of the most responsible citizens, brings the principles of hierarchy and subsidiarity into a republic. By entrusting the protection of the constitution to the Senate, Carrollton's system would have prevented the judicial activism that ran rampant in the late twentieth century. Unfortunately, Maryland abandoned Carroll's vision in 1837, and the United States Senate enjoyed only a brief period of independent authority.

The Electoral College, however, seems to have retained its potency. We know Carrollton invented the Maryland version: "The mode of choosing the Senate," he declared, "was suggested by me." The other Founding Fathers were so impressed with Carroll's idea that they created an Electoral College to choose the president of the United States. Hamilton, writing over Washington's signature in 1778, singled out Maryland for praise: "The powers of government are with her in full vigor." The sixty-third Federalist paper cited the example of Maryland to support the United States Senate. "The Maryland Constitution is daily deriving, from the salutary operation of this part of it, a reputation in which it will probably not be rivalled by that of any State in the Union."

The New Government Begins

Exhausted by the battle against the democrats, Carrollton sank into despair about the revolution. He told his father in October that "our affairs are desperate & nothing but peace with Great Britain on tolerably reasonable terms can save us from destruction." Even if the Americans won, "we shall be rent to pieces by civil wars & factions." Most of the new states "will be simple Democracies, of all governments the worst, and will end as all other Democracies have, in despotism." "Peace perhaps may be made this winter," Carroll hoped. "God send it."

As Washington retreated across New Jersey, he, too, despaired. "I am at the end of my tether," he wrote. "The game is up." The American retreat was the signal for increased loyalist activity on the eastern shore of Maryland. Trouble spread to four counties: Worcester, Somerset, Caroline, and Dorchester. As usual, the militia were the center of discontent. A militia captain led a salt riot in Dorchester County. The Anne Arundel militia was still trying to get rid of its aristocratic officers, one of whom was heard to say that "a poor man was not born to freedom but to be a drudge on earth."

Out of the army's desperation, however, came Washington's most brilliant tactics of the war. He followed his Christmas victory at Trenton by outmaneuvering Cornwallis at Princeton. The American successes ended the British threat to Philadelphia that winter and brought Congress back from Baltimore. More importantly, as former provincial secretary William Eddis wrote, the victories "gave spirits" to the patriots, "recruited their forces, and enabled their leaders to magnify" American prospects. Trenton and Princeton helped the Maryland Assembly to quell sedition when it met in February 1777.

The new government almost collapsed before it started, however. Carrollton was elected a senator. But as several senators failed to show up, Carroll feared the new constitution would become void. In that case, the power to create another constitution would have reverted to the people.

Most senators had good excuses, but Major Jenifer was waiting to see which way the political wind would blow. The Major complained that Carroll's system excluded so many citizens from office-holding that government could not run vigorously. The people would refuse to accept the decisions of the Senate, Jenifer wrote, since it was not "the Child of the people at large." Jenifer was concerned about his political survival. But he was correct in predicting that the new government would be plagued by apathy. It proved difficult to induce anyone to accept public office. The courts had to threaten jurymen and witnesses with heavy fines to make them appear, although they were paid.

The new government countered apathy by binding the citizens to the state through ties of interest. Maryland created 913 new government jobs at the county level between 1776 and 1778. Eddis acidly related this news to ex-governor Eden. "You know, Sir, it has long been popular in this Country to exclaim against Administration on account of the number of officers," Eddis wrote. "But most true it is, that exclusive of Army & Navy appointments, the persons now employed, greatly, very greatly exceed any former establishment." The new patronage was similar, but by no means identical to Old Corruption. It was based on the notion of public interest rather than honor.

Jenifer finally lent his support to the new regime. On February 1, 1777, the Senate achieved a quorum. However unjustly, Jenifer was chosen its president. The senators were addressed as "Your Honors," while the delegates, led by Chase, received the less exalted title of "Gentlemen." The assembly elected Thomas Johnson as governor.

Carrollton feared that he might be picked for the Governor's Council. He wasn't, but the results were even more distressing. On February 14, Carroll of Annapolis was named as a councillor. This was a sweet vindication for the lord of Doughoregan after his fifty years of struggle with the Protestant government. But the thought of having his father in Annapolis causing political trouble was too much for Carrollton. He told the senior Carroll to "politely decline the office & assign the true reason, your advanced age: the confinement would soon kill you." After a few days' suspense, the old Squire submitted to his son's wishes.

The assembly moved quickly to suppress dissent. On February 13, they ordered the resistance in Somerset and Worcester Counties to "disperse immediately." Within forty days, the Tory rebels had to surrender their weapons and swear loyalty to the state. General Smallwood was ordered to the eastern shore with two thousand troops.

At this stage of the war, Carrollton had little sympathy for Tories. He gloated that loyalist aristocrats, having fled to England, "are reduced to manual labour to support themselves... may all the enemies of Liberty & humanity meet with a similar treatment!" Though "I hate national reflections," Carroll held the Scots in particular contempt for their loyalty to the Crown. Callously, Carroll described how a Dr. Stevenson "cried like a child when he left his plantation...unfortunate, misguided men!"

But Carroll did not have the heart of a persecutor. In New York, he warned a Tory named Wallace to be careful, since he "gives great offence by his freedom of speech." With his recusant background, Carrollton especially mistrusted oaths as a means of social control. When the delegates passed a bill that censored the press, imposing an oath that went well beyond the provisions in the Declaration of Rights, the Senate amended the bill and struck out the oath. The new government also acted to prevent mob violence against Tories. After the Whig Club ordered Daniel Dulany to leave the state within three days on pain of death, Gov. Johnson issued a decree forbidding vigilante justice.

Molly Carroll's friendship with prominent loyalists, such as the Ridouts, influenced her husband toward greater leniency as the war progressed. And so did his own encounter with the new, terrifying power of public opinion, in the matter of the legal tender law.

Part III: Revolutionary

The Tender Law

Carrollton broke the news to his father on February 14, 1777. "A bill will certainly pass to make the Continental, & the currencies of this State a legal tender in all cases." This meant that creditors like the Carrolls, who had lent money in pounds sterling, could be repaid in paper money. Because of wartime inflation, this paper currency was worth a fraction of its face value. The Carrolls stood to lose a huge sum.

Carroll of Annapolis was infuriated. The tender law brought memories of the double tax, and the prospect of losing the fortune the Settler had managed to protect from the penal laws. "I shall look on every man who assents to such a law as infamous, & I would as soon associate with highwaymen & pickpockets as with them." He told his son to resign from the Senate if the law passed. "Quit a station which you cannot keep with honor."

Carrollton realized, however, that the new power of public opinion would not permit such a retreat. "Where shall I withdraw? The person who now withdraws himself from his country's service will be deemed its enemy." All revolutions, he argued, are attended with "much partial injustice & sufferings: I have long foreseen the consequences of this unhappy civil war."

Carrollton was unsettled by the terrifying new factor in politics, the offended "majesty of the people," as Jenifer called it. But he saw the matter differently from his father. For Carroll of Annapolis, debts fell within the realm of honor. Anyone who would cheat a creditor of his money was a thief. The Squire went so far as to recommend that his son concert an opposition to the law with the Dulanys, who epitomized the old politics of honor.

Carrollton rejected his father's emphasis on honor. He thought the Squire had let his passion for honor—and for money—get the better of his reason. Honor, thought Carrollton, was usually a smokescreen for pursuing one's own self-interest. A public man, on the other hand, "must be cool & dispassionate." Carrollton's politics transcended both honor and interest; he concerned himself only with the common good.

Carroll's politics of spirit were firmly embedded in the Catholic tradition. "The law will have its course," he wrote, "nor ought any individual to be above it." While the illegitimate English government ruled, men had been justified in their resistance to its tyranny. Now that a new social compact had been formed, all citizens had to obey the legitimate government of Maryland. "Although injustice be done to individuals," Carrollton wrote, "my country on the whole is in the right." In spite of the unjust tender law, "it behooves us to be just to our country & help it all we can."

Carrollton was the only senator to dissent from the tender law. He argued that the currency could be supported just as well if all future contracts were dischargeable in paper, "without giving it a retrospect." In his dissent, Carroll alluded to "the secret workings and devices of the avaricious and artful." But having made his point, he refrained from further criticism. By and large, the conservatives had had their way in setting up the new government. Radical economic legislation was the price they paid for popular support of the constitution.

The Squire, however, continued to pursue the supporters of the tender law as if it were an affair of honor. He demanded to know which senators had voted for the bill. "Invite none of them here," he ordered Carrollton, "for I shall turn them out of doors." When his son claimed not to remember who had been present when the law was passed, Carroll of Annapolis told him to consult the journal of the Senate.

The Squire then turned his anger against Samuel Chase, who had supported the tender law in the House of Delegates. On June 5, 1777, he accused Chase of "promoting a law which you know to be unjust...can you reflect on this with a tranquil conscience?" Chase exploded. "A man, Sir, may be neither a fool nor a villain, & yet differ from you in opinion." He claimed to be indifferent to what others might think about the law. The elder Carroll continued the attack. "A public strumpet taxed with her vices may say she is wholly indifferent what people say," the Squire replied. "Yet notwithstanding her pretended indifference...no one will scruple to call her a whore."

Carrollton was alarmed. He knew that if his father continued to make himself "obnoxious to the People," the old man would eventually be "confined in a gaol" or "knocked in the head by a mob." "I can not conceive that any individual is to turn Don Quixote," he told the Squire, "or that the point of honor obliges him to combat whole bodies of men, particularly the Legislature of the State: which even when it errs, ought to be treated, at least, with complaisance." He begged his father to remonstrate only with those debtors who took advantage of the law. "If you love me, you will pursue this conduct."

"Neither a prison nor death were I at Annapolis would deter me from saying publickly what I have said," the Squire trumpeted. "America is right, but that right is not to be asserted by unrighteous means." He criticized his son's "meekness of temper, you may think it prudence." "Are you not too fond of popularity," Carroll of Annapolis charged, "& has not that fondness biased your judgement?"

Carrollton responded mildly to his father's painful accusations. "I assure you I am not fond of popularity," he wrote, "because I am convinced it is often gained by the unworthy: I would wish to deserve the good opinion of the good & discerning; now I am sure the bulk of mankind are neither good, nor discerning, and 'tis for this very reason I wish you to avoid all publications relative to the tender bill." He counseled the Squire to accept political reality: "many wise & good men have acted so." They must bide their time. "I am never for showing my teeth till I can bite."

Carrollton held his ground. He refused the Squire's continued entreaties to resign from the Senate he had created. From this point forward he was a man in his own right. Father and son reversed roles in their correspondence. After the tender law dispute, it was Carrollton who instructed his father and made decisions. Finally, at age forty, he was the head of the family.

The Irish Presence

As 1777 wore on, Washington and his tiny army managed to keep Howe bottled up in New York. The general adopted the strategy Carroll of Annapolis had predicted. He realized that lines and fortifications were "a kind of trap" and resolved never to fight without urgent necessity.

The British tried to draw Washington closer to the coast to force an engagement. Carrollton wrote in late June of 1777 that "our cautious General has not given in to the trap." Washington would not give battle, Carroll wrote, unless the odds were a hundred to one in his favor. To dissuade Howe from attacking, Washington put out vastly inflated figures of his troop strength.

The size of Washington's army was one of the major concerns of the Congressional Board of War and Ordnance, to which Carrollton had been named on his first day in Congress. John Adams, the Board's chairman, commented that Carroll "is an excellent member, whose education, manners and application to business and study did honor to his fortune, the first in America." Reappointed to Congress, Carroll observed in June 1777 that most states had not filled their quotas of men. "I think the People grow tired of the war."

Some soldiers practiced "bounty-jumping," repeatedly enlisting and deserting in order to collect the bounties offered by the various states. One Maryland battalion of three hundred men suffered fifty desertions during a seventy-mile march. The Squire reported that "a meeting of our battalion was here last Friday, no men turned out." To set a good example, Carrollton promised to march to the front with the Doughoregan battalion. If Molly "regards the honor of her husband," Carroll wrote, "she must not keep him from the field this campaign."

The American difficulty with enlistments raises the question: Who were the American troops? Toward the end of the war, Lord George Germain believed that the British Army had enlisted more Americans than the Continental Army. James Galloway, the exiled loyalist, testified before Parliament that Continental soldiers were "scarcely one-fourth natives of America, about one-half Irish; the other fourth were English and Scotch."

This is in keeping with William Eddis' observation, in July 1777, that "a very great part of the troops lately raised in Maryland are convicts and servants." The General Assembly permitted the enlistment of indentured servants, a large percentage of whom were Irish. As far back as 1729, according to the anonymous French traveler, four-fifths of the immigrants to Maryland were Irish. They came, wrote the Frenchman, "to avoid the misery of their own country, where they are a thousand times worse than Guinea slaves."

Irishmen made up a large part of the troops of other states, as well. Proctor's Pennsylvania Artillery, for example, had 198 men in 1779: sixty-seven Irish, thirteen English, four Scotch, twenty-two Germans, and sixty-nine Pennsylvanians, the other twenty-two coming from other states. (Since presumably some of those listed as native-born in such surveys were of Irish descent, we have a very large Irish, partly Catholic, presence in the forces of the United States.)

The Royal army had large numbers of Irish, as well. In December 1777, the Crown sought thirty-three thousand new recruits, of whom five thousand were to be Irish Catholics. But the Irish did not go willingly. Carrollton heard that "the Irish R.C. will not enlist." Arthur Lee reported that an entire Irish regiment had to be shipped off "tied and bound." Howe realized that his Irish troops were unreliable, likely to desert. His successor, General Sir Henry Clinton, admitted that support for Britain was contrary to the Irishmen's interest.

Saratoga

In Philadelphia that summer, Carrollton thought he would stay on, "while the weather continues so pleasant." But Howe's army was at sea, on its way to take Philadelphia. The British entered the Chesapeake and landed at Head of Elk, Maryland, in late August. Carrollton told Governor Johnson that Washington's soldiers had foolishly begged their commander to attack Howe. Washington, however, "will not put all to the hazard of a battle: his intention is to harass the enemy & melt their numbers by frequent skirmishes."

True to his word, Carroll decided to join General Smallwood's army, en route to Washington's camp. At first, he found "this kind of sauntering life extremely disagreeable and fatiguing." But a few days later, Carroll declared that "I think I should like a military life when a little more used to it. The eager & solicitous expectation military men constantly experience, keeps the soul always on the spring, active, and enterprising."

This journey brought Carroll close to some of the hottest action of the war. At Brandywine Creek, on September 11, Washington was outmaneuvered, and the Maryland troops fled in confusion. The next night, in the infamous Paoli ambush, General Grey bayoneted and burned four hundred and fifty American soldiers, many of them after all resistance had ended. Carrollton joined Washington at headquarters on September 17 but soon had to depart for Lancaster, where Congress was sitting. It quickly moved to York.

On September 25, Carroll informed his father that Philadelphia had fallen. The respectable American showing at Germantown, on October 3, raised the army's spirits somewhat. Carrollton was far from impressed with the Continentals' discipline. But he believed that "our men are becoming more warlike, the blood already spilt will raise a spirit of obstinacy & revenge."

There was reason for optimism, even amid the American disaster. Benjamin Franklin, told that Howe had taken Philadelphia, replied, "I beg your pardon, Philadelphia has taken Howe." The comforts of the American capital would only increase Howe's legendary inertia. And Howe's sea voyage helped the American cause in the north.

Benedict Arnold's brilliant naval strategy on Lake Champlain had delayed the British invasion from Canada. But in July 1777, a force under General John Burgoyne pushed south, taking Ticonderoga on July 6 and Fort Edward on July 31. The original plan had called for Howe to march through New Jersey, cutting Washington off, while Clinton would link up with Burgoyne on the Hudson. But Washington's successes in New Jersey persuaded Howe to approach Philadelphia by sea. This meant that New York City, theoretically, was exposed to attack from Washington.

While the chances of an American assault on New York were infinitesimally small, Clinton respected Washington enough

Part III: Revolutionary

that he refused to budge from New York City. Meanwhile, Burgoyne's supply lines became strained. Schuyler's scorched-earth policy eliminated the possibility of foraging. Washington ordered Schuyler to fight a campaign of attrition.

As the Americans harassed Burgoyne's flanks and rear, British numbers dwindled. By September 20, Burgoyne had five thousand men against at least twelve thousand for Horatio Gates, who had assumed command. Patriot militia swelled Gates' numbers. After three weeks of delay, Clinton finally got around to telling Burgoyne that he would not advance in force up the Hudson. Two costly battles later, Burgoyne was surrounded at Saratoga, where he surrendered on October 17, 1777.

Valley Forge

The victory at Saratoga had little to do with Gates, and everything to do with Schuyler's preparations and Arnold's genius. Nevertheless, it put Gates in a position to challenge Washington's preeminence.

On the day of Burgoyne's surrender, Congress created a secondary Board of War and packed it with Washington's enemies. Horatio Gates was named its president. Gates had just refused Washington's urgent request for reinforcements. His friends in Congress, led by John Adams, forbade Hamilton to detach troops from Gates' army without his permission. As the president of the secondary Board of War, Gates was now in a sense Washington's superior.

Carrollton's presence on the Congressional Board of War and Ordnance became even more crucial. He had grown frustrated with Washington's exquisite sensibility and decorum. Congress had conferred "great, nay almost unlimited powers" on Washington, but the general hesitated to use them. "He is so humane & delicate that I fear the common cause will suffer." Still, Carroll supported Washington unconditionally and understood his military strategy. He and his congressional colleagues countered the partisans of Gates by creating another committee to visit Washington's winter camp at Valley Forge.

Carroll tried to use his influence with the commander in chief to spur Washington to action. "I am sorry to observe that two officers in high command in our Army are said to be much addicted to liquor," he wrote Washington. "What trust, what confidence can be reposed in such men?" Carroll recommended "severe punishments" to make "the commissaries and quartermasters attentive to their duty." "Your Excellency has the power," Carroll wrote, "and I hope will not want the will, to punish such as deserve punishment."

Carroll was also concerned with the army's "extremely defective" discipline. Fortunately, France took steps to secure her investment in the American troops. Baron von Steuben arrived at Valley Forge in December 1777 in order to teach the army European drill. He soon discovered that he had to temper his methods to the American spirit. In Europe, Steuben commented, "you say to your soldier, 'Do this,' and he doeth it, but here I am obliged to say, 'This is the reason why you ought to do that': and then he does it." Steuben composed a new military manual, called the "Blue Book," which adapted European drill to American realities.

Col. John Fitzgerald, an Irish Catholic officer, told the Carrolls on December 19 that the men had delayed building huts, focusing instead on the security of the surrounding country. The local residents failed to respond to the army's generosity by providing supplies. Carrollton contributed £50 for shoes and stockings, since the soldiers were "in great want of clothing." The locals were interested only in profiting from the army's needs. "Speculations, peculation, engrossing, forestalling," Washington mourned, "afford melancholy proofs of the decay of public virtue."

Under the influence of his aide Hamilton, the protégé of moral-sense Presbyterians, Washington was coming around to a more realistic view of human nature. "Men may speculate as they will, they may talk of patriotism," wrote the general, who now realized that patriotism was insufficient to wage a prolonged war. "It will not endure unassisted by Interest." The old code of honor had been replaced by the new bond of interest. It is one of the supreme ironies of American history that

Part III: Revolutionary

Alexander Hamilton, who did more than any man to promote the politics of interest, gave his life for the dead code of honor.

Hamilton prepared a report for the Valley Forge congressional committee, signed by Washington on January 29, 1778. This document, Hamilton's first major political statement, represents a turning point in the army's understanding of itself. "With far the greatest part of mankind," Hamilton wrote, "interest is the governing principle." "It is vain to exclaim against the depravity of human nature on this account," continued the young aide-de-camp. "We must in a great measure, change the constitution of man, before we can make it otherwise."

Thus, relying on Divine Providence to feed the army was a "dangerous and visionary experiment." Hamilton recommended that Congress take steps to improve the army's credit. He also picked up on Carroll's suggestion that the militia be drafted into regular battalions, eliminating the need to pay bounties. Military awards and honors would channel the "emulous love of glory and distinction" toward the common good. Congress should promote a "laudable rivalship" among the states to ensure an adequate supply of clothing.

Both Hamilton and Carroll took interest into account in their political theories. Both men were pragmatic about human nature. But Hamilton's ideas were more strongly influenced by the monarchical concept of honor. He believed that citizens would support the government, and public credit would rise, if government would attach men to itself by gratifying their ambitions. His master concept was "energy."

Carrollton, on the other hand, saw the destructive potential of such an arrangement. The monarchical code of honor, mixed with republican structures, would eventually lead to a dictatorship. In order for private interest to be channeled toward the public good, it was necessary to create a class of men with an interest in defending the constitution of the state. Such men, united in a Senate, could legislate according to the laws of nature. Carroll's ruling concept was not "energy" but "spirit."

Unfortunately, Carrollton was absent at the unveiling of Hamilton/Washington's radical document. Molly's health had collapsed, and Carroll had to return home before the committee departed for Valley Forge. Her nerves had deteriorated, forcing Carroll to buy land at Bath County, a spa in what is now Hot Springs, Virginia. Part of her stress lay in the tension between her patriotism and her friendships with Tories. After Saratoga, the Squire observed, "I think Molly was rather too insulting among her Tory acquaintance."

THE FRENCH ALLIANCE

Thomas Conway, a Frenchman of Irish descent, became inspector general of the army in November 1777. When Conway first arrived in America, he had impressed Carroll. But in February 1778, Col. Fitzgerald intercepted a letter from Conway to Gates. "I wish I could serve under you," Conway told Gates.

Fitzgerald alerted Washington, who forwarded the offending passage to Gates. Fitzgerald then consulted with Carrollton. He told Washington that Carroll was "very uneasy at a report having prevailed that a combination was formed in Congress against you." Carroll "gave me the strongest assurances that he never heard a member of this House utter a word which could be construed into the least disrespect for you, except once, and then the gentleman was so warmly replied to from different quarters that he has since been silent upon that head."

Carroll was back in York by June 1778, when Conway arrived to seek a promotion. Conway believed that Carroll would support him because of their common religion, but he had a rude awakening. Carrollton told Conway that "anybody that displeased or did not admire the commander in chief ought not to be kept in the army." On the floor of Congress, Carroll challenged Conway's lack of experience, asking "in a most despising manner" what Conway had done to deserve promotion. "Mr. Carroll might be a good papist," Conway told Gates, "but I am sure the sentiments he expressed are neither Roman nor Catholic."

After the Conway threat, Washington responded to Carroll's

prodding, taking a more assertive leadership stance. "I am determined," the general wrote Moylan in April 1778, "to make examples of those to whom this shameful neglect of the Cavalry has been owing." Having had some effect on the commander in chief, Carrollton tried to shame his countrymen into action. "Try, for God's sake and the sake of human nature," Carroll begged Gov. Johnson, "to rouse our countrymen from their lethargy." Americans must act "with a vigor & spirit suitable to the important & serious cause in which they are engaged," accepting "no terms short of independence."

Carrollton believed that the French would avoid war, "unless they should be drawn into it by some unforeseen accident." In Paris, Franklin was making sure that just such an accident would occur. With the playwright Beaumarchais, he concocted a private company to funnel French aid to America. Then Franklin began outfitting privateers, based in French ports, to attack English vessels. The British retaliated by seizing French ships in English ports, making conflict between George III and Louis XVI inevitable.

Charles Carroll's biographers have speculated much as to his role, or lack of a role, in securing the French alliance. There is little hard evidence of a direct Carroll influence on the negotiations, but we know that Carrollton destroyed much of his revolutionary correspondence. The delicate subject of the alliance is barely mentioned in his surviving correspondence with Franklin. (Referring to Franklin's famous theory that older women make the best mistresses, Carroll wrote the sage that Chase "has not had leisure to refute your reasons in favor of the old ladies.")

Certainly, though, Carrollton made the French alliance possible by diminishing the national prejudice against Catholics. Given the general hatred of French Popery, it is amazing that public opinion accepted the alliance. John Adams detested France and mistrusted Louis' intentions. So, predictably, did Jay. Baron de Kalb believed that if France attacked England, Americans' innate hatred of the French might lead them back to the English Crown. Carrollton showed his Protestant countrymen that Catholics could be loyal Americans. This realization, in turn, strengthened the American identity, as something distinct from its English and Protestant origin.

In Philadelphia, in May 1778, the British officers were engaged in festivities to honor General Howe, who was returning to England. These included the famous Meschianza ball, choreographed by Major John André. But in York, a different kind of triumph was taking place. France allied herself to the new American nation on December 16, 1777. A treaty was signed on February 6, 1778.

The letter announcing the alliance was borne through the streets of York. Congress joined in a solemn service of thanksgiving. They praised "the magnanimity and wisdom of His Most Christian Majesty" Louis XVI. The legislators hoped that "the friendship so happily commenced between France and the United States may be perpetual."

PART IV.

Senator.

CARROLLTON told his father that the French treaty "is bottomed on principles of the most liberal, wise, & generous policy; the only thing required of us, is the maintenance of our Independence." The United States promised to make no separate peace with England. But if war continued between France and England after the liberation of America, the United States had no obligation to fight.

More clothing and munitions were expected any day. In addition, "all the Great Powers of Europe are favourably disposed towards us." Under these circumstances, Carrollton permitted himself some guarded optimism. "If peace should soon take place, with proper economy in the expenditures of public money, a little skill in finance, heavy taxes, & a prosperous trade, we might soon put our paper money in a sure foundation."

THE DEPRECIATION OF CONGRESS

The public finances were certainly the most crucial problem facing the Congress. But that "noisy, empty & talkative assembly," as Carrollton called it, lacked the credibility to make much progress on any issue. Rev. Jacob Duché gave an anti-papist slant to the prevailing dissatisfaction with Congress. "The most respectable characters have withdrawn themselves," Duché sniped. "Maryland no longer sends a Tilghman and a Protestant Carroll." Gouverneur Morris quipped that "Continental money and Congress have both depreciated."

Carrollton favored heavy taxes, the redemption of all previous currencies, and the emission of one new currency. Making all interest payments in specie would also help the Continental credit in Europe. Carroll hoped against hope that Congress would act to retrieve public credit. "What cannot wisdom, perseverance, & virtue affect?" he asked. "Yet we abound not in either. I have more confidence of success from the blunders of our enemy than our own good conduct."

The point of heavy taxes was not to establish a big government. Carrollton always favored frugality on the part of the state. But the common good required drastic measures to improve the American credit rating, in order to carry on the war. High taxes would take a large amount of worthless paper out of circulation. They would also prop up the currency by creating demand for it.

Inflation during the Revolution has justly become legendary. In Maryland, between late 1777 and late 1780, salt prices increased by 3900 percent, wheat by 5043 percent, beef by 3900 percent, and tallow by 3900 percent. At Bath County in the summer of 1779, Carrollton found it more economical to buy things with specie. As inflation progressed, an even more dramatic expedient was widely adopted: reversion to a barter economy. When Carrollton was quoted a price of twenty dollars for a scythe that formerly cost seven shillings sixpence, he ended up paying three hundred bricks for it. "If we could deal in this way with the merchants," Carroll commented, "money would be almost useless."

Carroll of Annapolis successfully employed the barter strategy in exacting rents from his tenants. At Carrollton Manor, he asked for payment in kind in tobacco. The new rents were still lower than before, when inflation is considered, and Carrollton congratulated his father on his wise course of action. Some states also collected taxes in kind. Virginia asked for one bushel of wheat from every taxable resident.

Carrollton was skeptical of such plans. Paying taxes in kind would reduce the demand for paper money. Holders of useless currency would then lend it to the state, creating a large public debt, "destructive & contrary to the spirit of free governments." Carroll admitted that the public debt might "serve as a cement, or bond of Union." But in 1779, Carroll did not believe the various paper currencies could ever be redeemed at their face value, which amounted to upwards of £300 million. If the debt were funded, "it will enrich those, who have plundered the Public," namely speculators.

Later, Carroll would support Alexander Hamilton's plan for assuming the state debts and funding the currency. It should be noted that some of the paper emissions were called in before Hamilton's plan took effect, so that the amount of currency funded was less than Carrollton had expected in 1779. Carroll accepted the measure as a means of restoring public credit, but he never quite reconciled himself to currency speculation. Justice did not require that someone who sold £100 worth of merchandise, receiving £8,000 in paper for it, should ultimately be rewarded with thousands in hard money.

Interest: Private vs. Public

Carrollton proved his opposition to big government when, in December 1778, the House of Delegates attempted to raise their own salaries. After the Senate vetoed the bill, the delegates squawked that they were trying to create an aristocracy. Voters would have to choose "men of opulent fortunes, who may not be distinguished by their wisdom, probity, or zeal for the public good."

The Senate lost no time in replying. "Our form of government does not, we hope, altogether depend on granting to ourselves a further diurnal sum of fifteen shillings." Since the state constitution required assemblymen to own property, the raise was superfluous. The property qualification was not meant to establish a plutocracy, but to guarantee the "independence of legislators" from bribery. While not perfect, property qualifications were the "best security" of legislative integrity. The Senate agreed, however, to provide pecuniary assistance to worthy men who were too poor to run for the assembly.

During the following session, however, the assembly approved a pay hike. Carrollton dissented, "because this resolve sets a dangerous precedent for future legislators to vote the people's money into their own pockets." The pay raise, like the tender law, sprang from "the preference of private to the public interest."

We see here a further refinement of Carrollton's politics of interest. The common good often required the legislature to promote individual interests in the private sector and to protect the natural right to property. But Carroll balked at creating bureaucracies and pork-barrel programs, because he saw that such programs enriched individuals at the expense of the public. Big government is the politics of individual interest, applied to government itself. What was appropriate in the private sector did not apply to public officials, who should not seek financial gain from their posts.

Samuel Chase's career served as a cautionary tale. In 1778, he was suspected of profiting from inside information he received as a Congressman. Having heard that the army planned to buy flour, Chase had purchased a large quantity of flour and wheat. Carrollton sat on a committee to produce instructions for the congressional delegates that winter. Congressmen, Carroll's committee insisted, "ought not only to be honest, but free even from the imputation of dishonesty." Alluding to the the Chase scandal, the report suggested that delegates suspected of wrongdoing should not be returned to Congress. The delegates struck the committee's language from the final instructions, but Chase was excluded from the balloting for congressional delegates.

In July 1779, the assembly went even further, forbidding its members of Congress to engage in trade of any kind. Merchants had long been suspect in the political realm. Sixteen years earlier, Carrollton had said that talk of independence was "of a too delicate nature to be treated by a merchant." The act to restrain delegates from trade was a rare case in which the Senate overstepped its bounds. As Chase pointed out, the measure went beyond the state constitution, which already set the requirements for delegates to Congress.

But the Senate's policy was vindicated that very summer, when a letter from Chase to his business partner surfaced. "Hire more crafts, lose no time," Chase had written, "because the embargo here will be taken off." He planned to buy up crops, and much to the Carrolls' disgust, Chase even hoped to sell some of his hoarded tobacco to Carroll of Annapolis. Carrollton now called his former ally "the most prostituted scoundrel who ever existed."

Jenifer reported that Chase "has lost much of his influence, and what he has retained, he has done by keeping open house." The Major reflected the popular mood when he called speculators "harpies & scoundrels." In May 1778, a mob had assembled to seek revenge on speculators, who applied to the state for protection. It is a sign of the health of Maryland politics during the Revolution that popular discontent was generally channeled toward the common good.

The Articles of Confederation

Congress was in gridlock because of another type of private interest. The Articles of Confederation had lain on the table since 1777 because of a dispute over the back lands, the territory beyond the Appalachians. Virginia claimed them all, every square inch of territory between the mountains and the Pacific Ocean, based on her charter. Other states with land claims, led by Maryland, rejected the Articles' provision that "no State should be deprived to her territory for the benefit of the United States."

There was a problem with Maryland's position, however. Abrogating Virginia's charter claims would imply that the American claim to the west depended only on conquest, not on the charters. But the Maryland Assembly argued that the charters were now obsolete, having served their purpose as forerunners of the state constitutions. Instead of the charters, the Confederation should be based on "justice and perfect equality." Maryland proposed that the back lands be divided among the states in proportion to each state's tax burden.

To complicate matters, many Americans, including Washington and Jefferson, had invested in western land companies. These firms were itching to get hold of the lands that the Proclamation of 1763 and the Quebec Act had declared off limits. Carrollton, too, invested in the Illinois-Wabash, Indiana, and Vandalia land companies. He preferred that the back lands be apportioned among the states. Nevertheless, Carroll was willing to ratify the Articles even if Virginia retained its land claims, since confederation was a national necessity.

His committee to instruct the congressional delegates presented strong arguments for the nationalization of the back lands. The Marylanders emphasized the common good. The back lands should be a "common estate...granted out on terms beneficial to all the United States." Natural rights and the common good overrode states' rights in this case, without destroying the autonomy of the states. Carrollton's committee instructed the delegates "to promote the general welfare of the United States, and the particular interest of this State, where the latter is not incompatible with the former."

Domestic Crisis

Carroll of Annapolis was still running the family business while Carrollton sat in Congress and the assembly. He had to cope with inflation and with the spring drought of 1779, which left him unable to feed his horses. The only duty Carrollton regularly performed for the family was to receive paper money payments from debtors, who were terrified to approach the Squire.

Indeed, the old man was still fuming about the tender law. He published a petition against the law in 1779, which infuriated the delegates by exposing their venality. He was summoned before the House of Delegates and ordered to apologize or be arrested. Presumably at his son's urging, Carroll of Annapolis offered an apology. But when Carrollton suggested that the delegates might not appreciate being called "rogues," he received wounding criticism from his father. "I wish you had a great deal more warmth & earnestness in your temper," the Squire wrote. "You ought to be extremely warmed by your sufferings under the law."

Fortunately for her husband, Molly knew how to use psychology on the old man. She informed Carroll of Annapolis that Carrollton was losing his appetite as a result of the tender law controversy. The Squire immediately begged his son to "suffer not your spirits to be depressed by villains whom you cannot reform." Carrollton then sent his father a properly despondent letter, which drew the desired response. "I fear you take too much of the public business on yourself, drudge not," wrote Carroll of Annapolis. "Nothing is dearer to me than your health."

Molly proved less astute in her ongoing struggle with addiction. The Squire pleaded with her "never to touch laudanum which I hear she still takes, it is as bad as dram drinking." The patriarch implied that Carroll's reserved personality was to blame. "You, maybe, will not, but I desire Molly will kiss the children for me."

Carrollton made himself more available to his wife when Anne Brooke Carroll, their infant daughter, died in September 1778. Jenifer sympathized with Mrs. Carroll, "whose sensibility must have greatly increased her misery." Indeed, Molly immediately sought solace in opium. Her mother sent her a phial of laudanum.

By April of 1779, Carrollton admitted his wife's problem. A doctor had diagnosed Molly's addiction. "Let her avoid that poison laudanum," the Squire exclaimed, "or any thing else which may give only present ease." The couple went on a voyage, so that Molly could enjoy the purgative benefits of seasickness.

Later that summer, the Carrolls returned to Bath County, Virginia, where Molly was able to quit using opium. Her appetite improved, and she enjoyed a new friendship with Baroness Frederika von Riedesel, whose husband was one of the prisoners of Saratoga. The Baroness, who had braved the Adirondack wilderness in order to be near her beloved husband, adored Molly. But she found Carrollton "brusque and stingy."

Carrollton was trying hard to please Molly: he missed a Senate session in order to go to Bath. But he longed to return to the political arena. "I hate this idle, sauntering life," he complained. "Dancing & tea-drinkings take up the time of the ladies, & gaming that of the gentlemen." Carrollton has often been justly criticized for his emotional coldness toward his wife and children, which is amply documented in his correspondence with his father. Molly has been largely excused from blame. But one wonders to what extent she was emotionally available to her husband, given her high-strung and addictive personality.

In spite of the Squire's criticism, Carrollton did not lack "warmth & earnestness" when it came to politics, an interest which Molly did not share. His decision, then, to leave Congress in 1778 represents a sacrifice for his family. Carroll cited other reasons for his departure from Congress, in addition to "domestic concerns." Congress's "frivolous debates disgusted me," he told Franklin. The delegates' interminable speeches "neither edified, entertained, nor instructed me."

Carrollton left Congress at a time when he was spoken of, according to French Ambassador Gerard, as its next president. Arthur Lee, an American diplomat in Europe, favored Carroll as ambassador to France. "A man of sense, of honor, integrity and education may be found," Lee wrote. "In many respects I should think Mr. Carroll, the Catholic, a fit man. What objections there may be to him I know not."

Whether or not he was approached for the French job, Carrollton apparently refused the post of ambassador to Spain. "I wish your son could have been prevailed on to go to the Court of Spain," Jenifer wrote the Squire. "His reasons for not undertaking so hazardous an employment no doubt are weighty." The Spanish ambassadorship was a key post in 1778, because King Carlos III was trying to mediate among the belligerents. John Jay got the Madrid assignment.

Tory Confiscations

Even without his congressional duties, Carrollton had his hands full with Chase and the House of Delegates. Deprived of inside information from Congress, Chase's latest scheme involved confiscating lands of Tories. Once Tory property was in the hands of the state, it could be purchased by speculators at a low price in paper money.

Under Molly's influence, perhaps, Carrollton began to exert himself more openly on behalf of loyalists. As early as 1777, Carroll had offered a petition on behalf of the Eastern Shore loyalist Rev. John Bowie. In 1778, he helped a Mr. Brown obtain permission to move to England. The assembly had already imposed a triple tax on those who refused to take the oath of allegiance to the new state government. But in June 1778, the Senate refused to extend the triple tax to those who had taken the loyalty oath after the official deadline.

Congress, in 1779, gave the House of Delegates an excuse to push for confiscation of Tory property. They requested the astonishing sum of £14,220,000 currency from Maryland between February and October 1780. This was taking Carroll's high-tax plan too far. The Carrolls' assessment would come to at least £32,000. "When I reflect on these enormous requisitions," Carrollton wrote, "I can scarcely believe the Congress seriously think of or expect a compliance with them."

On December 21, the delegates struck. They estimated that the state would have to levy £54 in taxes on every £100 in property in order to meet Congress' demands. Since this was impossible, the delegates insisted on the necessity of confiscating all British property in the state. Without confiscation, Maryland residents would have to sell their own property to pay their taxes.

Carrollton and Matthew Tilghman replied for the Senate. They exposed the confiscation scheme as an attempt to enrich engrossers and speculators. The House had set no deadline for purchasers to pay for the Tory property. With delayed payments and inflation, the state would receive "next to nothing in the end." The senators refused "to raise great emoluments to a few individuals at a certain and heavy loss to the public."

Since the huge requisition was clearly impossible to meet, Carroll and Tilghman argued, the state should not try to meet it. Instead, Congress should raise the money itself by nationalizing the back lands and selling some of them. The back lands would also provide collateral for future European loans.

Carrollton also rejected price controls, which were "destructive of that freedom in dealing, which is the life & soul of trade." Instead of imposing confiscations and price controls, the Senate wanted to seize any goods being hoarded by engrossers and forestallers, and use them for the public benefit. The Senate closed their session with an address, written by Carrollton, which praised Gov. Johnson's "disinterestedness" and "close application to the public welfare" at a time when "dissipation and avarice have too generally prevailed."

The House of Delegates announced its intention to appeal to the public on the confiscation issue. Carrollton decided to beat them at their own game. On February 11, 1780, he began a series of articles in the *Maryland Gazette*, addressed "To the Public" and signed "A Senator."

Carrollton based his arguments against confiscation on the constitution, the natural law, and the law of nations. Declaring citizens born in Maryland to be enemy aliens would be an *ex post facto* law, and as such forbidden by the Maryland Bill of Rights. The natural law, as well as the Maryland constitution, protected property rights. And according to the law of nations, only property "belonging to the collective body of the guilty nation, or to the criminal members thereof" could be confiscated. The back lands, and not the private property of civilians, were subject to confiscation.

The delegates had implied that Marylanders owned their property only by right of conquest. "It is somewhat strange," Carrollton observed, "that the delegates…seem to have no other idea of right but what is founded on force, although mere force, unjustly exercised, can convey no right at all." Instead, the state must act according to the law of nature and of nations. "What of right ought not to be done, although we have the power, we should not do."

The Senator did not enjoy the same enthusiastic approval as the First Citizen. "A Sentry" called the senator pieces "damned Toryism." But Carrollton's writing had some effect. By May 1780, Carroll declared that "the people seem averse" to the confiscation of British property. Carroll's concept of the people was something of an abstraction, approximating what the

Church calls the *sensus fidei*. "The good sense of our people," as Carroll called it, was the opinion that all men would have, if they knew what was good for them. The Senate embodied the people in this sense. It did not merely represent the estate of the wealthy.

The March 1780 Assembly

The legislative struggles of 1779 made Carroll "wish most earnestly for peace." But as the March 1780 assembly session approached, he prepared for war with Chase and the House of Delegates.

He was aided by a congressional resolution, recommending that the states revise their laws making paper money a legal tender. On April 4, Carrollton joined a committee to reconsider the tender law. From that point, he refused payments in currency for old sterling debts. Official repeal would have to wait, however, for later sessions. The assembly partly repealed the tender law that June and fully revoked it in December 1780.

The delegates renewed their appeal for confiscation of Tory property on April 12. Two days later, the Senate rejected the confiscation. They did, however, make a counterproposal. They suggested offering refugees in Britain a year to take the loyalty oath, or suffer confiscation. But Tory property would be held as security for Maryland assets in Britain rather than sold.

In an eloquent message of May 14, the Senate defended the rule of law against the politics of will. Carrollton, most likely, spoke for his colleagues. "Such is the force of equity and justice," the Senate declared, "that the human heart, even in opposition to apparent interests, must silently, at least, approve of arguments flowing from such pure sources; natural equity dictates, that no man should be condemned and punished unheard."

The Maryland constitution was not intended to destroy rights acquired prior to the Revolution. Otherwise, the senators predicted, "upon every change or alteration of the government, all precedent right to property will be extinguished." The

Declaration of Independence, "made upon the very principle of preserving liberty and property, destroyed no right which might be possessed consistently with that principle." The Senate renewed its proposal for the confiscation and sale of the back lands, which had become more realistic since New York had empowered its delegates to cede lands.

The legislative session ended in gridlock. The delegates declared that they "return with anxiety to our homes." The Senate hoped that "our countrymen will, as our consciences do, acquit us of blame." In spite of the impasse, Carrollton must have been satisfied with his performance. He had stood firmly for justice against the demagogues.

The Army Struggles

Meanwhile, there was a war going on. The army, Carroll told Franklin, "reverence & love" Washington. The survivors of Valley Forge were "as tough as the knots of an old seasoned oak, well disciplined," and, with French help, "well armed, & pretty tolerably clothed." During the summer of 1779, Washington's troops successfully raided Stony Point, with the Maryland Line in the vanguard, and Paulus Hook, where Henry Lee reported that "the brave Marylanders stood by me faithfully."

But the primary theater of operations was shifting to the South, where Clinton planned to wage total war. With its national debt hovering around £200 million, and its economy on the verge of collapse, peace had become a necessity for England. The British took Savannah in the last days of 1778 and threatened South Carolina. Charleston fell on May 11, 1780. Two weeks later came the infamous Battle of Waxhaw, South Carolina, where Lieutenant Colonel Banastre Tarleton massacred more than a hundred Virginians after they asked for quarter.

There was worse to come. General Gates, with monumental arrogance, ordered his battered army to advance on Camden, South Carolina. He believed that the great Cornwallis "will not dare to look me in the face." The Battle of Camden, on August 16, 1780, was a disaster for the Americans. Baron de Kalb commanded eight hundred men from the Chesapeake against three times that number. De Kalb died, with eleven wounds.

While de Kalb fought to the death, Gates fled for his life to Charlotte, sixty miles away. Daniel Carroll related Gates' disgrace to his cousin of Carrollton. "The fugitive General" was "the first who carried an account of his own defeat...200 miles from the place of action." When Gates submitted a requisition for supplies to the state of Maryland, the Governor's Council turned him down in disgust.

In the wake of Camden, Maryland began to feel British pressure. Denied a Continental frigate, the assembly reinstated the Maryland Navy. Merchants commissioned a private armed flotilla. Washington continued to count on Maryland's assistance: "Maryland has made great exertions, but she can still do something more." Guerrilla warfare in the Carolinas helped the Americans to regroup. When one hundred fifty Maryland prisoners were liberated in South Carolina, Daniel Carroll praised the ragtag army's "spirit of enterprise."

Fortunately, a French squadron appeared off Newport in the summer of 1780. Franco-American relations were still tentative. In 1778, a no-popery mob had beaten several French sailors, one of whom died, because Admiral d'Estaing refused to support an American attack on Newport. The Tories claimed that France was sending holy water, chrism, relics, and indulgences in their ships, to convert America to Catholicism.

But the French soldiers' good behavior won public approval. At Newport in July 1780, Lafayette wrote Washington that the Americans "mingled so well with the French troops that every Frenchman, officer or soldier, took an American with him and shared with him, in a most friendly way, his bed and supper." The French troops never succumbed to the temptation to forage in the vicinity. General Rochambeau won hearts by declaring, upon arrival at Newport, that "I shall be only General Washington's lieutenant."

Rochambeau's deference was remarkable, given the embarrassing weakness and poverty of Washington's force. John

Hanson told Carrollton that the army in New Jersey received only one full meal every three days. With the inflated currency worthless, the Continentals were plundering the countryside. "Is it not most shameful that our army should be starving," Hanson wrote, "while the country abounds with provisions?"

The Arnold Treason

Back in 1778, Carrollton had offended General Charles Lee by refusing to support his promotion to lieutenant general. "He seemed chagrined & nettled at my frankness," Carroll noted. Lee recovered enough from his pique to get himself invited to Doughoregan Manor in the fall of 1780. Molly wished she could report that Lee had departed, "but am sorry to find there is no prospect of so much joy, the wretch is perfectly recovered, goes singing about the house, rides out every day, abuses General Washington." Finally, the Squire asked him when he intended to leave. Lee took the hint and exited promptly.

Another general with far greater abilities than Lee had also grown discontented with the new ruling powers. Benedict Arnold clung to the code of honor. In early 1777, Arnold was accused in a pamphlet of malfeasance in Canada. He asked Washington for a court of inquiry into his conduct. Arnold offered to resign "when I can no longer serve my country with honor."

Washington understood the new political reality. "I do not see upon what ground you can demand a court of inquiry," he replied. "Besides, public bodies are not answerable for their actions; they place and displace at pleasure." This was exactly what Carrollton had tried to teach his father during the legal tender controversy. On the Board of War, Carroll helped Arnold clear his name. But Arnold continued to embroil himself in futile disputes over honor and fulminated against "a set of men who, void of principle, are governed entirely by the private interest."

Ironically, Arnold's adherence to the code of honor made his name a synonym for dishonor. He offered West Point, which he commanded, to General Clinton. The capture of West Point became the linchpin of Clinton's northern strategy. In September 1780, Arnold was able to tempt the British with an additional coup. He offered to arrange the capture of Washington and his staff, on their way back from a meeting with Rochambeau.

The discovery of the plot, and the subsequent execution of the British go-between Major André, exposed the increasing divide between British ideas of honor and American sensibility. Arnold and Clinton accused Washington of indulging his passions by executing André as a spy. Clinton called the American commander a murderer and a Jesuit. Washington's comment on Arnold, however, was that the traitor lacked feeling.

After he joined the British, Arnold distributed a handbill that attacked Congress for attending the funeral Mass of Juan de Miralles, a Spanish agent, on May 8, 1780. Arnold "saw your mean and profligate Congress at Mass for the soul of a Roman Catholic in purgatory," he wrote, "and participating in the rites of a church against whose antichristian corruptions your pious ancestors would have witnessed with their blood."

Greene Takes Over

In spite of its papist leanings, Congress came up with a plan to save the currency during the summer of 1780. Old Continental money, amounting to £200,000,000, was called in and replaced by a new issue of £10,000,000.

Carrollton was skeptical. Congress should never have emitted £200,000,000 in currency, he wrote, but once they did, they should have continued printing money until the debt was impossible to redeem. Paradoxically, this would have helped the public credit, because then everybody would have known that the nation would never have to face the consequences of the debt.

Carroll doubted that all the old money would come in, and if the two currencies circulated together, the new would depreciate the old even more. He believed the French should subsidize the entire war, as a gift rather than a loan. The advantages France stood to reap from humbling its main rival outweighed the cost. But now that Congress had made up its mind, Carroll supported the new emission. He hoped the states would maintain the new money "wisely, honestly, frugally, & vigorously."

Carroll was frustrated because he saw that the new emission would not solve the real problem, which was a shortage of money to carry on business. In spite of the astronomical sums in circulation, the paper emissions were so worthless that they amounted to little in real money. "A situation," Carrollton wrote, "perhaps never experienced by any nation in the world." Ten million dollars was not a sufficient circulating medium for all the states, yet Congress' plan forbade each state to emit more than its percentage of the total.

When the "new Congress money" finally appeared, it came in large denominations, so that in early 1781 there was a change shortage. A group of black people, Carrollton told his father, complained about not receiving their change from one Meara. Still, the new emission showed that something was being done. Congress followed it up by admonishing the states to cede their hinterlands to the Union. Virginia complied on January 2, 1781.

The military situation in the South, while still desperate, no longer seemed hopeless. Americans defeated a loyalist army at Kings Mountain, and Nathanael Greene replaced Gates as commander of the Southern army. Cornwallis feared Greene, saying he was as dangerous as Washington. Greene did not disappoint. He drew Cornwallis away from the British base, while avoiding a major engagement. Greene followed Washington's strategy of attrition. The Americans never held the field in battle, yet the British gained nothing from their victories.

Greene had only eight hundred men fit for duty. Half of these were Maryland regiments commanded by Otho Williams and John Eager Howard. Greene's army included not one soldier from Georgia or the Carolinas. At the battle of the Cowpens on January 17, 1781, Howard won distinction by leading a bayonet charge. It was the first time the Americans

The Charles Carroll House
Annapolis, Maryland
Courtesy of the Carroll House of Annapolis

Here we see the Spartan simplicity of Carroll of Annapolis, as well as the Carroll cleverness: from the water, the lawn appears as a majestic expanse, while from the point of view of the house, Spa Creek seems quite close.

Elizabeth Brooke Carroll
ATTRIBUTED TO JOHN WOLLASTON
The Baltimore Museum of Art
Bequest of Caroline D. Pennington (BMA 1994.196)

The year after Charles Carroll of Annapolis finally married Carrollton's mother, Elizabeth Brooke, legally, he commissioned this portrait, as if to celebrate her new status as wife. The gentleness, intelligence, and femininity, which had captivated Elizabeth's wealthy husband, radiate from John Wollaston's canvas, currently displayed at Homewood House.

Charles Carroll of Carrollton
SIR JOSHUA REYNOLDS
Yale Center for British Art
Paul Mellon Collection

The most renowned English painter of his day gives Carroll, whose Catholicism and French education set him apart from Anglo-American culture, an air of foreignness and mystery. By 1763, when this portrait was painted, Carroll's political thought had already advanced far beyond English categories. The young Carroll proclaimed that America "will & must be independent" long before Franklin, Washington, or Jefferson expressed the thought.

Mrs. Charles Carroll of Carrollton
CHARLES WILLSON PEALE
The Baltimore Museum of Art

Mary Darnall (Molly) Carroll holds a copy of Locke's *Treatise on Education*, although the Carrolls' style of parenting was hardly ideal. Molly Carroll did her best to cope with her husband's frequent absences but turned increasingly to laudanum for solace.

Death of General Montgomery in the Attack on Quebec, December 31, 1775
JOHN TRUMBULL
Yale University Art Gallery

General Richard Montgomery's death during the New Year's Eve assault on Quebec in 1775 crippled the American cause in Canada and made Carroll's task as a commissioner to Canada much more difficult.

Archbishop John Carroll
GILBERT STUART
Georgetown University

Charles Carroll's cousin and companion on journeys to school in Europe and to Canada as a revolutionary commissioner, John Carroll became the first archbishop of Baltimore.

Charles Carroll of Carrollton
THOMAS SULLY
Maryland State Archives

Daniel Dulany publicly called Carroll a "monkey." This portrait does not hide Carroll's arms and legs, which were long in proportion to his torso. Instead, Thomas Sully makes a virtue of Carroll's physical defects. The hand that signed the Declaration of Independence receives special emphasis.

General George Washington Resigning His Commission
JOHN TRUMBULL
Architect of the Capitol

Trumbull's painting confirms Carroll's enlightened treatment of his daughters. Mary and Catherine Carroll watch the ceremony at their father's side, while Martha Washington and Nelly Parke Custis are relegated to the balcony. Washington resigned his military commission in the Old Senate Chamber of the Annapolis State House in December 1783, setting an important precedent for the young republic. Carroll deserved his place of honor, having been one of Washington's main defenders on the Congressional Board of War and Ordnance.

Charles Carroll of Carrollton
RICHARD E. BROOKS
Architect of the Capitol

This sculpture, which stands in Statuary Hall of the U.S. Capitol, bears no physical resemblance whatsoever to Carroll. Yet Brooks perfectly captures Carroll's noble spirit, his lonely struggle for Catholic civil rights, and the genius of his political inventions, such as the Electoral College.

The Departure of Charles Carroll of Homewood
ROBERT EDGE PINE
Frick Art Reference Library

Carrollton's heir embarked for Europe from the family's dock on Spa Creek in Annapolis. Although he, like his father, obtained a European education, Carroll of Homewood did not live up to his father's academic expectations.

George Washington
GILBERT STUART
National Portrait Gallery, London

When Washington sat for the "Athenaeum" portrait, on which this image is based, Harriet Chew joined him so that the President's face might have "its most agreeable expression." The future Mrs. Carroll of Homewood succeeded well enough to make this the most renowned likeness of Washington.

Charles Carroll of Homewood
C. B. J. F. DE SAINT-MEMIN
The Baltimore Museum of Art
Bequest of Ellen Howard Bayard
(BMA 1939.183)

Saint-Memin drew Carroll of Homewood in 1800 when the heir was still on top of the world: newly married to a famous beauty, destined to inherit a great fortune, compared to the Prince Regent George IV for his good looks and charming manners. Notoriety as an alcoholic and abusive husband would come later.

Homewood House
The Homewood House Museum
The Johns Hopkins University

Charles Carroll of Homewood's only significant accomplishment was the building of Homewood House, now on the campus of the Johns Hopkins University. The younger Carroll created one of the magnificent examples of Georgian architecture in America, but his extravagance cost him his father's confidence. Homewood House's precise, elegant symmetry masks its architect's mental chaos.

Charles Carroll of Carrollton
C.B.J.F. DE SAINT-MEMIN
The Maryland Historical Society
Baltimore, Maryland

Carroll's fortunes were at their lowest ebb when this drawing was made. Turned out of office in the Jeffersonian revolution of 1800, Carroll devoted himself to his personal affairs. He discovered that his long absences during the Revolution, and Molly Carroll's addictive personality, had left an indelible mark on his children's character.

Richard Caton
CHARLES VOLKMAR
Maryland Historical Society

Carrollton would have liked his daughter Mary to wed Daniel Carroll of Duddington, but he permitted her to marry Richard Caton instead, commenting that "I do not think myself at liberty to control her choice, when fixed on a person of unexceptionable character."

Emily Caton McTavish
PHILIP T. C. TILYARD
Maryland Historical Society
Courtesy of the Sisters of the Good Shepherd

Carrollton's preference for his granddaughter Emily McTavish caused strife within the family. The unglamorous younger sister of the "Three American Graces" later donated land for the convent that is now the home of the Sisters of the Good Shepherd.

Charles Carroll of Carrollton
MICHAEL LATY (AFTER ROBERT FIELD)
The Maryland Historical Society
Baltimore, Maryland

After his 1831 encounter with Carrollton, Alexis de Tocqueville recorded that Carroll's type of gentility "is disappearing now after having provided America with her greatest spirits. With them the tradition of cultivated manners is lost; the people is becoming enlightened, attainments spread, and a middling ability becomes common. The striking talents, the great characters, are rare."

Charles Carroll of Carrollton
CHESTER HARDING
Architect of the Capitol

Upon seeing this portrait, Carroll candidly admitted his own decrepitude: "A Mr. Harding has lately drawn my portrait, a most striking likeness of me in the ninety-first year of my life, a countenance with little meaning, the eyes dim and dull." The longest-living signer of the Declaration, Carroll had become a walking, talking museum piece, but he still wrote with force and power.

Doughoregan Manor
The Maryland Historical Society
Baltimore, Maryland

The Catholic Signer was buried in the chapel of his family estate where, so long before, he had spent his illegitimate childhood with his beloved mother. For many years, pilgrims came to pay their respects to the "Last of the Romans."

had beaten the British with the bayonet in the open field. The officers had to restrain their men, who pursued the enemy with cries of "Tarleton's quarter."

Williams had his hour at the battle of Eutaw Springs, where the half-naked American troops proved victorious. Williams' charge, Greene said, "exceeded anything I ever saw." By the end of his campaign, Greene had recovered the three southernmost states, with the exception of the cities of Wilmington, Charleston, and Savannah. Greene "has really done wonders," Carroll wrote. "I think his campaign hitherto a most brilliant one."

The War Comes to Maryland

Maryland strained itself to the utmost to fulfill its quotas of men and supplies. Lafayette, in March 1781, declared that the state "have made to me every offer in their power."

Congress recommended a draft, which met with much opposition. But the assembly, in late 1780, created a system that made property owners responsible for recruiting soldiers. It worked, but added to Carrollton's headaches. He was now forced to find, not only a substitute for himself, but men to meet his quota. Carroll resorted to a procurer, Mr. Todd, whose going rate was around £1,425 in old continental money for one recruit. Todd turned out to be a scoundrel, but Carroll eventually found a substitute.

By now, all vagrants were forcibly recruited. In spite of Washington's disapproval, indentured servants filled a good portion of the quotas. Even convicts were pardoned if they enlisted. Most startling of all, black slaves were permitted to bear arms after 1780. Anyone in Maryland who owned at least six black slaves between the ages of fourteen and forty-five could have one taken, with or without the owner's consent, as long as the slave was willing to enlist. The slave owner received a £100 certificate for specie.

Carrollton disapproved of enlisting African-American slaves, because he considered it a violation of property rights. One hundred pounds was inadequate compensation, he felt, for a healthy black male. But the policy continued, and the American army took on an extraordinary character in the eyes of the Europeans. "I cannot too often repeat how astonished I have been at the American army," commented Baron du Bourg. "It is inconceivable that troops nearly naked, badly paid, and composed of old men, negroes and children, should march so well, both on the road and under fire." Rochambeau, du Bourg said, shared his amazement.

Maryland prepared for invasion. In January 1781, the public records were removed to Carrollton's Elk Ridge plantation and his cousins' domain of Upper Marlborough. Carroll turned down a congressional seat but continued in the assembly. Not surprisingly, Molly complained that "I have a violent headache & have been greatly indisposed ever since you left me." But she too rose to the occasion, providing for the "Family" and participating in a drive to raise funds for the army.

In March, for the first time, the Carrolls themselves were struck. A British force under Admiral Marriot Arbuthnot, supporting Benedict Arnold, raided the Carrolls' Poplar Island plantation. Carroll of Annapolis was philosophical. "If we reflect on the distresses & total ruin of many opulent Gentlemen to the Southward," wrote the Squire, "we should be wanting in gratitude did we not return thanks to God that we & this State have suffered so little." But he was concerned about how Molly might react to the loss.

Carrollton replied that Molly was totally indifferent to the ransacking of Poplar Island, in her anxiety for her children, who had just been inoculated for smallpox. The disease was then raging around Annapolis. "The pox is come finely out," Carrollton reported after a few days, "Charles will have a good many of them." In spite of the successful inoculation, there were many other things to worry about. Molly went back on her drug.

The British had offered to take the Poplar Island slaves away with them, but all refused. As a reward for their loyalty, the blacks were transferred *en masse* to Doughoregan, "as they did not choose to be parted." Those slaves who did join Cornwallis faced an uncertain future; the *Maryland Gazette* reported that three-fourths of them died of disease and famine.

Still, the Poplar Island incident suggests that the Carroll slaves enjoyed a fair degree of contentment. The prevailing good will meant that Carrollton could use a light touch with those who were disaffected. Rather than punish James Sears, who planned to run away, Carroll transferred him to the manor. He monitored his servants' health, telling his father that "Jemima is out of all danger—she goes about & mends stockings."

That spring, an army of mutinous, disaffected Northern troops descended on Maryland. They were disgusted at being sent South. Their commander, the Marquis de Lafayette, borrowed £3,000 in gold to buy clothes for his army, in an attempt to win their affections. Lafayette no doubt unburdened himself to Carrollton when he and Smallwood came to dinner at the Spa Creek mansion on April 4.

Lafayette's force was supposed to defend Baltimore, but Carroll had no illusions that two thousand men could stop Cornwallis if he decided to cross the Potomac. The soldiers were "a great nuisance," Carroll wrote, "& I heartily wish they were gone." They stole chickens and burned Carroll's fence rails for firewood. Carroll had to ask his father to send provisions, since "it is short commons with us here."

The Dog in the Manger

The British threat helped the legislature resolve several long-standing controversies. Public opinion had turned against Carroll on the issue of Tory confiscation, after the British impounded bank stock owned by Maryland. The Senate agreed to the confiscation in late January. A few days later, the assembly "acceded to the confederation." Maryland's acceptance of the Articles cleared the way for their ratification in early March.

But by May 1781, the new money had fallen to five or six to one. It was "tumbling so fast" in June that Carroll thought no one would receive it. The only hope was the arrival of Frenchmen and French treasure. Marylanders scanned the horizon for the promised fleet from France.

At this moment, amid "so much confusion & hurry in the present agitation of men's minds," as Carrollton put it, Chase unleashed the resentment he had been harboring since 1778. He published a series of articles in the *Gazette*, signed "Censor." His target was the Senate, specifically Carrollton, whom he blamed for the committee report that had cost him his seat in Congress.

Although he epitomized the politics of interest, Chase tried to present the dispute as an affair of honor. He took offense that Carroll had not revealed the 1778 committee's intentions to him at the time. Chase called Carrollton "a calumniator and a villain." "The malice of enemies may be forgiven," he wrote, "but it requires some time to forget the ungenerous, perfidious conduct of false friends." Carroll fired back with a public letter over his own name. The correspondence dragged on until 1782. The threat of a duel was dispelled when Chase retracted his charge that Carroll had acted deceitfully.

Once again, Carrollton won an epistolary debate. His old enemy, Antilon, now lay prostrate in the dust. When Daniel Dulany refused to return and swear the loyalty oath, his estate was sold. The Dulany share of the Iron Works fell to the state of Maryland.

The confiscation of Tory lands helped tenant farmers to improve their position, while merchants snapped up the urban property. Indeed, the lot where Carroll spent his last days, on Lombard Street near Baltimore's Inner Harbor, was sold in the confiscation, though Carrollton was not the first buyer.

Yorktown

In late August 1781, wartime anxiety was compounded by family crisis. Molly's mother died. Rachel Brooke Darnall was buried out of the Doughoregan Chapel by Fr. John Carroll. Molly was distraught, perhaps reproaching herself for neglect. Carroll of Annapolis had complained earlier that summer that Molly had stopped writing her mother. "Mrs. Darnall may have foibles," the Squire wrote, "but I hope they are not such as to deserve to be slighted by her daughter."

Carrollton believed that the Comte de Grasse had no intention of bringing his twenty-five sail of the line, four hundred merchantmen, and seventeen thousand soldiers to the United States that year. But the fleet was Washington's only hope. Mutinies had broken out in the Pennsylvania and New Jersey lines. Cornwallis believed he had Lafayette trapped, though the Marquis held off four thousand redcoats with fifteen hundred militia. "The child cannot escape me," Cornwallis gloated.

Washington was in Chester, Pennsylvania, just southwest of Philadelphia, when he heard that the French fleet had arrived in the Chesapeake. Guillaume de Deux-Ponts recorded the scene as Washington gleefully waved his hat in the air. The commander in chief "divested himself of his character as the arbiter of North America and was satisfied for a moment with that of a citizen, happy in the happiness of his country." At that moment, Washington resembled "a child, all of whose wishes had been satisfied." Crowds gathered in front of the French Ambassador's house in Philadelphia, raising huzzas to Louis XVI.

De Grasse's stay would be short; timing was essential. Washington daringly sent half of his army south, while maintaining the fiction that he planned to lay siege to New York City. He allowed phony letters to be captured, in order to reinforce this impression. The armies, converging on Yorktown by land and sea, were aided by supplies from Maryland. Washington wrote Governor Thomas Sim Lee on October 12 that Maryland's liberal grants "remove any apprehension of want." But the American treasury was so depleted that even the Continental Army at Yorktown was paid out of French coffers.

The composition of the forces at Yorktown raises the question of how many allied troops were Catholic. Approximately half of the allied belligerents were French, and many of the Continentals were Irish. Carroll biographer Lewis Leonard estimated that seventy percent of the winning side was Catholic.

This is not implausible. Franklin believed that the Irish had become the majority in Pennsylvania. Jeffersonian polemicists later emphasized the role of the Irish during the Revolution. No doubt many of the Irish names on Revolutionary musters belonged to Scots-Irish Presbyterians rather than Irish Catholics. The question of how many Irish-American soldiers were actually Catholic has received little scholarly attention and awaits further research.

By October 15, Carroll reported that "the cannonading at York can be heard distinctly in Charles County." In a letter, Washington confided to Carroll that Cornwallis had been "passive beyond conception." The British surrendered on October 17, five days before Clinton appeared with seven thousand reinforcements. Colonel Tilghman carried the news to Congress in four days, crying out "a horse for the Continental Congress. Cornwallis is taken."

Carrollton had the joy of proclaiming victory to the citizens of Annapolis. He translated and read publicly the Comte de Grasse's letter to Gov. Lee. After Yorktown, Congress went to church. The French and American armies, appropriately, attended High Mass. On November 21, the Senate congratulated Washington. Again thanking Maryland for its leadership in the war effort, the commander in chief wrote that Yorktown "affords a rational ground of belief that under the favor of Divine Providence, the freedom, independence and happiness of America will shortly be established upon the surest foundation."

Peace

After Yorktown, life was more or less the same. Charles Carroll of Homewood, age six, had jaundice. "Charley has had a fever with little remission since last Saturday," the Squire reported. "He this day took a puke & discharged much bile." Homewood and his sister Mary had improved by the end of October, but were still "pulled down, pale & thin." As for Molly, she was "much as usual." Molly appended a note to one of her father-in-law's letters, saying she was "too much indisposed, my dear

Mr. Carroll, to write to you. I hope you are well, & God keep you so is my very sincere prayer."

Then tragedy struck. On May 30, 1782, Carroll of Annapolis stepped out onto the high east porch of the Spa Creek mansion. Losing his balance, the Squire fell, and died within an hour. The shock was too much for Molly, who witnessed the accident. She took to her bed, and eleven days later, followed her father-in-law in death. According to a friend, Henrietta Hill Ogle, Molly went willingly, saying "that her God called & she must go & wished to be with him & did not desire to live."

According to Mrs. Ogle, Carrollton was "in great grief." The only mention of the disaster in Carroll's writings comes in a letter to Joshua Johnson. "My Father died the 30th of May suddenly and my wife on the 10th ultimo after a short but very painful illness," Carroll wrote. "Be pleased to carry to my credit when paid the undernoted Bill of Exchange." This passage speaks of inexpressible loss, and also of anger. Carroll must have reflected on the melancholy truth that his wife preferred to join his father, rather than remain with her husband and children.

Mary, Charles, and Catherine Carroll, or Kitty, were turned over to a cousin, Nancy Darnall, who acted as governess. Carrollton sought solace, as usual, in work. As if to make up for the absence of his father from Maryland politics, he developed a more contrarian attitude. The phrase "Carroll dissenting," we are told, became a running joke in the Maryland Senate. Soon after his bereavement, dissenting to a tax law, Carroll called the bill's enforcement mechanism "menacing, yet ridiculous and illegal." He accused the executive branch of incompetence.

In spite of his habit of voting in the minority, Carrollton was highly esteemed by his peers. He continued to write many of the Senate's important messages. In the veto message for a civil list bill, Carroll demanded that the delegates make permanent provision for judicial salaries. He wrote addresses to Greene and Rochambeau. Under Carrollton's leadership, the Senate rejected yet another attempt by the delegates to raise their salary. They also stymied the House's effort to keep ex-Tories from returning to Maryland.

By the time the Treaty of Paris officially brought peace, Carroll was preeminent in Maryland life. The official celebration of the treaty was held at the Spa Creek mansion on April 24, 1783. "There is to be a grand dinner on Squire Carroll's Point," wrote Mrs. Walter Dulany, "a whole ox is to be roasted & I can't tell how many sheep and calves...liquor in proportion." Fireworks and a ball followed the banquet.

To complete Carroll's triumph, he was elected president of the Senate on May 22, 1783. That December, however, Carroll was overshadowed when the nation's spiritual and political leader came to Annapolis. George Washington attended Congress, which was then sitting in Annapolis, in order to resign his commission.

Washington's motto was *exitus acta probat*—"the departure proves the deeds." His resignation completed the aura of sacredness around his person. Hamilton had urged Washington to "guide the torrent" of dissatisfaction within the army, hinting that he should seize the reins of power. But Washington refused. Instead, he used his influence to promote a stronger federal government. Accordingly, the welcoming committee, led by Carroll, declared that if the Confederation's powers proved too weak, "we doubt not our constituents will readily consent to enlarge them."

The resignation took place in the small Senate chamber in the state house. A throng of visitors crowded around the senators' fifteen desks as Washington, clad in his buff and blue uniform, surrendered power to the nation's representatives. Carroll was there on the floor, with his daughters. Martha Washington and her two Custis grandchildren sat in the gallery overhead. John Trumbull's rendering of the scene adorns the United States Capitol Rotunda.

Washington asked his officers to retire. But many were unwilling to surrender their arms until they had received some guarantee of compensation for their efforts. After a mass meeting was scheduled by the dissidents, Washington called his own meeting at a place called the "Temple of Virtue." His pleas might have fallen on deaf ears, but for a casual remark. While putting on his glasses, Washington said, "I have already grown gray in the service of my country. I am now going blind." This inspired an outpouring of sensibility that won the general's point.

Lest one think that selfless virtue had made a sudden comeback, we should note that Washington had promised to support the soldiers' demands. His backing of lifetime half-pay for officers represents another stage in Washington's assimilation of the Hamiltonian politics of interest. By making a sizable chunk of the population into government pensioners, half-pay dealt a death blow to classical republicanism. From then on, there was only a liberal republicanism, which used moral-sense language to promote "attachment" to the new national government.

To be fair, Washington was an effective moral leader, who urged his people to exert themselves in the public interest. But the civil religion Washington promoted was hardly an orthodox Christian view. In his message to state governors, he wrote that "the foundation of our empire was not laid in the gloomy age of ignorance and superstition." Washington praised "the growing liberality of sentiment, and, above all, the pure and benign light of revelation."

The dream of a republican empire had been fulfilled. This empire of liberty was destined to supersede the Roman one, represented in modern times by the Catholic Church. Its citizens, approaching what Washington called "the last stage of perfection to which human nature is capable of attaining," would illuminate the dark and superstitious globe. America was not a nation-state like others. Rather, Washington envisioned "an asylum for the poor and oppressed of all nations and religions."

Light, heat, and electricity symbolized the power of human sympathy, emanating from America, overcoming all opposition. This illumination would unite mankind into "one soul," as expressed in a poem spoken at Dartmouth College on Commencement Day in 1795. The spark was channeled through the kite of Franklin, a Promethean light-giver. The sage of Philadelphia hoped in 1789 that "the fire of liberty... will act upon the inestimable rights of man, as common fire does upon gold; purify without destroying them." Once this took place, as a 1796 Massachusetts orator proclaimed, the "political millennium" would come, and "all nations shall be united in one mighty republic!"

Freemasonry had a great deal to do with all this. It is well known that the eye of Providence on the Great Seal of the United States and the motto *novus ordo seclorum* spring from Masonry. In an odd episode in 1781, Elkanah Watson, an American merchant in France, hired some nuns to make Masonic ornaments for Washington. Thanking Watson, Washington praised the "Grand Architect of the universe" for upholding His "superstructure of justice."

Rapprochement with Great Britain

The Treaty of Paris, as Carroll had predicted, rendered illegal many of the states' anti-Tory measures. For example, the treaty required that debtors pay their British creditors in sterling.

The treaty, along with the repeal of legal tender laws, meant that another circulating medium had to be found, since paper currency was no longer universally acceptable. Consequently, banks were established. Bank notes, backed by specie deposits, served as a form of currency. Having been burned by the tender law, Carrollton was skeptical about paper money. He declined to buy bank notes from the bank of Thomas Fitzsimons, a Pennsylvania Catholic.

The French alliance was showing signs of wear. France had been most generous, but it was not in her interest to help America attain the status of a great power. The American commissioners in Europe took steps to distance the new republic from France's tutelage. And in 1783, relations with England were already thawing. Joshua Johnson, resident in France during the fighting in America, rejoined his London firm. Since trade had resumed, Carrollton could again read the *London Magazine* and the *Parliamentary Register*. But merchandise sent to the United States was still overpriced and inferior, as it had been under the mercantile system. Some cheeses "are so much decayed, that they cannot be eat," Carroll complained.

Carroll told Johnson he regretted that anti-Tory laws had

driven "industrious" citizens to Nova Scotia. "Had they been suffered to remain...their animosities would have died away." He tried to chip away at the laws against Tories. Carroll dissented, in May 1783, to a bill that made it more difficult for former loyalists to practice law. He charged that the bill was really part of the ongoing attempt to evade British debts.

That master debt-evader Samuel Chase soon returned to plague Carroll. Chase got himself appointed commissioner to regain the bank stock belonging to Maryland that the English had impounded during the war. Carroll consoled Joshua Johnson, who had also sought the office. "I would not have you to solicit or engage in any public trust," Carroll advised. "You are a man of too much honor to make a job of a public character." In 1784, the assembly granted Chase a £500 advance on his commission for the recovery of the stock. Carroll dissented.

One one occasion, Carroll found himself allied with the House of Delegates against his fellow senators in an attempt to relieve the burden on former Tories. When the Senate vetoed a House bill to allow former nonjurors to vote, Carroll was alone in dissent. On January 15, 1785, Senator Thomas Stone filed a response to Carroll's dissent to the law banning loyalist attorneys. In March 1786, Carroll was permitted to bring in a "Reply to the Counter-Protest of Thomas Stone."

This document shows once again that Carroll, in spite of his supposed elitism, was not afraid to appeal to the public when necessary. When legislation of an "evil tendency" was passed, he said, the legislator had a duty to inform the public. Carroll believed that the assembly should trust the loyalty oaths sworn by former Tories. Man should not "arrogate to himself the attribute of the deity, emphatically styled the 'Searcher of Hearts.'" "Justice is the corner stone, the very foundation of legal government," Carroll declaimed. "What property can be secure if unjust laws are made, suffered to subsist, and the injury done by them be not repaired?"

Peace enabled Carrollton to maintain family tradition by sending his ten-year-old son, Charles Carroll of Homewood, to school at Liège. Entrusting the boy to Johnson's firm, he asked that they send him to the Continent "by the cheapest and readiest conveyance." Homewood's allowance was a frugal two guineas per year until 1791, when it increased to four. If Carroll was trying to teach his son fiscal responsibility through this tight-fistedness, he failed. Carroll of Homewood became a notorious wastrel. His academic career was lackluster. "I am told he begins to apply to his books," his father wrote hopefully, two years after Homewood's departure.

Carroll's parenting style was more effective with his daughters. Indeed, Carroll was enlightened for his time, in his insistence on educating his girls. In 1789, Kitty joined Charles at Liège, where she studied at the English convent. Carroll's oldest daughter, Mary, also enjoyed more latitude than the typical heiress. Although Carrollton favored their cousin Daniel Carroll of Duddington, Mary engaged herself in 1787 to an English merchant, Richard Caton. Carroll told Duddington that "I do not think myself at liberty to control her choice, when fixed on a person of unexceptionable character."

The Constitutional Convention

Washington's push for a stronger federal government was gaining momentum. The Potomac Company provided a spark for the Federalist movement. The Company was a coalition of Maryland and Virginia businessmen who sought to improve navigation on the Potomac. It had its origins in 1777, when the Maryland Senate proposed a joint commission with Virginia on the Potomac question.

By 1784, Carrollton sat on the board of the Potomac Company, along with Washington. Even Horatio Gates was included. Though powered by private capital, the Company was assisted by legislation such as the assembly's December 1784 act for improving the river. A letter from Washington to Carroll reveals that the Potomac Company encouraged legislative involvement. In November 1785, the Maryland Senate ratified a compact with Virginia concerning the Potomac. Cooperation over the river reduced the animosity between the two states, so that by the time the Constitutional Convention was summoned, Washington could refer to Maryland as Virginia's "nearly-allied sister."

The House of Delegates dragged its feet on appointing representatives to the 1787 convention. They were in a frenzy for another emission of paper currency. Maryland's paper money had risen almost to face value because of tight controls on the amount in circulation and improved tax collection. In December 1784, only £8,726 nineteen shillings ninepence of Maryland currency was still circulating. The money shortage caused hardship for debtors; foreclosures became commonplace. Under deflation, though, property sales rarely covered debts, and many citizens boycotted the auctions.

The Senate rejected paper emissions in December of 1785 and 1786, though it did allow debtors to pay in installments. The House, in turn, defeated a Senate bill to speed up debt executions. The assembly was once again at an impasse. Washington heard that some delegates were threatening secession if they did not get their way. The assembly adjourned in January 1787, as Carroll put it, to "consult their constituents, in other words to obtain instructions to force the Senate" to print more money. Carrollton feared that "our several Governments are on the eve of dissolution."

When the assembly got around to choosing convention delegates, Carrollton was on the list. But he dared not go. Without his presence in the Senate, the Chase faction might succeed in printing more paper money. A contemporary reported that Carroll and Thomas Johnson "remained at home, convinced their fellow citizens of their superior rectitude and wisdom, and defeated that favorite measure of Mr. Chase."

Sidelined in Maryland, Carrollton sent his recommendations to Daniel Carroll, the brother of Rev. John Carroll, and a delegate to the Philadelphia Convention. Each state should have only two delegates in Congress, he wrote, but the weight of each state's vote should correspond to its Treasury contributions. Carrollton was opposed to any kind of term limits.

Surprisingly, Carroll favored a unicameral federal legislature. But he wanted Congressmen chosen through a highly "refined representation." Each congressional delegate, he argued, should be elected by the state legislatures. All the state legislatures should consist of two houses. Suffrage should be restricted to those owning one hundred fifty acres of land.

"I may be singular in my way of thinking" about property qualifications, Carroll admitted. But "speculative rights, which cannot be exerted without detriment to the Community, ought they to be preserved?" Carrollton was trying to head off the explosion of new individual rights that resulted from freewheeling interpretations of natural law. There was, of course, no universal right to vote. Carroll consistently avoided speculative theory and political abstractions, focusing instead on the real needs of communities and individuals.

Indeed, if legislation were not to remain on the level of theory, a "good federal Executive" was needed to enforce the law. His proposal seems weak in hindsight: a president and an executive council elected by Congress. When Carroll read the proposed Constitution, however, he realized that the federal Senate removed the need for a council. The Senate would play the conciliar role of advice and consent on treaties and nominations. Carrollton thought that the president should command a standing army, which in peacetime would perform such public services as fixing roads.

Not surprisingly, Carroll wanted to take the power of coining and printing money away from the state legislatures and entrust it exclusively to Congress. Paper money should be emitted only in wartime, and only when backed by productive funds. But Carrollton thought the new federal superstructure depended on a sound base in the state governments. "Unless the several State Governments be well organized," he wrote, "I am confident the federal Government, however perfect it may appear in theory, will always be found very defective in practice."

Hamilton, meanwhile, was ready to take down classical republicanism once and for all. "We may preach till we are tired of the theme," he had written in 1782, "the necessity of disinterestedness in republics, without making a single proselyte." He saw clearly that the American "pursuit of happiness" would come to mean the pursuit of money on an unprecedented scale.

The question was whether the Articles of Confederation could channel these "private vices," in Bernard de Mandeville's dictum, into "public benefits."

Increasingly, the Articles were seen to have created an unhealthy state of nature, in which both individual rights and the common good were sacrificed to the states' tribal power. "Lycurgus" wrote that the Confederation was merely a "political union," not a union of "sentiment" or "interest." Hamilton and Washington wanted to bring this moral-sense language of attachment into the new government. An "energetic" power was needed, the general wrote, to slay the "many headed monster" of Confederation government. And Hamilton wanted a "mutually advantageous intercourse" among the states, harmonized by the national power.

Dogmatic religion was ebbing, and Masonry prevalent. It is hardly surprising, then, that when Franklin suggested daily prayer at the Constitutional Convention, Hamilton said there was no need to call in "foreign aid." Having admitted this, one should not overlook the virtues of the government the convention devised. It was both limited and mixed, without arrogating divine prerogatives to itself. As originally conceived, the new system more closely resembled the Roman Empire, as Carroll understood it, than the English. It was imperial in scope, but because of its multiple levels and complex checks, would remain humble before the natural law.

James Wilson, a Pennsylvania Scot, turned out to be the Founder most aware of Catholic teaching, aside from Carrollton. While serving on the United States Supreme Court, Wilson criticized the "ungracious silence" about the first Lord Baltimore, who deserved to be called "the father of his country." He also popularized Catholic corporatism, the idea of a state as a *corpus mysticum reipublicae*, or mystical body of the republic. A state is a "complete body," Wilson said, an "artificial person."

Thus, the common good was paramount: "The happiness of the society is the first law of every government." The government exists to serve the commonwealth, and not the other way around. "By some politicians, society has been considered as only the scaffolding of government," Wilson wrote. "In the just order of things, government is the scaffolding of society: and if society could be built and kept entire without government, the scaffolding might be thrown down, without the least inconvenience or cause of regret." Here we have an early formulation of the principle of subsidiarity, later defined by Pope Pius XI in *Quadragesimo anno*.

But Wilson's major contribution to the new government was his explanation of where the sovereignty lay. Not with the federal government, not with the states, not with the various legislatures, but with "we the people." The "citizens at large" had delegated sovereignty to the state and federal governments, but only to serve certain specific needs. This was indeed, as Wilson called it, a "revolution principle." Wilson's ideas are not entirely in keeping with Catholic thought, which holds that popular sovereignty ends when a new social contract is formed. However, the American concept of popular sovereignty does resonate with the Catholic idea of subsidiarity.

Daniel Carroll was responsible for the most important constitutional expression of popular sovereignty. As a member of the House of Representatives in the first Congress, he proposed adding the phrase "to the people" to the tenth amendment. The final text reads, "The powers not delegated to the United States by the Constitution, nor prohibited by it to the States, are reserved to the States respectively, or to the people." The Catholic politician followed Suarez, who argued that the people could delegate "power to a king and yet retain it in themselves for certain affairs and for things of greater moment."

The role of the general public in the election of the president, one of those matters "of greater moment," was a radical idea in 1787. It was Wilson who made the novel suggestion that rank-and-file voters should have a voice in the presidential election, and Wilson who borrowed Carrollton's concept of an electoral college.

The emphasis on popular sovereignty in the Constitution gradually vanquished the Whig notion that power resided in the legislature. Chief Justice John Marshall affirmed in

McCulloch vs. Maryland that government is "of the people. In form and in substance it emanates from them, its powers are granted by them and for their benefit."

THE MARYLAND RATIFYING CONVENTION

Daniel Carroll kept James Madison, who had played a crucial part at the convention, informed about the prospects for ratification in Maryland. He told Madison that Carrollton "is a warm friend" of the Constitution. Maryland Federalists suffered a setback when the assembly imposed no property qualifications for the state ratifying convention. But Carrollton was so confident of his own election to the ratifying convention that he began preparing a speech.

Then Carroll's political nemesis struck. Samuel Chase and his henchmen, including John Francis Mercer, went on the road to speak against Carrollton and the other Federalist candidates. "The people were alarmed at their positive assertions," Daniel Carroll reported to Madison, "and I am afraid when they attended the polls, a wildness appeared in many." Mercer had been circulating a list of those supposedly in favor of "Kingly Government," including Daniel Carroll.

Another Anti-Federalist, Luther Martin, had served as a delegate to the Philadelphia Convention. He refused to sign the Constitution, vowing that he would be hanged first. Martin was one of the first states' rights advocates: he objected to the preamble's "We the People." Martin noticed that "the powers are made to flow from them in the first instance.... This Government if ratified and established will be immediately from the People." He failed to recognize that the people had delegated a significant portion of their sovereignty to state governments, not just the national government, while retaining the residue for itself.

Carrollton lost the election, but his undelivered speech has survived. He enumerated certain basic truths of politics. "That government is the best," Carroll wrote, "which unites in its composition & frame the energy of monarchy, the wisdom of aristocracy with the integrity, common interest, & spirit of a democracy." The new constitution, when ratified, would "be founded on the express consent of a great majority of the People of the United States." And he believed that those "People of America will have the spirit & force" to thwart any abuses of governmental power.

Checks and balances would "produce that due admixture of energy & caution, of action & repose, which constitute the true, the invigorating health, the perfection of Government." Federalism would provide another safeguard. While the states would have various "interests," the "spirit of the federal Government will be one & entire; it will mix with, pervade, & animate the great body of the confederated Republic."

Carroll saw the Constitution as a worthy vehicle for his politics of spirit, which was rooted in Catholic corporatism. His idea of spirit was different from Hamilton's master concept of energy, though Carroll sometimes used the latter term as well. Energy represents a directing power from above, channeling the impulses of the citizenry in a desired direction. Spirit, on the other hand, pertains wholistically to the common good of the entire mystical body of the nation.

Maryland's convention came at a crucial time. Six states had already ratified, so Maryland would make a majority, though two more states would still be needed to establish the Constitution. Virginia, especially, watched Maryland's deliberations with interest.

The Maryland Federalists chose not to contest the elections of Chase, Martin, and others who were not resident in the counties they represented. This turned out to be a wise strategy, as the Federalists dominated the ratifying convention anyway. The opposition, which had seemed so potent at the polls—the bankrupt Chase, the paranoid Mercer, and the bibulous Martin—proved less formidable on the convention floor.

The Federalists refused to allow a discussion of the Constitution item by item. They would not entertain any amendments. The victors declined even to count yeas and nays on the final vote, which was, predictably, favorable to the new form of government. Subsequently, Virginia ratified by a narrow margin.

Part IV: Senator

The First United States Senate

After his defeat for the ratifying convention, Carrollton was vindicated when the assembly appointed him to the United States Senate. Carroll's career in the federal Congress is somewhat mysterious. The early Senate was highly secretive and kept no detailed record of its proceedings.

What little we know comes mostly from the journals of William Maclay, an Anti-Federalist curmudgeon from Pennsylvania. Early in the first Congress, Carrollton won Maclay's confidence by opposing titles of honor. Vice President John Adams, the president of the Senate, was obsessed with the need for titles. During one trifling debate over whether senators should be styled "right honorable" or merely "honorable," Maclay recorded that "Carroll and myself exchanged looks and laughs of congratulation."

On April 30, 1789, President Washington made his first appearance in the federal legislature. "This is a great, important day," Maclay minuted. "Goddess of etiquette, assist me while I describe it." John Adams kept Washington waiting while the Senate debated whether to stand or sit during the president's speech. Adams cited Parliamentary precedent, in which the Lords sat while the Commons stood. "Mr. Carroll got up to declare that he thought it of no consequence how it was in Great Britain; they were no rule to us."

Maclay appreciated Carroll's way of handling the pompous Adams. Carrollton admired the vice president's political ideas, but found his personality repugnant. One day Maclay and Carroll were "chatting on some common subject" in the Senate chamber. Adams descended from the chair and sidled up to Carroll. "How have you arranged your empire on your departure?" Adams asked. "What kind of administration have you established for the regulation of your finances? Is your government entrusted to a viceroy, nuncio, legate, plenipotentiary, or chargé d'affaires?"

Carroll told Adams that his son-in-law Richard Caton was managing his business. But Adams persisted, cataloguing all possible offices in a royal household. "I pared my nails," Maclay wrote, "and thought he would soon have done, but it is no easy thing to go through the detail of an empire."

Carroll's humility continued to impress Maclay. He voted against a bill to increase congressional salaries. Supporters of the pay hike seemed to argue "that all worth was wealth, and all dignity of character consisted in expensive living," Maclay wrote. "Mr. Carroll, of Maryland, though the richest man in the Union, was not with them." Deals and bargains also made Carrollton uncomfortable. He favored *viva voce* voting as a means of keeping the legislative process aboveboard.

When Franklin died, Carroll moved that the Senate wear mourning for a month. He still remembered their comradeship in the struggle for Canada and for the French alliance. But Franklin had become an icon of the democratic faction in the lower house, and it soon became clear that the Senate would not support Carroll. He withdrew his motion. On another occasion, Carroll "edged near" Maclay in the chamber, to tell him that France had eliminated titles of nobility. Maclay replied that he thought the French had been influenced by their own actions against titles. "A flash of joy lightened from his countenance," Maclay noted.

As the French Revolution progressed, however, Carroll became apprehensive. He wrote Jefferson that he feared "the side views and factions, combinations and cabals, amongst the popular party" in France would lead to disaster. (Oddly enough, a letter from Jefferson to Carroll written around that time is signed "Yours affectionately.") Carrollton soon proved that as a politician, he was no creature of the Anti-Federalists. His increasingly centralizing positions lowered Carroll in Maclay's esteem.

Carroll voted against the eleventh amendment, which prohibits lawsuits against the states. He wanted to increase the military, in order to protect settlers from Native American attack, although Pennsylvania's constitution forbade a standing army. Carroll "expressly said," Maclay fumed, that "we were not to be governed by any State Constitution." Quoting Montesquieu, Carroll favored allowing the president to remove appointees at will. He spoke of the "want of power in the President" and the "atrocious assumption of power in the States." "How strangely this man has changed!" Maclay lamented.

Carroll was merely expressing the full range of his political beliefs, in a way that surpassed the comprehension of an ideologue like Maclay. But his approach to parliamentary procedure had changed. Rejecting the temptation to become a legislative crank, Carrollton began to play political hardball. At this time, he urged Joshua Johnson to send him the memoirs of Frederick the Great, a purely Machiavellian document. "I must have them," Carroll wrote.

When Hamilton proposed that the federal government assume the debts of the states, Carroll moved into the thick of the negotiations. Hamilton's measure promised to restore public credit by turning the states' paper into a currency fully backed by the national government. Virginia opposed the assumption of debts, because it had already managed to fund its wartime emissions.

Hamilton struck a deal with Secretary of State Jefferson: assumption for a southern capital city. The temporary residence of the capital, until the federal city could be built, then became a bargaining chip. Residence came up in Congress before assumption. Maclay suspected that "Carroll & Company" planned to place the temporary capital in New York. The Pennsylvanian blamed Washington for the permanent capital's Potomac location. "He, by means of Jefferson, Madison, Carroll, and others, urged the business." Several of the great Catholic Maryland families, including the Carrolls of Duddington, owned land in what became the District of Columbia. Indeed, between the site of the White House and Capitol Hill, a stream called the Tiber ran through a tract known as Rome.

A few days after the residence bill passed, Maclay recorded, it dawned on everyone that a deal had been made. Carrollton chaired a committee to evaluate the merits of assuming state debts. After the committee reported favorably on assumption, Maclay lamented that "Hamilton has got his number made up. He wanted but one vote long ago." Carrollton was apparently that swing vote. "Since I am obliged to give up Carroll's political character," Maclay mourned, "I am ready to say, 'Who is the just man that doeth right and sinneth not?'"

Carroll was pleased with the state of affairs. Bills of exchange could now be bought at par, thanks to the improving public credit. "This government begins to gain confidence & respect: the opposition to it has in great measure subsided." By January 1791, Carrollton thought America "is now beginning to be in a flourishing condition." Congress was tedious—"I wish we could get into the way of doing a little faster"—but Carroll obviously found the new legislature more congenial than the wartime Congress.

Once again, however, the House of Delegates made Carrollton the object of their pettiness. The Maryland Senate had toned down the impassioned language of the delegates' petition to open the deliberations of the federal Senate. The delegates responded by passing a bill to prohibit dual office-holding. Carroll opposed the measure, but it passed the Maryland Senate on November 30, 1792. Carrollton immediately resigned his seat—in the United States Senate. Washington wrote right away to express his regret at "the loss of your services to the United States in your Senatorial capacity."

Carroll held the system of government in Maryland, which he had largely created, too dear to abandon it to the demagogues. But he hoped to stay in touch with issues in the national Congress. He wrote his fellow senator, John Henry, that "though not a player myself, I shall find myself interested in the game that is played."

Freedom of Religion

Before we leave Carroll's career in the United States Senate, something must be said about the freedom of religion clause of the First Amendment. We know little about Carroll's role in securing religious freedom. He always kept a low profile when religion became a subject of debate. He spoke against the Congress' attending an Episcopal service after Washington's first inaugural, but he did not press the issue. Carroll did, however, serve on a conference committee that hammered the Bill of Rights into its final form.

Based on their experiences under the Protestant establishment, both Carrollton and his cousin Daniel were wary of any state interference with religion. Matters of conscience, Daniel Carroll said in the House of Representatives, "will little bear the gentlest touch of governmental hand." It is doubtful, however, that either man foresaw the highly individualistic spin that would later be placed on the freedom of religion clause. Most Founders would have found it incredible that the First Amendment could be used to suppress, rather than to protect and encourage, religion.

The Northwest Ordinance of 1787, the great achievement of the Confederation government, provided for religious tolerance in the former back lands. It also declared that "religion, morality and knowledge" were necessary for good government, and suggested a special role for religion in the field of education. When the Maryland Senate protested certain privileges that the delegates granted the Episcopal Church, they made no claim that such privileges should not be granted by government, only that they should be conferred evenhandedly on all Christian religions.

The Catholic Church in America recognized the practical necessity for full religious toleration, which Rev. John Carroll thought was "the genuine spirit of Christianity." Writing in 1783 to *Propaganda Fide*, the Vatican's missionary congregation, which still supervised the American Church, John Carroll said that "in these United States our religious system has undergone a revolution, if possible, more extraordinary than our political one." Full tolerance was the norm. Interestingly, Carroll's language echoes the freethinker Thomas Paine's 1782 statement that "our style and manner of thinking have undergone a revolution, more extraordinary than the political revolution of the country."

Rev. Carroll told *Propaganda* that the elected leaders of the United States disapproved of the American Church being governed from Rome. On behalf of the American clergy, he requested a native hierarchy of some sort for the United States.

Carroll also informed Rome that American Catholics should remain "zealously attached to our government." The only foreign power they would admit was "that, which is essential to our Religion, the acknowledgement of the Pope's spiritual supremacy over the whole Christian world."

The papal nuncio at Versailles had approached Franklin to explore the possibility of sending a vicar apostolic to the United States. Franklin referred the question to Congress, who declined to pronounce on a "purely spiritual" matter. John Carroll thought a vicar apostolic, who would still report to *Propaganda Fide*, inadequate. Rome responded by broadening the vicar's faculties and allowing the local clergy to recommend a candidate. Carroll was appointed vicar apostolic, according to the official announcement, in order to "please and gratify many members of the republic, and especially Mr. Franklin."

But Franklin wanted his old traveling companion to be more than a vicar. Thomas Jefferson, Franklin's successor in Paris, agreed that America should have its own bishop. Jefferson told Cardinal Dugnani that Carroll could become bishop "without offense to our institutions or opinions." So in another American irony, the skeptical Franklin and the Deist Jefferson made John Carroll into a bishop. He was consecrated bishop of Baltimore on the feast of the Assumption in 1790, the second year of the Washington administration.

American Catholics lost no time in lobbying the new President. Carrollton, Daniel Carroll, Thomas Fitzsimons, and other prominent Catholic laymen signed an address to Washington that reminded the president of the efforts of Catholics during the war. "Whilst our country preserves her freedom and independence," the address states, "we shall have a well founded title to claim from her justice, the equal rights of citizenship, as the price of our blood spilt under your eyes." The memorialists prayed for the preservation of Catholic civil rights in the four states—Pennsylvania, Delaware, Maryland, and Virginia—where tolerance had been established, and hoped for "the full extension of them from the justice of those States, which still restrict them."

Washington's response of March 12, 1790, sees "liberality" as the answer to the Catholics' prayers. "As mankind becomes more liberal, they will be apt to allow that all those who conduct themselves worthy members of the community are equally entitled to the protection of Civil Government."

THE PRIVATE SECTOR

President Washington was less pleased when Carrollton, "the most monied man I was acquainted with," refused to grant him a loan. According to Washington, Carroll claimed that his "resources were not *more* than adequate to his own occasions; thenceforward I made no farther attempts, not knowing indeed where to apply." This was about as sarcastic as the courteous Chief Executive got. But the president was downright irritated when Carroll dunned him for £243 that Washington held in trust for the Carrolls, pending the result of a lawsuit among the partners in the Iron Works. "I have no desire to withhold the money from you one moment," the president replied sharply.

Carroll was certainly parsimonious, but he had less liquid cash than one might expect, since much of his estate consisted of land and slaves. He continued to lend money at interest, and his principal increased from £85,000 in 1788 to £128,705 ten years later. But he avoided speculations and was cautious about stocks and money markets. Disasters such as the failure of the Bank of New York confirmed Carroll's inclination to stay away from risky investments.

Carroll applied his concept of "spirit" to business, as well. He advised his colleagues that the Iron Works would become more profitable "if carried on with spirit." Later, he used the same term with respect to his Hockley Mills investment and the Potomac Company. Carroll continued to support public works, remaining a shareholder in the Potomac Company, although mismanagement of the concern lessened his enthusiasm. He joined the Susquehanna Canal Company in 1783. Carroll also became a member of the first public library in Baltimore, established in 1795.

His business affairs kept him from accepting political appointments, for which he was often mentioned. Washington considered naming Carroll ambassador to France in 1796, but concluded that "he has such large concerns of his own to attend to, and is so tenacious of them, that it is morally certain he would not be prevailed on to go." Washington did ask the fifty-five-year-old Carroll in April 1793 to negotiate with the Native Americans at Lower Sandusky, Ohio. Carroll declared he would be willing, except that "the infirmities of age are coming fast upon me; I do not think I could endure the fatigue of so long a journey."

Carroll's name was even brought forward as a potential successor to Washington, who had given some indications of retiring in 1792. James McHenry, Secretary of War and a Marylander, recommended Carroll to Hamilton. "I calculate that Mr. Carroll will not succeed, but it may produce more votes in this state for some man who ought," McHenry confided. "It should operate to detach Mr. Carroll from Mr. Jefferson, whose politics have in some instances infected him."

Hamilton replied that if Washington retired, he would promote Carroll "as one of the two who are to fill the two great offices." He spoke of his "real respect and esteem for the character" who had helped him gain the assumption of state debts. Carrollton was not a party to these intrigues. He reported to Hamilton that he had met with a potential Anti-Federalist candidate, probably Burr, who "left an unfavorable impression on my mind. He appeared to me not to want talents, but judgment and steadiness; and I suspect he possesses of ambition a *quantum sufficit* [sufficient amount] for any man."

Carroll grew increasingly disgusted with the French Revolution. "No real freedom can be enjoyed in France under the existing system," he wrote. "If the different factions, which distract & afflict that unhappy country would lay aside their animosities & unite in establishing a limited government, under the guidance of wisdom and law...France might yet be saved from the destruction to which she seems doomed." Some friends had joked that if Carroll possessed only £20,000 he would become a Jacobin.[3] "Perhaps was I worth *nothing* I might

---

[3] Jacobins were supporters of French revolutionary principles, not to be confused with Jacobites, who were loyal to the deposed Stuart kings.

affect to adopt their principles," Carroll retorted, ". . . in the hope of getting *something*."

Homewood and Kitty were exposed to the European upheaval, as the French army entered Liège in 1792. They escaped, only to find themselves in even greater danger when their ship was captured by a French privateer. Fortunately, the privateer's crew put the Carroll children on a ship bound for Boston.

Upon their return, Charles and Kitty took up residence with their sister Mary Caton near Baltimore. Unfortunately for the Catons, this meant that Carrollton suddenly took an intense interest in their household. He lectured Mary on the need to exercise instead of "lolling on the bed, & reading romances." Carroll discouraged his oldest daughter from "the chit chat of the tea table, dress and morning visits."

All three children had inherited their mother's love of society and pleasure. Carrollton now urged them to cultivate modesty and austerity. He bought clothes for Kitty that were "genteel, but not gaudy." The father hoped that Charles and Kitty "blend amusements with improvement, & that the latter applies in the mornings to Arithmetic."

All this parental concern proved too little, too late. Few sums were being done at the Caton house, where Kitty immediately fell into romantic intrigues. In May 1795, Carrollton told Mary Caton that her husband and Homewood had ridden to Georgetown to defend Kitty from "the blackest & most unfounded calumny that was ever invented & circulated." Kitty had suffered "several violent fits," said her "afflicted & loving father." That October, rumors circulated that both Kitty and Charles were betrothed, with Mary Caton's approval, to two house guests of the Catons. "I assured my informant that these tales were destitute of truth," Carrollton wrote. "I was confident you set too great a value upon my affection to countenance such alliances."

Disappointed in his children, Carrollton pinned his hopes on his four Caton granddaughters. "Does Mary Ann continue to make progress in reading & musick? I am sorry my little Betsy can't apply [to work]—she resembles her uncle in that respect."

At least Carroll had grown more affectionate in old age. "Give my love to them all, & kiss them for me," he asked.

Carroll of Homewood showed some signs of improvement in 1797. His father praised his resolution "to make a better use of your time than you have done." The following year, Homewood came near to making a splendid match with George Washington's step-granddaughter, Nelly Custis. The Carroll heir impressed Nelly's brother George Washington Parke Custis as "a young man of the strictest probity and morals, discreet without closeness, temperate without excess, and modest without vanity; possessed of those amiable qualities and friendship which are so commendable, and with few of the vices of the age."

The affair blew over, and Homewood later displayed all the vices of the age. Nelly Custis' diagnosis was more perceptive than her brother's. Carroll of Homewood "unfortunately has been told too often of his merit and accomplishments, and it has given him more affectation than is by any means agreeable." The heir was nagged by his father and spoiled by his sisters, hardly a promising combination. In 1798, Carrollton secured his son an appointment as an "extra aide-de-camp" to Washington, who had come out of retirement to lead the army during the "quasi-war" with France. But the war scare evaporated and Homewood lost another chance to make good.

The Slavery Question

Carrollton remained in the Maryland Assembly, which had less to do now that the federal government had power over money, trade, and warfare. He was usually the first or second to arrive, and had to wait for the other senators to trickle in. The Senate produced the occasional address in support of the president's policies. Instead of deliberating over paper emissions and property confiscations, they produced such momentous pieces of legislation as the 1797 "Act to prevent the going at large of swine." Fortunately, Samuel Chase was still around to liven things up occasionally.

Part IV: Senator

The most memorable aspect of Carroll's Senate career during the 1790s was his proposed solution to the problem of slavery. Jefferson acutely wrote that the United States was like the boy in the fable who had a wolf—slavery—by the ears. He was in trouble, whether he held on or let go. Carroll recognized the evil of slavery, but he also saw the impossibility of freeing the slaves all at once, turning them into a hostile society without skills or education.

In 1789, Nicholas Hammond introduced a bill in the assembly for the gradual abolition of slavery. Carroll joined his former political enemy John Hall in support of the bill. He recommended that a conference committee be created to discuss it. The House of Delegates refused. Carrollton brought in his own antislavery measure in 1797. He proposed that the state buy all female slave children, educate them, and free them at age twenty-eight. Gradually, under the influence of their educated sisters and wives, the men would become ready for freedom.

The plan died in the assembly, and having done what he could, Carroll left the issue alone. His record as a slave owner was mixed. He usually owned between three and four hundred slaves. The 1790 census counted 316. Unlike some other planters, Carroll had no qualms about selling slaves, but he tried to keep families together. Contrary to what some authors have claimed, Carroll did provide religious instruction for his slave family. He had no regular plan of manumitting slaves, and he became more, rather than less, dependent on plantation income as time passed. In 1816, however, Carroll freed all the slaves on his unprofitable Poplar Island plantation. Perhaps he remembered the wartime loyalty of an earlier generation of African-Americans there.

Foreign Entanglements

America in the 1790s had two vocal parties calling for war. The question was whom to support, France or England.

War fever flared up and died out in 1794. But passions ignited again in 1795 with the signing of the Jay Treaty. John

Marshall later wrote that even the Federalists were initially disappointed with the anglophile John Jay's effort. The treaty allowed England to tax American imports but rejected American tariffs on British imports. It made no provision for free trade with the West Indies, nor did it indemnify planters for the slaves who had joined the British during the war.

Carroll favored the treaty from the beginning, however, because it awarded disputed Northwestern outposts to the United States, and provided compensation for "illegal depredations on our trade." As the controversy raged on into 1796, the House of Representatives blocked appropriations needed to enforce the treaty. The beleaguered Washington ruled out a third term.

Carroll wrote the Chief Executive that "I am totally at a loss to account for the motives of the Majority. Do they wish to engross all power to themselves, to destroy the checks & balances established by the Constitution?" Carrollton argued that American foreign policy should play France off against England. It was not in America's "real interest" to allow either nation to obtain a "decided superiority."

Washington's reply attacked the House for its "assumption of power" at the expense of the president and the Senate. Carroll of Homewood had this letter published, and Carrollton noted that it was "repeatedly" reprinted. In his tell-all memoir, the *Anas*, Jefferson alludes to Washington's "letters to Mr. Adams and Mr. Carroll, over which in devotion to his imperishable fame, we must forever weep as monuments of mortal decay."

Virginia proposed constitutional amendments to enlarge the powers of the House of Representatives. Carroll devoted himself to defeating these amendments. He argued that a "passionate, prejudicial, or misguided majority" in the House of Representatives might subvert the Constitution if Virginia's amendments were adopted.

The Adams Administration

The Jay Treaty threw the presidential succession into confusion. Jefferson emerged from Monticello to challenge Adams.

Part IV: Senator

Carrollton had suggested that the Secretary of State's retirement was not entirely owing to his philosophic temperament. Rather, if Jefferson remained in office, the hostility of Hamilton's supporters might "throw obstructions in his way to the Presidential chair."

"The friends of the government," Carroll wrote McHenry in December 1796, "dread the election of Jefferson." The Anti-Federalists wanted "revolution & war.... A man must be blind indeed not to see through the designs of the party." The vice president's personality made him less than an ideal successor to Washington, but Carrollton supported Adams against a movement to elevate his running mate, Thomas Pinckney, to the presidency. The electoral rules of the time permitted such a maneuver.

Most of the political turmoil that followed was beyond President Adams' control. Adams would have preferred a bipartisan administration, sharing power with Jefferson. But he was stuck with three members of Washington's cabinet, including McHenry, who were anti-French war hawks. Unable to control his own administration, Adams was swept into the frenzy that led to the Alien and Sedition Acts. To be sure, the man from Braintree's distaste for foreigners was partly to blame for the sedition laws. His supporters attacked the "wild Irish," and Adams lamented that "we have no Americans in America."

The Anti-Federalists became more ideological in response. They distinguished the Federalist desire for mere "independence" from their own love for "liberty." Madison and Jefferson constantly used religious terminology to describe the political divide. They referred to their own "orthodoxy" as opposed to the "heretical" politics of the Federalists. Jefferson counseled "a little patience, and we shall see the reign of witches pass over, their spells dissolve, and the people recovering their true sight."

Washington maintained a statesmanlike reserve in public. At one Mount Vernon dinner, Colonel Fitzgerald, the Catholic war hero and member of the Potomac Company, tried to goad Washington into attacking Jefferson. "But he received no encouragement from the general, who led the conversation to the subject of the wonderful prosperity of the country."

On December 9, 1799, William Hindman observed to McHenry that "our friend Mr. Carroll wears remarkably well, and is in as good spirits as I ever knew him. He promises to live to a great age." Not so Washington, who was dead a week later. The Maryland Senate sent Carrollton to proclaim the news to the delegates.

Future Chief Justice Roger Taney recorded the scene as Carroll and another senator, whose identity is disputed, entered the hall. "The two honored senators with their gray locks stood at the bar of the House with the tears rolling down their cheeks," the Catholic Taney remembered. "Few were present who did not shed tears on that occasion. My eyes, I am sure, were not dry."

Washington's and Carroll's fates differed as concerns longevity, but not when it came to politics. Though Carrollton outlived the general by thirty-two years, his political career did not survive the *pater patriae*'s death. Neither man's virtues had any place in American politics after 1800.

The Jeffersonian Revolution

With Washington dead, Adams decided to rid himself of his political baggage. He treated McHenry to one of his legendary temper tantrums. Adams called Hamilton an "intriguant" and a "bastard." "You are subservient to Hamilton," Adams correctly charged, "who ruled Washington, and would still rule if he could. Washington saddled me with three Secretaries who would control me, but I shall take care of that."

Having fired the three disloyal cabinet members, Adams was determined to avoid war with France. For this, he has won the praise of most historians. Adams went so far as to disband the standing army in 1800. His about-face did little to placate the opposition, while it eroded the president's support within his own party. Hamilton started a campaign to elevate Charles Cotesworth Pinckney to the presidency over Adams. He composed a pamphlet that attacked Adams for his temper and instability.

Part IV: Senator

But Hamilton's plans were blasted from within his own state of New York, where Aaron Burr wrested control of the legislature away from the Federalists. Carroll wrote Hamilton on April 18, 1800, that "we have strange reports circulated among us concerning the prevalence of Jacobinical principles in your State." The legislature could throw all of New York's electoral votes to Jefferson, who "is too theoretical & fanciful a statesman to direct" the American nation. "He might try his experiments, without much inconvenience, in the little Republic of St. Marino, but his fantastic tricks would dissolve this Union." Carroll cited Jefferson's dictum that periodic revolutions were necessary to preserve liberty. "Possibly were he the Chief Magistrate," Carrollton quipped, "he might not wish for a revolution during his presidency."

Ever the gentleman, Carrollton nevertheless took the gloves off when he sensed danger impending. Some Federalists wanted the Maryland General Assembly, not the people, to choose the presidential electors, in order to deprive Jefferson of votes. Carroll approved of this step, foreseeing revolution, anarchy, and military despotism if the Anti-Federalists emerged victorious. On the other hand, Carroll considered Adams, according to McHenry, "totally unfit for the office of President." He praised Hamilton's pamphlet. "Let this console you," McHenry wrote Hamilton, "from one of the wisest, most prudent and best men in the United States."

But Carroll's popularity had waned in the backlash against the Adams administration. John Rutledge warned Hamilton that "Mr. Carroll's influence is great, but I do not believe it will be so operative in the present case as you seemed to imagine." McHenry complained that Carroll did not bother to leave Doughoregan to participate in assembly elections. Perhaps the Signer thought he could accomplish more in the backcountry, for he made a rare visit to Carrollton Manor. The *Republican Advocate* reported that "that hoary-headed aristocrat" had arrived at Carrollton. "Is he, old in iniquity as he is, to be the chief director of the people on the Manor? Citizens of Frederick County, set Charles Carroll at defiance!"

Times had changed. Jefferson won the election. Then, in

1801, the final blow at Carroll's political existence was struck. The assembly abolished property qualifications and established white manhood suffrage. Race was substituted for wealth as the criterion of voting, and free blacks with property were deprived of the franchise they had previously enjoyed in Maryland. Carrollton lost his seat in the Maryland Senate.

All he had worked for seemed to be disappearing. A commonplace incident crystallized Carroll's fears. In late October, Carrollton visited Belvedere, the home of Revolutionary War hero Gen. John Eager Howard. Belvedere was located in what is now the 1000 block of St. Paul Street in downtown Baltimore. Instead of taking a carriage back to Doughoregan Manor, Carroll rode. Richard Caton accompanied him.

The journey was about sixteen miles from Belvedere to the manor, near present-day Ellicott City, Maryland. About three miles before reaching Doughoregan, a storm blew up. Carroll and Caton took refuge in a small cottage.

The woman of the house invited them in, the old-school Southern gentleman and the young English businessman. She was giving supper to her three children. "It consisted of boiled Irish potatoes and milk," Carrollton observed.

The scene crystallized Carroll's fears for the future. "It occurred to me," he wrote, "that in the course of a few years, I might be driven into exile by the prevalence of an execrable faction, and forced to shelter in as poor a hovel the remnant of a life, a considerable part of which had been faithfully devoted to my country's service."

Yet Carroll knew that this humiliation would not mean the end of all his hopes. He told himself that it was well to entertain such thoughts. "They serve to prepare the mind for adversities, and enable us to bear frowns and snubs of Fortune with resignation and fortitude."

"Can the pitiful pleasure resulting from a fine equipage and the gratification of wealth, which the greatest villains may enjoy," Carrollton asked, "be compared with this firm and steady temper of the mind, and its advantages?"

PART V.

Patriarch.

CHARLES CARROLL was not turned out of his home, but he never regained his Senate seat after the democratic revolution of 1800. Of the prominent Federalists, only Chief Justice John Marshall retained the power to oppose Jefferson. With most property qualifications eliminated, the United States Senate became the tool of the ruling party. For this reason, the guardianship of the Constitution passed from the Senate to the Supreme Court, which first enunciated the principle of judicial review in 1803. Carrollton recognized that the Supreme Court was now the only bastion against the demagogues.

RELIGIOUS SEEKING

He also took more notice of the Supreme Being. Like Hamilton, Carroll began to explore religion more deeply after his political fall. Bishop Carroll supplied his cousin with a list of Catholic apologists, to counter the freethinkers in the library at Doughoregan. Carrollton embarked on three years of inquiry, comparing Catholicism with other religions and with atheism. He finally concluded that the claims of the Church were valid.

At first, Carroll embraced religion largely for its social utility. Without religion, "the encouragement of the good, the terror of evil doers, and the consolation of the poor, the miserable, and the distressed," society would collapse. "Remove the hope and dread of future rewards & punishments, [and] the most powerful restraint on wicked actions, & the strongest inducement to virtuous ones is done away."

On this foundation, Carrollton built a solid and attractive piety, based on humility, true devotion, and grace. Late in life he remarked that "on the mercy of my Redeemer I rely for salvation; and on his merits; not on the works I have done in obedience to His precepts."

But when Carroll began sharing his new devotion with his son, Charles Carroll of Homewood, it was a hard sell. Handsome, charming, sensitive, alcoholic, amoral, Homewood had his admirers. John H. B. Latrobe praised Homewood's "noble presence" and "most gracious manner." The heir possessed "the most scholarly acquirements, [was] ready in conversation, full of anecdote and ready at repartee—it was impossible to be in his presence without admiring him." Latrobe compared Homewood to the Prince Regent of England, later George IV.

Carrollton recommended that his son "study the grounds of the Catholic faith." "If the Christian religion be true, it can be but one," the Signer argued. "For if revealed of God, he could not reveal different and inconsistent doctrines and variant: now all the attended reform Churches have varied and departed from the doctrine with which they set out." As Homewood's moral difficulties increased, Carrollton set about reforming him. "Without virtue there can be no happiness," he urged, "and without religion no virtue." To avoid sin, Homewood should "consider yourself as always in the presence of the Almighty."

In 1800, the heir became engaged to Harriet Chew of Philadelphia. Harriet's father, Benjamin Chew, the loyalist chief justice of Pennsylvania, owned the house that the British used as their stronghold during the battle of Germantown. Her older sister Peggy, known for her flirtation with Major André during the British occupation, eventually married the Maryland war hero John Eager Howard. But Harriet Chew had become a beauty in her own right, so much so that Washington supposedly asked her to attend him while he sat for the artist Gilbert Stuart, so that his face would have "its most agreeable expression."

The Chews were Protestant. Carrollton raised no objection to his daughter-in-law's religion, but he insisted on July 3 that the marriage be delayed until he approved the financial settlement. The Signer, who hated hot weather and feared "pestilential fevers," refused to go to Philadelphia for the wedding. Bishop Carroll, however, rushed north to make sure the couple was not married by a Protestant minister. The great "influence and preponderance" of the Carrolls in American Catholicism, the Bishop said, made such an irregularity highly undesirable.

Upon his arrival, Bishop Carroll discovered that the couple expected him to marry them in the morning, while the Episcopal Bishop would wed them again that night, "in a more ceremonious style." John Carroll refused. Although such arrangements were common in England, as a way to make Catholic marriages legal, no such necessity existed in the United States. Mary and Kitty supported Bishop Carroll in his stand, believing that a Protestant ceremony would lead to Homewood's alienation from the Catholic Church.

Homewood House

Bishop Carroll conducted the nuptials on July 17, 1800. Soon afterward, the younger Carroll embarked on his only lasting endeavor. Homewood House, which now stands on the campus of the Johns Hopkins University in Baltimore, is one of the finest Georgian houses in America. The building, with its central hall and two connecting wings, reflects the period's passion for symmetry.

Small by modern standards, the house is exquisite in detail. Intricate handcarving adorns the molding and mantelpieces, which are made of black walnut rather than the more usual pine. Wooden baseboards are carefully painted to resemble marble. All of this is in sharp contrast to Carrollton's urban headquarters on Spa Creek. Although the Annapolis mansion boasted such luxuries as looking glasses, clocks, portraits, and an extensive collection of plate, the building itself is austere. Its lack of decoration is a monument to the Spartan virtue of Carroll of Annapolis.

Harriet's relatives were impressed with the young Carroll's zeal to complete the house. "It is a much handsomer & better house than I could have expected & more done than I could have believed in the time," wrote her parents. "Mr. C. is indefatigable." John Chew described Charles as "a most worthy young fellow, with an honest benevolent heart." He was "a kind affectionate husband, and as well calculated as any young man I ever knew for the enjoyment of domestic happiness."

But as so often happens, Carroll of Homewood's energetic efforts to impress his father had the opposite effect. The fantastic expense of Homewood House did much to sour their relationship. Carrollton initially offered his son ten thousand dollars for the project, to be deducted from his share of the inheritance. By the time the house was completed, forty thousand dollars had vanished, approximately half a million dollars today. This sum does not include the value of the land. And, of course, much of the labor was done by slaves for free. Homewood House was "a most improvident waste of money," Carroll declared, "and which you will have reason, as long as you live, to look back upon with painful regret."

Worse, the young architect alienated his father by lying about expenses. Carrollton would agree to a purchase, only to find out that the actual price was much higher than his son had claimed. A $1,200 coach turned out to cost $1,400, "a monstrous charge." Homewood tried to sneak in various expenses under the category of "improvements," including provisions, a saddle, a gig, and theater tickets.

At first, the elder Carroll was polite. But he erupted when his son billed him £47.7 sterling for books. "If you would really read and acquire useful knowledge by study and reading, this would be money well laid out," the father wrote. But knowing his son, Carrollton was sure that "these books which you have imported without my knowledge...were intended more to decorate your book-case than for you." Finally, in May 1802, the Signer refused to spend another penny on improvements to

Homewood House. The heir had to cut corners, buying pine doors instead of mahogany.

The American Narcissus

While Homewood's project was to build a house, Carrollton's was to rebuild his son's character. And Carroll's zeal, like his son's, backfired. The more the father preached virtue to Homewood, the deeper the heir sank into hopelessness.

Carroll told his son to keep strict accounts. Homewood's body and mind, he said, would become "torpid and diseased, if exercise and study be neglected and disused." When his son was ill, Carrollton prescribed "the refreshing air of the morn." "A person who rises at 8 o'clock only," Carroll lectured, "loses two or 3 hours every day...and these hours thus wasted in drowsiness can never be recalled."

It was good advice, but ill-suited for its recipient. Homewood could no more get up at five a.m. than he could fly across the Atlantic. He had been raised until the age of seven by his drug-addicted mother and ignored by his father. One wonders whether Molly took laudanum during her pregnancy; if so, Homewood's addictive personality is no mystery. In any case, her anxieties, combined with Carrollton's emotional distance and absences, crippled the boy.

A letter of 1807 offers a revealing glimpse into the heir's childhood. "Had your mother lived some years longer," Carrollton wrote his son, "her anxiety and too much care about you would have ruined your constitution." Carroll recalled that a family friend, Dr. Scott, had advised him "to let you run more about and be more exposed to the open air; I followed his advice and in a short time you grew stout and hardy." In other words, it took the intervention of an acquaintance to secure for Charles any semblance of a normal boyhood.

Carroll of Homewood was not the only victim of Revolutionary fathers' absenteeism. John Adams' two alcoholic sons caused the second president much grief. The practical impact of the Revolution in sundering families was only part of a broader revolution in social mores. The formal, ordered world of the Enlightenment gave way to the dominion of sensibility and emotion, much of it contrived.

Something similar happened when commercialism and narcissism followed the hardships of the Great Depression and World War II era. American culture after Yorktown was awash in narcissism. In order to purchase "domestic tranquillity," parents of the revolutionary generation spoiled their children, only to find them ungrateful for their parents' sacrifice. Like many men of his generation, the Signer could not understand why his family was not at peace. He wrote Mary Caton, "how strange that a coolness should subsist between a brother & sisters without any *real* cause for such coolness."

Too late, he tried to undo the example of his and Molly's overprotectiveness. He told his son that there had never been "two more affectionate parents" than Homewood and Harriet, who had seven children between 1801 and 1809. This was a backhanded compliment. The patriarch observed that the couple were "too anxious, too solicitous and too easily alarmed about your children's health." In 1801, Charles Carroll of Doughoregan was born. Carrollton warned his son that if he raised the boy "too tenderly," "you will greatly injure a constitution which is now good."

Carroll saw the same narcissism in his son's management of his slave family. A typical pattern of the narcissistic family, in which parents lose their temper and abuse their spoiled children instead of giving them solid discipline, was repeated on the Homewood plantation. Carrollton cautioned Homewood about a slave called Izadod, who was inclined to drink. His advice proved ineffectual; the heir became enraged and struck Izadod.

Carrollton was disturbed. He told his son "never to strike a servant in anger." Instead, "when your negroes commit a fault deserving punishment, and not to be overlooked," they should receive twenty-five lashes, thirty-nine for a heinous offense. "Correct but seldom," the patriarch advised, "but when you do correct, let not the correction be a trifling one."

This recommendation may be offensive to us. But an orderly

system of rational, predictable punishments was certainly preferable to a cycle of permissiveness followed by random violence. Such a dysfunctional cycle could easily lead to the murder of a slave by an irate master. As a slave owner, Homewood was both permissive and unfeeling. He allowed one Christopher to fornicate with a girl named Harriet, but was known to separate husbands from wives.

The younger Carroll seems to have realized his incompetence to manage a plantation on his own. No sooner was Homewood completed than its master asked his father to build him another house on the Doughoregan lands. Carrollton rejected the proposal. "Two masters on the same estate will never answer," he said. But the son's desire to return to the parental nest was eventually gratified, if only for one month out of the year, by the building of the Folly Farm next to Doughoregan.

Narcissism is a condition in which an infant never fully separates from his mother, whom he sees as omnipotent. The narcissist never develops a sense of himself as an individual, nor does he acquire a realistic view of his parents. Instead of "self" and "other," he sees the world in terms of "good" and "bad." Those who gratify his desires are "good." He becomes enraged with those who do not meet his needs. Because he has no personal boundaries, he has no respect for those of others, and no compassion. His imperial ego seeks to control and annihilate other people.

Narcissism is played out in society through the politics of will. It made itself known in the Carroll family through Homewood's incredible behavior. Richard Caton went bankrupt in 1802. Carrollton decided to give his daughter Mary Caton a $2,500 annuity, to be charged against her portion of the estate. Up to that point, the Catons had received nothing from Carroll except for rents on the properties Caton managed and some gifts.

Carroll of Homewood objected to the Catons' annuity. His father had to remind him that Homewood's annuity of $5,000, unlike the Catons', was not being charged against his estate. It was Homewood's wastefulness in his building program, Carrollton charged, that had caused his financial problems. In any case, few men in Maryland had an annual income of $5,000, about $116,000 in today's money. This may not seem like much, but most planters were land rich and cash poor. And, of course, they produced most of their own food and other necessities.

The heir could see none of this. He expected his father to raid the principal of the estate in order to make further improvements to Homewood House. Carrollton refused. "This would be eating the calf in the cow's belly; I have the interest of my grandchildren too much at heart to persevere in so inconsiderate a course of expenditure." Defeated, Carroll of Homewood finally discharged his workmen in August 1803.

The Education of Women

Homewood's profligacy was, in part, a reaction to his father's parsimonious and controlling personality. Nevertheless, Carrollton must be praised for protecting his daughters' inheritance. He laid down the law when Robert Goodloe Harper, a Federalist Congressman, came courting, burdened with £4,000 in debt. Carroll insisted that "I shall never suffer any part of Kitty's fortune to be applied to the payment of her husband's debts."

Carroll invested Kitty's portion of the estate in land, which brought little revenue, but which guaranteed her something to live on when he died. Harper, a lawyer, was required to have "an *established* practice & income," as well as a house and carriage, before he could marry Kitty. Harper bargained with the patriarch, offering a modest dwelling, a net income of between three and four thousand dollars, and "reasonable certainty of carriage." "I shall never attempt to seduce a daughter from her duty towards her father," Harper wrote indignantly, "nor to thrust myself into a family by the head of which I am repelled."

Carrollton accepted Harper's conditions, provided that Kitty's children would be raised Catholic. Harper ought "to excuse the prudential views disclosed in this writing; they are solely dictated by my affection for a dutiful and beloved child."

Part V: Patriarch

The suitor admitted that "every father ought to entertain" such views. Carroll would later have to hold the line against Harper's requests to turn his wife's lands into ready cash. "Every trifle which can be saved decently, ought to be saved," the Signer counseled, "for a prudent economy is one of the foundations of Independence, & consequently of happiness."

Kitty Harper remained Catholic throughout her life, and Carroll also guided his granddaughters toward the Faith. His letters to them are remarkable for his acknowledgement of their dignity as women. He saw women as persons with souls, rather than objects or decorations, though he by no means sought to suppress their God-given femininity.

Carrollton wrote the fifteen-year-old Mary Ann Caton in 1803 that "piety towards God is the *first* of all duties; without it those acquirements, which adorn the person, & improve the mind, are but frivolous amusements at best, & frequently pernicious." A poet "personified virtue as *female*, plainly intimating it should ever be the attendant of your sex." Carroll treated his granddaughter "not as a child, but as a rational being capable of judging correctly, and desirous of acting rightly."

Mary Ann's sister Louisa, three years younger, also benefited from Carroll's attention and, in her case, correction. He told Louisa that she and her sister would be sent back home from their Annapolis school "if you do not apply, & improve yourselves." Her baby cousin Charles "is in fine health & spirits, but a little fractious, & does not like contradiction; in this respect he resembles a little cousin of his."

But Carroll's favorite granddaughter was Emily Caton, later McTavish. She devoted herself to the patriarch in later years and thus consoled him for his disappointment with Homewood. Carroll was generous with her in return, inspiring jealousy within the family. In paradoxical fashion, Carrollton told Richard Caton "how essential kindness and affection are in the desolate state of age; they cannot be bought, and are entitled to reward."

On one occasion, Emily said to her father, "Alas, my dear Papa, what bad doings there are in this world!" Hearing about this, her grandfather gently chided Emily for her world-weariness at the age of nine. But Carrollton admitted that "you must expect to meet with crosses, & some affliction, which I hope you will have virtue enough to bear with resignation to the will of God."

Burr

It was a different kind of will, narcissistic and imperial, that entered the White House with Jefferson, or "Thomas the great man," as Carrollton called him. With exquisite sensibility, Jefferson called for "harmony and affection" in his first inaugural address. But the 1803 purchase of Louisiana, to Carroll's mind, revealed the darker side of this moral-sense language: the desire for dominion. Montesquieu had warned that large accessions of territory were fatal to republics.

With the Federalist party in disarray, the only political alternative to Jefferson was vice president Aaron Burr. Indeed, as Jefferson's running mate, Burr had come close to being elected president by the House of Representatives in 1801. His coy refusal to rule out the possibility earned him Jefferson's enmity.

Carroll hoped the House would pick Burr. He found the Colonel "not less a hypocrite than Jefferson; but he is a firm, steady man, and possessed, it is said, of great energy and decision." Despite his character flaws, Burr would act assertively on behalf of the nation, while Jefferson could do nothing for fear of offending the states and public opinion. "Thus will the powers of the general government...be benumbed," Carroll predicted, "and gradually usurped by the larger states and so will terminate the Union."

Burr spent the Christmas of 1803 with Carrollton and the Harpers. The vice president and Harper were working together to stop Jefferson's assault on the judiciary. The president wanted a constitutional amendment to allow Congress to remove judges by majority vote. As president of the Senate, Burr chaired the impeachment trial of Judge Pickering for mental incompetence, while Harper served as a defense attorney.

Jefferson's next target on the bench was Samuel Chase. In another stunning metamorphosis, Chase had resurfaced as an arch-Federalist justice of the United States Supreme Court. He incurred Jefferson's wrath by denouncing manhood suffrage and defending the judiciary's independence in a charge to a grand jury. Harper served on Chase's defense team for his Senate trial, which convened in early 1805. Although he had recently killed Alexander Hamilton in the famous duel on the cliffs of Weehawken, New Jersey, Burr still presided over the Senate, and ran the trial with great dignity.

Carroll followed the Chase trial with great interest. He had forgiven his rival for past wrongs. "This day has determined whether a sense of justice has overcome the blindness and bitterness of party zeal in one-third of the judges of Mr. Chase." On March 3, Carroll rejoiced over Chase's acquittal, calling the verdict "a triumph over party spirit."

The Chase trial was Burr's swan song. Although his relations with Jefferson thawed—Carrollton was astonished to hear that "Col. Burr is very intimate at the President's"—Jefferson dropped Burr from the 1804 ticket. In his eloquent farewell to the Senate, Burr called that institution a "sanctuary and a citadel of law, of order, of liberty" against "the storms of popular frenzy and the silent arts of corruption." He predicted that, should the Constitution ever be overthrown, "its expiring agonies will be witnessed on this floor."

Carrollton was summoned one last time by the Maryland Assembly to serve the public. He was named to a committee on the future of Washington and St. John's Colleges. The demagogues in the assembly had tried several times to defund the colleges, saying they were elitist. The colleges fulfilled a necessary role in the young republic and possessed an exalted sense of mission. Washington College's first valedictorian called the school a "temple of virtue and knowledge."

The two Maryland colleges also taught young Catholics the classics as a preparation for seminary, until Bishop Carroll in 1786 founded a specifically Catholic institution, which became Georgetown University. Carrollton supported Georgetown financially. Late in life, he donated land and shares of stock to build St. Charles' Seminary near Doughoregan Manor, asking only that Mass be said for him once a month.

Embargo

The conflict in Europe between Napoleon and the English had Carroll on his guard. The Jefferson administration favored the French, a policy Carrollton expected to produce "anarchy, & civil war." Jefferson's solution to the problem of protecting American shipping from the French and the British was not to trade with anybody. In 1808, the United States placed a general embargo on foreign trade.

Foreseeing "a derangement in the finances of the U.S." and the suspension of interest payments on the national debt, Carrollton retrenched. He refused to enlarge his interest in the Susquehanna Canal Company and tried to pull out of the Baltimore Company, the successor to the Iron Works. His fortune stayed mainly in bonds and other low-risk investments. He continued to lend money, taking six-percent interest and insisting on land as security.

Carrollton had nothing but contempt for the Jeffersonian politics of will. "The Democrats are a servile and timid crew, and to keep themselves in place they would make a treaty with the Devil himself, and would break it." He ridiculed Madison's proposal that American shippers take over the trade between France, Spain, and their colonies. This was asking the British to seize American ships and cargoes. It was "impossible," Carroll said, "for a man tainted with democratic principles to possess an elevated soul and dignified character; in all their actions and in all their schemes and thoughts there is nothing but what is mean, selfish, and snivelling."

Carrollton ordered his employees to support Federalist candidates for the Maryland electoral college. He assured Horatio Ridout that "I will speak to my manager & to my clerk & prevail upon them to vote for you & Col. Mercer, and to obtain as many votes for you both...as their influence & exertions can procure...but all I fear without success." Even the Maryland Senate, which Carroll had created, could no longer be trusted. He hoped one assembly session would be short. "In that case they will not have time to do much mischief; for as to their doing any good, it is out of the question."

It had become critical to stop Napoleon, and the English were the only nation who could do it. In Carroll's opinion, the United States "should make an alliance offensive & defensive" with Great Britain. A combined Anglo-American force should invade and liberate the Spanish colonies in Latin America, cutting off a vital source of Napoleon's income. "Europe must feel its degraded state," Carroll wrote, "and its sovereigns, if possessed of energy & wisdom, and a sense of honor, will endeavour to emancipate themselves from the thralldom of France."

There was no chance that the Jeffersonians would treat with Britain, since "the whole faction from top to bottom detests the English and their Constitution." Before the embargo hit, Congress had passed an act banning all British manufactures. "The general opinion is that the Act will be repealed," Carrollton wrote his new factor, William Murdoch. "On what this opinion is founded, I know not, unless the folly of having passed such an Act."

Jefferson's appeasement of Napoleon would enable the emperor to "impose on us his iron yoke." Should Bonaparte's "universal dominion" be established, "what event more disastrous could happen to the world! What a train of events would overwhelm the human race should the plans of this mighty conqueror be realized!" But Carroll, like Churchill in the years leading up to the Second World War, was a voice crying in the wilderness.

The embargo, which ruined the American economy, was finally lifted in 1809. Nonintercourse with Britain and France was retained. The money lost in the embargo would have been sufficient to protect American shipping worldwide. "A more miserable set of statesmen could not be selected to disgrace our country," Carrollton fumed. But in spite of his hatred of Napoleon, Carroll kept his innate courtesy. He hoped the French vessel *Patriot* would cross the Atlantic safely, since he had befriended several of its officers during their stay in Maryland.

Families Divided

Carrollton continued to urge his son toward "exercise and temperance." Homewood avoided his father's nagging. "I shall be very happy to see my son on Wednesday," the Signer once wrote, "if he will favor me with his company."

As with the Catons, Carroll turned his attention to his grandchildren. Homewood did not obstruct his father's attempts to keep the children Catholic. "Unfortunately though at present he has little religion himself," Carrollton told Harriet, "he is quite in earnest that his daughters should be religious; he and many others under the influence of passions know and feel the importance of religion though they do not live up to its precepts."

Harriet Carroll was still an anxious mother. Carrollton advised her that "over anxiety is hurtful, nay blameable: we should not set our hearts too much on anything in this world." To be fair, Harriet was not the only overprotective parent in the family. Robert Harper showed the same concern for his son Charles Carroll Harper. When Richard Caton wanted to take the little boy out on a sleigh ride, Carrollton had to assure Harper that "he will be warmly wrapped up in blankets."

Soon, though, Carroll's advice to Harriet would be tested when her infant son, Benjamin Chew Carroll, died in 1806. "I much fear that my dear little Ben had quitted this world before your arrival," Carrollton wrote Homewood. "The will of God must be submitted to, bear up with fortitude against this visitation and afford poor Harriet all the comfort you can." He reminded his son that the baby was certainly "enjoying a glorious immortality." "I hope your indispositions proceed solely from sorrow," Carrollton concluded. In other words, he hoped his son had not been drinking.

The child's death created a temporary harmony between father and son. Of course, Carroll's agreeing to advance Homewood an additional thousand dollars per year, to be charged against his estate, probably had something to do with their reconciliation. Carrollton praised his son for bearing a painful operation "with great fortitude," and thanked him for inquiring about his health. Homewood let his father take care of the five-year-old Carroll of Doughoregan for a while. The patriarch notified the parents that the boy walked in his sleep.

Meanwhile, all were diverted by the marriage of Mary Ann Caton to Robert Patterson, in April 1806. Patterson was a Protestant, and Bishop Carroll lamented that "one after the other, all this family drops into the hands of Protestant partners for life, and must in the end lose all attachment to the religion of their forefathers." He was wrong in the case of Mary Ann, who kept her Catholic faith.

Robert Patterson's chief claim to fame was his sister Betsy, also known as Madame Jerome Bonaparte. Betsy Patterson had married the emperor's brother. She was cast aside when Napoleon annulled the marriage by fiat. Nevertheless, she styled her son the King of Westphalia. Her revealing clothes were the scandal of Baltimore. Carrollton wrote in 1804 that "we hear strange reports of Madame Bonaparte's dress on public occasions, I might rather say, *of her no dress*, for if the reports are not much exaggerated, she goes to public assemblies nearly naked."

The rapprochement between Carroll and his son did not last long. Homewood quarreled with Harper over a lawsuit. Harper was representing the family against one Madewell, who sued over property lines. Although Harper had a solid reputation as an attorney, the heir insisted that his father add another lawyer to the suit. He feared that if the Carrolls lost, a flood of similar suits would follow, diminishing his inheritance. Carrollton disagreed, but Homewood hired the extra lawyer anyway, and let his father break the news to Harper.

Not surprisingly, Carroll of Homewood continued to have chilly relations with his sisters. Carrollton told his son that "they have indeed often expressed with strong feelings in my presence their regret for your want of affection for them." Carroll hastened to add that Mary and Kitty were not trying to increase their share of the inheritance by telling him this. The old man increasingly sided with his daughters. Because Homewood was "completely destitute" of the "habit of business, and of method," his income "melts away like snow before a warm sun."

Carroll's slave family also had its difficulties. Carrollton was indicted in January 1811 by "the grand Inquest for the Body of the City of Annapolis" for letting one of his slaves ride up the street in a wagon. It is ironic that Catholic corporatist theory, the political "Body," was used in such a context (see above, p. 199.)

But ironies abounded in Carroll's attitude toward his African-American slaves. His desire to help and improve their lot in life was always balanced by the recognition that they were his property. In July 1811, Harry, a carpenter, asked Carroll to prevent his daughter Flavia from being sold into Georgia. Carrollton had sold Flavia, her husband, Rezin, and their children to a Dr. Mathews. He had stipulated that the family must be allowed to go free if they paid Mathews their purchase price, plus interest and expenses. This was apparently a standing policy of Carroll's. He let two friends of Rezin, Daniel and John, buy their freedom.

But Mathews went bankrupt, so that Carroll never got paid. Furthermore, Rezin defaulted on a contract he had made with Mathews. Rezin was in jail, while Daniel and John risked losing their freedom, which they had offered as security for Rezin's performance of the contract. Carroll intervened, but he was only able, or willing, to help Flavia. He offered to buy her for $140 "merely out of compassion for the woman," though he did not want her. "The children I consider as a mere encumbrance: I would not have them as a gift." It is not clear what happened to Flavia's family.

Carroll showed consideration for his slaves, such as Charity, who was working for one Burgess. Carroll instructed Burgess never to take Charity to Homewood House, fearing perhaps that the heir would molest her. But the patriarch also spoke of his workers casually, in terms that objectified them. If Mrs. Caton still wanted a girl, he wrote, "she shall have the girl Nelly now in the manufactory; she is well grown, & likely."

When some slaves complained about an overseer, Sears, Carrollton admitted that "things are not as they should be." But he promised only to replace Sears at some later date, because he was deficient in "farming and the management of stock." Carroll refused to let the plaintiffs confront Sears directly, fearing such an encounter would lead to "ill treatment of my negroes."

The War of 1812

Carroll had long been convinced that "there is a secret understanding between our government & that of France." The last straw came in 1811, when the Bank of the United States lost its charter, over the objections of Treasury Secretary Albert Gallatin. Carroll took the money he had invested in the Bank and put it into English stock. And not just any stock. He purchased £3,400 worth of English Navy stock, and held on to it even after Congress declared war against Great Britain. Prominent New York bankers were also defying the Madison Administration, which Carroll called "perfidy personified," by sending their dollars to England.

Carroll obviously felt that the British Navy was the only hope of defeating Bonaparte. He let it be known as late as July 1815 that he had no intention of selling the Navy stock. Carrollton "and a large number of others" from Annapolis submitted a futile protest to the United States Senate after the declaration of war.

On June 22, 1812, four days after the declaration of war against Britain, the offices of the anti-war *Federal Republican* newspaper were levelled by a Baltimore mob. Alexander Contee Hanson, the paper's editor, created a private militia, led by Revolutionary War hero General "Light-Horse Harry" Lee, father of five-year-old Robert E. Lee. On July 27, Hanson and his cronies distributed an issue of the *Federal Republican*, then barricaded themselves in a house at 45 Charles Street.

A Republican crowd stormed the stronghold, and one of the demonstrators died. The Federalists surrendered on the morning of the 28th and were taken to jail. That evening, the jailhouse doors were opened to the Republican mob. Hanson, Lee, and the other Federalists were beaten senseless and pitched down the steps of the jail, where they lay in a tangled heap for nearly three hours. Hooligans stuck penknives into their bodies and dripped candle wax into their eyes as they lay helpless.

The only Federalist fatality was General James Maccubin Lingan, a hero of the Maryland Line during the Revolution and a survivor of the hellish British prison ship *Jersey*. As Lingan pleaded to live, a vigilante stomped him to death.

The 1812 Baltimore riot blackened the city's reputation for years to come. The Federalist Party swept the Republicans from office on a wave of public revulsion. A number of leading citizens fled Baltimore until the unrest dissipated. Carrollton briefly considered joining the exodus. He told Homewood that he would depart "if the state of politics does not soon grow better and men be suffered to speak their sentiments on the measures of the present rulers of our country and to take what newspapers they please."

But like his father before him, Carroll withdrew his plan to leave Maryland. When James McHenry, one of the refugees, notified Carroll of his escape from Baltimore's "rogues and riot," Carrollton counseled his friend to return to the city. Poetically, Carroll told McHenry, who had chosen an Appalachian retreat, not to "heave a sigh how politics may end."

> Yet for a time when Science needs thine aid,
> Leave meditation's lonely mountain shade,
> To bears & wolves their gloomy forests give
> And learn that life was given us—to live.

On August 1, 1812, another round of pro-war riots broke out in Baltimore. Carroll met Peggy Chew Howard on the road, fleeing from the city. The patriarch calmed her down and took her to Doughoregan Manor. He notified John Eager Howard of his wife's whereabouts and asked Howard to see that all the Carroll funds in the Bank of Maryland were transferred to Philadelphia.

Carroll was skeptical about the American *casus belli*, the impressment of American seamen and execution of British deserters found on American ships. According to the law of nations, he believed, the British had a right to reclaim their citizens and to punish deserters with death. Carrollton saw war as "a great calamity & having a stronger influence in corrupting the morals of a nation, even than a long peace." Only the "most weighty & just" reasons would justify making war. But Carroll thought Madison's real motive in prosecuting the war was to seize Canada and suppress internal dissent.

In 1813, rumors of Napoleon's death in Russia reached Annapolis. Carroll was dubious, "although no one desires his death more than I do." He hoped that the emperor's captured papers would reveal the Madison administration's collusion with France. News of Bonaparte's first fall from power came in May 1814. Should Napoleon be exiled, Carrollton remarked, "I know of no place in which he could find so kind a reception and protection as under the fostering care of the grateful democracy of this country."

But hard on the heels of this good news came the destruction of Washington by the British. Carroll wrote his son on August 25, 1814, that "the fire at Washington was plainly seen by several of my people about ten o'clock last night." The British burned Washington to retaliate for a similar American raid on York, now Toronto. Otherwise, Carroll noted, "the enemy keep up the strictest discipline and do not suffer their soldiers to plunder."

The English had no interest in continuing the war after Napoleon's fall. Carroll expected the British to offer "just conditions." He was proven right by the 1815 Treaty of Ghent, which restored the *status quo ante bellum*. Looking back on the war, Carroll was despondent. "I say nothing of politics," he wrote, "indeed I hate to think of them, for in viewing the general complexion & temper of these United States, I see nothing to console but much to alarm me for the present & future welfare of my country."

Decline of the Heir

Carroll could have been talking about his son's condition.

Harriet Carroll's sister Sophia visited her in 1812. She hinted to her brother Benjamin Chew, Jr., that something was wrong.

The patriarch had been supporting Harriet, she wrote, and "*exalting in her conduct*—through trials that have been fully *guarded* from public observation as far as possible." In a desperate attempt to divert his son, Carroll permitted Homewood to build the Folly Farm house.

But by the spring of 1813, Harriet could no longer bear her ordeal. With the Signer's approval, she separated from her husband in order to escape what Carroll called "the afflicting scene she has daily witnessed." Homewood's addiction to alcohol would "shorten a miserable life, and that of an affectionate wife." Carrollton begged his son to "call in religion to your aid; never rise or go to bed without humbling yourself in fervent prayer before your God, and crave his all-powerful grace to overcome your vicious and inveterate habit."

Carroll offered to let his son stay at the manor while he struggled with "the habit, which embitters your days." This was generous, but the father undermined his message by letting old resentments creep in. "I shall be glad to see you there," he wrote, "and to have more of your company than you have been accustomed to give me." John Carroll, now an archbishop, also made himself available to the heir for "frequent conversations."

It was all to no avail. Homewood kept up a façade of urbanity and sensibility. He wrote Mary Caton in 1814 that "you are very dear to my heart." But he had to resign his commission in John Eager Howard's militia corps. Soon, Carrollton asked Howard to take over his son's affairs. Howard would receive $4,500 of the annuity, while Richard Caton would hold the other $1,500 for Homewood's immediate needs. The Signer stipulated that when Harriet returned to Philadelphia, she would receive $4,000 in alimony from her husband's annuity.

In February 1814, Homewood agreed to go to a sanitarium called Magotty. By early March, there were signs of improvement. "There is now room for hope," Carrollton wrote, "but not for entire confidence, so great is the difficulty of conquering a rooted habit."

Homewood resumed his responsibilities. But after reviewing some accounts, the elder Carroll realized that his son had relapsed. "I do suspect that you do not know what you are about."

Part V: Patriarch

Homewood was keeping entirely to himself, in order, he claimed, to take care of business. Carrollton asked whether he was indulging his "fatal propensity in secret." If this was the case, "the more you keep out of the view of the world and the less you are observed, pitied, or despised, the better." Bitterly, Carroll declined to sign this letter "your affectionate father," because "your course of life has nearly extinguished my affection."

There was worse to come. Local gossip accused Homewood of worse crimes than drunkenness. Rosalie Stier Calvert reported that the heir "is drunk from morning to evening. He has treated his wife in the most impossible way, beating her almost daily and on one occasion almost strangling her." Mrs. Calvert claimed that, when confronted, Homewood protested that he had inherited his alcoholism from his Darnall grandfather.

We should take this with a grain of salt. Rosalie Calvert was no doubt jealous of the Carrolls' dominance in Maryland society. She treated the whole clan as *nouveau riche* upstarts and referred, falsely, to Elizabeth Brooke Carroll as "a woman of the lowest class." Mrs. Calvert also spread the story of Carrollton's illegitimacy, with fanciful details, and predicted that the Caton girls would marry badly because of their ill breeding.

However, when Carrollton forbade Homewood, in the summer of 1814, to come to the manor unless he were sober, he told Mary Caton that "I will not in any manner be accessory to his brutality." The word could mean simply his alcoholic degradation, or something more. And John Eager Howard spoke of Homewood's total lack of "active affection for any human being, even (I might say) for his very children." Howard expected that insanity would shortly return the heir "to the guardianship of those whose early error it was that they never taught him to walk alone, but turned him, a grown baby, loose into the world."

Homewood rallied in 1815. His father told Charles that June that he was "quite as you should be." Archbishop Carroll promoted a reconciliation with Harriet, as the best means of keeping Homewood sober. But he soon succumbed to temptation. By April 1816, Homewood was drunk again, and all hope of saving the marriage disappeared. With Carrollton's blessing,

Harriet Carroll moved permanently to Philadelphia with her daughters.

The patriarch obtained guardianship of Carroll of Doughoregan, the next heir. He hired a man to oversee Homewood House and its occupant. And he continued to offer his son the hope of forgiveness. Carrollton told Homewood he would come to visit when the heir had been sober for a month. "When reformed you will find me as ever, your affectionate father."

While Carroll had taken pains to provide for his daughters, he wanted to transmit the estate largely intact to Carroll of Doughoregan. Other great fortunes had been divided to the point of disappearing. Carroll's daughters and their husbands resented the old man's policy of primogeniture. Caton thought it "unjust" that the goods and chattels of the various plantations should descend in the male line. In 1812, Kitty Harper demanded diamonds that she believed her father had promised her. Carrollton remembered offering pearls and gave Kitty $1,000 instead.

By late 1813, Carroll had had enough of his family's importunity. He informed Caton and Harper that he would refuse to endorse any of their notes in the future. Carrollton transferred $11,838 worth of previously signed notes to another financier, Robert Oliver. "This measure," he informed Harper, "will save you the disagreeable trouble of frequent renewals." In other words, Oliver, unlike Carroll, would expect the notes to be paid within the stated term. After 1813, the patriarch only endorsed notes for his sons-in-law to purchase property, and then only if they mortgaged the property to him.

In spite of such disputes, Carroll retained his affection for his troublesome family. He told Mary Caton in 1816 that he had no attachment "to the world & its vanities, but to my near & dear connections perhaps too much."

THE THREE GRACES

Amazingly, given his private sorrows and his political alienation, Carrollton maintained his equanimity. Fr. Charles C.

Part V: Patriarch

Pise, a frequent visitor to Carroll's home on Lombard Street in Baltimore, observed that the Signer had no "moroseness, or crabbed impatience. He was neither *querulus*, nor *difficilis*."

During the "Era of Good Feeling" that followed the War of 1812, the public began to notice Carroll. George Ticknor published an account of his 1815 meeting with Carrollton. The Signer still wore gold buckles on his shoes and lace ruffles over his hands and chest, "the fashion, I suppose, of the year '60." Carrollton's "tact and skill in conversation lead him to the subjects most familiar to his hearer; while he is so well read that he appears to have considered each himself." James K. Paulding, in 1816, found the patriarch "sprightly and intelligent in a most extraordinary degree," easily provoked to laughter. "I never saw a finer old fellow."

Carrollton began to receive official invitations. He declined to lay the cornerstone of Baltimore's Washington Monument in 1815, but he praised "the moral, civil, and military virtues of that illustrious man." Carroll was somewhat mollified with the administration when the Bank of the United States was reestablished in 1816. He invested a large portion of his monied estate in the new national bank. After Napoleon's final defeat, Carroll sold his British Navy stock.

The Signer made Baltimore his new urban headquarters. It was said that he moved from Annapolis because of high taxes. This is not implausible, from the man who was known to remove the wheels from his coaches in order to avoid Hamilton's coach excise. But Carroll's main motivation for the move was probably his business concerns. Baltimore had become a major center of commerce. Basil Hall quoted Carrollton as saying that "Baltimore, which now contains seventy thousand inhabitants, was a village of only seven houses within his memory."

Carroll's grandchildren helped console him for the selfishness of his children. "The liberal heart of my dearest Grandfather is ever ready to relieve the unfortunate," Emily Caton wrote. "I know that you are charity itself." The pious Mary Diana Harper, who attended St. Elizabeth Seton's Emmitsburg school before her early death, thanked God "for preserving us such a good Grandpapa."

After the war ended, Mary Ann Patterson, with her sisters Betsy and Louisa Caton, went to England. They achieved stunning success in English society, becoming known as the "Three American Graces." Supposedly, when Mary Ann was presented to King William IV, a bystander asked, "Do you come from that part of America, where they 'guess' and where they 'calculate'?" (Referring, I guess, to the American habit of saying "I guess.") The monarch put in that Mary Ann "comes from where they 'fascinate.'"

Carrollton corresponded with Col. Sir Felton Bathurst Hervey, who had written him a lengthy account of Waterloo. Hervey was a close associate of the Duke of Wellington, the victor of that battle. Wellington became the Graces' chief sponsor in England. He lent his house for the wedding of Louisa Caton to Hervey on March 1, 1817. Widowed in 1819, Louisa later married the Duke of Leeds.

Mary Ann conquered the heart of Wellington himself. Her jealous sister-in-law, Betsy Patterson Bonaparte, told a friend that "you would be surprised if you knew how great a fool she [Mary Ann] is, and at the power she exercises over the Duke." Another socialite wrote that Louisa Caton Hervey had become fashionable "because the Duke of Wellington is in love with Mrs. Patterson." Wellington even consented to show the Caton sisters around the Waterloo battlefield, a rare occurrence. Afterwards, Mary Ann regretted the tour. She wrote that the Duke had displayed "mental anguish" at the scene of the battle.

Carrollton was delighted with his granddaughters' success, especially their connection with Wellington, whom he admired. But he qualified his approval, saying that to him the life of high society "appears incompatible with real happiness; for that depends on the love of God, [and] a good conscience." Carroll told Betsy Caton that "the continued round of amusements and dissipation" worked against "those duties which we owe to society, to the stations of life we fill, and to those with whom we are intimately connected." Betsy, too, married into the aristocracy, becoming Lady Stafford.

Part V: Patriarch

Two Grandsons

Carroll also, naturally, devoted much attention to the upbringing of his grandsons. Only two lived long enough to make their mark in the world: Carroll of Doughoregan and Charles Carroll Harper. Carrollton was determined that neither of them would follow in the footsteps of his son. Indeed, Homewood's example seems to have scared both of the boys away from vice. An 1806 letter of Carrollton's unwittingly supplies an apt image for the Carroll generations. "These cold bleak winds, I fear, have blasted the forward buds of the fruit trees," he wrote, "but may be the means of preserving those which were not so forward and expanded."

Carrollton kept his grandsons on a tight leash, even when they were away at college. He thought about enrolling them in Harvard, but the vacations were "too many & too long." After the restoration of the Bourbon monarchy, Carroll decided to send the boys to Europe. First, however, he inquired whether the "morals of youth" were "strictly attended to in the College of Paris? This is a most material consideration."

The new heir was a handsome but diffident youth who died serving the Confederacy as a colonel. Few of his letters have been preserved. In contrast, his cousin Charles Carroll Harper was a dynamo. Carrollton thought his Harper namesake showed "decision & energy." Charles Harper was probably the most hearty and "American" of the family. He objected to European education, because expatriates come home "full of 'His Majesty,' his Lordship and her Ladyship, the which sounds very badly in the ears of an American." Harper offended his schoolmates and professors by hoping for revolutions against European monarchs.

Carrollton allowed the boys to tour the French countryside during their vacations, but he hustled them out of Paris as soon as they had completed their course of study in 1820. Should they miss the boat from Le Havre, they were to proceed directly to Liverpool, avoiding London. All this, presumably, to protect them from urban vice. Carrollton made it clear that Carroll of Doughoregan would retain his affection only "if by good conduct, you should merit it." "The inheritance will never be yours," the old man warned his grandson, "unless you render yourself deserving of it."

Carroll used the power of the purse strings to control his grandsons when they were away from Maryland. Upon their return from Europe, Carrollton sent them both to Harvard. But he pinched them so much on their journey that they had to borrow $100 from Archibald Gracie, of Gracie Mansion in New York, for traveling expenses. Carroll's children were used to such tactics. When Robert and Kitty Harper wanted to prolong a European jaunt, the patriarch speedily brought them back by cutting off their funds.

Part of this parsimony was motivated by Carrollton's concern for the common good of society. He paid for his grandsons' education, he told them, "to fit you both for the station you may hereafter occupy." Carroll was capable of generosity when he believed the recipient was "industrious and good." Ann Hollyoke wrote in 1826 that she had "often experienced the blessings of your liberal hand." But instead of giving money away, Carrollton preferred to invest in public works that would give others a livelihood. Thus, he declined John Weems' 1827 loan request, since he had just subscribed $30,000 to the Baltimore & Ohio Railroad.

As a creditor, Carrollton was occasionally severe, but not merciless. He responded curtly to a widow who had stopped by to ask for a forbearance, asking her to name a date when her debt would be discharged or face a lawsuit. On the other hand, when William Darne pleaded for an extension after a poor harvest, Carroll obliged. "Be not discouraged," he counseled Darne. "The succeeding year may produce better crops & prices." The patriarch saved his anger for those who tried to take advantage of him, such as Rembrandt Peale, who mortgaged the Baltimore Museum to someone else when Carroll already held the mortgage.

SLAVERY QUESTIONS

Carrollton used the same mixture of patience and firmness in his plantation management. He saw the necessity of discipline on his plantations, to protect the more vulnerable among his "family." When Moses "behaved outrageously and without the least provocation to Tom," Carrollton ordered an investigation. Moses would receive fifteen lashes if the story turned out to be true. In 1825, Ben received a whipping "for telling me a gross falsehood."

Carrollton never punished without solid evidence of wrongdoing, and he rewarded slaves for good conduct. He promoted Moses to a position of responsibility. "It is a proof of confidence placed in his good conduct & integrity." Carroll advised an overseer to bear with Patience, who "is old and of a passionate temper." "When we reflect on the evils resulting from slavery," he wrote, "and that slaves are subject to passions as well as ourselves, the instruction & patience of a Christian should learn how to excuse and to forgive."

Carroll tried to prepare his slaves for a general manumission, should the state take such a measure. He forbade nighttime dances and the drunkenness that attended them. According to Richard Caton, Carrollton appointed teachers to instruct the slave children daily in the catechism and Christian morality. The patriarch dreaded the consequences, Caton said, of "letting loose on society a race of beings, who, nine out of ten are incapable of providing for themselves."

Carrollton quickly grew weary of the debate over the Missouri Compromise, which raged in 1820. Focusing on the extension of slavery simply postponed the major question, when and how to get rid of slavery entirely. Missouri kept Congress from dealing with other important issues, such as bankruptcy regulation, reform of western land sales, and elimination of corruption in government. "Why keep alive the question of slavery?" Carroll asked. "It is admitted by all to be a great evil, let an effectual mode of getting rid of it be pointed out, or let the question sleep for ever."

In the absence of a plan for gradual manumission, Carrollton saw no alternative but African colonization. Encouraged by Harper, Carroll joined the American Colonization Society. Other supporters of the Society were Madison, James Monroe, and Henry Clay. In 1830, Carrollton was elected its president.

He thus incurred the wrath of William Lloyd Garrison, who deplored the fact that the slaveholding Carroll was "lauded beyond measure as a patriot, a philanthropist, and a Christian!"

For his part, the patriarch had a clear conscience. When a mill burned in a suspicious manner, he declared that "I have injured no one, and I am at a loss to account why any one should be my enemy." Carroll had a good relationship with his slaves, partly because he kept close track of his overseers' doings. When it came to money, the octogenarian Carroll had an extraordinary memory. He pored over his employees' accounts, questioning charges such as $2.50 for removing a dead horse. He remembered the debt a butcher owed him for some sheep, twelve months after the fact.

Carrollton still had a keen eye for the weather and how it would affect his crops. He offered homely advice, requesting that cider be bottled only on a cool, clear day, with the wind in the northwest. Hogs were not to be slaughtered until the decrease of the moon. Carroll used "nox vomica," "oil of Rhodium," and musk to kill pests. As age began to overtake him, he grew philosophical about his memory lapses. A receipt he mislaid "will be found some day, when it is not looked for, and I will then return it to you."

Manifest Destiny

Other men's fortunes eclipsed Carroll's during his lifetime because of his conservative investment strategy. The patriarch was fascinated with Stephen Girard's $10,000,000 nest egg. "A great deal of money in one man's life," he would say.

Though Carroll invested cautiously, his business instincts were by no means sentimental or old fashioned. The Potomac Company transformed itself into the Chesapeake & Ohio Canal Company, with the goal of connecting the Potomac and the Ohio by water. Carroll thought such a canal would be pointless. "A railroad from the great falls on the Potomac" would fill the same need. Instead, the Chesapeake & Ohio Company should get into hydropower, constructing mills along the Potomac.

Part V: Patriarch

The Signer threw all his prestige behind the Baltimore and Ohio Railroad, or B&O. At age ninety, he chaired a committee to petition the assembly on behalf of the railroad, and then he served on its board of directors. The project fit Carrollton's political ideas as well as his business interests. He thought government should support private projects that promoted the common good, without creating bureaucratic programs. With the railroad, Carroll believed, Baltimore would become "one of the largest and most commercial cities in the United States" within fifty years.

Baltimore was in a "fever of excitement," John H. B. Latrobe recorded, as the Fourth of July, 1828, approached. The laying of the cornerstone for the B&O Railroad was scheduled for that day. Carroll presided at the ceremony. Two young men dressed as Mercury handed out copies of the Declaration of Independence, while a band played the "Carrollton March." Execrable poetry was composed for the occasion:

> Then swear to be just, while a Carroll remains
> To gaze on the giant that broke from his chains!

John B. Morris spoke on the patriarch's behalf. Morris claimed that, among the "proudest act[s] of his life," Carroll ranked the laying of the cornerstone second only to his signing of the Declaration. The B&O, Morris said, "is to perpetuate the union of the American States, to make the east and the west as one household in the facilities of intercourse and the feelings of mutual affection." Appropriately enough, after this moral-sense rhetoric, the cornerstone was laid with Masonic ritual.

Where did the Church fit into the new America? Catholicism in America was veering toward orthodoxy. In 1822, Carrollton supported Bishop Conwell of Philadelphia against the schismatic Fr. Hogan. He received in his home the fathers of the 1829 Provincial Council of Baltimore, which outlawed lay control of parishes in the United States.

But while the Church became more hierarchical, it remained engaged with the American political experiment. Carroll told the council fathers that he rejoiced "to see that the Church which he loved was so visibly keeping pace with the rapid movements of the country." Speaking to Congress in 1826, Bishop John England used Carrollton to prove that the Church was truly American. "It is again urged that at least our Church is aristocratic, if not despotic, in its principles," England observed. "Men who make these assertions cannot have read our Declaration of Independence."

Carrollton's later pronouncements on the issue of Church and state emphasize charity. In them, one hears the voice of the second Lord Baltimore. Carroll wrote in 1827 that "to obtain religious, as well as civil liberty, I entered zealously into the Revolution." He hoped "that all believing in the religion of Christ may practice the leading principle of charity, the basis of every virtue."

During Carroll's life, the campaign to integrate the Church and the American system proved successful. Shortly after Carroll's death, Charles Constantine Pise was selected as a congressional chaplain. Carroll told Pise that of all the blessings he had enjoyed during his long life, "what I now look back on, with greatest satisfaction to myself, is that I have practised the duties of my religion."

Carroll did support the Church materially. He gave land adjacent to his Annapolis mansion for the building of St. Mary's Church and made a significant contribution to the Baltimore Cathedral. Carrollton also funded orphanages and contributed to a school for the education of poor children. He balked, however, when Robert Harper asked him to donate land to the Trappists. Carroll drolly suggested that the monks might like some of Kitty's dowry land.

Family Tragedy and Triumph

The tragedy of Carroll's son was reaching its conclusion. Occasionally the master of Homewood would bestir himself and resolve, as he told Harper in 1821, to resume his "station in society." "From a libertine like St. Augustine, I may be too made a Saint at last!" Homewood told Harper. "I have serious thoughts of going to mass every Sunday, unless the weather should prove too damp, or too cold."

This was hardly a recipe for sainthood, and Homewood continued to sink. Carrollton seemed to have made peace with the situation; he returned to signing his letters "Your Affectionate Father." In 1823, Carroll judged Homewood unfit to see his daughters, yet invited the heir to visit the manor. "He knows he is always welcome at my house, and his residence in it with me will restrain that fatal propensity, which his seclusion at Homewood encourages."

In 1824, Carrollton ordered his steward never to grant his son any cash. Meanwhile, the family suffered a blow when Robert Goodloe Harper died suddenly after breakfast, on January 14, 1825. "I have lost a son-in-law whom I loved & esteemed," Carroll mourned. Soon afterwards, Carroll of Homewood was forcibly removed to Emmitsburg.

The end came in April. "My Dear Harriet," Carroll wrote on April 12, 1825, "Your son has informed you of the death of his Father, and I presume that he expressed anguish and repentance for the life he led; the course of which both of us have more cause to lament than his end. He has appeared before a judge, the Searcher of Hearts, and most merciful; let us pray that he has found mercy at that dread Tribunal."

Perhaps Carrollton searched his own soul and asked mercy for his failings as a father. John Eager Howard's comments were just. Carroll had given his children no discipline, because of his frequent absences. His emotional reserve deprived them of affirmation. Carroll compensated by exerting tight control over his son's affairs as an adult. As a result, Homewood never became a man in his own right. When confronted by adversity, he had no inner resources, and he gave way to despair.

This is not to say that Homewood bore no blame. He might have resisted his father's domination, but he was too attached to the prospect of an inheritance. Or he might have forgiven Carrollton for his defects as a father and done the best he could with what he had been given. But deprived of the sacraments and alienated from religion, Homewood had little incentive to leave his resentments behind. He ignored his father's advice to humble himself before the only Power that could save him. Carrollton himself had accomplished much, in spite of his difficult youth, by humbly asking God for the grace to fulfill his role as a man in society.

Carrollton buried his son, not in the chapel at Doughoregan, but in the family graveyard a few miles from Annapolis. He continued to pay Harriet $3,500 annually. Gratefully, Harriet offered to return to Maryland if her father-in-law wished. Carroll recommended that she remain in Philadelphia, where her daughters would have a better chance of making good marriages.

The patriarch made sure his new heir got the message. He warned Carroll of Doughoregan "that in this republic personal merit alone gives consideration and weight of character." Perceiving "a want of steadiness and reflection" in Doughoregan, Carrollton refused to give him any rope with which to hang himself. He put the heir on a $2,500 annual allowance. "I cannot increase it," said Carroll, "and if I could, I would not."

One of the Carroll family's greatest triumphs, however, took place just after its worst disaster. The Marquis of Wellesley was the Duke of Wellington's brother. Back in 1807, Carroll had spoken of the Marquis as the only man who could organize an opposition to Napoleon. Now he was governor-general of Ireland, with viceregal rank, and he fell in love with Mary Ann Patterson, a widow since 1822.

The Duke of Wellington tried to dissuade Mary Ann from marrying his brother, whom he called "totally ruined," "violent," "jealous," and "profligate." Betsy Patterson Bonaparte felt she had been trumped by her sister-in-law. "I married the brother of Napoleon, the conqueror of Europe," wrote Mrs. Bonaparte. "Mary has married the brother of Napoleon's conqueror."

An eight-page prenuptial agreement was signed on October 28, 1825, and the ceremony took place a few days later. Two ceremonies, in fact. The Anglican primate of Ireland married the couple. Afterwards "their Excellencies" excused themselves and showed no signs of returning, whereupon the bishop took the hint and departed. On his way out he met the Catholic archbishop of Dublin, Dr. Murray, who had come to perform a Roman Catholic ceremony. King George IV was outraged at the celebration of Mass in the viceregal home. "That house is as much my palace as the one in which I am," blustered the monarch, who was secretly married to the Roman Catholic Maria Fitzherbert, "and in my palace Mass shall not be heard."

The new Marchioness' Irish ancestry pleased her subjects, as did her strict observance of the Catholic faith. The viceregal couple wore crowns on occasion. Bishop England had this in mind when he toasted Carrollton: "in the land from which his grandfather fled in terror, his granddaughter now reigns a queen." Lady Wellesley made one small adjustment to suit her new image, changing her given name to "Marianne."

Carrollton wrote the Marquis an elegant letter. "The partiality of the Marchioness has, I perceive, impressed you with a favourable opinion of my character," he remarked. "I wish I was really deserving of it, and of your esteem; from all accounts of your character, there is no one whose esteem I more covet and would endeavour to gain." But Carroll realized that he would never have the pleasure of meeting Wellesley or seeing his granddaughter again. He told her that their separation was part of the "mixture of good and evil in this world, which all must experience, wisely ordained to wean our affections from it."

On a more down-to-earth note, Carrollton asked the Marchioness to draw no more money on his account. But he made an exception in 1830, when the former Mrs. Patterson was appointed first lady-in-waiting to the new Queen, Adelaide. This coup triggered a check for ten thousand dollars.

Carroll was not so dazzled by aristocracy that he forgot his political convictions. He objected to Wellington's Irish policy, which kept "a large portion of the population of the empire in a state of distrust and degradation." The Marquis of Wellesley agreed and notified Carrollton in 1829 that "the perverted policy, so long pursued towards Ireland, seems expiring in its own weakness." Wellington, stifling his personal opinion, forced Catholic emancipation through Parliament that year for political reasons.

John H. B. Latrobe

Carrollton was pleased with the success of the Three Graces, but his favorite granddaughter remained Emily McTavish, their unglamorous younger sister. Carroll's preference for Emily would lead to the first major family quarrel after Homewood's demise.

The patriarch petitioned the House of Delegates in 1825 to name Emily's husband, John McTavish, one of his executors. The delegates refused. The furious Signer wrote Carroll of Doughoregan that "I consider myself a fitter judge whom to appoint my executor than the House of Delegates." He added ominously that "it has been whispered that I ought to appoint one of my grandsons or both of them; be assured that neither will be appointed."

Undaunted, Carrollton hired Latrobe to draft a codicil to his will, which his other lawyer, Roger Taney, had drafted. He gave the McTavishes a thousand acres of the Folly Farm. Carroll of Doughoregan challenged the bequest on the grounds that his grandfather was senile. Carrollton then offered his heir five thousand additional acres, on condition that Harriet Carroll give up her dowry rights. Doughoregan asked for a deed to the land, which Carroll granted, stipulating that the deed would take effect only after his death.

Latrobe took pains to prove that the old man was still mentally competent. Although his memory of "recent events was almost wholly gone," Carrollton still spoke "clearly and understandingly" on topics of interest. The Signer told Latrobe "that he hoped his mind would be preserved as long as he lived—he would not wish to live a moment longer."

John H. B. Latrobe was an innocent bystander, but being drawn into the Carrolls' family quarrels would profoundly affect his life. He was the son of Benjamin Henry Latrobe, the architect whose Basilica of the Assumption in Baltimore is a masterpiece of American architecture in the classical style. The younger Latrobe studied law in Robert Goodloe Harper's office. He and Charles Carroll Harper became inseparable. Latrobe thought of Carrollton's grandson as a "very dear brother." He was "on the footing of a relative" with the Carrolls.

The young lawyer first met Carrollton when the old man was eighty-six. His verbal portrait of the patriarch is more realistic than some others. Carroll was "weak and emaciated, his voice thin and feeble." But he moved quickly and listened eagerly to all that was said. Latrobe saw the Signer as "a shadow from past days, when manner was cultivated as essential to a gentleman." He wrote with trembling hand, but always signed his name "Charles Carroll of Carrollton."

Carroll's view of himself, interestingly enough, agrees with Latrobe's. He did not credit the flattery of those who portrayed him as the picture of vitality. His aspect, which "partial friends thought intelligent and expressive, has lost whatever lustre it once might have had. A Mr. Harding has lately drawn my portrait, a most striking likeness of me in the ninety-first year of my life, a countenance with little meaning, the eyes dim and dull." Nor was Latrobe blind to Carroll's petty faults, as when the old man sent out of the house for change rather than overpay the lawyer by a few cents.

Latrobe's intimacy with the Carrolls changed suddenly when he drew up Codicil 3 to the patriarch's will. The codicil stated that anyone who questioned the will's validity would lose his inheritance. This provision sent Charles Carroll Harper's wife, Charlotte, into such a fury that she insisted her husband cut off all relations with the lawyer. Latrobe was devastated. Years later, he wrote that no man had ever filled Harper's place in his affections. "There are women who desire that their husbands concentrate all their affection on themselves," Latrobe wrote. "I think Mrs. Charles Harper was such a woman." Charlotte Harper would soon share Latrobe's grief; her husband died in 1837, ending a promising career.

Latrobe did more than anyone else to encourage the growing Carrollton cult. His 1826 biographical sketch in Sanderson's compendium of the lives of the signers of the Declaration increased Carroll's celebrity. The patriarch read the biography. "Well, Mr. Latrobe," he remarked, "you have certainly made me out a much greater man than I fancied myself to be; and yet, really, I hardly think that the facts you have stated are otherwise than strictly true." Of course, this is Latrobe's account of their conversation.

Rehabilitation

In 1818, it seemed unlikely that Carrollton would become an icon. Carroll referred in that year to his "little influence" with the legislature and canceled two newspaper subscriptions, saying he had "lost all relish for news & politics."

By 1820, his political rehabilitation had begun. The Signer was asked to carry a copy of the Declaration in a procession to the Washington Monument in Baltimore. Soon politicians were jockeying for his endorsement. John Quincy Adams was disappointed when the Signer's vote went to Andrew Jackson in 1824. Carrollton believed that the junior Adams, who had split with the Federalist Party, would retaliate against the Federalists for rejecting him. "I regretted much that Mr. Carroll, for whose character I entertained a profound veneration," Adams told his diary, "should harbor such opinions of me."

Jackson won the popular vote in 1824 but took only a plurality, not a majority, of the electoral votes. The election was thrown into the House of Representatives. When the House elevated Adams to the presidency, rumors of a corrupt deal with House Speaker Henry Clay were widespread. Clay wound up as Secretary of State. The disputed election turned Jackson's campaign into a populist crusade, as he geared up for the 1828 contest.

Carrollton's support for Jackson resembles his former flirtation with Aaron Burr. Indeed, the Tennessean had spoken on Burr's behalf when Burr was accused of treason in 1807. Like Burr, Old Hickory was a spokesman for the popular will, not for the states.

Carrollton agreed with Jackson's emphasis on the good of the whole nation, as opposed to states' rights. The Anti-Federalists had feared the national government would destroy the autonomy of the states, Carroll recalled in 1826. "I wish to God the very reverse may not happen. I already discover the seeds of such an event." Of course, the Signer wanted the states, as well as the central government, to retain their legitimate prerogatives. "Both must be preserved to ensure the continuance of Liberty in the spirit of the Constitutions of both."

But Carroll soon caught on to the general, who perfected the politics of popular will. Andrew Burstein says that Jackson melded "sentiment and power" into an "ideology of benevolent aggressiveness," which still endures. Witness his semiprivate war against the Native Americans of Florida, the first in a long series of imperialistic American conquests. Old Hickory represents the triumph of individual rights, especially the "pursuit of happiness," over the common good. With Jackson, an individualistic interpretation of natural law, in the moral-sense tradition, definitively replaced the Christian concept.

After the Supreme Court overturned an illegal seizure of Native American land, President Jackson declared that "John Marshall has made his decision; now let him enforce it." Jackson also vetoed a bill renewing the charter of the Bank of the United States. The destruction of the Bank, as Alasdair MacIntyre points out, was done in the name of radical democracy. But as a result, Jackson "unleashed the power of money on that democracy." Ignoring authentic human rights and the common good, the general made the abuses of nineteenth-century industrial capitalism possible.

Carrollton distanced himself from Jackson in 1828. He told *Niles' Weekly Register* that "of course I give no opinion which of the candidates should be the choice of the people." He hoped only "that it may fall on him whose measures will be solely directed to the public good." Carroll emphasized more and more the need for government to promote public morality. "What government, the principal object of which should be the preservation of morals, can subsist amid their general corruption?" He continued to extol Washington's virtues, and to recommend the first president's farewell address as a textbook on good government.

August 2, 1826

Carroll's newfound celebrity gave him opportunities to express these ideas. In October 1824, the Signer played a prominent role in the welcome given to General Lafayette on his return to Maryland. The tent of Washington was erected at Fort McHenry. Carroll rode with Lafayette and John Eager Howard from the fort to Baltimore.

But it was the strange event of July 4, 1826, which assured Carroll's importance. On the fiftieth anniversary of the Declaration of Independence, not only its author, Jefferson, but his fellow signer John Adams died. The news that two of the three surviving signers, two of the first three presidents, had died on the fiftieth Independence Day spread to every American town. Carrollton served as the chief mourner at a Baltimore ceremony commemorating the two "praised & dispraised Presidents." "Their services should be remembered," Carroll commented, "and their errors forgotten & forgiven."

Considerable anxiety surrounded the progress of the American experiment. Thus, the nation was eager to adopt the amazing coincidence as a sign of divine favor. Speaking to a gathering at Boston's Faneuil Hall on August 2, 1826, the fiftieth anniversary of the Declaration's signing, Daniel Webster capitalized on this mood. "As their lives themselves were the gifts of Providence," Webster orated, "who is not willing to recognize in their happy termination...proofs that our country and its benefactors are objects of His care?"

Webster seized the opportunity to offer a moral-sense version of American history. True to his roots in the New Light movement, he employed the image of light. "A superior and commanding human intellect," Webster stated, has "power to enkindle the common mass of human kind; so that when it glimmers in its own decay, and finally goes out in death, no night follows, but it leaves the world all light, all on fire, from the potent contact of its own spirit." This metaphor had been employed, as we have seen, since the founding of the republican empire.

With a certain condescension, Webster paused to speak of the only remaining signer. "He seems an aged oak, standing alone on the plain," declaimed the orator. "Venerable object! We delight to gather round its trunk, while yet it stands, and to dwell beneath its shadow." Webster speculated on the "interesting reflections" within Carrollton's "elevated and devout soul." "If he glance at the future, how does the prospect of his country's advancement almost bewilder his weakened conception! Fortunate, distinguished patriot! Interesting relic of the past!"

Webster's choice of the word *relic* is significant. Only the Catholic Church's defense of concrete reality, epitomized in the veneration of relics, stood in opposition to the transcendental world-spirit which Webster was preaching. "It cannot be denied," he declared, "but by those who dispute against the sun, that with America, and in America, a new era commences in human affairs." The United States was more than a nation-state or a place. It was an idea, "inseparably connected, fast bound up" with the concepts of representative government, religious liberty, free inquiry, and the spread of knowledge.

To close, Webster sketched a divine sound and light show, starring Washington, Adams, and Jefferson as points of light in the new creation. "Washington is in the clear, upper sky. These other stars have now joined the American constellation; they circle round their centre, and the heavens beam with new light."

Meanwhile, the man who stubbornly refused to join this celestial pageant sat down to write. Showing no sign of a "weakened conception," and in his own hand, he drafted a statement to commemorate the day of the signing.

Carrollton first thanked God "for the blessings which, through Jesus Christ our Lord, he has conferred on my beloved country in her emancipation, and upon myself." He recommended "the principle of that important document," the Declaration, "as the best earthly inheritance their ancestors could bequeath to them; and pray[ed] that the civil and religious liberties they have secured to my country may be perpetuated to the remotest posterity and extended to the whole family of man."

DEMOCRACY IN AMERICA

Carrollton was now, in the words of John Quincy Adams, "the last surviving signer of the Great Charter of Mankind." The *National Journal* gushed that "every expression, every fragment of a phrase from such a man, is now of inestimable value." A United States senator remembered in 1903 that, during his boyhood, "the schoolboy used to be asked the question in the school, to name the only man living of that illustrious band."

Webster's astronomical cliché got a good workout in newspapers and speeches. Rev. P. C. Hay: "that bright constellation, the light of which has shone upon the world for fifty years, is now reduced to a single star, whose beams feebly twinkle on the horizon, and soon will be seen no more." C. D. Arfvedson: "His star continued bright after all the others had set, and the rising generation looked up to it with an almost religious veneration."

Carrollton's home on Lombard Street in Baltimore became a place of pilgrimage. Josiah Quincy came in 1826 and was amazed when "this very active patriarch...started from his chair, ran down the stairs before me, and opened the front door." Quincy apologized for having inspired such exertion. "Exertion!" Carroll exclaimed. "What do you take me for? I have ridden sixteen miles on horseback this morning, and am good for as much more this afternoon."

He again pulled the staircase trick on the British actor Macready, joking that "I shall never see you again, and so I will see the last of you!" Macready said that "in my life's experience I have never met with a more finished gentleman." Behind his urbanity, the attentive guest could glimpse the Signer's private sorrow. America would be great, Carroll told Macready, "if not marred by faction and the vice of intemperance in the use of ardent spirits."

People were fascinated with Carrollton's personal habits.

They never failed to remark on his daybreak plunge into a cold bath. Guests observed that Carroll drank madeira, champagne, and claret, but that he always left the table hungry, his secret of health. He continued to read the classics, especially Horace, but also purchased a set of Franklin's works.

Carrollton good-naturedly offered himself as the guinea pig for new inventions. The "friction wheel" moved him a great distance by means of a tiny weight attached to a pulley. The famous chess-playing automaton let Carroll win. He was elected to societies, such as the New-York Historical Society. Numerous gifts came: an "American Box" made of native trees, a beaver hat from the Philadelphia hatters. A newspaper, the *Carrolltonian*, bore his name. Carroll told Mary Caton that "I am too deeply impressed with the knowledge of my own defects to be elated by the praises bestowed on me in the public prints." But he sent the paper $50 anyway.

Of course, Carrollton participated in Fourth of July ceremonies. Parades typically wound past his Lombard Street mansion, and Carroll reviewed them from the porch. It is strange today to visit the sturdy, unpretentious red brick house that was once the focal point of public celebrations in Baltimore. Its windows are shuttered, the door locked. Nearby, curtains blow out of the broken windows of an abandoned housing project, a testament to the effects of the politics of will.

The most significant visitor to Lombard Street, perhaps, was Alexis de Tocqueville, who came in late 1831. He wrote down his lengthy exchange with Latrobe, an analysis of the transformation of Maryland into a democracy, which could be quoted in its entirety. A record remains of Tocqueville's meeting with Carrollton. "A mere Democracy is but a mob," Carroll told the Frenchman. Of all forms of government, constitutional monarchy "is the only one suitable for you; if we tolerate ours, that is because every year we can push our innovators out west."

Tocqueville's encounter with Carrollton started a train of thought that influenced his conclusions about American democracy. Carroll was "just like a European gentleman," Tocqueville recorded. But this type of Southern planter "is disappearing now after having provided America with her greatest spirits.

With them the tradition of cultivated manners is lost; the people is becoming enlightened, attainments spread, and a middling ability becomes common. The striking talents, the great characters, are rare." He wondered what had caused this change. "I do not yet see clearly."

Last of the Romans

Doubt settled over the nation during 1832. The future was uncertain, as South Carolina debated whether it had the power to nullify federal laws. Henry Clay's National Republican party confronted Jacksonian Democrats in a bitter presidential campaign. Carrollton was the last living symbol of national unity. It was as if the entire people expected, and dreaded, Carroll's death.

Just that June, he had finally turned over his affairs to McTavish, Caton, and Carroll of Doughoregan. Carrollton declined to officiate at the centennial celebration of George Washington's birth, pleading that "I should be afraid of exposure to a cold air." The centennial procession passed down Lombard Street, heads bared.

Carroll seemed to give Clay his blessing when he received National Republican youths at his home. Their spokesman trotted out the celestial metaphor. Among the "galaxy of talent" in the Continental Congress, "no star burned with a more intense, yet mild and steady luster than that which we contemplate, still bright, descending in the horizon of freedom, and shedding its benignant luster on admiring millions."

As winter approached, Fr. Pise visited Carrollton. "You find me very low," the old man whispered. "I am going, Sir, to the tomb of my Fathers!" The ladies were alarmed, and Carroll managed a joke to console them.

Dr. Stewart, Carrollton's physician, recorded that the weather was very cold. Around sundown on November 14, a priest, Rev. John M. Chanche, set up a table with candles, holy water in an antique silver vessel, and a crucifix. Carroll sat in a chair before the table. His descendants knelt around him, and

Part V: Patriarch

in the rear, "three or four old negro servants, all of the same faith, knelt in the most venerating manner."

Stewart noticed that Carroll leaned forward to receive the Host, without opening his eyes. His soul was clearly "alive to the act."

Afterward, the doctor offered Carroll something to eat. "Thank you, doctor, not just now," the patriarch replied. "This ceremony is so deeply interesting to the Christian that it supplies all the wants of nature. I feel no desire for food."

Upon being laid in the bed, Carroll said, "Thank you, that is nicely done."

Mrs. Caton then brought a glass of jelly, a gelatin-like dessert. Carroll declined. Mary was importunate: "Papa, you must take it, as the doctor says you ought to do so."

"Mary, put it down, I want no food," said Carroll.

He slept, fitfully. Dr. Stewart helped him find a more comfortable position. Carrollton thanked him.

Sometime after midnight, "without a struggle, he breathing as calmly as if falling into a gentle sleep," Carroll died.

All parties concurred in displays of respect. The South Carolina convention wore mourning for three weeks, Congress for three months, an honor previously accorded only to Washington. Carroll was buried out of the great Cathedral of the Assumption in Baltimore. He was laid to rest in the chapel at Doughoregan Manor, where he had spent his lonely boyhood so many years before. President Jackson could not attend the funeral because of the nullification crisis, but he closed the offices of the United States on November 16. Amid the outpouring of newspaper prose, the *Baltimore American* put it simply: Carrollton was "the last of the Romans."

But to those who, for many years, visited the Manor Chapel, which holds the Catholic Signer's relics, the crypt did not have the final say. Nor had the metaphor of starlight obscured the true meaning of Carroll's career. To be sure, the tableau placed over his tomb had thirteen stars. But above them all was the cross.

Notes.

PART I: Exile

17 *one of the two richest*: Col. Edward Lloyd was reputedly richer; Peter Joseph Paul, *The Social Philosophy of Charles Carroll of Carrollton* (dissertation, University of Chicago, March 1947), 65.

17 *take the Carroll fortune*: See Thomas O'Brien Hanley, *Revolutionary Statesman: Charles Carroll and the War* (Chicago: Loyola University Press, 1983), 6, and Ronald Hoffman, *Charles Carroll of Carrollton: The Formative Years, 1748–1764* (Working Paper Series 12:3, Fall 1982), 38.

17 *"only a b. son"*: "Journal of a French Traveller in the Colonies, 1765, II," *American Historical Review* 27:1 (October, 1921), 74.

17 *"is an illegitimate son"*: Margaret Law Callcott, ed., *Mistress of Riversdale: The Plantation Letters of Rosalie Stier Calvert, 1795–1821* (Baltimore: Johns Hopkins University Press, 1991), 267.

17 *"those happy days"*: Charles Carroll of Carrollton [hereafter CCC] to Charles Carroll of Annapolis [hereafter CCA], June 10, 1761, *Charles Carroll Papers*, Thomas O'Brien Hanley, ed. [hereafter Hanley], microfilmed 1971, 95. Carroll of Carrollton later wrote of a friend who "knew me well & was often with me up at Elk ridge": CCC to CCA, December 19, 1761, *Maryland Historical Magazine* [hereafter MHM] 11, 187–189.

18 *"the most moneyed man..."*: "Journal of a French Traveller II," 74.

The Origins of the English Reformation

18 *"chiefs of Ely"*: Ronald Hoffman and Sally D. Mason, *Princes of Ireland, Planters of Maryland* (Chapel Hill: University of North Carolina Press, 2000), 3. See also Kate Mason Rowland, *The Life of Charles Carroll of Carrollton, 1737–1832* (New York: G. P. Putnam's Sons, 1898), I:1.

18 *The ius...ordering of society*: Brian Tierney, *The Idea of Natural Rights* (Atlanta: Scholars Press, 1997), 17, 19.

18 *It declared...null and void*: J. Moss Ives, *The Ark and the Dove* (London: Longmans, Green, 1936), 81–84.

18 *"A law has as much force..."*: Thomas Aquinas, ST q. 95, art. 2, in R. J. Henle, ed. *Saint Thomas Aquinas, the Treatise on Law* (Notre Dame, Ind.: University of Notre Dame Press, 1993), 287.

18f. *William of Ockham...politics of will*: Tierney, *Idea*, 29–30.

19 *William Tyndale supplied...*: Gerard B. Wegemer, *Thomas More: A Portrait of Courage* (Princeton, N.J.: Scepter, 1995), 132.

19 *"Since he had not..."*: Thomas Aquinas, "On Kingship," in William Baumgarth and Richard Regan, eds., *St. Thomas Aquinas on Law, Morality, and Politics* (Indianapolis: Hackett Publishing, 1988), 269.

19 *professional informers*: Ives, 17.

19 "*a kind of harpies*": David Hume, *The History of England, from the Invasion of Julius Caesar to the Revolution in 1688*, Rodney W. Kilcup, ed. (Chicago: University of Chicago Press, 1975), 149.
19 "*surrender and regrant*": Hoffman, *Formative Years*, 10; Michael A. Mullett, *Catholics in Britain and Ireland, 1558–1829* (Houndmills, Basingstoke, Hampshire: Macmillan Press Ltd., 1998), 126.
19 *King James I seized...*: Hoffman, *Formative Years*, 11.
19 *1641 rebellion*: Ronald Hoffman, "'Marylando-Hibernus': Charles Carroll the Settler, 1660–1720," *William and Mary Quarterly*, Third Series, 45:2 (April 1988), 209.
19f. *Irish Catholic landholdings...Catholic hands*: Hoffman, *Formative Years*, 18.
20 *being reconciled...or reconciling*: Hubert Chadwick, S.J., *St Omers to Stonyhurst* (London: Burns & Oates, 1962), 1–2.
20 *students in continental seminaries*: ibid., 2.
20 *could travel no more*: ibid., 11. For these penal laws, see also Henry Care, "*Draconica*" (London: George Larkin, 1687); William Cawley, *The Laws of Q. Elizabeth, K. James, and K. Charles the First concerning Jesuites, Seminary priests, Recusants, &c.* (London: John Wright and Richard Chiswell, 1680).
20 *The Mass was prohibited*: Hoffman, *Formative Years*, 69.
20 *taken from their parents*: Chadwick, 11.
20 *financially dependent*: Ives, 100; Michael Mullett, 26.
20 "*a participation...*": Robert Bellarmine, *De Laicis or the Treatise on Civil Government*, ed. Kathleen Murphy (New York: Fordham University Press, 1928), 46.
20 *when a human law...ceases to bind*: ibid., 52.
20 *the application...to particular cases*: ibid., 27.
20 "*no claim to such...*": ibid., 38.
21 "*an excellent ground...*": ibid., 27.
21 *They routinely..."Puritan-Papists"*: Brian Tierney, *Religion, Law, and the Growth of Constitutional Thought, 1150–1650* (Cambridge, Mass: Cambridge University Press, 1982), 3–4.
21 *King James...for his son*: Ives, 19.
21 *Privy Council*: ibid., 30.
21 *negotiations failed*: ibid., 38.
21 *When James placed...publicly*: ibid., 41.
21 *James elevated him*: ibid., 42.

Lord Baltimore's Experiment

21 *James later told...amnesty for Catholics*: ibid., 51–52.
21 *1625*: ibid., 44.
21 *a palatinate*: ibid., 46.
21 "*God's Holy and True Religion*": ibid., 49.
22 *under the same roof*: ibid., 52.
22 "*Popish doings*": ibid., 54.
22 *paid tribute*: Lewis A. Leonard, *Life of Charles Carroll of Carrollton* (New York: Moffat, Yard & Company, 1918), 26.
22 *Like Moses*: Ives, 64.
22 *in an Anglican church*: ibid., 92.

Notes

22 "*to be silent*"..."*take place privately*": ibid., 106.
22 "*to love one another*": Patrick W. Carey, *The Roman Catholics in America* (Westport, CT: Praeger, 1996), 15.
22 "*trouble, molest*"..."*punish his persecutor*": Ives, 146.
22 *Religious Toleration Act*: ibid., 230.
22 *took the Protestants' side*: ibid., 150.
22f. *locking up a Protestant chapel*: ibid., 153.
23 *triple damages*: Leonard, 29.
23 "*an heretic, schismatic....*": George Petrie, "Church and State in Early Maryland," *Johns Hopkins University Studies in Historical and Political Science*, 10th series (April 1892), 212.
23 *Nearly all...were Jesuits*: Ruth Bradbury LaMonte, *Early Maryland Education* (dissertation, Ohio State University, 1976), 100.
23 *could not openly assist*: Ives, 102–103.
23 *to evangelize Native Americans*: Edward Terrar, "Was There a Separation Between Church and State in Mid-17th Century England and Colonial Maryland?" *Journal of Church and State* 35, 1 (Winter 1993): 70.
23 *to serve as pastors*: ibid., 72, 81.
23 *unique devotional practices*: LaMonte, 136; Carey, 14.
23 *personal conversion*: Michael Mullett, 4, 23, 71.
23 "*ecclesiastical laws of England*": Petrie, 196.
23 "*written technicalities*": ibid., 199.
23 "*natives and liege-men*": ibid., 198.
23 "*importation, custom or other taxation*": Ives, 86.
24 "*of and with the advice...*": ibid., 67.
24 *1637*: ibid., 158.
24 *to initiate all legislation*: ibid., 85.
24 *propose legislation...dissolve the assembly*: Francis Edgar Sparks, "Causes of the Maryland Revolution of 1689," *Johns Hopkins University Studies in Historical and Political Science*, 14th series (Nov.–Dec. 1896), 481.
24 "*consonant to reason*": Petrie, 198.
24 "*patronages and advowsons*": Ives, 90.
24 *barely mentions religion*: ibid., 177.
24 *Massachusetts Bay*: ibid., 155.
24 *Because Lord Baltimore...political role*: David W. Jordan, "'God's Candle' Within Government," *William and Mary Quarterly*, 3rd series, 39:4 (October 1982), 634.
24 *Hussites*: Ives, 242.
24 *Dr. Jacob Lumbrozo*: ibid., 246.
24 *A 1664 act*: ibid., 193.
24 "*are both spitting...one fire of Hell*": ibid., 196.
24 *noted with some disgust*: Petrie, 215.

The Plundering Begins

25 *caught between Puritans...Cavaliers*: Ives, 133.
25 *refused to trade...in his colony*: ibid., 134.
25 *Virginia dissenters*: Jordan, 629; Ives, 233.
25 *naval assault*: Ives, 137.

25 *Richard Ingle*: ibid., 202.
25 *deposing the governor...of the vote*: ibid., 235.
25 *"not to busy themselves..."*: ibid., 237.
25 *pardoned the insurgents*: ibid., 238.
25 *renew the Toleration Act*: LaMonte, 83.
25 *potentially explosive situation*: Petrie, 200.
25 *They controlled...by 1649*: Ives, 231.
25 *freed servants*: ibid., 168.
25 *men without property*: ibid., 174.
25 *"Protestant Declaration"*: ibid., 234.
25 *the situation worsened*: Chadwick, 173.
26 *Catholic relatives*: Sparks, 516.
26 *removing laws...veto power*: ibid., 517.
26 *pocket veto*: ibid., 527.
26 *new offices*: ibid., 519.
26 *restricting the electoral franchise*: ibid., 520.
26 *Cecilius Calvert*: ibid., 535.
26 *affirmed...toleration*: ibid., 534.
26 *conspiring to exclude*: Chadwick, 195.
26 *divine-right language*: Michael Graham, S.J., "Popish Plots: Protestant Fears in Early Colonial Maryland, 1676–1689," *Catholic Historical Review* 79:2 (April 1993), 200.
26 *liveried lackeys*: Joseph Gurn, *Charles Carroll of Carrollton, 1737–1832* (New York: P. J. Kenedy & Sons, 1932), 24.
26 *Protestant gentry and poor whites*: Sally D. Mason, "Charles Carroll of Carrollton and His Family, 1688–1832," in Ann C. Van Devanter, *"Anywhere So Long As There Be Freedom"* (Baltimore: Baltimore Museum of Art, 1975), 14.
26 *three Anglican ministers*: Jordan, 633.
26 *all were notoriously lax*: Petrie, 229.
26 *Baltimore expressed support*: ibid., 229, 234.
26 *Protestants were dissenters*: Sparks, 544.
26 *The citizens...disturb the peace*: Petrie, 233.
27 *"guilt of permission"*: ibid., 219.
27 *"Complaint from Heaven"*: Sparks, 539–540.

The "Glorious Revolution"

27 *Inner Temple*: Hoffman, *Formative Years*, 14.
27 *Lord Powis*: Hoffman, "Marylando-Hibernus," 211.
27 *"affairs are going on very badly"*: Rowland, I:3–4.
27 *in the Tower*: Hoffman, *Formative Years*, 14.
27 *changed his family's motto*: Ellen Hart Smith, *Charles Carroll of Carrollton* (Cambridge, Mass.: Harvard University Press, 1942), 9; Rowland, I:8.
27 *presented his credentials*: Hoffman, *Formative Years*, 15.
27 *"the first principle..."*: Tierney, *Idea*, 322.
27 *"by nature it is..."*: ibid., 328.
27 *collapse into the desires*: Charles F. Mullett, *Fundamental Law and the American Revolution* (New York: Octagon Books, 1966; reprint of 1933 edition), 27.

Notes

28 *such men as Roger Williams*: Peter Paul, 47–48.
28 *"the King in Parliament"*: see Tierney, *Religion*, 82.
28 *awarded the throne*: Charles Mullett, 197.
28 *unitary sovereign*: Peter S. Onuf, ed., *Maryland and the Empire, 1773* (Baltimore: Johns Hopkins University Press, 1974), 22.
28 *troop of horse*: Sparks, 570–571.
28 *died en route*: LaMonte, 15; Ives, 253.
28 *conspiring with the Native Americans*: Graham, 202.
28 *Boatloads of Irish*: ibid., 209.
28 *indictment against Baltimore*: ibid., 205.
28 *"honest…their irregularities"*: Charles Carroll the Settler [hereafter CCS] to Lord Baltimore, September 25, 1689, Leonard, 38.
28 *a hard seasoning*: ibid.
28 *"high misdemeanors"*: LaMonte, 152; Hoffman, *Formative Years*, 20.
29 *a considerable private establishment*: Hoffman, *Formative Years*, 19
29 *huge tracts of land*: see Thomas Meagher Field, ed., *Unpublished Letters of Charles Carroll of Carrollton* (New York: United States Catholic Historical Society, 1902), 13.
29 *to keep him company*: Ives, 263.
29 *fifty pounds a year*: Hoffman, "'Marylando-Hibernus,'" 213.
29 *His grandfather…during the 1650s*: Hoffman and Mason, 33.
29 *Battle of the Boyne…to the authorities*: Hoffman, "'Marylando-Hibernus,'" 208; Hoffman, *Formative Years*, 16.
29 *only three*: Hoffman, *Formative Years*, 18.
29 *Irish identity*: Hoffman, "'Marylando-Hibernus,'" 235.
29 *taxes designed to discourage*: Ives, 267–268; LaMonte, 56.
29 *"Marylando-Hibernus"*: CCS to CCA and Daniel Carroll, Rowland, I:10–11.
29 *"duty all Irishmen owe"*: CCA to CCC, July, 1761, Field, 61.
29 *"how unavailing to remember"*: CCC to CCA, March 28–29, 1761, Hanley 87.
29 *Protestant Revolution*: Hanley, *Revolutionary Statesman*, 4.
29 *small minority…forty pounds of tobacco*: Ives, 256; LaMonte, 51.
29 *The assembly failed…in force in Maryland*: LaMonte, 97–98; Jordan, 649.
30 *no laws concerning religion*: LaMonte, 51.
30 *"arbitrary will and pleasure"*: Ives, 254.
30 *"Act to Prevent the Growth of Popery"*: LaMonte, 98.
30 *converting Protestants…inherit land*: ibid., 99.
30 *private homes*: Ives, 264–265.
30 *confirmed this privilege*: LaMonte, 99.
30 *Crown's approval*: Ives, 257.
30 *subject to Parliament*: Thomas O'Brien Hanley, *Charles Carroll of Carrollton: The Making of a Revolutionary Gentleman* (Washington, D.C.: Catholic University of America Press, 1970), 3.
30 *"It is we…"*: Charles A. Barker, "Maryland before the Revolution," *American Historical Review* 46:1 (October 1940), 11.
30 *Bill of Rights*: Peter Paul, 30.
30 *circumvent the process*: ibid., 33–34.

1715

31 *a rich widow*: Hoffman, "'Marylando-Hibernus,'" 216.
31 *Mary Darnall*: Hoffman, *Formative Years*, 21.
31 *agent and receiver general...land office*: ibid.; Hoffman, "'Marylando-Hibernus,'" 221.
31 *Chancery and Prerogative Courts*: Hoffman, "'Marylando-Hibernus,'" 218.
31 *"Attorney in fact"*: ibid., 223.
31 *47,777 acres...20,000 more*: ibid., 219.
31 *store in Annapolis*: ibid., 225.
31 *Benedict Calvert...Church of England*: Ives, 269; Hoffman and Mason, 79.
31 *he too died*: Hoffman, *Formative Years*, 22.
31 *"lose his estate"*: Chadwick, 251.
31 *assumed the full proprietorship...lost the attorney-generalship*: Hoffman, *Formative Years*, 22.
32 *Protestant Irishman*: Hoffman, "'Marylando-Hibernus,'" 226.
32 *Carroll had promised*: ibid., 229.
32 *railroaded... an act*: ibid., 232.
32 *blithely continued to exercise*: ibid., 231.
32 *toasted the Stuart Pretender's*: Hoffman and Mason, 84.
32 *Gov. Hart protested*: Hoffman, *Formative Years*, 22–23.
32 *"Papist in Masquerade"*: Hoffman, "'Marylando-Hibernus,'" 233.
32 *Carroll's commission was revoked*: Hoffman, *Formative Years*, 23.
32 *cost...privilege of voting*: Hoffman, "'Marylando-Hibernus,'" 228, 234.
32 *right up to 1776*: Mason in Van Devanter, 15.
32 *state house...swords*: David Ridgely, ed. *Annals of Annapolis* (Baltimore: Cushing and Brother, 1841), 94–95.
32 *social stratification*: Hoffman, "'Marylando-Hibernus,'" 215.
33 *sank into peonage*: Peter Paul, 32.
33 *never founded a Harvard*: Barker, Maryland before the Revolution, 2; LaMonte, 77.
33 *"that the people...make tobacco!"*: Gurn, 62–63.

Building an Empire

33 *more cosmopolitan outlook*: Barker, Maryland before the Revolution, 3.
33 *"take much the same...awkward appearance"*: CCS to CCA and Daniel Carroll, Rowland I:10–11.
33f. *sacrifice his legal education*: ibid., I:14.
34 *manage the family's affairs*: LaMonte, 155.
34 *consolidate his patrimony...five-percent commission*: Hoffman, *Formative Years*, 4.
34 *"men of pleasure..."*: Michael Mullett, 84.
34 *thirty thousand pounds sterling*: Hoffman, *Formative Years*, 4.
34 *one-fourth of the land*: William Voss Elder III, "The Carroll House in Annapolis and Doughoregan Manor," in VanDevanter, 60.
34 *Two-thirds of its residents*: LaMonte, 156.
34 *23,230 pounds sterling...eighteen hundred pounds sterling*: Hoffman, *Formative Years*, 5.

34 *"activity, thought..."*: Susan Eugenia Kwilecki, *Through the Needle's Eye* (dissertation, Stanford University, 1982).
34 *tried to help Acadians*: see CCA to CCC, July 26, 1756, Rowland, I:26; Hanley 14.
34 *"I was never genteeler..."*: "Journal of a French Traveller II," 74.
34 *Baltimore City*: Leonard, 49.
34 *"immorality, drunkenness..."*: Andrew Burstein, *Sentimental Democracy* (New York: Hill & Wang, 1999), 38.
34 *political power...economic clout*: Hanley, *Making*, 12, 17.
35 *Iron Works was organized...the Elder*: Keach Johnson, "The Genesis of the Baltimore Iron Works," *Journal of Southern History* 19:2 (May 1953), 170.
35 *medicine to commerce*: ibid., 163.
35 *nonpayment of quitrents*: Rowland, I:17; Hanley, *Making*, 13.
35 *Squire Carroll alleged*: CCA to Baltimore Company, February 13, 1748, Letterbook 1684–1771, Carroll Family Papers, Library of Congress.
35 *vehemently denied this charge*: Charles Carroll the Surgeon to Baltimore Co., n.d., Letterbook 1684–1771, Carroll Family Papers, Library of Congress; Charles Carroll the Surgeon to Baltimore Co., March 21, 1748, Letterbook 1684–1771, Carroll Family Papers, Library of Congress.
35 *all the partners must consent*: CCA to Richard Croxall, n.d., Letterbook 1684–1771, Carroll Family Papers, Library of Congress.
35 *before the Surgeon left*: Ives, 279.
35 *developed scruples*: Hanley, *Making*, 10, 43.
35 *"which reflected...character"*: Gov. Sharpe to Lord Baltimore, December 16, 1758, Ridgely, 95–100.
35 *to the state house*: Hoffman, *Formative Years*, 71.
35 *"that the papists..."*: Gov. Sharpe to Lord Baltimore, December 16, 1758, Ridgely, 95–100.
35 *under house arrest...public jail*: June 4–5, 1751, Proceedings and Acts of the General Assembly of Maryland 1748–1751, *Archives of Maryland* 46, 572–583.
36 *have all Masses forbidden*: Ives, 284.
36 *"one of the largest..."* Johnson, 157.
36 *later industrial innovations*: ibid., 178.
36 *mercantilist ideology*: ibid., 161.
36 *"iron plantation"*: ibid., 175.
36 *smiths, carpenters*: Ronald L. Lewis, "Slavery on Chesapeake Iron Plantations before the American Revolution," *Journal of Negro History* 59:3 (July 1974), 244.
36 *extra work*: ibid., 246.
36 *company commissary*: Johnson, 167.
36 *"white servants seldom..."*: CCC to CCA, January 7, 1763, in Rowland, I:52.
36 *more than twenty percent*: Johnson, 177.
36 *third largest*: Lewis, 242.

St. Omers

36 *Bohemia Manor*: LaMonte, 105.

37   *bookkeeping, surveying...Sewalls*: ibid., 114.
37   *John Carroll*: ibid., 107.
37   *left for Flanders*: ibid., 115.
37   *1592 by Fr. Robert Persons*: Hoffman, *Formative Years*, 40.
37   *"Iesu, Iesu..."*: Chadwick, 87.
37   *"packs of merchandise"*: ibid., 256.
37   *1685 with one hundred eighty*: ibid., 166.
37   *the only obstacle*: ibid., 55.
37   *Fr. Andrew White*: ibid., 21.
37   *Anthony, James, and Henry*: Hoffman, *Formative Years*, 70.
37   *"mightily beloved"*: CCC to CCA, March 1750, Hanley 2.
37   *"is gone up..."*: Ives, 296.
37   *Jesuit novitiate*: LaMonte, 135.
37   *Bellarmine's reply*: Chadwick, 142.
38   *rather than a seminary*: ibid., 45, 220, 241.
38   *free choice*: ibid., 308.
38   *Christian gentlemen*: ibid., 72, 214.
38   *riding horses*: Hanley, *Making*, 27.
38   *continuous surveillance*: Chadwick, 85–86.
38   *"that education..."* CCC to CCA, December 19, 1761, *Maryland Historical Magazine* 11, 187–189.
38   *conversation was in Latin*: Chadwick, 40.
38   *translations between Latin and Greek*: ibid., 215.
38   *ratio studiorum*: Chadwick, 69.
38   *humane letters*: LaMonte, 118, 123.
38   *ratio et oratio*: Chadwick, 70.
38   *moral, political, and intellectual leadership*: LaMonte, 122.
38   *vented their competitive instincts...falling short academically*: ibid., 126–127.
38   *"circumstances of time..."*: ibid., 123.
38   *emotions found an outlet*: ibid., 134.
38   *generally in Latin*: Chadwick, 374.
38   *history and geography...prose and poetry*: ibid., 77.
38   *five A.M....5:30*: ibid., 80.
38   *a quarter hour...major feast days*: ibid., 40.
38   *Tuesday and Thursday..."Bread and Beer"*: ibid., 83.
39   *"the family"*: Hanley, *Making*, 28.
39   *spiritual exercises...Fr. Levinas Browne*: ibid., 24.
39   *"he could rise...cheerfulness"*: Charles Constantine Pise, "Oration in Honor of the Late Charles Carroll of Carrollton" (Georgetown: Joshua N. Rind, 1832), 9–10.

"Aut Caesar Aut Nullus"

39   *Most of the records...Sack of Louvain*: LaMonte, 128.
39   *"I cannot be better satisfied..."*: CCC to CCA and Elizabeth Brooke, September 4, 1749, Hanley 1.
39   *Aut Caesar aut nullus*: CCA to CCC, October 10, 1753, Rowland, I:11.
39   *"increase the love..."*: CCA to CCC, October 10, 1753, Rowland, I:22.
39   *"I hope to be always..."*: CCC to CCA, March 22, 1750, Hanley 3.

Notes

39 "*I can easily see*": CCC to CCA, March 1750, Hanley 2.
40 *personal tutor*: see Chadwick, 367.
40 *Anthony Carroll*: LaMonte, 165.
40 "*Cousin Anthony forced me…*": CCC to CCA, March 23, 1751, Hanley 8.
40 "*giddy…*": Anthony Carroll to CCA, February 26, 1751, Hanley 7.
40 "*I believe you will mind very little…*": John Carroll to CCC, September 6, 1757, Maryland Historical Society [hereafter MHS] collection 4191, 109.
40 *writing a journal*: CCA to CCC, October 1, 1762, MHS 4192, 276.
40 "*If you remember…*": Onorio Razolini to CCA, November 17, 1757, in Sally D. Mason, "Mama, Rachel, and Molly: Three Generations of Carroll Women," in Ronald Hoffman and Peter J. Albert, eds., *Women in the Age of the American Revolution* (Charlottesville: University Press of Virginia, 1989), 254–255.
41 "*universal good character*": J. Jenison to CCA, October 21, 1757, Hanley 24.
41 "*degenerate into the mean…*": Leonard, 73.
41 "*gave me the greatest…*": J. Jenison to CCA, October 21, 1757, Hanley 24.
41 *one lasting, intimate relationship*: see Mason in Van Devanter, 16.
41 "*For what may I…*": Elizabeth Brooke to CCC, September 8, 1756, Hanley 15.
41 *by a Jesuit priest*: Hoffman and Mason, 132.
41 "*Elizabeth Carroll, late…*": Hoffman, *Formative Years*, 33–34.
41 *had had to settle*: ibid., 39.
41 "*Is he in great esteem…*": Hoffman and Mason, 135.
41f. "*clandestine marriage*"…*eyes of the Church*: ibid., 137–138.

Suarez and Montesquieu

42 *followed St. Thomas*: Tierney, *Idea*, 32.
42 *Suarez, therefore… balance state power*: ibid., 288.
42f. *True individual rights…right to life*: ibid., 25–26, 307–308; Henle, 93.
43 *obedience to legitimate authority*: Tierney, *Idea*, 301–305, 310–311; Peter Paul, 49–52.
43 *to depose tyrants*: Tierney, *Idea*, 314.
43 *poetry, history, geography, and heraldry*: LaMonte, 169.
43 *Enlightenment thinkers*: Kwilecki, 135.
43 *Universal History*: list of books, June 26, 1759, Hanley 58.
43 *Voltaire's works*: CCC to CCA, June 22, 1759, Hanley 56; see also *Catalogue of the Library of Charles Carroll of Carrollton, Embracing Many Old, Curious and Rare books, to Be Sold at Auction, Commencing on Monday Evening, December 5, 1864.* (Baltimore: Gibson & Company, 1864), 91; John C. Carpenter, "Charles Carroll of Carrollton," *Magazine of American History with Notes and Queries* II (New York and Chicago: A. S. Barnes & Co., 1878), 103; CCC to William Graves, February 7, 1768, Hanley 225.
43 *Rousseau*: *Catalogue of the Library*, 68.
43 *Gibbon, Godwin*: ibid., 29.
43 *Rapin*: ibid., 66.
43 *Hume*: ibid., 35.
43 *opposed religious toleration*: Hanley, *Making*, 47.
43 *incompatible with the English constitution*: Evarts B. Greene, "Persistent

Problems of Church and State," *American Historical Review* 36:2 (January, 1931), 262.
43 *"you need not buy..."*: CCC to CCA, July 26, 1757, MHM 10, 150.
43 *seminal influence...was Montesquieu*: see Peter Paul, 14; Thomas O'Brien Hanley, "Young Mr. Carroll and Montesquieu," MHM 62:4 (December 1967), *passim.*
43 *humor of its people*: Montesquieu, *The Spirit of Laws* I.3.9, Thomas Nugent, trans., David Wallace Carrithers, ed. (Berkeley: University of California Press, 1977), 104.
44 *"each diversity..."*: ibid., I.1.7, 99.
44 *"events that incessantly arise..."*: ibid., X.14.4, 195.
44 *regulates even virtue...check power*: ibid., XI.4.1–2, 200.
44 *"master-piece of legislation"*: ibid., V.14.30, 147.
44 *"Abolish the privileges..."*: ibid., II.4.3, 113.
44 *Church must be left alone*: ibid., II.4.5–6, 113.
44 *includes marriage*: ibid., XXVI.13.3–4, 361.
44 *"mediocrity"*: ibid., V.3.7, 134.
44 *"spirit of extreme equality"*: ibid., VIII.2.1–2, 171.
44 *"Such is the difference..."*: ibid., VIII.3.3, 172.
44 *"wisdom or in grace..."*: Bellarmine, 35–36.
44 *"most repugnant to reason..."*: Leo XIII. Encyclical on Freemasonry *Humanum Genus* (April 20, 1884), 26. Vatican website. www.vatican.va.
45 *"next to nothing"*: Montesquieu, XI.6.32, 206.
45 *"exact letter...private opinion"*: ibid., XI.6.17, 203; see also VI.3.2, 156.
45 *"Senate"*: ibid., V.7.3–4, 139.
45 *power to veto*: ibid., XI.6.34–35, 206.
45 *tribunal of impeachment*: ibid., XI.6.50, 210.
45 *executive branch to be strong*: ibid., XI.6.42–43, 208.
45 *Republics cannot function*: ibid., VIII.16.1, 176.
45 *for republics is to confederate*: ibid., IX.1.3, 183.
45 *"a certain subsistence"*: ibid., XXIII.29.3, 317.
45 *industry and commerce*: ibid., XXIII.29.4, XXIII.29.8, 317–318.
45 *"he is paying himself"*: ibid., XIII.13.1, 236; see also XIII.12.1, 235.
45 *"real wants...of the State"*: ibid., XIII.1.2, 230.
45 *"the power of the people..."*: ibid., XI.2, 199; see also XII.1.3, 216.
45 *"In societies directed...not to will"*: ibid., XI.3.1, 200.

The Persecution Revives

46 *universal philosophy*: Peter Paul, 14.
46 *John the Baptist*: Mason in Van Devanter, 8.
46 *southwestern Arkansas*: LaMonte, 172.
46 *announced from the pulpit*: Gov. Sharpe to Lord Baltimore, December 16, 1758, in Ridgely, 95–100.
46 *black people...officer's dress*: ibid.
46 *"guard your holy Religion"*: Smith, 37.
46 *Driven by this..."many other restraints"*: Gov. Sharpe to Lord Baltimore, December 16, 1758, in Ridgely, 95–100.
46 *the two houses...could not agree*: Hoffman, *Formative Years*, 72.

Notes

46 *"if I was asked..."*: Gov. Sharpe to Lord Baltimore, December 16, 1758, in Ridgely, 95–100.
47 *"all French America..."*: CCA to CCC, November 27, 1758, Hanley 49.
47 *"our late glorious success..."*: CCC to CCA, May 16, 1760, Hanley 74.
47 *militia duty...used as a pretext*: J. William Black, "Maryland's Attitude in the Struggle for Canada," *Johns Hopkins University Studies in Historical and Political Science*, 10th series (July 1892), 371.
47 *"sundry Roman Catholics...privilege of voting"*: *Maryland Historical Magazine* 5:1, 46–57.
47 *governor had not bothered*: Hoffman, *Formative Years*, 28.
47 *"if [Carroll] is inclined..."*: ibid.
47 *"I think of you..."*: CCC to CCA, January 1, 1758, Hanley 32.
47 *too grand...sizeable tract*: Leonard, 54.
48 *received aid*: Hoffman, *Formative Years*, 73.
48 *"the only Frenchman..."*: Hanley, *Making*, 109.
48 *grief..."melancholy"*: CCC to CCA, January 1, 1758, Hanley 32.
48 *Roman and French civil law*: Hanley, *Revolutionary Statesman*, 6.
48 *twice a week*: CCC to CCA, December 28, 1757, Hanley 30.
48 *"there is no instruction...perfect stranger"*: CCC to CCA, February 4, 1758, Hanley 35.
48 *"I find no [other] conversation...Great, Good, & Just"*: CCC to CCA and Elizabeth Brooke, June 14, 1758, Hanley 41.
48 *"very dry and tedious"*: CCC to CCA, December 28, 1757, Hanley 30.
48 *Justinian's Institutes*: ibid.; CCC to CCA and Elizabeth Brooke, June 14, 1758, Hanley 41.
48 *escaped Bourges*: CCC to CCA, January 17, 1759, Hanley 50.; Smith, 45.
48 *"young, pretty, witty daughter"*: CCC to CCA and Elizabeth Brooke, June 14, 1758, Hanley 41.
48 *soaking the bed*: Hanley, *Making*, 57.
49 *"no desire of ease...improper place"*: CCC to CCA, January 17, 1759, Hanley 50.
49 *He promised not to sell..."our people"*: CCA to CCC, April 1759, Hanley 55.
49 *"injustice and ungratefulness...groundless"*: CCC to CCA and Elizabeth Brooke, June 14, 1758, Hanley 41.
49 *"I suppose you will..."*: CCC to CCA, June 22, 1759, Hanley 56.
49 *"uncultivated insolent rabble...more civilised"*: CCC to CCA, August 14, 1759, Hanley 60.
49 *"I can't conceive...holds it"*: CCC to CCA, December 10, 1759, Hanley 66.

France Expels the Jesuits

50 *"property, liberty...injustice"*: CCC to CCA, May 16, 1760, Hanley 74, MHM 10, 323.
50 *Jansenists...Madame de Pompadour*: Chadwick, 277.
50 *"They are not only..."*: CCA to CCC, April 16, 1759, Field, 31.
50 *"destitute of common sense"*: CCC to CCA, June 22, 1759, Hanley 56.
50 *"a blind impetuosity...the Catholic church"*: CCC to CCA, October 22, 1761, Hanley 106, MHM 11, 182–183.
50 *"things innocent..."*: CCA to CCC, April 6, 1762, in Field, 64–67.

50 *technically "boundless"...these assemblies*: Hanley, *Making*, 69.
50 *forbade the Jesuits...anti-Jesuit pamphlets*: ibid., 91.
50f. *"men of republican principles..."*: CCC to CCA, August 8, 1763, MHM 11, 342–343.
51 *void of republican virtue*: Hanley, "Young Mr. Carroll," 409.
51 *"the injustice, violence..."*: CCC to CCA, June 14, 1763, MHM 11, 335–336.
51 *"The name of liberty..."*: CCC to CCA, June 14, 1763, MHM 11, 335–336.
51 *"The decisions & proceedings..."*: CCC to CCA, February 5, 1763, MHM 11, 326–327.
51 *John Carroll...were arrested*: Chadwick, 344.
51 *replacement priests*: ibid., 292.
51 *The Bourbons...August 16, 1773*: ibid., 334–336.

Carrolls and Calverts

52 *"to gratify a faction...honor and justice"*: CCA to CCC, October 6, 1759, Rowland, I:38–39.
52 *"he was much offended"...not pursuing the point*: CCC to CCA, April 10, 1760, Hanley 70.
52 *"What you said..."*: CCA to CCC, July 14, 1760, in Field, 45–46.
52 *"It is necessary..."*: CCA to CCC, October 13, 1760, Hanley 81, MHM 10, 330.
52 *Henry Darnall III*: Field, 56.
52 *"Should [Calvert] show..."*: CCA to CCC, October 13, 1760, Hanley 81, MHM 10, 330.
52 *"was advised to it"*: CCC to CCA, February 13, 1761, Hanley 85, MHM 10, 334.
52 *"injustice & pusillanimity"*: CCC to CCA, October 13, 1761, MHM 11, 178.
52 *"I do not care..."*: CCA to CCC, May 20, 1761, in Field, 58–60.
53 *"I know of no Catholic country..."*: CCC to CCA, January 1, 1761, Hanley 84.
53 *"True happiness...not going unrewarded"*: CCC to CCA, February 30, 1760, Hanley 69.
53 *"one not to be awed..."*: CCC to CCA, September 16, 1760, Hanley 79.
53 *"if the Roman Catholics..."*: CCC to CCA, February 13, 1761, Hanley 85.
53 *General Montcalm*: Benson Bobrick, *Angel in the Whirlwind* (New York: Penguin Books, 1998), 29.

"We Live in the World"

53 *"I am naturally timid...intimate with nobody"*: CCC to CCA, July 15–16, 1761, Hanley 97, MHM 10:70–71.
54 *"very circumspect...ever appearing virtuous"*: CCA to CCC, October 6, 1759, in Field, 32–33.
54 *"be reserved"*: CCA to CCC, October 6, 1759, in Field, 34–35.
54 *"intimacy or familiarity..."*: CCA to CCC, August 30, 1758, in Field, 28–29.
54 *"I often wish..."*: CCA to CCC, August 30, 1758, MHM 10, 226.
54 *Governor Thomas Bladen*: Smith, 55; Hanley, *Making*, 82.

Notes

54   "*to which...am unlucky*": CCC to CCA, March 30, 1761, Hanley 88, MHM 10, 342.
54   "*remarkably handsome*": CCC to CCA, October 13, 1761, MHM 11, 181.
54   "*A too great intimacy*": CCC to CCA, July 15, 1761, Hanley 97, MHM 10, 70.
54   *Mr. Jenison*: CCC to CCA, May 16, 1760, MHM 10, 324.
54   "*The frequenting of company...*": CCC to CCA, March 17, 1762, MHM 11, 261–264.
54f.   "*A man can hardly...towards you*": CCA to CCC, April 16, 1762, in Field, 68–70.
55   "*We live...conversation*": CCA to CCC, December 29, 1762, in Field, 74–77.
55   "*A knowledge of it...*": CCA to CCC, n.d., in Field, 64–65.
55   "*Should you for example...*": CCA to CCC, December 29, 1762, in Field, 74–77.
55   *impishly forwarded*: CCA to CCC, May 12, 1762, MHM 11, 266–267.
55   "*in a proper genteel...*": CCC to CCA, November 13, 1759, Hanley 65, MHM 10, 242.
55   "*easy and genteel carriage...*": CCC to CCA and Elizabeth Carroll, February 17, 1759, Hanley 53.
55   *to slouch*: CCC to CCA, September 16, 1760, Hanley 79.
55   "*this carriage, this manner...*": CCA to CCC, August 30, 1758, in Field, 28–29.
55   "*fops*": CCA to CCC, October 10, 1753, Rowland, I:20.
55   "*some excursions...*": CCC to CCA, May 22, 1760, Hanley 75.
55   *Pitt's mannerisms*: CCC to CCA, December 8, 1763, MHM 12, 22–26.
55   *with Edmund Burke*: Pise, 11.
55   "*Charly is very well...*": Michael Macnamara to CCA, July 20–22, 1761, Hanley 99.
55   "*elegant way of living*": Rowland, I:65.
56   *Sir Joshua Reynolds*: Van Devanter, 2.
56   "*Initium Sapientiae...*": CCA to CCC, July 26, 1756, Hanley 14.
56   "*Prayer does not consist...*": CCA to CCC, August 30, 1758, MHM 10, 226.
56   "*A pipe of wine...*": Hanley, *Making*, 94.
56   "*A good conscience...wish to do*": CCC to CCA, January 17, 1759, Hanley 50; Ronald Hoffman et al., eds., *Dear Papa, Dear Charley*, vol. 1 (Chapel Hill: University of North Carolina Press, 2001), 90.
56f.   *Carroll never developed...gentry*: Hanley, *Making*, 21, 113.
57   *mired in the Jacobite resistance*: Michael Mullett, 85–86, 96.
57   *penniless, drunken Jacobite exile*: CCC to CCA and Elizabeth Brooke, June 14, 1758, Hanley 41.
57   *Gothic ruin*: Michael Mullett, 97.
57   *Pragmatic action*: Hanley, *Making*, 20.
57   *William Paca and John Hammond*: Peter Paul, 22.
57   *including Hammond*: C. E. A. Bedwell, "American Middle Templars," *American Historical Review* 25:4 (July 1920), 684.
57   *Lloyd Dulany*: ibid., 685.
57   *Richard Tilghman*: ibid., 686.

57 *Edward Tilghman*: ibid., 687.
57 *John Dickinson*: ibid., 684.
57 *Thomas McKean*: ibid., 685.
57 *John Laurens and Arthur Lee*: ibid., 687.
57 *Daniel Dulany, Jr.*: ibid., 683, 686; Rowland, I:64.
57 "*indisputably the best...designing*": CCA to CCC, April 17, 1761, Hanley 91, MHM 10, 343.
57 "*Dulany has...*": CCC to CCA, November 11, 1762, MHM 11, 275–278.
57f. "*Common civility...good sense*": CCC to CCA, April 26, 1762, MHM 11, 264–266.
58 "*politician*": CCA to CCC, April 17, 1761, Hanley 91, MHM 10, 343; CCC to CCA, May 16, 1760, Hanley 74, MHM 10, 323.
58 *mutual lawsuits*: CCA to CCC, April 28, 1763, Rowland, I:55–56.

The Common Law

58 *Carrollton told..."farther than words"*: CCC to CCA, November 13, 1759, Hanley 65.
58 "*Disgusted with the difficulties...*": CCC to CCA, January 7, 1763, Hanley 127.
58 "*What, must I live...*": CCC to CCA, April 10, 1760, Hanley 70.
58 "*It is a shame...*": CCA to CCC, October 6, 1759, in Field, 33.
59 "*Your welfare, interest...*": CCA to CCC, December 29, 1762, 74–77.
59 "*I love you entirely...*": CCA to CCC, April 16, 1762, in Field, 68–70.
59 "*well regulated love...tenderest parent?*": CCC to CCA, September 16, 1760, Hanley 79.
59 "*depended only on desires...*": CCC to CCA, December 26, 1759, Hanley 67.
59 "*disgust[s] a liberal mind*": CCC to CCA, July 2, 1763, MHM 11, 340–341.
59 "*agreeable*": CCC to CCA, June 14, 1758, Hanley 41, MHM 10, 221.
59 "*mere chaos*": CCC to CCA, January 29, 1760, Hanley 68.
59 "*jargon...barbarous language*": CCC to CCA, May 15, 1761, Hanley 93.
59 "*the strictness of geometrical...*": CCC to CCA, July 2, 1763, MHM 11, 340–341.
60 "*mankind's experience...arts of chicane*": CCC to CCA, September 16, 1760, Hanley 79.
60 "*This is in my own hand...*": CCA to CCC, July 24, 1762, MHM 11, 271–272.
60 "*lay resident...*": Peter Paul, 16.
60 *devised his own...bookkeeping*: LaMonte, 187.
60 *surveying..."much fatigue"*: CCC to CCA, January 31, 1763, MHM 11, 323–326.

Bereavement

60 *gave in*: CCA to CCC, 1763, in Field, 79–80.
60 "*a very long...make me amends*": CCC to CCA, January 1, 1761, Hanley 84.
61 "*Your Papa's love...your satisfaction*": Elizabeth Brooke to CCC, September 30, 1754, MHS 4191, 72.

Notes

61 *"no parent can have...tenderness & affection"*: Elizabeth Brooke to CCC, August 29, 1758, MHS 4191, 139.
61 *"You was always"*: Elizabeth Brooke to CCC, September 8, 1756, Hanley 15.
61 *"great uneasiness"*: CCC to CCA, April 10, 1760, Hanley 70.
61 *"what you used to tell me..."*: Elizabeth Carroll to CCC, September 10, 1760, Hanley 78.
61f. *"attended with a dizziness...best of parents."* CCC to Elizabeth Carroll, March 31, 1761, Hanley 89.
62 *"the only solid comforter"*: CCA to CCC, March 22, 1761, Hanley 86; see also Hanley, *Making*, 104.
62 *"I loved my Mama...this was denied me"*: CCC to CCA, June 10, 1761, Hanley 95.
62 *"The loss of my dear mother..."*: CCC to CCA, July 15, 1761, Hanley 97, MHM 10, 72.
62 *"Your mention of your Mama..."*: CCA to CCC, July 10, 1761, MHS 4192, 235.
62 *"I could not say less..."*: CCA to CCC, November 10, 1761, MHM 11, 184.
62 not to speak: Hanley, *Making*, 102.
63 *"Pray do not talk...live happy together"*: CCC to CCA, July 23, 1761, Hanley 100.
63 *"surrounded with enemies..."*: CCC to CCA, March 17, 1762, MHM 11, 261–264.
63 *"Take care of your health"*: CCC to CCA, January 8, 1762, Hanley 113.
63 *"Dear Charley, I am convinced..."*: CCA to CCC, December 29, 1762, in Field, 74–77.
63 he made his will: CCA to CCC, May 20, 1761, in Field, 58–60.
63 *"The sending a copy...order to be done"*: CCC to CCA, October 13, 1761, MHM 11, 178.

Marriage Negotiations

64 his father cautioned him: CCA to CCC, February 9, 1759, Hanley 52.
64 assured the Squire: CCC to CCA, January 29, 1760, Hanley 68, MHM 10, 251.
64 *"on no consideration..."*: CCA to CCC, September 1, 1762, MHM 11, 272–274.
64 *"no consideration whatever..."*: CCC to CCA, February 19, 1763, MHM 11, 327–328.
64 *"your wife be virtuous..."*: CCA to CCC, September 1, 1762, MHM 11, 272–274.
64 *"follow me to a barbarous...never shall be"*: CCC to CCA, February 19, 1763, MHM 11, 327–328.
64 *"What, not one...fond doting husbands"*: CCC to CCA, June 22, 1763, MHM 11, 339–340.
64f. *"Her youth & inexperience..."*: CCC to CCA, October 11, 1763, MHM 11, 344–346.
65 *"bred in a monastery"*: CCA to CCC, September 1, 1762, MHM 11, 272–274.

65 *Ursuline convent...postpone his return home*: CCC to CCA, October 11, 1763, MHM 11, 344–346.
65 *send him his fortune*: Hanley, *Making*, 116.
65 "*The situation of our affairs...must be independent*" CCC to CCA, November 12, 1763, MHM 12, 21–22.
65 "*A thing...*": CCA to CCC, January 9, 1764, MHM 12, 26–28.
65 *manor of Carrollton*: CCA to CCC, April 10, 1764, MHM 12, 166–168.
65 "*get the [Baker] estate...*": CCA to CCC, January 10, 1764, MHM 12, 28–29.
65 "*which is not improbable...*": CCC to CCA, October 3, 1763, MHM 11, 346–348.
65 *payment of eighteen hundred pounds*: Hanley, *Making*, 109.
65 *large cash dowry*: ibid., 109.
65 "*I think I feel...*": CCC to CCA, January 27, 1764, MHM 12, 31–36.
66 "*If the daughter's temper...*": CCC to CCA, January 27, 1764, MHM 12, 31–36.
66 *Louisa's older sister*: Hanley, *Making*, 120.
66 "*was pleased to form...given the world*": CCC to the Countess of Auzouer, October 6, 1766, in Rowland, I:80.
66 "*the anxiety your passion...*": CCA to CCC, February 12, 1764, in Field, 84.
66 "*promote your happiness*": CCA to CCC, February 27 [misdated March 27 in Field], 1764, MHM 12, 36, Field, 85.
66 "*so unnatural a proposal...make a parent miserable*": CCC to CCA, March 21, 1764, MHM 12, 38–41.
66 "*I find myself much mended...*": CCC to CCA, February 27, 1764, MHM 12, 37–38.
66 *three or four years*: CCC to CCA, April 19, 1764, MHM 12, 168–170.
66 "*I should choose...*": CCC to CCA, May 1, 1764, MHM 12, 170–171.

PART II: First Citizen

67 "*tossed about...30 days*": CCC to CCA, December 8, 1764, MHM 12, 175.
67 *Finally arriving...shortly*: CCC to CCA, December 20, 1764, MHM 12, 175.
67 *But harsh weather...Tilghman family*: CCC to CCA, January 25, 1765, MHM 12, 177.
67 *Tuesday, February 12*: *Maryland Gazette*, February 14, 1765, MHM 12, 178; Ives, 300.
67 *give a ball*: Elizabeth Carroll to CCC, September 10, 1760, Hanley 78.
67 *King George...March 22, 1765*: Gurn, 27.

Parliamentary Tyranny

67 *unitary sovereign*: Onuf, 22–24.
67 "*King in Parliament*": Tierney, *Religion*, 82–83.
67 *every seven years...to vote*: H. Trevor Colbourn, *The Lamp of Experience*

Notes

(Chapel Hill: University of North Carolina Press, 1965), 52–54.
68 *"uncontrollable"*: Hume, 370.
68 *"middle power...disarmed"*: ibid., 155.
68 *made the government more absolute*: ibid., 309.
68 *Parliament had granted...forty-five year reign*: ibid., 158.
68 *"metaphysically endowed..."*: Charles Mullett, 53–56.
68 *"when an act..."*: ibid., 45.
68 *"no human laws..."*: Onuf, 8–9.
68 *Most justices...all law*: Charles Mullett, 37.
69 *misty Teutonic past*: Colbourn, 8.
69 *"no new declaration"*: ibid., 36.
69 *"that ancient constitution..."*: ibid., 55.

The Saxon Myth

69 *supposedly elected their kings...degenerate Roman Empire*: ibid., 25.
69 *Petyt and...Sidney*: ibid., 8–9.
69 *racial ideologies*: see ibid., 195.
69 *labor of peasants*: ibid., 196.
69 *originated in Christendom*: see Tierney, *Religion*, 9.
69 *"the first writer..."*: Colbourn, 25.
69 *preferred Rapin's...to Hume's*: ibid., 177.
69 *"An incarnate God!!!..."*: Paul C. Nagel, *Descent from Glory: Four Generations of the Adams Family* (New York: Oxford University Press, 1983), 128.
70 *"rights of nature"*: Peter Paul, 108; Colbourn, 97.
70 *"antecedent to all..."*: Colbourn, 90.
70 *"on the frame...of the Universe"*: Peter Paul, 61.

The Mental Revolution

70 *"the Revolution was..."*: Onuf, 4.
70 *the concept of a written constitution*: John W. Blassingame, "American Nationalism and Other Loyalties in the Southern Colonies, 1763–1775," *Journal of Southern History* 34:1 (February, 1968), 53; Peter Paul, 43.
70 *identified with natural rights*: Colbourn, 189; Charles Mullett, 6, 90.
70 *"end of law..."*: Thomas Aquinas, ST q. 96, art. 1, in Baumgarth and Regan, 65.
70 *corpus mysticum reipublicae*: Tierney, *Religion*, 20.
71 *as Christ had been born*: ibid., 66–67.
71 *the people delegated sovereignty*: ibid., 45.
71 *maior et sanior pars*: Tierney, *Idea*, 23.
71 *"but by the common..."*: Ives, 86–87.
71 *"the body of the whole realm"*: Tierney, *Religion*, 21.
71 *direct divine mandate*: see Colbourn, 40.
71 *"the consent of the people..."*: Wegemer, 131.
71 *few men in the colonies*: Charles Mullett, 87.
71 *"was incorporated into..."*: Everett Adams, *A Critique of the Concepts "Life, Liberty, and the Pursuit of Happiness" as They Are Discussed in Sermons of Selected American Preachers from 1750 to 1783* (dissertation: Southwestern Baptist Theological Seminary, 1993), 20.

72 "to such bodies...": Tierney, Religion, 55.
72 "one is set...": ibid., 89.
72 "should take account...": Thomas Aquinas, ST q. 96, art. 1, in Baumgarth and Regan, 65.
72 established by Moses...based on the Exodus: Tierney, Religion, 88.
72 resemblance to the Catholic Church: ibid., 64, 90–91.
72 Pillars of Priestcraft...: Colbourn, 62.
73 "Turks, Jews...": Bobrick, 209–210.

The Republican Empire Stirs

73 Catholics did not join: "Journal of a French Traveller II," 73.
73 John Jay claimed: Gurn, 79.
73 "I never had heard...": ibid., 79–80.
73 "must and will be": LaMonte, 194.
73 "No nation whatsoever...": "Journal of a French Traveller II," 84.
73 damned before they would pay: ibid., 72.
73 "lay aside their religion...": ibid., 75.
73f. "The power of this continent...superfluities of life": CCC to [Christopher Bird?], September 28, 1765, Rowland I:73–74.
74 "the only matter...affluence can do": William Graves to CCA, January 14, 1770, MHM 12, 287–293.
74 "I do not intend...to be industrious": CCC to William Graves [misidentified as Henry Graves], September 15, 1765, in Field, 88–92.
74 "to make the oppressors feel it": CCC to Mr. Bradshaw, December 8, 1765, in Field, 101–102.
74 "an argument rather levelled...": CCC to Daniel Barrington, March 17, 1766, in Field, 108–114.
75 "an empty point..." CCC to Daniel Barrington, March 17, 1766, in Field, 108–114.
75 "their own interest...": CCC to ?, October 5, 1765, in Field, 95.
75 the key ideological shift...with public virtue: Cathy Matson and Peter Onuf, "Toward a Republican Empire: Interest and Ideology in Revolutionary America," American Quarterly 37:4 (Autumn 1985), passim.
75 "great and lucrative posts...to public liberty": CCC to Edmund Jennings, March 9, 1767, in Field, 138–142.
75 "Liberty will maintain...": CCC to Mr. Bradshaw, November 21, 1765, in Field, 96–97.
75 "not yet corrupt enough...": CCC to Mr. Bradshaw, December 8, 1765, in Field, 101–102.

The Mercantile System

76 "An argument that proves...": CCC to Daniel Barrington, May 29, 1766, in Field, 121–123.
76 "If I could make...": CCC to Edmund Jennings, May 29, 1766, in Field, 116–120.
76 pretended not to notice: Bobrick, 62.
76 the tax...on molasses: Willard Sterne Randall, Benedict Arnold: Patriot and Traitor (New York: William Morrow & Co., 1990), 43.

Notes

76   *will to enforce*: see Onuf, 3.
76   *Sugar Act of 1764*: Randall, 46.
76   *not enough money*: Ronald Hoffman, *A Spirit of Dissension* (Baltimore: Johns Hopkins University Press, 1973), 36.
77   *Currency Act had forbidden*: Randall, 41.
77   *importation of specie…balance of trade*: Hoffman, *Spirit*, 35.
77   *lumber and iron production*: ibid., 30.
77   *inflated what little was left*: ibid., 34.
77   *worth one hundred pounds sterling*: Black, 44.
77   *Bills of exchange*: Hoffman, *Spirit*, 26.
77   *paid £52 annually*: ibid., 32.
77   *Even Gov. Sharpe regretted*: ibid., 35.
77   *Carrollton realized…financial woes*: CCC to Edmund Jennings, May 29, 1766, in Field, 116–120.
77   *To circumvent…of the council*: Hoffman, *Spirit*, 57.
77   *$173,733*: ibid., 59.
77   *"A medium of trade…so useful a measure"*: CCC to Edmund Jennings, March 9, 1767, in Field, 138–142.
77   *"Our factors…oppress us"*: CCC to William Graves, September 15, 1765, in Field, 88–92.
77   *provided a pretext*: Hoffman, *Spirit*, 38.
78   *"draw from it…"*: CCC to Mr. Bradshaw, December 8, 1765, in Field, 101–102.
78   *"slaves and beasts…spirit"*: CCC to William Graves, August 12, 1766, in Field, 126–131.
78   *"To judge from the number…"*: CCC to ?, September 30, 1765, in Rowland I:74–75.

The Spirit of Liberty

78   *"harpies, id est…political death"*: CCC to Mr. Bradshaw, December 8, 1765, in Field, 101–102.
78   *"mechanical company"*: Hoffman, *Spirit*, 38.
78   *"a busy, restless incendiary…"*: Hanley, *Making*, 225.
78   *denied membership…chronic financial trouble*: Hoffman, *Spirit*, 48.
78   *"is hated & despised…Old Nick"*: CCC to Daniel Carroll, September 5, 1765, Hanley 165.
79   *"the clamorous public"*: CCC to Daniel Barrington, May 29, 1766, in Field, 121–123.
79   *"some expressions…at that juncture"*: CCC to Daniel Barrington, March 17, 1766, in Field, 108–114.
79   *descended on the capital*: Hoffman, *Spirit*, 55.
79   *April 1, 1766…"than they usually are"*: CCC to Daniel Barrington, March 17, 1766, in Field, 108–114.
79   *fled Maryland in disgrace*: CCC to Christopher Bird, September 28, 1765, in Field, 93–94.
79   *"They begin to think…"*: Hoffman, *Spirit*, 58.
79   *"men of little note"*: ibid., 39.
79   *"The clamour of the People…"*: CCC to Daniel Barrington, March 17, 1766, in Field, 108–114.

79 *"condescending"*: CCC to [Christopher Bird?], September 28, 1765, in Rowland I:73–4; see also CCC to Edmund Jennings, May 29, 1766, in Field, 116–120.
79 *"England can never be..."*: CCC to William Graves, August 12, 1766, in Field, 126–131.
79 *"No stretch of the..."*: CCC to Edmund Jennings, March 9, 1767, in Field, 138–142.
80 *"The genuine principles...in its stead"*: CCC to William Graves, August 12, 1766, in Field, 126–131.
80 One desultory riot: "Journal of a French Traveller II," 83.
80 *"does not in the least...put it in practice"*: CCC to Daniel Barrington, May 29, 1766, in Field, 121–123.
80 *"this act of justice..."*: CCC to Edmund Jennings, May 29, 1766, in Field, 116–120.
80 rediscovered their charter rights: Ives, 300–301.
80 Citing Lord Baltimore's...unconstitutional: ibid., 89.
80 claimed the right of home rule: Charles Mullett, 129, Peter Paul, 89.
80 *"a competent legislature..."*: CCC to William Graves, August 12, 1766, in Field, 126–131.

The Habit of Business

80 *As an attorney...by other lawyers*: Hanley, *Making*, 142.
81 *"Providence"*: ibid., 205.
81 *"Among all the disadvantages...hatred than envy"*: CCC to CCA, June 14, 1763, MHM 11, 335–337.
81 willing to accept a permanent exclusion: Hanley, *Making*, 201.
81 *"My views reach...my paternal acres"*: CCC to William Graves, in Rowland, I: 71.
81 *"My poor little thin..."*: CCC to William Graves, August 14, 1772, MHM 32, 214–218.
81 *58,621 acres...Pennsylvania*: Peter Paul, 211.
81 £2,272 sterling...£100,000 sterling: Kwilecki, 12.
81 £1,000 to the Potomac Company: Rowland, I:95.
81 *With the Stamp Act...£40,000 sterling*: Edwin J. Perkins, *The Economy of Colonial America* (New York: Columbia University Press, 1988), 32.
81f. *When the Maryland Assembly...in paper money*: see Joseph A. Ernst, "The Political Economy of the Chesapeake Colonies, 1760–1775," in Ronald Hoffman, et al. eds., *The Economy of Early America, The Revolutionary Period, 1763–1790* (Charlottesville: University Press of Virginia, 1988), 217.
82 *The Carrolls...terms of wealth*: Perkins, 131–133.
82 never actually lived at Carrollton: Rowland, I:69.
82 *"perfect understanding...from each other"*: CCC to Christopher Bird, March 8, 1767, in Field, 137.
82 *"the spirits of youth...happy & easy"*: CCC to the Countess of Auzouer, September 20, 1771, MHM 32, 203–208.
82 *"Not only 40,000 pounds..."*: CCC to William Graves, September 15, 1765, in Rowland, I:77.
82 *"I have been poring...the fatigue"*: CCC to Christopher Bird, September 17, 1765, Hanley 167.

Notes

82 *"you cannot without fatigue…"*: CCA to CCC, April 20, 1770, MHM 12, 348–351.
82 *"Never do anything…very disagreeable"*: CCA to CCC, May 22–25, 1770, MHM 12, 359–362.
83 *"The way to do it…"*: CCA to CCC, April 20, 1770, MHM 12, 348–351.
83 all the rent rolls…*"indolent & careless"*: CCA to CCC, October 21, 1773, MHM 15, 283–284.
83 *"penny wise & pound foolish"*: CCA to CCC, August 12, 1770, MHM 12, 367–369.
83 watch the markets: CCA to CCC, April 25, 1770, MHM 12, 351–353.
83 say nothing: CCA to CCC, August 31, 1770, MHM 13, 57–60.
83 until the buyers…to his price: CCA to CCC, September 5, 1770, MHM 13, 60–61.
83 As economists Lawrence H. Officer and Samuel H. Williamson have shown through their "Measuring Worth" project (www.measuringworth.com), the relative worth of money in different time periods is a vexed question. Following the RPI or Retail Price Index, we can say that £100,000 would equal about $15,385,000 today in terms of relative purchasing power. However, using another method proposed by Officer and Williamson, Carroll's net worth translates into £185.4 million today in "economic status value" or "prestige value," calculated on "the income index of the per-capita GDP." And Carroll's "economic power"—or his ability to control the "composition or total amount of production in the economy," considering his wealth as a share of GDP—becomes a striking £1.37 billion in 2017.

Labor, Free and Unfree

83 *"It is true…well-looking slaves"*: CCA to CCC, September 15, 1771, MHM 14, 135.
83 *"There are some light…"*: CCA to CCC, June 12, 1772, MHM 14, 150–151.
83 *"I lost a pair…"*: CCA to CCC, October 19, 1772, MHM 14, 358–360.
83 *"It is with great…"*: CCA to CCC, September 28, 1774, MHM 16, 136.
84 *"have been well whipped…"*: CCC to CCA, October 2, 1769—November 5, 1769, MHM 12, 283–286.
84 *"was not whipped…off soon"*: CCA to CCC, August 31, 1770, MHM 13, 57–60.
84 mostly Irish…more legal protection: Hanley, Making, 177.
84 *"to purchase 5 negroes…shoemaker"*: Clement Brooke to Baltimore Iron Works, February 4, 1774, Hanley 406.
84 buying a Scot: CCC to CCA, October 2—November 5, 1769, MHM 12, 283–286.
84 Magdalen's struggle: CCA to CCC, October 11, 1770, MHM 13, 61–63.
84 worms…one Antony: CCA to CCC, September 17, 1772, MHM 14, 286–287.
84 *"Poor old creature…"*: CCC to CCA, April 3, 1773, MHM 15, 62–65.
84 *"to pamper my horses…"*: CCA to CCC, June 1, 1772, MHM 14, 145–147.
84 Carrollton proposed…be stopped: CCC to Baltimore Iron Works, November 2, 1767, Carroll Family Papers, Library of Congress.

84   *threatened to withdraw*: CCC to Baltimore Iron Works, November 20, 1767, Carroll Family Papers, Library of Congress.
84f. *"to carry on...our interest"*: CCC to Baltimore Iron Works, n.d., Hanley 369.
85   *usurious and illegal..."one thing besides"*: CCC to CCA, July 4, 1762, MHM 11, 267–271.
85   *"in conscience, justice, & reason"*: CCA to CCC, December 24, 1762, MHM 11, 322–323.
85   *1798 List of Assets*: Edward C. Papenfuse, "Charles Carroll of Carrollton: English Aristocrat in an American Setting," in Van Devanter, 44.

Marriage

85   *"The most beautiful..."*: CCC to CCA, January 29, 1760, Hanley 68, MHM 10, 251.
85f. *"A man of common sense...station of life"*: CCC to Mr. Bradshaw, November 21, 1765, in Rowland, I:77–78.
86   *"obliging temper..."* CCC to the Countess of Auzouer, October 6, 1766, Hanley 183.
86   *"no ways inferior...strengthened by Philosophy"*: CCC to Christopher Bird, September 17, 1765, Hanley 167.
86   *dispensation*: a second dispensation is dated October 14, 1766, in Field, 135.
86   *"fever...into that state"*: CCC to William Graves, July 16–22, 1766, Hanley 176.
86   *fiancé at her bedside*: Leonard, 84.
86   *November 25*: CCC to Charles Digges, November 28, 1766, in Field, 136.
86   *"I loved her...melancholy subject"*: CCC to William Graves, November 27, 1766, Hanley 190.
86   *"It was this gentleman's..."*: CCC to William Graves, April 16, 1768, in Rowland, I:90–92.
87   *Baltimore apparently warned*: Hanley, *Making*, 85–86.
87   *convicted of embezzlement...£1,000 deposit*: Mason in Van Devanter, 26.
87   *Darnall's son...married Rachel Brooke*: Hanley, *Making*, 85.
87   *"worthless good for nothing...yet awhile"*: Elizabeth Carroll to CCC, March 4, 1759, Hanley 54.
87   *"low spirited"*: CCA to CCC, September 6, 1772, MHM 14, 281–282.
87   *a dispensation*: from Thomas Digges, June 3, 1768, Hanley 231.
87   *on both sides*: Rowland, I:88.
87   *"Indenture"*: ibid., I:87.
87   *"how disagreeable such a delay...Reason & Justice"*: CCC to William Graves, January 16, 1768, Hanley 221.
88   *"When your letter I read..."*: Ronald Hoffman, "Charles Carroll of Carrollton: Conservative Revolutionary, 1776–1781," in Van Devanter, 36.
88   *"on Sunday evening..."*: *Maryland Gazette*, June 9, 1768, in Rowland, I:88.
88   *"You cannot be...at this season"*: CCA to CCC, September 15, 1771, MHM 14, 135.
88   *"Can fine furniture...of any sort"*: CCA to CCC, November 30, 1770, MHM 13, 71–72.
88   *When Molly begrudged*: CCA to CCC, April 12, 1771, MHM 13, 175–176.

Notes

88f. *"a child's temper..."*: CCA to CCC, April 10–13, 1774, Hanley 411.
89 *She became addicted*: Mason in Van Devanter, 27–28.

The Search for Harmony

89 *"golden age"*: ibid., 25.
89 *famous gardens*: Elder in Van Devanter, 59.
89 *"merry set of gentlemen..."*: Leonard, 82.
89 *"election to the Homony Club..."*: Smith, 87; Hanley, *Revolutionary Statesman*, 10.
89 *never before admitted Catholics...Eden...Eddis*: Mason in Van Devanter, 25.
89 *Boucher...Paca...Dulany...Chase*: Hanley, *Making*, 147.
89 *forbidden subject*: ibid., 249.
89 *Charles Willson Peale*: Rowland, I:95.
90 *"I long to hear..."*: CCC to William Graves, April 16, 1768, Hanley 229.
90 *"why friends should not..."*: CCC to Edmund Jennings, April 14, 1768, Hanley 228.
90 *"Dear Sir...the last..."*: CCC to Christopher Bird, September 10, 1767, Hanley 206.
90 *"as fatal to private..."*: CCC to William Graves, [August 9, 1771?], MHS 4193, 478.
90 *"I am determined..."*: CCC to William Graves, September 7, 1773, MHM 32, 219–220.
90 *"no, unless I..."*: CCC to William Graves, August 15, 1774, MHM 32, 220–225.
90 *"Honest & well-meaning..."*: CCC to Edmund Jennings, December 18, 1770, Hanley 286.
91 *"It happens to be gunpowder..."*: CCC to Edmund Jennings, October 14, 1766, in Field, 132–134.
91 *"Well, I see...singular in that"*: CCC to William Graves, August 15, 1774, MHM 32, 220–225.
91 *"have not reformed..."*: CCC to Edmund Jennings, October 14, 1766, in Field, 132–134.
91 *"Those against whom..."*: CCC to Edmund Jennings, August 13, 1767, in Field, 142–143.
91 *"I read no controversy"*: CCC to William Graves, August 12, 1766, in Field, 126–131.
91 *During Lent...confession and Communion*: CCA to CCC, April 2, 1771, MHM 13, 172–173.
91 *dominated by the lay gentry*: Hanley, *Revolutionary Statesman*, 25.
91f. *When it was rumored...similar complaint*: Carey, 16.
92 *popular at the time*: Barker, 19.

Deadly Potential

92 *"Mr. Carroll thinks..."*: William Deards to CCA, September 29, 1769, MHM 12, 276.
92 *"your language...with pistols"*: CCC to Lloyd Dulany, September 29, 1769, MHM 12, 279–280.
92f. *"I did not know...to my person"*: note from CCC to CCA in ibid.

Charles Carroll of Carrollton

93 *Molly's father…another set*: Hanley, *Making*, 183–185.
93 *shoes and a stretcher*: William Deards to CCA, September 30, 1769, MHM 12, 280–281.
93 *"the deep stain…jesuitical forge"*: Lloyd Dulany to CCC, September 29, 1769, MHM 12, 277–278.
93 *as a witness…"hurt my rest"*: CCC to CCA, September 30, 1769, MHM 12, 281–282.
93f. *"If the grossest…on the occasion"*: CCC to CCA, October 2, 1769, MHM 12, 283–286.
94 *"silly pride…indentured servant"*: CCC to CCA, October 1, 1769, MHM 12, 282–283.

The Townshend Acts

94 *new market for colonial wheat*: Hoffman, *Spirit*, 19–20.
94 *little opposition*: Bobrick, 80–81.
94 *"I do not as yet…"*: CCC to William Graves, November 7, 1767, Hanley 218.
94 *which Carroll supported*: Hanley, *Revolutionary Statesman*, 10.
94 *Boston and New York…both were acquitted*: Hoffman, *Spirit*, 83–85, 91.
94 *would not act on principle*: ibid., 3, 27.
94 *"half of the nation…"*: Kwilecki, 16.
95 *bribe the…government*: Colbourn, 131.
95 *in 1769…began to widen*: Hoffman, *Spirit*, 20.
95 *planters united in 1770*: ibid., 81.
95 *factors in the colonies*: ibid., 22.
95 *extra taxes*: ibid., 30.
95 *mysteriously lost weight*: CCC to Wallace and Company, June 10, 1775, Charles Carroll of Carrollton Letterbook, Arents Tobacco Collection, S0767, New York Public Library [hereafter Arents Letterbook].
95 *tobacco market collapsed*: Hoffman, *Spirit*, 99.
95 *"Such a conflagration…"*: ibid., 100.
95 *Maryland native*: ibid., 24.
95 *"I should not be surprised…"*: ibid., 103.
95 *Carroll the Barrister…Annapolis boycott*: letter of May 23, 1769, *Archives of Maryland* 62, 457–458.
95 *refusing a seat*: David Curtis Skaggs, "Maryland's Impulse Toward Social Revolution: 1750–1776," *Journal of American History* 54:4 (March, 1968), 778.
95 *this association…colonial self-taxation*: Charles Mullett, 105.
95 *"The society of a few…"*: CCC to Charles Carroll, Barrister, December 3, 1771, MHM 32, 208–210.
95f. *A Carroll kinsman…of Mary Digges*: Hoffman and Mason, 128.
96 *"Many in court…"*: CCC to CCA, late April or early May, 1771, MHM 13, 249–252.
96 *"that he supposed…"*: CCA to CCC, May 7–10, 1771, MHM 13, 254–258.
96 *Digges won £1,500*: Hoffman and Mason, 129.
96 *£50*: CCA to CCC, April 15, 1771, MHM 13, 177–178.
96 *debate with Daniel Dulany*: CCA to CCC, November 13, 1769, MHM 12, 286–287.

Notes

96   *"Had I not seen..."*: Hanley, *Making*, 232.
96   *still held back*: Leonard, 88.
96   *Anglican clergy salaries*: see CCA to CCC, November 8, 1771, MHM 14, 136.
96   *led astray by a Papist*: Hanley, *Making*, 226, 228.
96   *"This is dead time..."*: CCC to Charles Carroll, Barrister, August 9, 1771, MHM 32, 200–203.
96   *"joined two things..."*: CCC to William Graves, August 27, 1767, in Field, 145–149.
96   *"to see all the powers..."*: CCC to Edmund Jennings, August 9, 1771, MHM 32, 197–199.
96   *George Washington...October, 1772*: Dorothy Twohig, ed. *George Washington's Diaries: An Abridgment* (Charlottesville: University Press of Virginia, 1999), September 27, 1771, 165; October 10, 1772, 175.

The Fee Controversy

97   *Delegates passed...sale of offices*: Hoffman, *Spirit*, 93.
97   *assembly had fixed*: Hanley, *Revolutionary Statesman*, 11.
97   *Late that year...in 1763*: Onuf, 13.
97   *The opposition members...of the electorate*: ibid., 14.
97   *"robbery"*: Hoffman, *Spirit*, 95.
97   *"Could you imagine...of this Province"*: CCC to Charles Carroll, Barrister, December 3, 1771, MHM 32, 208–210.
97   *surpassed that in any other colony*: Onuf, 14.
97   *Even Walter Dulany...naval officer*: Hoffman, *Spirit*, 54.
97   *"Independent Whigs"...Maryland Gazette*: Hanley, *Revolutionary Statesman*, 11.
97   *the Popular Party*: ibid., 28.
98   *quite conservative*: Hoffman in Van Devanter, 36.
98   *upheld the concept...court party*: Hanley, "Young Mr. Carroll," 418.
98   *Nor did...as a party*: Hanley, *Making*, 228.
98   *tax revolt*: Hoffman, *Spirit*, 118.
98   *a form of currency...resume the inspections*: ibid., 122–123.
98   *"Bacon Face"*: Richard M. Ketchum, *Saratoga* (New York: Henry Holt & Co., 1997), 9.
98   *needed a leader...and planter*: Hoffman, *Spirit*, 117.
98   *Truth Teller...Dr. Richard Steuart*: Rowland, I:100–101.
98   *"we have the better...of the dispute"*: John H. B. Latrobe, "Charles Carroll of Carrollton," in John Sanderson, ed. *Biography of the Signers to the Declaration of Independence* (Philadelphia: R.W. Pomeroy, 1827), 246–247.
98   *"great power...of their proceedings"*: Hanley, *Making*, 224.
99   *"Act with the governor..."*: CCA to CCC, October 28, 1772, MHM 14, 360–364.
99   *when he wrestled...a miscarriage*: Hanley, *Making*, 152.
99   *strongly recommended Dulany's pamphlet*: CCC to Mr. Bradshaw, November 11, 1765, in Field, 96–97; Peter Paul, 40.
99   *"rare talent..."*: John H. B. Latrobe, "Biographical Sketch of Daniel Dulany," *Pennsylvania Magazine of History and Biography* III:1 (1879), 6.

Charles Carroll of Carrollton

99   *"a diamond of the first..."*: Rowland, I:102.
99   *"Persecution...starts at it"*: Daniel Dulany, "Military and Political Affairs in the Middle Colonies in 1755," December 9, 1755, *Pennsylvania Magazine of History and Biography* III:1 (1879), 27–28.

The Challenger Scores

99   *draws out infection*: Smith, 104–105.
99f.   *Antilon's first letter...ordained by God*: Onuf, 43–50.
100f.   *replied to Antilon..."best of natures"*: ibid., 53–60.
101   *"honest freedom...upon the community"*: Rowland, I:105–106.

The Champion Retaliates

101f.   *Dulany fired back..."reach of it"*: Onuf, 65–75.
102f.   *"all the strangers...the First Citizen"*: CCA to CCC, March 17, 1773, MHM 14, 368–369.
103f.   *First Citizen attacks..."soul like thine"*: Onuf, 77–98.
104   *"every eye...pleasure I feel"*: CCA to CCC, March 17, 1773, MHM 14, 368–369.
104   *"let me have..."*: CCA to CCC, March 17, 1773, MHM 14, 369–370.
104   *"I suppose Antilon...renew the attack"*: Daniel of St. Thomas Jenifer to CCA, March 28, 1773, MHM 15, 58.
104   *did not trust Jenifer*: CCC to CCA, April 3, 1773, MHM 14, 369–370.
104   *his father cultivated the Major*: CCA to CCC, April 8, 1773, MHM 15, 194–196.

The Contest Continues

104f.   *rode out...excuse of illness*: CCC to CCA, April 3, 1773, MHM 14, 369–370.
105   *Antilon's third effort..."our religious establishment"*: Onuf, 102–122.
105   *"The preposession is..."*: CCA to CCC, April 16, 1773, MHM 15, 197–198.
106   *"ought to be active..."*: Onuf, 107.
106   *The fee proclamation...was lawful*: ibid., 119.
106   *First Citizen falls back..."remember, and forgive"*: ibid., 124–151.
106   *"their thanks to the First..."*: Leonard, 92.
106   *"a distinguished advocate..."*: Charles Carroll of Carrollton Biography from the New York "Truth Teller," 1827, MHS.
106   *"was an author..."*: CCA to CCC, May 20, 1773, MHM 15, 200–201.
106f.   *one final assault..."way they please"*: Onuf, 159–191.
107   *fourth and last..."original intent"*: ibid., 192–226.
107f.   *"They are obliged..."*: CCC to CCA, April 3, 1773, MHM 15, 62–65.
108   *"The union of all...directs the storm"*: CCC to CCA, October 27, 1774, MHM 16, 40; Hanley, *Making*, 260.

The Tea Act

108   *Lewis Leonard...make himself indispensable*: Leonard, 59.
108   *"I will serve them..."*: CCC to William Graves, August 15, 1774, MHM 32, 220–225.
108   *"give offence..."*: CCA to CCC, June 18, 1773, MHM 15, 275.
108   *"enemies to their Country"*: CCA to CCC, June 24, 1773, MHM 15, 275–277.

Notes

108 *"very silly idle..."*: CCA to CCC, August 26, 1773, MHM 15, 280–281.
108 *"he may perhaps meet..."*: CCA to CCC, July 20, 1773, MHM 15, 277–278.
109 *"The pains you've been at..."*: Gurn, 46.
109 *"Consistent Protestant"...confessional state*: Hanley, *Making*, 258.
109 *"a Protestant people..."*: Hoffman and Mason, 291.
109 *"political parricide..."*: Hanley, *Making*, 250.
109 *proclamations were permissible..."guardians of the people"*: ibid., 259.
109 *lost their leverage...inspection bill*: Onuf, 15.
109 *in 1774...against the party leadership*: see CCA to CCC, April 15, 1774, MHM 16, 29–30.
109 *The Tea Act...smuggled Dutch tea*: Hanley, *Revolutionary Statesman*, 22; Hoffman and Mason, 294.
109f. *Assembly resolved...in July 1773*: Charles Mullett, 107.
110 *Committee of Correspondence*: Hanley, *Revolutionary Statesman*, 17.
110 *dissolved in rancor*: Smith, 112.
110 *proprietary party disappeared*: Skaggs, 780.
110 *"there is a schism"...of Hammond land*: Hoffman, *Spirit*, 127.
110 *At a May 25, 1774...was repealed*: ibid., 128–129.
110 *In August...nonimportation*: CCC to Wallace and Company, August 17, 1774, Arents Letterbook.
110 *"a general scheme...and the Colonies"*: CCC to Wallace and Company, June 5, 1774, Arents Letterbook.
110 *"total redress..."*: CCC to Wallace and Company, August 17, 1774, Arents Letterbook.

The First Continental Congress

110 *"I hope the Colonies"*: CCA to CCC, May 27, 1774, MHM 16, 31.
111 *"This congress is really"...with delegates*: CCC to CCA, September 12, 1774, MHM 16, 35–36.
111 *"a little on politics"*: Hoffman and Mason, 353.
111 *"happy reconciliation"*: Hanley, *Revolutionary Statesman*, 75.
111 *The metaphor...adult prerogatives*: Colbourn, 110.
111 *Carrollton accepted*: Hanley, *Revolutionary Statesman*, 44, 57.
111 *King could not...Parliament*: Charles Mullett, 167, 197.
111 *Galloway's Plan of Union...one vote*: Journal of the Continental Congress, September 28, 1774, in Peter Force, ed. *American Archives* (Washington, 1837), 4th series, v. 1, 905–906.
112 *"I still think..."*: CCC to CCA, September 12, 1774, MHM 16, 35–36.
112 *"Boston, it is said..."*: CCC to CCA, September 7, 1774, MHM 16, 31–32.
112 *"the smallest incident..."*: CCC to CCA, September 9, 1774, MHM 16, 32–33.
112 *Congress called...December 1*: CCC to Messrs. Lawton & Browne, October 30, 1774, Arents Letterbook.
112 *postponed for a year*: Hoffman, *Spirit*, 132–133.
112 *The delegates dispersed...cannon salute*: Leonard, 107.
112 *praised Daniel Dulany*: Hoffman and Mason, 354.

The Peggy Stewart

112 "*It has been represented...*": CCC to CCA, September 30, 1774, MHM 16, 38.
112 *On October 15...three-month voyage*: Rowland, I:128.
112 *Stewart had already...British creditors*: Hoffman, *Spirit*, 130.
112f. "*daring insult...friends of America*": Rowland, I:129.
113 *Charles Ridgely...if Stewart complied*: Hoffman, *Spirit*, 135–136.
113 *Carroll the Barrister and Chase objected*: ibid.; Skaggs, 781.
113 *According to Annapolis lore...was decisive*: Elihu S. Riley, "*The Ancient City*": *A History of Annapolis, in Maryland, 1649–1887* (Annapolis, 1887; reprinted, Baltimore: Genealogical Publishing Company, Inc., 1995), 171.
113 "*moderate measures*": Ronald Hoffman et al., eds., *Dear Papa, Dear Charley*, vol. 2 (Chapel Hill: University of North Carolina Press, 2001), 749.
113 "*It will not be...to the water's edge*": Latrobe in Sanderson, 248–249; Charles Carroll Biography from the "*Truth Teller*"; Gurn, 55–56.
113 "*the fair Scotch Peggy*": Rowland, I:130.

PART III: Revolutionary

115 *Annapolis legend..."same kind of tea"*: Riley, 309.
115 "*I assured him...or a knave*": CCA to CCC, November 21–23, 1774, Hanley 440.

The Provisional Government of Maryland

115 *The Maryland Convention...Arundel County*: Hanley, *Revolutionary Statesman*, 32.
115 *committees of correspondence and of observation*: John Archer Silver, "The Provisional Government of Maryland (1774–1777)," *Johns Hopkins University Studies in Historical and Political Science*, 13th series, no. x (October 1895), 487.
116 *correspondence committee in December*: Hanley, *Revolutionary Statesman*, 64.
116 *selected the delegates*: "At a full meeting of the inhabitants of Anne-Arundel County...on Monday the 16th day of January, 1775" (Annapolis: Anne Catharine Green and Son, 1775, Evans 13817).
116 "*all former differences...*": Ives, 312.
116 *rejected the...to stop debt collections*: Silver, 504.
116 *backlash against the...incendiaries*: Hoffman, *Spirit*, 136.
116 *With a clear...after the war began*: Silver, 484–492.
116 "*courtly principles*": CCC et al. to Committee of Correspondence of Baltimore County, March 26, 1775, MHS 4194, 624.
116 "*prevent any punishment...*": Journal of the Maryland Convention, *Archives of Maryland* 11, 66–67; see also Silver, 496–497.
117 "*Legion*": Hoffman, *Spirit*, 165.
117 *Robert Christie..."rebels"*: Silver, 496.
117 "*your life will be...*": Hoffman, *Spirit*, 190.
117 "*truest though absurdest...*": ibid., 140.

Notes

117 "*What think you…*": ibid., 137.
117 *prosecuted by the British*: CCC to William Graves, August 15, 1774, MHM 32, 220–225.
117 *statute of Edward III…treasonable*: CCC to CCA, July 2, 1776, Hanley 534.
117 *In April, 1775…loyal to him*: Silver, 493.
117 *He began promoting…two thousand men*: Hoffman, *Spirit*, 143–144.
117 "*great temper and moderation*": ibid., 141.
117 "*all power is getting fast…*": ibid., 150.

The Council of Safety

117 *What soured Eden…Major Jenifer*: Hanley, *Revolutionary Statesman*, 60.
117 *who became president*: Hoffman, *Spirit*, 142.
117 *immediately took action…September 1 advertisement*: *Journal of the Maryland Convention, Archives of Maryland* 11, 74–77.
118 "*As the exigency…*": CCC to Daniel of St. Thomas Jenifer, September 10, 1775, Hanley 477.
118 *Dunmore had…for his militia*: see Hanley, *Revolutionary Statesman*, 81.
118 *Patriots who…quartering them*: Hoffman, *Spirit*, 185.
118 *Dunmore later sold…slavery*: Bobrick, 163.
118 *Richard Henry Lee…proprietary government*: Hanley, *Revolutionary Statesman*, 149.
118 *Samuel Purviance…of Observation*: Hoffman, *Spirit*, 158.
118 *arresting the governor*: Silver, 512.
118 *They remonstrated…unmolested*: ibid., 515; Smith, 155.
118 "*immediate anarchy and convulsion*": Hoffman, *Spirit*, 159.
118 "*highly applauded…common Cause*": ibid., 161–165.
118 *to receive all Loyalists*: Sir Robert Eden [to CCC?], June 24, 1776, Hanley 532.
119 "*So scandalous a transaction…*": CCC to CCA, June 28, 1776, Hanley 533.
119 "*the namby pambys…*": Hoffman, *Spirit*, 157–158.
119 *William Neill applied*: William Neill to CCC, February 12, 1776, *Journal and Correspondence of the Maryland Council of Safety, Archives of Maryland* 11, 156–157.
119 *So did Purviance*: ibid., 227.
119 "*unless you have express…*": CCC to Thomas Dorsey, March 8, 1776, ibid., 223; Rowland, I:142.
119 *His subcommittee*: Leonard, 116.
119 *proposed…powder mill*: Rowland, I:140.
119 *invested…saltpeter mill*: Hanley, *Revolutionary Statesman*, 161.
119 *expanded the…Works*: ibid., 112.
119 *Carrollton later wrote…serve the Revolution*: ibid., 258.
120f. "*as certainly that intelligence…*": CCC to Wallace and Company, June 4, 1775, Arents Letterbook.
120 "*regulate your conduct…*": CCC to Wallace and Company, October 4, 1775, Arents Letterbook.
120 "*we shall prove victorious*": CCC to Wallace and Company, September 18, 1775, Arents Letterbook.

120 *"my hand is far..."*: CCA to William Graves, May 29, 1775, Hanley 458.
120 *Carrolls transferred...Joshua Johnson*: see CCA to CCC, August 14, 1775, Hanley 471.
120 *established himself in France...John Quincy Adams*: Nagel, 62–63.

Sense and Sensibility

120 *first surviving daughter*: for the Carroll genealogy, see charts in Van Devanter.
120 *after Carroll's former loves*: Smith, 90.
120 *"is now big with..."*: CCC to William Graves, August 15, 1774, MHM 32, 220–225.
120 *March 2, 1775*: Hanley, *Revolutionary Statesman*, 67.
120 *"my dear little"...milk supply*: CCA to CCC, April 6, 1775, Hanley 451.
120 *"Are such risks..."*: CCA to CCC, December 1, 1775, Hanley 488.
120 *Charles Willson Peale...Treatise on Education*: Hanley, *Revolutionary Statesman*, 235.
121 *foreign to the American mind*: Henry F. May, *The Enlightenment in America* (New York: Oxford University Press, 1976), 41, 119, 132.
121 *Common Sense theory*: ibid., 38.
121 *medical and moral ideas...moral decision-making*: Burstein, 11.
121 *American colleges...Scottish universities*: May, 33.
121 *American Society...in 1766*: ibid., 84.
121 *sentimental fiction*: Burstein, 15.
121 *"the best course..."*: ibid., 110.
122 *"expect to escape..."*: CCC to William Graves, August 15, 1774, MHM 32, 220–225.
122 *"attachment...advantage"*: Hanley, *Revolutionary Statesman*, 71.
122 *"Torn from the body..."*: Geoffrey Gilbert-Hamerling, *Exitus Acta Probat: George Washington and the American Civil Religion* (dissertation, University of California at Berkeley, 1993), 39.
122 *"our attachment..."*: Journal of the Continental Congress, July 6, 1775, accessed May 11, 2000, http://memory.loc.gov.
122 *"Parliament has a right..."*: Charles Mullett, 169.

North Meets South

122 *"the man singled out..."*: CCC to Washington, September 26, 1775, Thomas Addis Emmet Collection, 978, New York Public Library.
122f. *"When I reflect..."*: CCC to CCA, August 18, 1775, Hanley 472.
123 *"It is certainly..."*: CCA to CCC, June 24, 1775, Hanley 464.
123 *"an illustrious school..."*: Gilbert-Hamerling, 126; see also 93.
123 *"one hour's service..."*: Washington to Lund Washington, August 20, 1775, in J. Thomas Scharf, *History of Maryland from the Earliest Period to the Present Day* II (Baltimore: John B. Piet, 1879), 249–250.
123 *"Notwithstanding all the public..."*: Washington to Joseph Reed, February 10, 1776, in ibid., II:259.
123 *"suffer nothing..."*: Washington to Lund Washington, September 30, 1776, in ibid., II:249.

Notes

123   *"The deficiency of public..."*: Martin I.J. Griffin, *Catholics and the American Revolution*, 3 vols. (Ridley Park, Penn.: published by the author, 1907–1911), II:249.
123   *"must shake..."*: ibid., II:242.
123   *"to curry favour"*: Washington to Richard Henry Lee, August 29, 1775, in ibid., II:236.
123   *"next under providence"*: Gilbert-Hamerling, 121.
123   *one hundred to five*: ibid., 117.
124   *"have introduced...run away"*: Scharf, II:260.
124   *"the unhappy..."*: Washington to Philip Schuyler, July 17, 1776, in ibid., II:257.
124   *forbade...Guy Fawkes' Day*: Kwilecki, 124.
124   *"ridiculous and childish...at this juncture"*: Ives, 317–318.
124   *breach of military etiquette*: see Ketchum, 202, 406.
124   *smallpox-infested...and slaves*: Bobrick, 184.
124   *"there is not the least..."*: Griffin, II:247.
124   *Bunker Hill...finding their mark*: Bobrick, 331.
124   *lack of gunpowder..."I have done"*: Griffin, II:258–259.

"CX"

125   *"That which was esteemed..."*: "Countryman," "To the people of Maryland" (Baltimore: Mary Katherine Goddard, 1776), Evans 15111.
125   *Boldly, Carroll...and judicial powers*: "CX" [CCC], *Dunlap's Maryland Gazette*, March 26, 1776.
125f.   *The second CX paper...lead to mob rule*: "CX" [CCC], *Dunlap's Maryland Gazette*, April 12, 1776.

The Quebec Act

126   *June 13, 1774*: Brantz Mayer, ed. *Journal of Charles Carroll of Carrollton During His Visit to Canada in 1776...* (Baltimore: John Murphy for Maryland Historical Society, 1876; reprinted, New York: New York Times and Arno Press, 1969), 13.
126   *established the Catholic Church...sit on the council*: David Milobar, "Quebec Reform, the British Constitution and the Atlantic Empire: 1774–1775," *Parliamentary History* 14:1 (1995), 67.
126   *150,000...360 Anglicans*: Rowland, I:145–146.
126   *"absolutely a dissolution..."*: Blassingame, 74.
126   *"Roman Catholic, nay..."*: Griffin, II:137.
126   *A hissing mob...sign the Act*: Milobar, 78–79.
126f.   *All of the English...system of land tenure*: ibid., 67–76; Ketchum, 15.
127   *"clear beyond a doubt..."*: Griffin, I:250.
127   *"False Frenchmen"*: Burstein, 39.
127   *"Virginius" expected the Inquisition*: William Everett Pauley, Religion and the American Revolution in the South: 1760–1781 (dissertation, Emory University, 1974), 144–145.
127   *"torture at the hands...with slavery"*: Burstein, 40–43.
127   *"We much fear..."*: Griffin, II:98.
127   *promised to obtain...their support*: ibid., II:97, 118.

127f. *Dickinson penned...the Catholic Church*: Gurn, 60.
128 *"Nor can we suppress..."*: Allan S. Everest, ed. *The Journal of Charles Carroll of Carrollton as One of the Congressional Commissioners to Canada in 1776* (Fort Ticonderoga, N.Y.: Champlain—Upper Hudson Bicentennial Committee, 1976), 2.
128 *"The decent manner...unbroken curses"*: Gurn, 61.
128 *"so shallow a politician..."*: ibid., 65.
128 *When the 1774...returned to Maryland*: Hanley, *Revolutionary Statesman*, 50–51.

The Canadian Campaign

128 *"We have received...to fall upon us"*: Journal of the Continental Congress, July 6, 1775, accessed May 11, 2000, http://memory.loc.gov.
129 *to justify...Fort Ticonderoga*: Randall, 93.
129 *"The safety and welfare..."*: Bobrick, 169.
129 *"the Inhabitants of America...best friends"*: George Washington to Canadian Citizens, September 6, 1775, accessed February 25, 2000, http://memory.loc.gov.
129 *"look with compassion..."*: Randall, 145.
129 *strike up Lake Champlain...attack Montreal*: Bobrick, 169–170; Randall, 212.
129 *unreliable maps...twice that far*: Bobrick, 171.
129 *a division...returned to Cambridge*: Randall, 177–178.
129 *whose father...Princeton University*: ibid., 435.
129 *"Golden Thighs"*: Bobrick, 171.
129 *An American minister...thanksgiving or prayer*: Randall, 212.
130 *withhold the sacraments*: Everest, 3; Randall, 208.
130 *"best of sovereigns..."*: Griffin, II:173.
130 *Carleton had to threaten*: Randall, 110.
130 *hated the feudal...starving army*: ibid., 193, 239.
130 *reinforced on November 12*: ibid., 203.
130 *"Had I been ten..."*: ibid., 205.
130 *on November 13 occupied Montreal*: Hanley, *Revolutionary Statesman*, 94.
130 *Montgomery had assumed command*: Everest, 3.
130 *expired on January 1..."on that Providence"*: Bobrick, 173.
130 *killing Montgomery*: Randall, 219.
130 *wounding Arnold*: Everest, 3.
130 *keeping Montgomery's death a secret*: Randall, 224.
130 *The Americans...promissory notes*: Everest, 4.
131 *"enemies and rascals"*: Smith, 148.
131 *abusing the clergy*: Randall, 231; Everest, 5–6.
131 *"possessing Canada...schemes"*: CCA to CCC, October 11, 1775, Hanley 482.
131 *Carrollton...in exchange*: Journal of the Maryland Convention, *Archives of Maryland* 11, 131–132.
131 *about £120 sterling*: Rowland, I:143.

The Canadian Commission

131 *The army begged...to the commission*: Everest, 5–7.

[294]

Notes

131   *"prevail on Mr. John Carroll..."*: Journals of the Continental Congress, February 15, 1776, accessed October 14, 1999, http://memory.loc.gov.
131   *£800*: Hanley, *Revolutionary Statesman*, 103.
131   *eight tons of powder*: Journals of the Continental Congress, February 15, 1776, accessed October 14, 1999, http://memory.loc.gov.
131   *"a Roman Catholic but..."*: Leonard, 104.
131   *"to communicate the circumstances..."*: Paul Eston Mundey, *"Beware of False Allegiance": Origins of Civil Religion in the United States, 1776–1791* (honors thesis: Towson State College, 1973), 37.
131   *"They have not...change of government"*: Griffin, III:303–304.
132   *March 2, 1776...weaken the commission*: Hanley, *Revolutionary Statesman*, 103–106.
132   *"These public honors..."*: ibid., 117.
132   *"quite charmed"*: CCC to CCA, March 29, 1776, Hanley 502.
132   *"What a man!..."* Leonard, 111.
132   *His 1746...Popish domination*: *American Catholic Historical Researches*, XVIII, 121–122.
132   *change with the times*: see Bobrick, 74.
132   *get away with anything*: see ibid., 362.
132   *complained...in return*: CCC to CCA, April 18, 1776, Hanley 510.
132   *to share the letters*: CCC to CCA, April 1, 1776, Hanley 503; CCC to CCA, April 8, 1776, Hanley 506.
132   *"long letters...little to do"*: CCC to CCA, April 30—May 1, 1776, Hanley 513.
132   *women of Philadelphia...pairs of shoes*: CCC to CCA, March 18–19, 1776, Hanley 497.
133   *including Carrollton*: CCC to CCA, March 29, 1776, Hanley 502; CCC to CCA, March 21–22, 1776, Hanley 498.
133   *"it will not be..."*: CCC to CCA, March 8, 1776, Hanley 493.
133   *"as countrymen & friends"*: CCC to CCA, March 25, 1776, Hanley 500.
133   *"urge the necessity"...for their neutrality*: Instructions and Commission from Congress, March 20, 1776, *The Papers of Benjamin Franklin*, vol. 22, *March 23, 1775 through October 27, 1776*, ed. William B. Willcox (New Haven, Conn: Yale University Press, 1982), 382–383.
133   *All officers...in their tasks*: Journals of the Continental Congress, March 20, 1776, accessed October 14, 1999, http://memory.loc.gov.
133   *"the application..."* CCC to CCA, April 30—May 1, 1776, Hanley 513.
133   *"what if we..."*: CCC to CCA, March 21–22, 1776, Hanley 498.
133   *"neither interest nor...of the sword"*: CCC to CCA, March 18–19, 1776, Hanley 497.

The Journey to Canada

133f.   *"Gentlemen of the first...unconquerable"*: CCC to CCA, March 29, 1776, Hanley 502.
134   *The party...five days later*: Ketchum, 19.
134   *"this river seems intended..."*: Everest, 20.
134   *£50,000 sterling*: ibid., 24.
134   *"fine manufactory"*: ibid., 40.
134   *"enjoys a good government"*: ibid., 49.

134 "*I am afraid...*": Franklin to John Hancock, April 13, 1776, *Papers of Benjamin Franklin* 22, 400.
134 *The goals...could hope for*: Hanley, *Revolutionary Statesman*, 120.
135 *if the British...rest of the colonies*: Ketchum, 18.
135 *a fort...Richelieu*: CCC to CCA, April 30—May 1, 1776, Hanley 513.
135 *pickets in the lake...Noix*: Everest, 45; Mayer, 86.
135 "*we may defy...*": Mayer, 76.
135 *Lac du Saint Sacrement*: Ketchum, 28.
135 *Franklin facetiously...him off*: Franklin to Josiah Quincy, April 15, 1776, in Everest, 25.
135 "*If they could not...*": Franklin, in CCC to Mary Carroll, April 15, 1776, Hanley 509.
135 "*Mr. Chase and I...*": Rowland, I:148.
135 *He became violently...gunboat*: Everest, 30–31.
135 *went ashore..."Commissioners' Point"*: Mayer, 81.
135 "*the snow's not dissolving...*": Everest, 46.
135f. "*amazing...horrifying prospects*": CCC to CCA, April 8, 1776, Hanley 506.
136 "*swollen...terrifying spectacle*": Everest, 23.
136 *a French abatis...twenty years earlier*: Mayer, 74, 78.
136 *alarmed*: Commissioners to Canada to William Heath, April 5, 1776, *Papers of Benjamin Franklin* 22, 398.
136 *On April 27...on the 29th*: Mayer, 90–92.
136 "*the affections...*": CCC to CCA, April 15, 1776, Hanley 508.
136 "*good taste and politeness...great man*": CCC to CCA, April 30—May 1, 1776, Hanley 513.
136 "*ease and softness*": CCC to CCA, April 30—May 1, 1776, Hanley 513.
136 *He made an excursion...Sorel River*: Mayer, 94.
136 "*If the Congress...*": CCC to CCA, May 6, 1776, Hanley 516.

The Commmissioners Take Charge

136 *Arnold's proclamation...to Americans*: Randall, 210.
137 "*have recourse to violences...*": Commissioners to Canada to John Hancock, May 6, 1776, *Papers of Benjamin Franklin* 22, 417–419.
137 "*Not the most trifling service...into silver*": Commissioners to Canada to John Hancock, May 1, 1776, in ibid., 413–415.
137 *he reported...were sick*: Mayer, 62.
137 *the British...into the camp*: Bobrick, 173.
137 *enlistments expired*: Mayer, 62.
137 *John Hancock...to Quebec*: John Hancock to Commissioners to Canada, April 26, 1776, *Papers of Benjamin Franklin* 22, 402–403.
137 *five days later...from Wooster*: Bobrick, 176.
137 *only one thousand...downriver*: Mayer, 35–36.
137 "*We were employed...make a sally*": John Thomas to Commissioners to Canada, May 7, 1776, *Papers of Benjamin Franklin* 22, 421–423.
137 *The Americans fled...also captured*: Commissioners to Canada to Philip Schuyler, May 10, 1776, in ibid., 427–429.

Notes

137 *"we have lost...many of them"*: CCC to CCA, May 10, 1776, Hanley 518.
137 *"We are afraid..."*: Commissioners to Canada to John Hancock, May 10, 1776, Papers of Benjamin Franklin 22, 426–427.
137 *Franklin left*: Everest, 50.
137 *"become generals, commissaries..."*: CCC and Chase to Philip Schuyler, May 17, 1776, in Rowland, I:162.
138 *Carroll tried...leave it unprovided*: Commissioners to Canada to John Hancock, May 8, 1776, Papers of Benjamin Franklin 22, 424–426.
138 *only ten days' provisions*: CCC and Chase to Philip Schuyler, May 11, 1776, in Rowland, I:158–159.
138 *"For God's sake..."*: CCC and Chase to Philip Schuyler, May 14 [17?], 1776, in ibid., 161–162.
138 *"If further reinforcements..."*: CCC and Chase to Philip Schuyler, May 11, 1776, in ibid., I:158–159.
138 *"The officers are not..."*: CCC and Chase to John Thomas, May 26, 1776, in ibid., I:166–168.
138 *to make a buck*: they were gouging the British as well; see Ketchum, 106.
138 *"It is very difficult..."*: Commissioners to Canada to Hancock, May 6, 1776, Papers of Benjamin Franklin 22, 417–419.
138 *"a violent remedy...plundering the inhabitants"*: CCC and Chase to John Thomas, May 26, 1776, in Rowland, I:166–168.
138 *"neither abilities nor inclination"*: CCC and Chase to Congress, May 17, 1776, in ibid., I:163.
138 *On May 11...St. Johns*. CCC and Chase to Franklin, May 11, 1776, Papers of Benjamin Franklin 22, 430–431.
138 *"great importance"*: CCC and Chase to John Thomas, May 15, 1776, Hanley 520.
138 *the dying Thomas*: Mayer, 36.
138 *to inoculate the troops*: CCC and Chase to John Thomas, May 15, 1776, Hanley 520.
138f. *a smallpox inoculation...quarantine*: Ketchum, 35.
139 *"is, in our opinion..."*: Everest, 55.
139 *"is now shamefully"...his arrest*: CCC to CCA, May 17, 1776, Hanley 522.
139 *He perished...in 1777*: Randall, 333.
139 *compared the commissioners... "Apostles of Confusion"*: Everest, 11–12.
139 *like good fortune*: Bobrick, 177.
139 *"uneasiness"*: CCC to CCA, May 27, 1776, Hanley 525.
139 *The Native Americans...stormy night*: Everest, 63; CCC to CCA, May 28, 1776, Hanley 526.
139 *"that detestable government...for themselves"*: Hanley, *Revolutionary Statesman*, 136.
139 *Half were sick...fortifying Ticonderoga*: CCC to CCA, July 20, 1776, Hanley 537.
139f. *"a singular dispensation...can prevail"*: Peter Guilday, *Life and Times of John Carroll* (New York: Encyclopedia Press, 1922), I:99–101.
140 *"entrenching, making abbaties..."*: CCC to Horatio Gates, June 14, 1776, in Rowland, I:174–176.
140 *"Doctor Franklin is gone..."*: CCC to CCA, November 8, 1776, Hanley 556.

Maryland Declares Independence

140 *"The lady had...by Tories"*: note by John Carroll on Franklin to CCC and Chase, May 27, 1776, *Papers of Benjamin Franklin* 22, 439–440.

140 *"one of the most..."*: John Carroll to Franklin, April 2, 1787, in Griffin, III:257.

140 *urged his cousin*: John Carroll to CCC and Chase, May 28, 1776, Hanley 527.

140 *Conservatives had taken control*: Smith, 153.

141 *Franklin also...new governments*: Franklin to CCC and Chase, May 27, 1776, Emmet Collection, 1598, New York Public Library.

141 *"my old acquaintance"...quartermaster-general*: Everest, 58.

141 *made their official report*: Journals of the Continental Congress, June 11, 1776, accessed October 14, 1999, http://memory.loc.gov.

141 *"done as much..."*: Hanley, *Revolutionary Statesman*, 137–138.

141 *"foreign alliance"*: Gurn, 81.

141 *"to disavow..."*: Rowland, I:141.

141 *"county after county..."*: Hoffman, *Spirit*, 166.

141 *the next day...on the 28th*: Hanley, *Revolutionary Statesman*, 150–151.

141 *Carrollton...the decision*: Peter Paul, 119.

141 *Carrollton's Declaration..."monarch"*: CCC, July 3, 1776, draft of "A Declaration of the Delegates of Maryland," Hanley 535.

141 *"The point..."*: Owen Dudley Edwards, "The Writers of the American Revolution—Variations on a Theme by Auden," in David Noel Doyle and Owen Dudley Edwards, eds. *America and Ireland, 1776–1976* (Westport, CT: Greenwood Press, 1980), 37.

141 *"ministerial army"*: Griffin, II:238.

142 *"cruel war..."*: Burstein, 5.

142 *The central passage..."nothing is concealed"*: CCC, July 3, 1776, draft of "A Declaration of the Delegates of Maryland," Hanley 535.

142 *"sacred and undeniable...self-evident"*: Burstein, 108.

142 *"last stab...unfeeling brethren"*: ibid., 5.

143 *Genuine Principles...Constitution*: Colbourn, 191.

143 *Jefferson...new body politic*: Gilbert-Hamerling, 46.

143 *vandalizing King George's portraits...lower Manhattan*: ibid., 52.

Carroll the Signer

143 *Carrollton was selected*: CCC to CCA, July 5, 1776, Hanley 536.

143 *"is to be celebrated..."*: CCC to CCA, June 26—July 4, 1776, Hanley 602.

144 *"the war of the pen..."*: Edwards in Doyle and Edwards, 19.

144 *"malady of Bibliomania"..."estate in books"*: Colbourn, 12.

144 *Male literacy...mother country*: May, 35.

144 *The roster...for every gentleman*: Colbourn, 14.

144 *"A Man of Words...of a perfume"*: May, 126–127.

144 *"the sacred rights..."*: Ives, 89.

145 *On July 19*: Leonard, 133.

145 *as an 1826...affirms*: Latrobe in Sanderson, 256.

145 *According to Latrobe...a bystander*: ibid., 256–257; see also Rowland, I:181.

Notes

145 *"In the cause...figure in America"*: Hanley, *Revolutionary Statesman*, 148.
145 *"All who took part...our Independence"*: *American Catholic Historical Researches* XXVIII, 380.
145 *"Reflecting...our holy religion"*: CCC to George Washington Parke Custis, February 20, 1829, in *American Catholic Historical Researches* XIV, 27.
146 *"the basis of every virtue"*: CCC to Rev. John Standford, October 9, 1827, *American Catholic Historical Researches* XV, 131.

The Maryland Line

146 *"distinguished by the most...Silk Stocking Infantry"*: Scharf, II:255–257.
146 *"an exceeding fine..."*: ibid., II:241.
146 *The Maryland Line's...Cortelyou House*: ibid., II:249–250.
146 *"sons of the best..."*: ibid., II:245; Thomas W. Spalding, in "'A Revolution More Extraordinary': Bishop John Carroll and the Birth of American Catholicism," MHM 84:3 (Fall 1989), 202–203, claims there were "a large number of Catholics" in Smallwood's force.
146 *256 Marylanders*: Scharf, II:246.
147 *"I don't know whether...in their way"*: ibid., II:253–254.
147 *"We shall give them..."*: ibid., II:252.
147 *At White Plains...British troops*: ibid., II:262.
147 *"it is not..."*: CCC to CCA, September 13, 1776, Hanley 547.
147 *The faith in militia...that summer*: see Gilbert-Hamerling, 118.
147 *Against Washington's wishes...cavalry in December*: Bobrick 221–225.
147 *"Everything is at stake..."*: Scharf, II:251.
147 *eight more battalions*: Silver, 531.
147 *"to turn out every..."*: Scharf, II:293.
147 *Maryland responded...20,636 men*: James McSherry, *History of Maryland: From Its First Settlement in 1634, to the Year 1848* (Baltimore: John Murphy, 1849), 391.
147f. *This figure does...Legion*: Scharf, II:350.
148 *formed in Baltimore...of 1778*: ibid., II:345.
148 *"Maryland excepted..."*: ibid., II:351.

Planters vs. Populists

148 *"is it not amazing..."*: Daniel of St. Thomas Jenifer to CCA, June 16, 1776, Hanley 531.
148 *one-twelfth*: Skaggs, 771.
148 *"by far the greatest..."*: Griffin, III:238.
148f. *"solely by...good Whigs"*: Ives, 321.
149 *the average delegate...eight thousand acres*: Barker, 8.
149 *artisans and mechanics*: Philip Crowl, "Maryland During and After the Revolution: A Political and Economic Study," *Johns Hopkins University Studies in Historical and Political Science*, Series LXI, no. 1 (1943), 18.
149 *ninety-five percent*: Hoffman, *Spirit*, 9.
149 *Tory/democrat*: Hanley, *Revolutionary Statesman*, 179.
149 *"the ring leaders...Papist"*: Hoffman, *Spirit*, 177.
149 *"for the purpose..."*: ibid., 156.
149 *In December...own officers*: Skaggs, 782.

149 When the June...in the convention: Hoffman, *Spirit*, 167.
149 "*absurd*": CCC to CCA, June 28, 1776, Hanley 533.
149f. Encouraged...universal manhood suffrage: Hoffman, *Spirit*, 171–173.
150 stoppage of debt collections: Hanley, *Revolutionary Statesman*, 178.
150 plural executive...of the poll tax: Skaggs, 783.
150 Pennsylvania...elected judges: Peter Paul, 136.
150 "*mild mercies*...": CCC to CCA, October 4, 1776, Hanley 548.
150 "*Feeble beyond conception*...": CCC to CCA, May 27, 1777, Hanley 587.
150 pitched battle: May, 201.
150 "*the most perfect*...": CCC to CCA, October 4, 1776, Hanley 548.
150 "*The seeds of disunion*...": CCC to CCA, October 10, 1776, Hanley 550.

The Maryland Constitution

150 Fifty acres...August 1, 1776: Silver, 521.
150 these levels...provincial government: Crowl, 29.
150 viva voce: Scharf, II:239.
150 Hammond and Hall...qualifications: Hanley, *Revolutionary Statesman*, 167.
150 electoral revolt: Skaggs, 784.
150f. Five counties dismissed...Anne Arundel County: Hoffman, *Spirit*, 169–170.
151 "*If they can find*...": CCC to CCA, July 29, 1776, Hanley 541.
151 convention set aside...elections: Silver, 525.
151 eighteen of the twenty...in Annapolis: Hoffman, *Spirit*, 170-2.
151 they resigned: Crowl, 31.
151 "*weak, impudent...very wicked*": CCC to CCA, August 17, 1776, MHS 4194, 707.
151 returned Chase...John Hall: Hoffman, *Spirit*, 175.
151 "*exert themselves...in this State*": CCC to CCA, August 20, 1776, Hanley 543.
151 "*I long to see you*...": CCC to CCA, September 13, 1776, Hanley 547.
151 Carrollton sat...of government: Hoffman, *Spirit*, 178.
151f. His influence...to become a delegate: see Peter Paul, 134; Hanley, *Revolutionary Statesman*, 173; "Declaration of Rights," *Proceedings of the Conventions of the Province of Maryland, Held at the City of Annapolis, in 1774, 1775, & 1776* (Baltimore: J. Lucas & E. K. Deaver; Annapolis, Md.: J. Green, 1836), November 3, 1776, 311–316; "Constitution and Form of Government," *Proceedings of the Conventions*, November 8, 1776, 349–365.
152 the convention considered...29–24: Hoffman, *Spirit*, 183.
152 £30 currency: "Constitution and Form of Government," *Proceedings of the Conventions*, November 8, 1776, 349–365.
152 The Lockean connection...intact: Hanley, *Revolutionary Statesman*, 168.
152 viva voce voting: Crowl, 33.
152 fifty-five percent: Skaggs, 774.
152 The drafting committee...five members: Hanley, *Revolutionary Statesman*, 198.
152 "*God knows what...of legislation*": CCC to CCA, October 20, 1776, Hanley 552.
152f. "*If we can not*...": CCC to CCA, October 20, 1776, Hanley 552.
153 The militia...their own officers: Crowl, 34.

Notes

153   *A motion...was defeated*: *Proceedings of the Conventions*, November 8, 1776, 348–349.

153   *The convention stopped..."acceptable to him"*: Hanley, *Revolutionary Statesman*, 202–203; "Declaration of Rights," *Proceedings of the Conventions*, November 3, 1776, 311–316.

153   *Maryland abandoned...in 1837*: Rowland, I:196.

153   *"The mode of choosing..."*: CCC to Virgil Maxcy, December 29, 1817, in Peter Paul, 139.

153   *"The powers of government..."*: George Washington [Hamilton] to Congress Conference Committee, January 29, 1778, accessed October 14, 1999, http://memory.loc.gov.

153   *"The Maryland Constitution...in the Union"*: Rowland, I:193.

The New Government Begins

154   *"our affairs are desperate...in despotism"*: CCC to CCA, October 4, 1776, Hanley 548.

154   *"Peace perhaps...send it"*: CCC to CCA, October 18, 1776, Hanley 551.

154   *"I am at...the game is up"*: Griffin, II:270.

154   *Trouble spread..."drudge on earth"*: Hoffman, *Spirit*, 186–190.

154   *outmaneuvering Cornwallis*: Scharf, II:292.

154   *back from Baltimore*: ibid., II:305.

154   *"gave spirits...to magnify"*: ibid., II:312–315.

155   *But several senators...plagued by apathy*: Daniel of St. Thomas Jenifer to Maryland Senate, February 2, 1777, MHS 4194, 724.

155   *It proved difficult...they were paid*: Beverly W. Bond, "State Government in Maryland, 1777–1781," *Johns Hopkins University Studies in Historical and Political Science*, series 23, nos. 3–4 (March–April, 1905), 144.

155   *913 new government jobs*: Hoffman, *Spirit*, 223.

155   *"You know, Sir..."*: Scharf, II:312–315.

155   *"Your Honors...Gentlemen"*: Leonard, 145.

155   *The assembly elected..."soon kill you"*: CCC to CCA, February 13–14, 1777, Hanley 561.

156   *the old Squire submitted*: CCA to CCC, February 20, 1777, Hanley 463.

156   *"disperse immediately"...to the state*: "By the General Assembly of Maryland, a proclamation..." February 13, 1777, Early American Imprints, first series, 43273.

156   *General Smallwood...two thousand troops*: Scharf, II:299–301; Hoffman, *Spirit*, 195.

156   *"are reduced to manual..."*: CCC to CCA, March 15–16, 1776, Hanley 496.

156   *"I hate national..."*: CCC to CCA, August 18, 1775, Hanley 472.

156   *"cried like a child..."*: CCC to Thomas Johnson, September 8, 1777, in Rowland, I:215–216.

156   *"gives great...freedom of speech"*: CCC to CCA, March 29, 1776, Hanley 502.

156   *mistrusted oaths*: CCC to CCA, November 15, 1777, Hanley 645.

156   *the delegates...Declaration of Rights*: Hanley, *Revolutionary Statesman*, 230–231.

156   *the Senate amended...the oath*: CCC to CCA, April 15, 1777, Hanley 579.

156 After the Whig...vigilante justice: Scharf, II:308, 312–315.
156 Molly Carroll's friendship...Ridouts: Smith, 131.

The Tender Law

157 "A bill will certainly...": CCC to CCA, February 13–14, 1777, Hanley 561.
157 "I shall look on...with honor": CCA to CCC, March 13, 1777, Hanley 565.
157 "Where shall I...civil war": CCC to CCA, March 15, 1777, Hanley 566.
157 "majesty of the people": Daniel of St. Thomas Jenifer to CCA, July 20, 1778, Hanley 701.
157 concert an opposition...Dulanys: CCA to CCC, March 19, 1777, Hanley 568.
157 Carrollton rejected..."dispassionate": CCC to CCA, March 28, 1777, Hanley 572.
158 "The law will have...": CCC to CCA, June 26, 1777, Hanley 602.
158 "Although injustice be done...": CCC to CCA, March 28, 1777, Hanley 572.
158 "it behooves us...": CCC to CCA, June 2, 1777, Hanley 589.
158 "without giving...avaricious and artful": Votes and Proceedings of the Senate, April 9, 1777.
158 Radical economic...of the constitution: see Hoffman, Spirit, 210.
158 "Invite none of them...": CCA to CCC, April 13, 1777, Hanley 578.
158 his son claimed...passed: CCA to CCC, April 15, 1777, Hanley 579.
158 consult the journal: CCA to CCC, April 16, 1777, Hanley 580.
158 "promoting a law...": CCA to Samuel Chase, June 5, 1777, Hanley 590.
158 "A man, Sir...": Samuel Chase to CCA, June 6, 1777, Hanley 591.
158 "A public strumpet...a whore": CCA to Samuel Chase, June 9, 1777, Hanley 593.
159 "obnoxious to the People...by a mob": CCC to CCA, November 13, 1777, Hanley 641.
159 "I can not conceive...with complaisance": CCC to CCA, June 26, 1777, Hanley 602.
159 "If you love me...": CCC to CCA, June 16, 1777, Hanley 596.
159 "Neither a prison...": CCA to CCC, March 22–23, 1777, Hanley 570.
159 "America is right...": CCA to CCC, April 1, 1777, Hanley 573.
159 "meekness of temper...": CCA to CCC, November 7, 1777, Hanley 636.
159 "Are you not...your judgement?" CCA to CCC, November 14, 1777, Hanley 643.
159 "I assure you...can bite": CCC to CCA, November 15, 1777, Hanley 645.

The Irish Presence

159 keep Howe bottled up: Washington to CCC, June 22, 1777, Hanley 600; Bobrick, 237.
160 "a kind of trap": Bobrick, 255.
160 "our cautious General...": CCC to CCA, June 26, 1777, Hanley 602.
160 a hundred to one: CCC to CCA, June 28, 1777, Hanley 603; CCC to Franklin, August 12, 1777, The Papers of Benjamin Franklin, vol. 24, May 1 through September 30, 1777, ed. William B. Willcox (New Haven, Conn.: Yale University Press, 1984), 417–421.
160 Washington put out...troop strength: Bobrick, 300.

Notes

160 *Carrollton had been...day in Congress*: Journals of the Continental Congress, July 18, 1776, accessed October 14, 1999, http://memory.loc.gov.
160 *"is an excellent..."*: Hanley, *Revolutionary Statesman*, 161.
160 *"I think...tired of the war"*: CCC to CCA, June 7, 1777, Hanley 592.
160 *"bounty-jumping"*: Gilbert-Hamerling, 163.
160 *One Maryland battalion...seventy-mile march*: Hoffman, *Spirit*, 203.
160 *"a meeting of our..."*: CCA to CCC, February 6, 1777, Hanley 560.
160 *promised to march*: CCC to CCA, August 27—September 1, 1777, Hanley 608.
160 *"regards the honor...this campaign"*: CCC to CCA, June 23, 1777, Hanley 601.
160 *Lord George Germain...Continental Army*: Griffin, II:165.
160 *"scarcely one-fourth..."*: Griffin, III:245.
160 *"a very great part"...of indentured servants*: Scharf, II:312–315.
161 *the anonymous French..."than Guinea slaves"*: "Journal of a French Traveller II," 80.
161 *Proctor's Pennsylvania...from other states*: Griffin, II:203.
161 *thirty-three thousand...Irish Catholics*: Griffin, I:329.
161 *"the Irish R.C...."*: CCC to CCA, March 15–16, 1776, Hanley 496.
161 *"tied and bound"*: Griffin, I:34.
161 *likely to desert*: Griffin, II:248.
161 *contrary to the Irishmen's interest*: Griffin, I:343.

Saratoga

161 *"while the weather..."*: CCC to CCA, June 20–21, 1777, Hanley 598.
161 *Head of Elk*: Griffin, II:285.
161 *begged their commander*: CCC to Thomas Johnson, August 22, 1777, ibid., II:373.
161 *"will not put all..."*: CCC to CCA, September 8, 1777, Hanley 612.
161f. *"this kind of sauntering..."*: CCC to Thomas Johnson, September 8, 1777, in Rowland, I:215–216.
162 *"I think I should...and enterprising"*: CCC to CCA, September 11, 1777, Hanley 613.
162 *fled in confusion*: Scharf, II:320.
162 *General Grey bayoneted...had ended*: Griffin, II:191; Bobrick, 266.
162 *Carrollton joined...September 17*: CCC to CCA, September 18, 1777, Hanley 616.
162 *soon had to depart...was sitting*: CCC to CCA, September 23, 1777, Hanley 618.
162 *On September 25...had fallen*: CCC to CCA, September 25, 1777, Hanley 620.
162 *respectable American showing*: Bobrick, 267–269.
162 *the Continentals' discipline*: CCC to CCA, October 8, 1777, Hanley 624.
162 *"our men are becoming..."*: CCC to CCA, October 12, 1777, Hanley 629.
162 *"I beg your pardon..."*: Bobrick, 307.
162 *Howe's sea voyage...in the North*: ibid., 312.
162 *The original plan...on the Hudson*: Ketchum, 257, 259.
162 *This meant that...from Washington*: ibid., 284.

163 *Schuyler's scorched-earth policy*: ibid., 242.
163 *Washington ordered...of attrition*: ibid., 290.
163 *By September 20...twelve thousand*: ibid., 383.

Valley Forge

163 *Congress created...named its president*: Rowland, I:224–225.
163 *Gates had...without his permission*: Leonard, 162.
163 *"great, nay...will suffer"*: CCC to CCA, September 23, 1777, Hanley 618.
163 *creating another committee*: Leonard, 170.
164 *"I am sorry to observe...deserve punishment"*: CCC to Washington, September 27, 1777, in Rowland, I:217–218.
164 *"extremely defective"*: CCC to CCA, October 5, 1777, Hanley 623.
164 *to secure her investment*: Bobrick, 332.
164 *"you say to your"..."Blue Book"*: ibid., 334.
164 *delayed building huts*: John Fitzgerald to CCA, December 19, 1777, Hanley 658.
164 *Carrollton contributed £50*: CCC to CCA, December 6, 1777, Hanley 655.
164 *"in great want..."*: CCC to CCA, November 28, 1777, Hanley 653.
164 *"Speculations, peculation..."*: Bobrick, 292.
164 *"Men may speculate..."*: ibid., 329.
164 *The old code...new bond of interest*: James Lovell, a New England congressional delegate, correctly observed that the issue of honor vs. interest in Arnold's resignation was really "a question between monarchial and republican principles"; Randall, 343.
165 *"With far...laudable rivalship"*: Washington [Hamilton] to Continental Congress Conference Committee, January 29, 1778, *Papers of George Washington* accessed October 14, 1999, http://memory.loc.gov.
165f. *Molly's health had collapsed*: J. Henry to Thomas Johnson, January 27, 1778, *Journal and Correspondence of the Council of Safety, January 1–March 20, 1777...*, Archives of Maryland 16, 475–476.
166 *forcing Carroll...at Bath*: Hanley, *Revolutionary Statesman*, 234.
166 *now Hot Springs*: Hoffman and Mason, 327.
166 *"I think Molly..."*: CCA to CCC, January 7, 1777, Hanley 636.

The French Alliance

166 *had impressed Carroll*: CCC to CCA, May 12, 1777, Hanley 584.
166 *"I wish I could..."*: Griffin, II:379.
166 *"very uneasy...upon that head"*: John Fitzgerald to Washington, March 17, 1778, in Gurn, 93.
166 *to seek a promotion*: *American Catholic Historical Researches*, XXII, 8–9.
166 *"anybody that displeased..."*: Thomas Conway to Horatio Gates, June 7, 1778, in Gurn, 94–95.
166 *"in a most despising manner"*: Leonard, 164–165.
166 *"Mr. Carroll might..."*: Thomas Conway to Horatio Gates, June 7, 1778, in Gurn, 94–95.
167 *"I am determined..."*: Washington to Stephen Moylan, April 11, 1778, in Griffin, II:293.
167 *"Try, for God's sake..."*: Hanley, *Revolutionary Statesman*, 291.

Notes

167 *"with a vigor..."*: CCC to Thomas Johnson, April 21, 1778, in Rowland, I:237–238.
167 *"no terms short..."*: CCC to Thomas Johnson, April 27, 1778, in ibid., I:240–241.
167 *"unless they should be..."*: CCC to CCA, April 20, 1778, Hanley 668.
167 *concocted a private company*: Leonard, 182.
167 *Then Franklin...English vessels*: Richard N. Rosenfeld, *American Aurora: A Democratic-Republican Returns* (New York: St. Martin's Press, 1997), 303, 318, 323, 324–325, 326–327.
167 *Carrollton destroyed...correspondence*: CCC to Robert Gilmor, October 15, 1826, in *American Catholic Historical Researches* XIX, 177.
167 *The delicate subject..."the old ladies"*: CCC to Franklin, August 12, 1777, *Papers of Benjamin Franklin* 24, 417–421.
167 *John Adams detested...intentions*: Rosenfeld, 322.
167 *So...did Jay*: ibid., 430.
167 *Baron de Kalb...English Crown*: Bobrick, 193.
168 *the British officers...Meschianza ball*: Leonard, 158.
168 *France allied...February 6, 1778*: ibid., 185.
168 *"the magnanimity...perpetual"*: Gurn, 97–98.

PART IV: Senator

169 *"is bottomed on principles..."*: CCC to CCA, May 3, 1778, Hanley 677.
169 *The United States...with England*: CCC to CCA, May 4, 1778, Hanley 678.
169 *if war continued...obligation to fight*: CCC to CCA, May 3, 1778, Hanley 677.
169 *"all the Great Powers..."*: CCC to CCA, May 3, 1778, Hanley 677.
169 *"If peace should soon..."*: CCC to CCA, May 11, 1778.

The Depreciation of Congress

169 *"noisy, empty..."*: CCC to CCA, October 5, 1777, Hanley 623.
169 *"The most respectable..."*: Griffin, III:259.
169 *"Continental money..."*: Bobrick, 290.
169 *Carrollton favored...new currency*: CCC to CCA, November 28, 1777, Hanley 653.
169f. *Making all interest...in Europe*: CCC to CCA, June 7, 1777, Hanley 592.
170 *"What cannot wisdom...good conduct"*: CCC to CCA, June 7, 1777, Hanley 592.
170 *between late 1777...by 3900 percent*: Elizabeth Cometti, "Inflation in Revolutionary Maryland," *William and Mary Quarterly*, 3rd series, 8:2 (April, 1951), 234.
170 *Carrollton found...with specie*: CCC to CCA, July 24, 1779, Hanley 754.
170 *Carrollton was quoted..."be almost useless"*: CCC to CCA, May 3, 1779, Hanley 733; for the use of specie and payment in kind, see also CCC in the *Maryland Gazette*, February 18, 1780.
170 *congratulated his father*: CCC to CCA, April 29, 1779, Hanley 731.
170f. *Virginia asked..."plundered the Public"*: CCC to CCA, July 24—August 2,

Interest: Private vs. Public

171 *"men of opulent fortunes..."*: Votes and Proceedings of the Senate, December 13, 1778.
171 *"Our form of government"...for the assembly*: ibid., December 14, 1778.
171f. *"because this resolve...to the public interest"*: ibid., March 21, 1779.
172 *purchased...flour and wheat*: see CCC in the Maryland Gazette, August 23, 1781.
172 *"ought not only..."*: Votes and Proceedings of the House of Delegates, December 12, 1778.
172 *Chase was excluded*: Votes and Proceedings of the Senate, November 13, 1778.
172 *forbidding its members...of any kind*: ibid., July 23, 1779.
172 *"of a too delicate..."*: CCC to CCA, January 31, 1763, MHM 11, 323–326.
172 *the measure went beyond...to Congress"*: Samuel Chase in the Maryland Gazette, June 21, 1781.
172 *"Hire more crafts..."*: Daniel of St. Thomas Jenifer to CCA, August 12, 1779, Hanley 762.
173 *to sell some...of Annapolis*: Hoffman, Spirit, 249.
173 *"the most prostituted scoundrel..."*: CCC to CCA, November 9, 1779, Hanley 782.
173 *"has lost much..."*: Daniel of St. Thomas Jenifer to CCA, August 12, 1779, Hanley 762.
173 *"harpies & scoundrels"*: Daniel of St. Thomas Jenifer to CCA, June 21, 1779, Hanley 745.
173 *In May...for protection*: Daniel of St. Thomas Jenifer to CCA, May 24, 1779, Hanley 742.

The Articles of Confederation

173 *Virginia claimed...on her charter*: see CCA to CCC, November 3, 1776, Hanley 555; CCC to CCA, June 23–24, 1777, Hanley 601; CCC, "Notes on the injustice of Virginia's claim to the back lands," ca. 1778, MHS, 4227A, 6964.
173 *"no State..."*: Rowland, II:9.
173 *Abrogating...not on the charters*: ibid., II:10.
173 *"justice and perfect equality"*: Votes and Proceedings of the Senate, June 18, 1778.
173 *the back lands...tax burden*: Rowland, II:12.
173 *Washington and Jefferson...off limits*: Burstein, 45.
174 *Carrollton, too...land companies*: Hoffman, Spirit, 243; see also CCC to CCA, August 12, 1779, Hanley 763.
174 *He preferred...national necessity*: Rowland, II:44.
174 *"common estate...the former"*: Votes and Proceedings of the Senate, December 15, 1778.

Domestic Crisis

174 *still running the family business*: see CCA to CCC, March 29, 1779, Hanley 717.

Notes

174 *drought of 1779*: CCA to CCC, May 3, 1779, Hanley 773.
174 *unable to feed his horses*: CCA to CCC, May 7, 1779, Hanley 734.
174 *The only duty...from debtors*: see, for example, CCC to CCA, April 29, 1779, Hanley 731.
174 *published a petition*: CCA, "petition to the House of Delegates," Hanley 748.
174 *infuriated the delegates...an apology*: Hoffman and Mason, 327.
174 *"rogues"*: CCC to CCA, November 7, 1779, Hanley 781.
174 *"I wish you had..."*: CCA to CCC, November 9, 1779, Hanley 782.
175 *"suffer not your spirits..."*: CCA to CCC, December 3, 1779, Hanley 784.
175 *properly despondent letter*: CCC to CCA, December 4–5, 1779, Hanley 785.
175 *"I fear you take..."*: CCA to CCC, December 8, 1779, Hanley 786.
175 *"never to touch...children for me"*: CCA to CCC, April 28, 1778, Hanley 675.
175 *Anne Brooke Carroll*: Hanley, *Revolutionary Statesman*, 301.
175 *"whose sensibility must..."*: Daniel of St. Thomas Jenifer, October 1, 1778, Hanley 706.
175 *sought solace...of laudanum*: CCC to CCA, November 18, 1778, Hanley 713.
175 *doctor had diagnosed*: CCC to CCA, April 17–18, 1779, Hanley 726.
175 *"Let her avoid..."*: CCA to CCC, April 22–24, 1779, Hanley 727.
175 *voyage...benefits of seasickness*: CCC to CCA, April 25, 1779, Hanley 730; CCA to CCC, May 3, 1779, Hanley 733; CCC to CCA, May 8, 1779, Hanley 735.
175 *Her appetite improved*: CCC to CCA, July 15, 1779, Hanley 750.
175 *new friendship...adored Molly*: Hoffman and Mason, 374–376.
175 *"brusque and stingy"*: ibid., 377.
175 *"I hate this idle..."*: CCC to CCA, August 19, 1779, Hanley 767.
176 *"domestic concerns...instructed me"*: CCC to Franklin, December 5, 1779, *The Papers of Benjamin Franklin*, vol. 31, *March 23, 1775 through October 27, 1776*, ed. Barbara B. Oberg (New Haven, Conn.: Yale University Press, 1995), 198–202.
176 *he was spoken...president*: M. Gerard to M. Vergennes, November 10, 1778, in Ives, 342.
176 *"A man of sense..."*: Arthur Lee to Samuel Adams, May 22, 1779, in Griffin, III:241.
176 *"I wish your son..."*: Daniel of St. Thomas Jenifer to CCA, June 21, 1779, Hanley 745.

Tory Confiscations

177 Rev. *John Bowie*: *Journal and Correspondence of the Maryland Council*, March 28, 1777, *Archives of Maryland* XVI, 192.
177 *Mr. Brown*: CCC to Thomas Johnson, May 11, 1778, in Rowland, I:241–242; see also J. Henry to Thomas Johnson, May 11, 1778, in *Journal and Correspondence of the Council of Maryland, Archives of Maryland* 21, 76.
177 *The assembly had...new state government*: Bond, 226, 229.
177 *refused to extend*: *Votes and Proceedings of the Senate*, June 23, 1778.

177 They requested..."compliance with them": CCC to CCA, October 23, 1779, Hanley 775.
177 On December 21...to pay their taxes: Votes and Proceedings of the Senate, December 21, 1779.
177 Carrollton and Matthew Tilghman...future European loans: ibid., December 23, 1779.
178 "destructive of that freedom...": CCC to Franklin, December 5, 1779, Papers of Benjamin Franklin 31, 198–202.
178 Instead of...public benefit: Votes and Proceedings of the Senate, December 10, 1779.
178 written by Carrollton: CCA to CCC, December 3, 1779, Hanley 784.
178 "disinterestedness...too generally prevailed": ibid., November 17, 1779.
178 The House...confiscation issue: Votes and Proceedings of the Senate, December 30, 1779.
178 Carrollton based..."we should not do": CCC in the Maryland Gazette, February 11, 18, 25, 1780.
178 "damned Toryism": Scharf, II:389.
178 "the people seem averse": CCC to Joshua Johnson, May 1, 1780, Arents Letterbook.
179 "The good sense...": CCC in the Maryland Gazette, February 25, 1780.

The March 1780 Assembly

179 "wish most earnestly...": CCC to CCA, November 7, 1779, Hanley 781.
179 a congressional resolution: CCA to CCC, April 16, 1780, Hanley 793.
179 On April 4, Carrollton joined: Votes and Proceedings of the Senate, April 4, 1780.
179 From that point...sterling debts: CCC to CCA, April 17, 1780, Hanley 794.
179 The assembly...in December, 1780: Hoffman and Mason, 331–332.
179 The delegates renewed...on April 12: Votes and Proceedings of the Senate, April 12, 1780.
179 rejected the confiscation: ibid., April 14, 1780.
179 a counterproposal: ibid., April 17, 1780; CCC to CCA, April 17, 1780, Hanley 794.
179f. "Such is the force"...sale of the back lands: Votes and Proceedings of the Senate, May 14, 1780.
180 New York...to cede lands: Bond, 162.
180 The delegates declared..."of blame": Votes and Proceedings of the Senate, May 16, 1780.

The Army Struggles

180 "reverence & love...tolerably clothed": CCC to Franklin, December 5, 1779, Papers of Benjamin Franklin 31, 198–202.
180 Maryland Line...vanguard: Scharf, II:354.
180 "the brave Marylanders...": ibid., II:356.
180 total war: see Bobrick, 373.
180 With its national...collapse: ibid., 397.
180f. "will not dare...": ibid., 401.
181 Baron de Kalb...that number: Scharf, II:364–365.
181 De Kalb died...wounds: Bobrick, 402.

181 "*The fugitive General…of action*": Daniel Carroll to CCC, September 10, 1780, Hanley 831.
181 *When Gates…in disgust*: Bond, 198.
181 *Denied a Continental frigate*: Scharf, II:384; *Votes and Proceedings of the Senate*, June 12, 1780.
181 *reinstated the Marland Navy*: Bond, 215–216.
181 "*Maryland has made…*": Scharf, II:379.
181 "*spirit of enterprise*": Daniel Carroll to CCC, September 18, 1780, Hanley 833.
181 *a French squadron…of 1780*: CCC to Joshua Johnson, July 22, 1780, Arents Letterbook.
181 *a no-popery mob…on Newport*: Bobrick, 357.
181 *The Tories claimed…to Catholicism*: ibid., 341.
181 "*mingled so well*"*…in the vicinity*: Marquis de Lafayette to Washington, July 31, 1780, in Thomas Balch, *The French in America During the War of Independence of the United States, 1777–1783*, v. 1 (Boston: Gregg Press, 1972; reprint of Philadelphia: Porter & Coates, 1891–1895 edition), 114.
181 "*I shall be only…*": ibid., 115.
181f. *John Hanson told…"abounds with provisions?"*: John Hanson to CCC, September 18, 1780, Hanley 834.

The Arnold Treason

182 "*He seemed chagrined…*": CCC to CCA, May 17–19, 1778, Hanley 681.
182 "*but am sorry…*": Mary Carroll to CCC, October 22, 1780, Hanley 839.
182 *the Squire asked…promptly*: CCA to CCC, October 26, 1780, Hanley 841.
182 "*when I can…*": Randall, 329.
182 "*I do not see…at pleasure*": ibid., 330.
182 *Carroll helped Arnold*: *American Catholic Historical Researches*, XVIII, 133; Randall, 337.
182 "*a set of men…*": Randall, 469.
183 *linchpin of Clinton's…strategy*: ibid., 531–532.
183 *capture of Washington*: ibid., 540.
183 *indulging his passions*: ibid., 567.
183 *murderer and a Jesuit*: ibid., 570.
183 *the traitor lacked feeling*: ibid., 564.
183 "*saw your mean…*": Mundey, 38.

Greene Takes Over

183 *plan to save the currency*: CCC to William Carmichael, August 9, 1780, Hanley 824.
183 *Congress should never…even more*: CCC to John Hanson, August 15, 1780, Hanley 826.
183f. *He believed…outweighed the cost*: CCC to John Hanson, August 15, 1780, Hanley 826.
184 "*wisely, honestly…*": CCC to William Carmichael, August 9, 1780, Hanley 824.
184 *Carroll was frustrated…"in the world"*: CCC to John Hanson, August 15, 1780, Hanley 826.

184   *"new Congress money"*: Daniel Carroll to CCC, August 26, 1780, Hanley 828.
184   *A group of black people...one Meara*: CCC to CCA, April 12, 1781, Hanley 868.
184   *Congress followed it up...January 2, 1781*: Bond, 162–163.
184   *Cornwallis feared...major engagement*: Bobrick, 428–430.
184   *never held...their victories*: ibid., 441.
184   *eight hundred men...John Eager Howard*: Nathanael Greene to Marquis de Lafayette, December 29, 1780, in Scharf, II:398.
184   *not one soldier...or the Carolinas*: ibid., II:412.
184f.   *At the battle...open field*: ibid., II:399.
185   *"Tarleton's quarter"*: ibid., II:407.
185   *half-naked American troops*: Bobrick, 441.
185   *"exceeded anything..."*: Scharf, II:425.
185   *Greene had recovered...and Savannah*: ibid., II:427.
185   *"has really done wonders..."*: CCC to Thomas Sim Lee, August 11, 1781, MHS 4196, 1062.

The War Comes to Maryland

185   *"have made to me..."*: Scharf, II:439.
185   *recommended a draft*: Bond, 186.
185   *much opposition*: ibid., 167.
185   *in late 1780...recruiting soldiers*: ibid., 169.
185   *added to Carrollton's headaches...meet his quota*: CCA to CCC, January 21–22, 1781, Hanley 855.
185   *a procurer...for one recruit*: CCA to CCC, April 3–6, 1781, Hanley 864.
185   *Todd turned out...a substitute*: CCC to CCA, April 15, 1781, Hanley 870.
185   *all vagrants were...recruited*: Bond, 43.
185   *Washington's disapproval*: ibid., 172.
185   *Even convicts were pardoned*: ibid., 172.
185   *black slaves...after 1780*: ibid., 43.
185f.   *Anyone in Maryland who owned...healthy black male*: CCC to CCA, June 4, 1781, Hanley 891.
186   *"I cannot too often"...shared his amazement*: Balch, 162–163.
186   *In January...of Upper Marlborough*: Votes and Proceedings of the Senate, January 13, 1781.
186   *turned down a...seat*: ibid., November 17, 1780.
186   *"I have a...Family"*: Mary Carroll to CCC, October 22, 1780, Hanley 839.
186   *Admiral Marriot Arbuthnot*: Hoffman and Mason, 338.
186   *"If we reflect..."*: CCA to CCC, March 30, 1781, Hanley 862.
186   *Molly was totally...for smallpox*: CCC to CCA, March 31, 1781, Hanley 863.
186   *was then raging*: CCA to CCC, April 3-4, 1781, Hanley 864.
186   *"The pox is come...of them"*: CCC to CCA, April 5, 1781, Hanley 865.
186   *back on her drug*: CCA to CCC, May 7-9, 1781, Hanley 876.
186   *The British had..."to be parted"*: CCC to CCA, April 11-12, 1781, Hanley 867.
186f.   *Those slaves...disease and famine*: Scharf, II:463.
187   *Rather than punish...to the manor*: CCC to CCA, April 5, 1781, Hanley 865.

Notes

187 *"Jemima is out..."*: CCC to CCA, May 21-22, 1781, Hanley 885.
187 *disgusted at being sent South*: Scharf, II:444-445.
187 *Their commander...their affections*: CCA to CCC, April 18-20, 1781, Hanley 871.
187 *Lafayette no doubt...on April 4*: CCC to CCA, April 5, 1781, Hanley 865.
187 *Carroll had no illusions...cross the Potomac*: CCC to CCA, June 1, 1781, Hanley 890.
187 *"a great nuisance"...for firewood*: CCC to CCA, April 5, 1781, Hanley 865.
187 *"it is short commons..."*: CCC to CCA, May 11, 1781, Hanley 877.

The Dog in the Manger

187 *The Senate agreed*: Votes and Proceedings of the Senate, January 30, 1781.
187 *"acceded to the confederation"*: ibid., February 2, 1781.
187 *"tumbling so fast"*: CCC to CCA, June 4, 1781, Hanley 891.
188 *"so much confusion..."*: CCC to CCA, June 4, 1781, Hanley 891.
188 *"a calumniator...false friends"*: Samuel Chase in the *Maryland Gazette*, June 21, 1781.
188 *Carroll fired back*: CCC in the *Maryland Gazette*, August 23, 1781.
188 *Chase retracted his charge*: Chase to CCC, February 11, 1782, Hanley 921.
188 *the loyalty oath*: Bond, 202.
188 *his estate was sold*: Crowl, 51.
188 *the state of Maryland*: Hoffman and Mason, 348–349.
188 *The confiscation...the first buyer*: ibid., 47–48.

Yorktown

188 *Molly's mother...Fr. John Carroll*: CCC to Thomas Sim Lee, August 26, 1781, MHS 4196, 1064.
189 *"Mrs. Darnall may have..."* CCA to CCC, May 29—June 1, 1781, Hanley 889.
189 *Carrollton believed...that year*: CCC to Thomas Sim Lee, August 11, 1781, MHS 4196, 1062.
189 *Mutinies...New Jersey lines*: Balch, 130.
189 *"The child cannot..."*: ibid., 165.
189 *"divested himself..."*: ibid., 177.
189 *huzzas to Louis XVI*: Scharf, II:457.
189 *stay would be short*: Bobrick, 447.
189 *half of his army*: see ibid., 446, 449; Balch, 157.
189 *He allowed...this impression*: Balch, 146, 166.
189 *"remove any apprehension..."*: Washington to Thomas Sim Lee, October 12, 1781, in Scharf, II:462.
189 *the Continental Army...French coffers*: Rosenfeld, 416.
189 *seventy percent*: Leonard, 201.
190 *Franklin believed...in Pennsylvania*: Rosenfeld, 451.
190 *the role of the Irish*: ibid., 177.
190 *"the cannonading at York..."*: CCC to CCA, October 15, 1781, Hanley 901.
190 *"passive beyond conception"*: CCC to CCA, October 18, 1781, Hanley 903.
190 *five days before...seven thousand*: Bobrick, 464.
190 *"a horse for the..."*: Leonard, 199.

190 *Carrollton had the joy*: CCC to CCA, October 20, 1781, Hanley 905.
190 *Congress went to church*: Bobrick, 466.
190 *High Mass*: May, 116.
190 *congratulated Washington*: Hanley, *Revolutionary Statesman*, 395.
190 *"affords a rational…"*: Scharf, II:464.

Peace

190 *"Charley has had…"*: CCA to CCC, October 23, 1781, Hanley 906.
190 *"pulled down, pale…"*: CCA to CCC, October 30, 1781, Hanley 908.
190f. *"much as usual…sincere prayer"*: CCA to CCC, November 7, 1781, Hanley 909.
191 *Then tragedy struck…"Bill of Exchange"*: CCC to Messrs. Wallace, July 9, 1782, Arents Letterbook; Hoffman and Mason, 386–388.
191 *Nancy Darnall*: Smith, 217.
191 *"Carroll dissenting,"* ibid., 200.
191 *"menacing"…incompetence*: Rowland, II:59–61.
191 *Carroll demanded…salaries*: *Votes and Proceedings of the Senate*, December 11, 1782.
191 *Greene*: ibid., January 15, 1783.
191 *Rochambeau*: Leonard, 210.
191 *rejected yet another…salary*: *Votes and Proceedings of the Senate*, January 10, 1783.
191 *They also stymied…to Maryland*: ibid., January 3, 1783.
192 *"There is to be…"*: Smith, 218.
192 *elected president*: *Votes and Proceedings of the Senate*, May 21–22, 1783.
192 *exitus acta probat*: Gilbert-Hamerling, 3, 5.
192 *"guide the torrent"*: ibid., 185.
192 *promote a stronger federal government*: Bobrick, 477.
192 *"we doubt not…"*: Ives, 344.
192 *the gallery*: Gurn, 112.
192 *Washington asked…retire*: Griffin, II:355.
192 *meeting was scheduled*: Bobrick, 474.
192 *"Temple of Virtue"*: Gilbert-Hamerling, 197.
192f. *"I have already grown…"*: Bobrick, 475.
193 *half-pay…classical republicanism*: Gilbert-Hamerling, 167–168, 171.
193 *"the foundation of our empire…of revelation"*: ibid., 28; Burstein, 126.
193 *"the last stage…"*: Gilbert-Hamerling, 204.
193 *"an asylum for…"*: ibid., 211.
193 *"one soul"*: Burstein, 168.
193 *"the fire of liberty…"*: Rosenfeld, 495.
194 *"political millennium…republic!"*: Burstein, 168.
194 *Elkanah Watson…"superstructure of justice"*: Griffin, III:365–367.

Rapprochement with Great Britain

194 *the treaty required…in sterling*: Crowl, 68.
194 *The treaty…form of currency*: Scharf, II:374–375.
194 *He declined…Thomas Fitzsimons*: CCC to Thomas Fitzsimons, April 28, 1783, Hanley 926.

Notes

194   *France had been...tutelage*: Bobrick, 472.
194   *London Magazine...Parliamentary Register*: CCC to Messrs. Wallace, February 9, 1784, Arents Letterbook.
194   *"are so much decayed..."*: CCC to Messrs. Wallace, November 11, 1784, Arents Letterbook.
195   *Carroll told Johnson..."died away"*: CCC to Joshua Johnson, October 18, 1783, Arents Letterbook.
195   *Carroll dissented...evade British debts*: Votes and Proceedings of the Senate, May 30, 1783.
195   *"I would not...public character"*: CCC to Joshua Johnson, October 18, 1783, Arents Letterbook.
195   *assembly granted...advance*: Votes and Proceedings of the Senate, December 21, 1784; January 17, 1785.
195   *When the Senate...alone in dissent*: ibid., January 15, 1785; January 18, 1785.
195   *filed a response*: ibid., January 15, 1785.
195   *"evil tendency...be not repaired?"*: CCC, "Reply to the Counter-Protest of the Honourable Thomas Stone, Esquire," March 10, 1786, typescript, February 1938, MHS.
195f.   *"by the cheapest..."*: CCC to Messrs. Wallace, July 31, 1785, Arents Letterbook.
196   *two guineas*: CCC to Messrs. Wallace, July 6, 1789, Arents Letterbook.
196   *four*: CCC to Joshua Johnson, September 6, 1791, Arents Letterbook.
196   *"I am told..."*: CCC to Daniel Carroll of Duddington, March 13, 1787, in Rowland, II:104–106.
196   *Kitty joined Charles...English convent*: CCC to Messrs. Wallace, February 17, 1789, Arents Letterbook.
196   *"I do not think..."*: CCC to Daniel Carroll of Duddington, March 13, 1787, in Rowland, II:104–106.

The Constitutional Convention

196   *spark for the Federalist movement*: ibid., II:82–83.
196   *Maryland Senate...the Potomac question*: Votes and Proceedings of the Senate, November 25, 1777, December 21–22, 1777.
196   *By 1784...Horatio Gates*: Rowland, II:80.
196   *assisted by legislation...improving the river*: Votes and Proceedings of the Senate, December 28, 1784.
196   *A letter from Washington...legislative involvement*: Washington to CCC, January 10, 1785, George Washington Papers, accessed October 14, 1999, http://memory.loc.gov.
196   *In November...concerning the Potomac*: Votes and Proceedings of the Senate, November 22, 1785.
197   *"nearly-allied sister"*: Crowl, 161.
197   *dragged its feet*: Votes and Proceedings of the Senate, January 20, 1787.
197   *Maryland's paper...hardship for debtors*: Crowl, 87–90.
197   *many citizens boycotted*: ibid., 93–94.
197   *December of 1785*: ibid., 90–91.
197   *and 1786*: ibid., 102.
197   *it did allow...in installments*: Rowland, II:98.

197   House, in turn...debt executions: Crowl, 92.
197   Washington heard that...their way: Gurn, 116.
197   Carrollton was on the list: Records of the Federal Convention of 1787, May 19, 1787, accessed October 14, 1999, http://memory.loc.gov.
197   dared not go: Hoffman, Spirit, 268.
197   "remained at home...": Gurn, 116–117.
197f. Sidelined in Maryland..."defective in practice": CCC to Daniel Carroll, July 23, 1787, in "Charles Carroll's Plan of Government," ed. Philip A. Crowl, American Historical Review 46:3 (April 1941), 590–594.
198   "We may preach...": Joseph J. Ellis, Passionate Sage: The Character and Legacy of John Adams (New York: W. W. Norton, 1993), 149; Gilbert-Hamerling, 231.
198f. He saw clearly..."public benefits": ibid., 232.
199   the Articles were seen..."interest": Matson and Onuf, 526.
199   "energetic": Smith, 226.
199   "many headed monster": Gilbert-Hamerling, 174.
199   "mutually advantageous intercourse": Burstein, 88.
199   "foreign aid": Thomas Fleming, Duel: Alexander Hamilton, Aaron Burr and the Future of America (New York: Basic Books, 1999), 5.
199   the Roman Empire: see CCC, n.d., MHS 4227B, 7043.
199   humble before the natural law: see CCC, "Notes on natural-born subjects," n.d., MHS 4227B, 7041.
199   "ungracious silence...of his country": James Wilson, "Introductory Lecture of the Study of the Law in the United States," in Selected Political Essays of James Wilson, Randolph G. Adams, ed. (New York: Knopf, 1930), 188.
199   "complete body...artificial person": Ives, 408.
199   "The happiness of...": Colbourn, 120.
199f. "By some politicians...": Wilson, 210.
200   "citizens at large...revolution principle": ibid., 196, 199.
200   Daniel Carroll was responsible..."to the people": Ives, 404.
200   "power to a king...": ibid., 407.
200   It was Wilson...an electoral college: ibid., 368–370.
201   "of the people...": ibid., 411–412.

The Maryland Ratifying Convention

201   "is a warm friend": Daniel Carroll to James Madison, October 28, 1787, in Gurn, 118.
201   no property qualifications...convention: Votes and Proceedings of the Senate, November 26, 1787; Crowl, 118.
201   "The people were alarmed...Kingly Government": Daniel Carroll to James Madison, May 28, 1788, in Papers of James Madison 11, Robert A. Rutland et al., eds. (Charlottesville: University Press of Virginia, 1977), 62–66.
201   he would be hanged: Smith, 231.
201   "We the People...from the People": Luther Martin before the Maryland House of Representatives [sic], November 29, 1787, in Max Farrand, ed. Records of the Federal Convention of 1787 III (New Haven, Conn.: Yale University Press, 1911), 151–159.
201f. "That government is...confederated Republic": CCC, "Remarks on the Pro-

Notes

posed Federal Constitution," in "An Undelivered Defense of a Winning Cause," Edward C. Papenfuse, ed. MHM 71:2 (Summer 1976), 229–251.
202 *Six states had already ratified*: Crowl, 149.
202 *The Maryland Federalists...they represented*: ibid., 151.
202 *The Federalists...yeas and nays*: Rowland, II:111.
202 *Virginia ratified...margin*: Crowl, 161–162.

The First United States Senate

203 *the assembly appointed...Senate*: Bernard C. Steiner, *Life and Correspondence of James McHenry* (Cleveland: Burrows Brothers, 1907), 115; *Votes and Proceedings of the Senate*, December 9–10, 1788.
203 *Senate was highly secretive*: Gurn, 122.
203f. *What little we know...Maclay noted*: William Maclay, *Journal*, accessed June 27, 2000, http://memory.loc.gov.
204 *"the side views..."*: CCC to Jefferson, April 10, 1791, in Gurn, 147.
204 *"Yours affectionately"*: Jefferson to CCC, April 15, 1791, in ibid., 148.
204f. *Carroll voted against...Maclay lamented*: Maclay, *Journal*.
205 *"I must have them"*: CCC to Joshua Johnson, April 1, 1790, Arents Letterbook.
205 *Virginia opposed...wartime emissions*: Rowland, II:164.
205 *Hamilton struck...southern capital city*: Fleming, 96, 110; Rowland, II:160.
205 *"Carroll & Company...the business"*: Maclay, *Journal*.
205 *Several of the great...tract known as Rome*: Thomas W. Spalding, *The Premier See: A History of the Archdiocese of Baltimore, 1789–1994* (Baltimore: Johns Hopkins University Press, 1989), 34.
205f. *A few days..."sinneth not"*: Maclay, *Journal*.
206 *"This government begins..."*: CCC to Captain James Hannick [Hanrick?], January 11, 1790, Arents Letterbook.
206 *"is now beginning..."*: CCC to Joshua Johnson, January 14, 1791, Arents Letterbook.
206 *"I wish we could..."*: CCC to William Tilghman, March 29, 1792, Hanley 969.
206 *The Maryland Senate...the federal Senate*: Rowland, II:178–179; *Votes and Proceedings of the Senate*, December 13, 1791, December 15, 1791.
206 *The delegates responded...November 30, 1792*: *Votes and Proceedings of the Senate*, November 30, 1792.
206 *"the loss of..."*: Washington to CCC, December 9, 1792, *George Washington Papers*, accessed October 14, 1999, http://memory.loc.gov.
206 *"though not a player..."*: Smith, 244–245.

Freedom of Religion

206 *He spoke against...press the issue*: Maclay, *Journal*.
207 *serve on a conference committee*: Ives, 398.
207 *"will little bear..."*: Robert J. Allison, ed. *American Eras: Development of a Nation, 1783–1815* (Detroit: Gale, 1997), 331.
207 *"religion, morality"...field of education*: Mundey, 17–18.
207 *the Maryland Senate...all Christian religions*: *Votes and Proceedings of the Senate*, November 21, 1788.

207 "*the genuine spirit...*": James Hennessey, "An American Roman Catholic Tradition of Religious Liberty," *Journal of Ecumenical Studies* 14 (Fall 1977), 604.
207 "*in these United States...*": Ives, 351–352.
207 "*our style and manner...*": Gilbert-Hamerling, 8.
208 "*zealously attached...whole Christian world*": Spalding, "A Revolution," 204.
208 "*purely spiritual*"...*recommend a candidate*: ibid., 205–6.
208 "*please and gratify...*": Ives, 353.
208 *Franklin wanted...its own bishop*: ibid., 357.
208 "*without offense...*": Gurn, 69–70.
208 "*Whilst our country...restrict them*": "Address of the Roman Catholics to George Washington, Esq....." in Thomas O'Brien Hanley, ed. *John Carroll Papers* (Notre Dame, Ind.: Notre Dame University Press, 1976), I:410–411.
208f. "*liberality...Civil Government*": Washington, "To the Roman Catholics in the United States of America," March 12, 1790, *American Catholic Historical Researches* XXVIII, 298.

The Private Sector

209 "*the most monied man...where to apply*": Washington to Charles Carter, September 14, 1790, *George Washington Papers*, accessed October 14, 1999, http://memory.loc.gov.
209 *Carroll dunned him...in the Iron Works*: CCC to Washington, July 16, 1791, Hanley 965; Twohig, 74.
209 "*I have no desire...*": Washington to CCC, August 28, 1791, *George Washington Papers*, accessed October 14, 1999, http://memory.loc.gov.
209 *his principal increased...ten years later*: Papenfuse in Van Devanter, 52.
209 *Disasters such as...risky investments*: see CCC to Mary Caton, April 12, 1792, Hanley 970.
209 "*if carried on with spirit...*": CCC to Baltimore Iron Works, August 11, 1783, in Rowland, II:74–75.
209 *he used...and the Potomac Company*: CCC to Daniel Carroll of Duddington, October 26, 1797, CCC to Daniel Carroll of Duddington, January 12, 1799, and CCC to Daniel Carroll of Duddington, July 11, 1799, Daniel Carroll Papers, Library of Congress.
209 *remaining a shareholder*: CCC to Washington, August 5, 1799, Rowland, II:229–231.
209 *mismanagement...lessened his enthusiasm*: CCC to Daniel Carroll of Duddington, July 11, 1799, Daniel Carroll Papers, Library of Congress.
209 *Susquehanna Canal Company*: Rowland, II:79.
209 *Carroll also became...1795*: ibid., II:200–201.
210 "*he has such large...*": Kwilecki, 61.
210 *Washington did ask...with the Native Americans*: Washington to CCC, January 23, 1793, *George Washington Papers*, accessed October 14, 1999, http://memory.loc.gov.
210 "*the infirmities of age...*": CCC to Washington, January 28, 1793, Emmet Collection, 9676, New York Public Library.

Notes

210   "*I calculate that...infected him*": James McHenry to Hamilton, August 16, 1792, in Steiner, *Life and Correspondence*, 136–137.

210   "*as one of the two...for the character*": Hamilton to James McHenry, September 10, 1792, *American Catholic Historical Researches* XVII, 137.

210   "*left an unfavorable impression...*": CCC to Hamilton, October 22, 1792, in Gurn, 153.

210   "*No real freedom...*": CCC to John Henry, December 23, 1792, in Rowland, II:193–196.

210   "*If the different...*": CCC to Joshua Johnson, March 5, 1793, Arents Letterbook.

210f.   "*Perhaps was I...*": CCC to John Henry, December 23, 1792, in Rowland, II:193–196.

211   *Homewood and Kitty...in 1792*: CCC to Joshua Johnson, March 5, 1793, Arents Letterbook.

211   *captured by a French...bound for Boston*: CCC to Joshua Johnson, October 8, 1794, Arents Letterbook.

211   "*lolling on the bed...morning visits*": CCC to Mary Caton, April 18, 1796, Hanley 987; Field, 167–169; MHS 4197, 1202.

211   "*genteel, but not gaudy...*": CCC to Joshua Johnson, February 27, 1794, Arents Letterbook.

211   "*blend amusements with improvement...*": CCC to Mary Caton, October 15, 1795, Hanley 983.

211   "*the blackest...*": CCC to Mary Caton, May 21, 1795, Hanley 981.

211   "*I assured my informant...alliances*": CCC to Mary Caton, October 15, 1795, Hanley 983.

211f.   "*Does Mary Ann...kiss them for me*": CCC to Mary Caton, January 28, 1798, Hanley 993.

212   "*to make a better...*": CCC to Charles Carroll of Homewood [hereafter CCH], August 13, 1797, MHS 203, 1.

212   "*a young man...*": Gurn, 165–166.

212   "*unfortunately has been told...*": Eleanor Parke Custis to Elizabeth Bordley, May 30, 1797, in Twohig, 415.

212   "*extra aide-de-camp*": Gurn, 192–193.

The Slavery Question

212   *occasional address...of the President's policies*: *Votes and Proceedings of the Senate*, November 27, 1798, December 13, 1796; Rowland, II:231.

212   "*Act to prevent...*": *Votes and Proceedings of the Senate*, November 17, 1797.

213   *Jefferson acutely wrote...or let go*: Smith, 266.

213   *In 1789...House of Delegates refused*: Rowland, II:143–144; Jeffrey R. Brackett, "The Negro in Maryland," *Johns Hopkins University Studies in Historical and Political Science*, extra volume VI (1889), 52–55; *Votes and Proceedings of the Senate*, December 5, 1789.

213   *Carrollton brought in...died*: Peter Paul, 178; Rowland, II:215.

213   *316*: Crowl, 25.

213   *tried to keep families together*: Peter Paul, 182.

213   *religious instruction*: ibid., 179.

Foreign Entanglements

213 In 1816...Poplar Island plantation: Papenfuse in Van Devanter, 49.
213 *War fever*: see John Adams to CCC, December 10, 1794, Hanley 979.
213f. *John Marshall...Jay's effort*: Gurn, 158.
214 *to tax American...British imports*: Ellis, *American Sphinx*, 159.
214 *made no provision...joined the British*: Rowland, II:202.
214 *Carroll favored..."on our trade"*: CCC to Upton Scott, September 26, 1795, Hanley 982.
214 *"I am totally...decided superiority"*: CCC to Washington, April 23, 1796, Hanley 988.
214 *"assumption of power"*: Washington to CCC, May 1, 1796, in Rowland, II:204–206.
214 *Carroll of Homewood..."repeatedly"*: ibid., II:206–207.
214 *"letters to Mr. Adams..."*: Peter Paul, 163.
214 *"passionate, prejudicial..."*: CCC, n.d., MHS 4196, 1139; see also CCC, "Notes on the second and fourth amendments to the Constitution," 1796, MHS 4227B, 6989.

The Adams Administration

215 *Carrollton had suggested..."the Presidential chair"*: CCC to Upton Scott, September 26, 1795, Hanley 982.
215 *"The friends...revolution & war"*: CCC to James McHenry, December 5, 1796, in Steiner, *Life and Correspondence*, 204–205.
215 *"A man must be blind"...to the presidency*: CCC to James McHenry, December 12, 1796, in ibid., 206.
215 *"wild Irish"*: Rosenfeld, 43.
215 *"we have no Americans..."*: ibid., 901.
215 *"independence...liberty"*: ibid., 127.
215 *"orthodoxy"*: ibid., 904.
215 *"heretical"*: ibid., 510, 662, 750.
215 *"a little patience..."*: Burstein, 191.
215 *the Catholic...of the Potomac Company*: Griffin, II:383.
215 *"But he received..."*: ibid., 386.
216 *"our friend Mr. Carroll..."*: William Hindman to James McHenry, December 9, 1799, in Gurn, 167.
216 *sent Carrollton*: *Votes and Proceedings of the Senate*, December 17, 1799.
216 *"The two honored...not dry"*: Gurn, 168.

The Jeffersonian Revolution

216 *"intriguant...care of that"*: James McHenry to John Adams, May 31, 1800, reporting a conversation of May 5, 2000, in *The Papers of Alexander Hamilton*, vol 24, *November 1799 – June 1800*, ed. Harold C. Syrett (New York: Columbia University Press, 1977), 557.
216 *determined to avoid war*: Nagel, 76–77.
216 *disband the standing army*: Rosenfeld, 812.
217 *"we have strange reports...dissolve this Union"*: CCC to Hamilton, April 18, 1800, in *Papers of Alexander Hamilton*, 24, 412.

Notes

217 *Jefferson's dictum*: Conor Cruise O'Brien, *The Long Affair: Thomas Jefferson and the French Revolution, 1785–1800* (Chicago: University of Chicago Press, 1996), 41.
217 "*Possibly were...during his presidency*": CCC to Hamilton, April 18, 1800, in *Papers of Alexander Hamilton*, 24, 412.
217 *Carroll approved*: CCC to Hamilton, August 27, 1800, in *The Papers of Alexander Hamilton*, vol 25, *July 1800–April 1802*, ed. Harold C. Syrett (New York: Columbia University Press, 1977), 93–95.
217 "*totally unfit...*": James McHenry to Oliver Wolcott, September 1, 1800, in Gurn, 171.
217 "*Let this console...*": James McHenry to Hamilton, November 19, 1800, in *Papers of Alexander Hamilton*, 25, 242–244.
217 "*Mr. Carroll's influence...*": John Rutledge Jr. to Hamilton, July 17, 1800, in ibid., 25:34.
217 *McHenry complained...assembly elections*: James McHenry to Oliver Wolcott, October 12, 1800, in ibid., 25:158.
217 "*hoary-headed aristocrat...at defiance*": Gurn, 173.
218 *established white manhood suffrage*: Crowl, 84.
218 *Race was substituted...enjoyed in Maryland*: Bernard C. Steiner, *Roger Brooke Taney, Chief Justice of the United States Supreme Court* (Westport, Conn.: Greenwood Press, 1970, reprint of Baltimore: Williams & Wilkins, 1922), 56.
218 "*It consisted...its advantages?*" CCC to CCH, October 23, 1800, in Field, 170–172.

PART V: Patriarch

219 *tool of the ruling party*: see CCC to CCH, March 13, 1807, MHS 203, 82.
219 *Carrollton recognized...against the demagogues*: CCC to Richard Peters, June 28, 1824, *American Catholic Historical Researches* XIX, 56–57.

Religious Seeking

219 *Bishop Carroll supplied...Church were valid*: Carpenter, "Charles Carroll of Carrollton"; Kwilecki, 139; see also Fr. John McCaffrey's eulogy of December 20, 1832, in Gurn, 189.
219 "*the encouragement...is done away*": CCC to James McHenry, November 11, 1800, in Steiner, *Life and Correspondence*, 473–476.
220 "*on the mercy...*": Leonard, 226.
220 "*noble presence...without admiring him*": Semmes, 70–71.
220 "*study the grounds...they set out*": CCC to CCH, December 13, 1801, MHS 203, 23.
220 "*Without virtue...of the Almighty*": CCC to CCH, MHS 203, 10.
220 *Benjamin Chew...battle of Germantown*: Rowland, II:3, II:242.
220 *flirtation with Major André*: Randall, 383.
220 *eventually married...Howard*: Rowland, II:241–242.
220 "*its most agreeable expression*": *American Catholic Historical Researches* XXIX, 208. See also Charles M. Mount, *Gilbert Stuart* (New York: W. W. Norton, 1964), 201.

221 *but he insisted...financial settlement*: CCC to CCH, July 3, 1800, MHS 203, 2.
221 *"pestilential fevers"*: CCC to CCH, July 7, 1800, MHS 203, 3.
221 *"influence and preponderance"...from the Catholic Church*: John Carroll to CCC, July 15, 1800, *John Carroll Papers* II, 310–311.

Homewood House

221 *one of the finest*: Smith, 262.
221 *looking glasses...plate*: Hoffman and Mason, 77.
222 *"It is a much...indefatigable"*: Elizabeth Oswald Chew and Benjamin Chew, Sr. to Benjamin Chew, Jr., August 16, 1802, Chew Family Papers, courtesy of Homewood House.
222 *"a most worthy young fellow...domestic happiness"*: John Chew to Benjamin Chew, Jr., February 18, 1801, Chew Family Papers, courtesy of Homewood House.
222 *Carrollton initially...of the inheritance*: CCC to CCH, November 3, 1800, MHS 203, 6.
222 *forty thousand dollars had vanished*: Mason in Van Devanter, 29.
222 *half a million*: using the method in McCusker.
222 *"a most improvident...painful regret"*: CCC to CCH, July 31, 1803, MHS 203, 31.
222 *"a monstrous charge"*: CCC to CCH, November 29, 1800, MHS 203, 7.
222 *"improvements"...theater tickets*: CCC to CCH, January 24, 1801, MHS 203, 9.
222 *"If you would really..."*: CCC to CCH, July 17, 1801, MHS 203, 17.
222 *refused to spend another penny*: CCC to CCH, May 8, 1802, MHS 203, 24.
223 *The heir...instead of mahogany*: J. Gilman D'Arcy Paul, "The History of Homewood" (Baltimore: Johns Hopkins University, pamphlet, October 1939).

The American Narcissus

223 *"torpid and diseased..."*: CCC to CCH, MHS 203, 10.
223 *"the refreshing air of the morn"*: CCC to CCH, April 28, 1801, MHS 203, 13.
223 *"A person who rises..."*: CCC to CCH, July 3, 1800, MHS 203, 2.
223 *"Had your mother lived...stout and hardy"*: CCC to CCH, March 18, 1807, MHS 203, 83.
223 *Adams' two alcoholic sons*: Nagel, 5.
224 *The formal, ordered...and emotion*: see May, 353–357.
224 *parents of the revolutionary...not at peace*: Jan Lewis, "Domestic Tranquillity and the Management of Emotion among the Gentry of Pre-Revolutionary Virginia," *William and Mary Quarterly*, third series, 39:1 (January, 1982), 143.
224 *"how strange..."*: CCC to Mary Caton, September 19, 1803, Hanley 1084.
224 *"two more affectionate parents"*: CCC to CCH, March 18, 1807, MHS 203, 83.
224 *"too anxious..."*: CCC to CCH, July 31, 1803, MHS 203, 31.
224 *"too tenderly...now good"*: CCC to CCH, September 12, 1802, MHS 203, 28; see also CCC to CCH, September 18, 1802, MHS 203, 29.

Notes

224 *inclined to drink*: CCC to CCH, MHS 203, 47.
224 *"never to strike...a trifling one"*: CCC to CCH, February 1, 1808, MHS 203, 89.
225 *He allowed...to fornicate*: CCC to CCH, September 30, 1808, MHS 203, 96.
225 *to separate husbands from wives*: CCC to CCH, September 30, 1808, MHS 203, 96.
225 *"Two masters..."*: CCC to CCH, February 12, 1801, MHS 203, 12.
225 *Richard Caton went bankrupt...and some gifts*: Richard Caton, "A Brief Statement of Facts in the Management of the Late Mr. Carroll of Carrollton's Moneyed Estate," December 11, 1832, MHS, 2–3, 27.
225 *His father had...of $5,000*: CCC to CCH, August 29, 1803, MHS 203, 34.
226 "about $116,000 in today's money": Again, following Officer and Williamson, and using the method of conversion in McCusker at <https://www.measuringworth.com/uscompare/>, accessed November 30, 2017.
226 *"This would be..."*: CCC to CCH, August 8, 1803, MHS 203, 32.
226 *discharged his workmen*: CCC to CCH, August 9, 1803, MHS 203, 33.

The Education of Women

226 *Carrollton must...daughters' inheritance*: see Mason in Van Devanter, 26–27.
226 *"I shall never"...house and carriage*: CCC to Richard Caton, September 8, 1800, Hanley 1006.
226 *Harper bargained..."I am repelled"*: Robert Harper to Richard Caton, October 2, 1800, Hanley 1007.
226 *accepted Harper's conditions..."and beloved child"*: CCC to Richard Caton, October 4, 1800, Hanley 1008.
226f. *"every father ought..."*: Robert Harper to Richard Caton, November 5, 1800, Hanley 1013.
227 *"Every trifle which..."*: CCC to Robert Harper, December 5, 1801, Hanley 1016.
227 *Kitty Harper remained Catholic*: Gurn, 187.
227 *"piety towards God...of acting rightly"*: CCC to Mary Ann Caton, February 2, 1803, MHS 4197, 1304.
227 *"if you do not...cousin of his"*: CCC to Louisa Caton, September 19, 1803, Hanley 1085.
227 *"how essential kindness..."*: Caton, 28.
227f. *"Alas, my dear Papa"..."will of God"*: CCC to Emily Caton, March 4, 1802, Hanley 1051.

Burr

228 *"Thomas the great man"*: CCC to Robert Harper, December 10, 1802, Hanley 1073.
228 *"harmony and affection"*: Burstein, 3–4.
228 *Montesquieu had warned...fatal to republics*: Montesquieu, X.6.3, 193.
228 *"not less...terminate the Union"*: CCC to CCH, February 8, 1801, in Rowland, II:248–249.
228 *Burr spent...and the Harpers*: Mary Jo Kline and Joanne Wood Ryan, eds. *Political Correspondence and Public Papers of Aaron Burr* (Princeton, N.J.: Princeton University Press, 1983), II:813–814; Fleming, 92.
228 *working together*: see also Fleming, 277.

228 *assault on the judiciary*: see ibid., 180.
228 *The President wanted...majority vote*: ibid., 367.
228 *As President...a defense attorney*: ibid., 134.
229 *He incurred...to a grand jury*: James Haw, et al., *Stormy Patriot: The Life of Samuel Chase* (Baltimore: Maryland Historical Society, 1980), 214–215.
229 *Harper served...defense team*: Robert Harper to Mr. Bayard and General Hamilton, January 22, 1804, Hanley 1087.
229 *"This day has determined...over party spirit"*: CCC to Robert Harper, February 28—March 3, 1805, Hanley 1112.
229 *"Col. Burr is..."*: CCC to Robert Harper, January 12–14, 1805, Hanley 1104.
229 *"sanctuary and a citadel...on this floor"*: Fleming, 369.
229 *Carrollton was summoned...St. John's Colleges*: Leonard, 225.
229 *The demagogues...were elitist*: Crowl, 85; *Votes and Proceedings of the Senate*, December 28, 1793, December 12, 1794, December 20, 1797; Rowland, II:214.
229 *"temple of virtue..."*: Burstein, 196.
229 *taught young Catholics...Georgetown University*: Spalding, "A Revolution," 211.
229 *supported Georgetown financially*: Leonard, 253.
229f. *donated land...once a month*: Rowland, II:362; CCC to Rev. Deluol, March 27, 1830, Arents Letterbook.

Embargo

230 *"anarchy, & civil war"*: CCC to Robert Harper, May 5, 1804, Hanley 1097.
230 *"a derangement in the finances..."*: CCC to CCH, April 14, 1804, MHS 203, 39.
230 *refused to enlarge...Canal Company*: CCC to Daniel Carroll of Duddington, June 7, 1805, Daniel Carroll of Duddington Papers, Library of Congress.
230 *tried to pull out...Iron Works*: CCC to Daniel Carroll of Duddington, February 4, 1808, Daniel Carroll of Duddington Papers, Library of Congress.
230 *taking six-percent...as security*: Rosalie Stier Calvert to H.J. Stier, August 30, 1810, in Callcott, 228.
230 *"The Democrats are..."*: CCC to CCH, January 16, 1806, MHS 203, 50.
230 *He ridiculed...ships and cargoes*: CCC to Robert Harper, February 24, 1806, Hanley 1142.
230 *"impossible for a man..."*: CCC to CCH, September 3, 1806, MHS 203, 68.
230 *"I will speak..."*: CCC to Horatio Ridout, August 22, 1806, Hanley 1160.
231 *"In that case..."*: CCC to CCH, November 21, 1806, MHS 203, 74.
231 *"should make an alliance...thralldom of France"*: CCC to Robert Harper, March 14, 1806, Hanley 1145.
231 *"the whole faction..."*: CCC to CCH, January 23, 1807, MHS 203, 79.
231 *"The general opinion...such an Act"*: CCC to William Murdoch, October 17, 1806, Arents Letterbook.
231 *"impose on us..."*: CCC to CCH, February 12, 1808, MHS 203, 90.

231 "*universal dominion*"...*France was retained*: CCC to William Murdoch, March 14, 1809, Arents Letterbook.
231 *The money lost...shipping worldwide*: Fleming, 396.
231 "*A more miserable...*": CCC to CCH, April 29, 1810, MHS 203, 112.

Families Divided

232 "*exercise and temperance*": CCC to CCH, April 12, 1806, MHS 203, 53.
232 "*I shall be very happy...*": CCC to Robert Harper, April 30, 1804, Hanley 1096.
232 "*Unfortunately though...to its precepts*": CCC to Harriet Carroll, August 29, 1810, in Guilday, I:5.
232 *an anxious mother*: CCC to CCH, June 1, 1804, Hanley 1098.
232 "*over anxiety is hurtful...*": CCC to CCH, October 31, 1805, MHS 203, 46.
232 "*he will be warmly...*": CCC to Robert Harper, January 12–14, 1805, Hanley 1104.
232 "*I much fear...comfort you can*": CCC to CCH, August 11, 1806, MHS 203, 62.
232 "*enjoying a glorious...solely from sorrow*": CCC to CCH, August 12, 1806, MHS 203, 63.
232 *an additional thousand...against his estate*: CCC to CCH, April 18, 1806, MHS 203, 54.
232 "*with great fortitude*": CCC to CCH, December 24, 1806, MHS 203, 77.
233 *inquiring about his health*: CCC to CCH, August 28, 1806, MHS 203, 66.
233 *walked in his sleep*: CCC to CCH, January 4, 1807, MHS 203, 78.
233 "*one after the other...*": John Carroll to Ambrose Marechal, April 29, 1806, *John Carroll Papers*, II:514.
233 *kept her Catholic faith*: Gurn, 231.
233 "*we hear strange reports...*": CCC to CCH, February 14, 1804, MHS 203, 36.
233 *the heir insisted...diminishing his inheritance*: CCH to CCC, June, 1805, Hanley 1119.
233 *Carrollton disagreed*: CCC to Robert Harper, June 16, 1805, Hanley 1122.
233 *Homewood hired...news to Harper*: CCC to Robert Harper, June 19–20, 1805, Hanley 1123.
233 "*they have indeed*"...*telling them this*: CCC to CCH, January 29, 1811, MHS 203, 119.
233f. "*completely destitute*"..."*of method*": CCC to CCH, November 19, 1808, MHS 203, 97.
234 "*melts away...*": CCC to CCH, January 29, 1811, MHS 203, 119.
234 "*the grand Inquest*"...*in a wagon*: City of Annapolis to CCC, January 31, 1811, Hanley 1240.
234 *In July 1811...losing their freedom*: CCC to Robert Harper, July 15, 1811, Hanley 1250.
234 "*merely out of compassion...as a gift*": CCC to Robert Harper, November 21, 1811, Hanley 1254.
234 *Carroll instructed...would molest her*: CCC to Robert Harper, October 29, 1814, Hanley 1340.

234 *"she shall have... & likely"*: CCC to Richard Caton, August 21, 1811, Hanley 1251.
234f. *"things are not...of my negroes"*: CCC to Robert Harper, January 16, 1814, Hanley 1311.

The War of 1812

235 *"there is a secret..."*: CCC to Robert Harper, February 6, 1811, Harper Papers, MSS 24950, Library of Congress.
235 *£3,400 worth...Navy stock*: CCC to William Murdoch, October 24, 1812, Arents Letterbook.
235 *Prominent New York bankers*: Fleming, 399.
235 *"perfidy personified"*: CCC to CCH, May 28, 1812, MHS 203, 131.
235 *as late as July 1815*: CCC to William Murdoch, July 7, 1815, Arents Letterbook.
235 *"and a large number..."*: *Journal of the Senate of the United States of America*, 1789–1873, Saturday, June 13, 1812, accessed October 14, 1999, http://memory.loc.gov.
235 *On June 22...doors were opened*: Frank A. Cassell, "The Great Baltimore Riot of 1812," *Maryland Historical Magazine* 70:3 (Fall 1975), 241–256.
235f. *pitched down the steps...stomped him to death*: "Affidavit" in Henry Lee, "A Correct Account of the Conduct of the Baltimore Mob" (Winchester, Va.: John Heiskell, 1814), 15–16.
236 *"if the state..."*: CCC to CCH, August 5, 1812, MHS 203, 135.
236 *"rogues and riot"..."to live"*: Oral S. Coad, "A Signer Writes a Letter in Verse," *Journal of the Rutgers University Library* 32:1 (December, 1968), 33–35.
236 *Carroll met Peggy Chew Howard...to Philadelphia*: CCC to John Eager Howard: August 1, 1812, MHS 4198, 1533.
236f. *According to the...with death*: CCC to Robert Harper, December 9–10, 1813, Hanley 1304.
237 *"a great calamity... & just"*: CCC to Robert Harper, April 17, 1816, Hanley 1363.
237 *to seize Canada...dissent*: CCC to Robert Harper, January 16, 1814, Hanley 1311.
237 *"although no one..."*: CCC to Robert Harper, March 5, 1813, Hanley 1286.
237 *He hoped...with France*: CCC to Robert Harper, March 9, 1813, Hanley 1287.
237 *"I know of no..."*: CCC to Mary Caton, May 19, 1814, in Field.
237 *"the fire at Washington..."*: CCC to CCH, August 25, 1814, in Rowland, II:304.
237 *"the enemy keep up..."*: CCC to CCH, August 27, 1814, MHS 203, 151.
237 *"just conditions"*: CCC to Robert Harper, March 7, 1814, Hanley 1318.
237 *"I say nothing..."*: CCC to Robert Harper, September 11, 1816, Hanley 1378.

Decline of the Heir

238 *"exalting in her conduct"...Folly Farm house*: Sophia Philips to Benjamin

Notes

Chew, Jr., June 29, 1812, Chew Family Papers, courtesy of Homewood House.
238 *"the afflicting scene...inveterate habit"*: CCC to CCH, April 27, 1813, MHS 203, 140.
238 *"the habit...to give me"*: CCC to CCH, May 8, 1813, MHS 203, 141.
238 *"frequent conversations"*: CCC to CCH, December 5, 1813, MHS 203, 146.
238 *"you are very..."*: CCH to Mary Caton, February 8, 1814, Hanley 1313.
238 *But he had...militia corps*: CCH to John Eager Howard, June 25, 1813, MHS 4198, 1567.
238 *Carrollton asked Howard...her husband's annuity*: CCC to John Eager Howard, February 21, 1814, Hanley 1315.
238 *"There is now...habit"*: CCC to Robert Harper, March 7, 1814, Hanley 1318.
238f. *"I do suspect...extinguished my affection"*: CCC to CCH, May 15, 1814, MHS 203, 147.
239 *Rosalie Stier Calvert...their ill breeding*: Rosalie Stier Calvert to Henri J. Stier, June 10, 1814, in Callcott, 267.
239 *"I will not..."*: CCC to Mary Caton, June 12, 1814, Hanley 1322.
239 *"active affection...loose into the world"*: John Eager Howard to Benjamin Chew, Jr., March 18, 1813, Chew Family Papers, courtesy of Homewood House.
239 *"quite as you..."*: CCC to CCH, June 1, 1815, MHS 203, 153.
239 *Archbishop Carroll promoted*: John Carroll to Richard Caton, September 1, 1815, *John Carroll Papers*, III:357–358.
239 *drunk again*: CCC to Mary Caton, April 26, 1816, Hanley 1364.
240 *Harriet Carroll moved*: CCC to Robert Harper, June 8, 1816, Hanley 1368.
240 *He hired...occupant*: CCC, Directions to Captain Craig, June 11, 1816, Hanley 1369; CCC to John Eager Howard, Richard Caton, and Robert Oliver, June 11, 1816, MHS 203, "Requests."
240 *"When reformed..."*: CCC to CCH, June 18, 1816, MHS 203, 157.
240 *"unjust"*: Richard Caton to Robert Harper, January 10, 1813, Hanley 1281.
240 *demanded diamonds...$1,000 instead*: CCC to Robert Harper, May 15, 1812, Hanley 1266.
240 *"This measure..."*: CCC to Robert Harper, November 25, 1813, Hanley 1302; CCC to Robert Oliver, November 25, 1813, MHS 4198, 1578.
240 *the patriarch only...property to him*: CCC to Jonathan Pinkney, December 20, 1813, Hanley 1306.
240 *"to the world..."*: CCC to Mary Caton, April 26, 1816, Hanley 1364.

The Three Graces

241 *"moroseness...nor difficilis"*: Pise, 20.
241 *"the fashion, I suppose...each himself"*: Gurn, 195.
241 *"sprightly and intelligent...old fellow"*: ibid., 213.
241 *"the moral, civil..."*: ibid., 197.
241 *reestablished in 1816*: Papenfuse in Van Devanter, 54.
241 *invested a large portion*: see ibid., 55.

241 *sold his British Navy stock*: CCC to William Murdoch, August 14, 1817, Arents Letterbook.
241 *It was said...taxes*: Riley, 276.
241 *to remove the wheels...coach excise*: CCC to Thomas Simpson, December 9, 1814, Hanley 1341.
241 *"Baltimore, which now..."*: Gurn, 255.
241 *"The liberal heart..."*: Emily Caton to CCC, May 14, 1812, Hanley 1265.
241 *"for preserving..."*: Mary Diana Harper to Charles C. Harper, July 22, 1816, MHS 430.
242 *"Do you come...they 'fascinate'"*: Semmes, 219.
242 *lengthy account of Waterloo*: Col. Sir Felton Bathurst Hervey to CCC, n.d., in Field, 176–179; in "A Contemporary Letter on the Battle of Waterloo," *The Nineteenth Century* (March, 1893). This letter is dated July 3, 1815.
242 *He lent...March 1, 1817*: Semmes, 220.
242 *"you would be surprised..."*: Elizabeth Longford, *Wellington: Pillar of State* (New York: Harper & Row, 1972), 32.
242 *"because the Duke..."*: ibid., 46.
242 *"mental anguish"*: ibid., 32.
242 *"appears incompatible...good conscience"*: CCC to Mary Ann Patterson, October 16, 1816, in Field, 183–185.
242 *"the continued round...intimately connected"*: CCC to Betsy Caton, October 23, 1816, in ibid., 185–187.

Two Grandsons

243 *"These cold bleak winds..."*: CCC to CCH, March 14, 1806, MHS 203, 51.
243 *"too many & too long"*: CCC to Robert Harper, May 16, 1816, Hanley 1365.
243 *"morals of youth...material consideration"*: CCC to Rev. George Persigny, February 19, 1817, Arents Letterbook, MHS 4200, 1834.
243 *"decision & energy"*: CCC to Robert Harper, July 21, 1816, Hanley 1373.
243 *"full of 'His Majesty'..."*: Charles Carroll Harper to Mary Diana Harper, September 29, 1816, MHS 430.
243 *Harper offended...European monarchs*: Charles Carroll Harper to CCC, July 28, 1820, Hanley 1468.
243 *hustled them out*: CCC to Michael O'Maly, February 20, 1820, Arents Letterbook.
243 *Should they miss...avoiding London*: CCC to William Murdoch, March 27, 1820, Arents Letterbook.
243 *"if by good conduct..."*: CCC to Charles Carroll of Doughoregan [hereafter CCD], April 9, 1819, MHS 203, 162.
243f. *"The inheritance will..."*: CCC to CCD, November 1, 1821, MHS 4201, 2122.
244 *$100 from Archibald Gracie*: CCH to Robert Harper, November 19, 1820, MHS 1225.
244 *When Robert...their funds*: CCC to Robert Harper, November 3, 1818, Hanley 1432; CCC to William Murdoch, February 2, 1819, MHS 4201, 2066.

Notes

244   *"to fit you both..."*: CCC to CCD, November 1, 1821, MHS 4201, 2122.

244   *"industrious and good"*: MHM 10, 73; see also CCC to Thomas Sim Lee, February 8, 1795, in Charles Carroll Personal Miscellanous file, MHS.

244   *"often experienced..."*: Ann Hollyoke to CCC, November 14, 1826, Hanley 1651.

244   *Weems' 1827 loan request*: John Weems to CCC, March 12, 1827, Hanley 1676.

244   *just subscribed $30,000*: CCC to John Weems, March 14, 1827, Hanley 1679.

244   *He responded...face a lawsuit*: CCC to "Madam," n.d., MHS 215.

244   *"Be not discouraged...crops & prices"*: CCC to William Darne, August 8, 1822, Hanley 1522.

244   *such as Rembrandt Peale*: CCC to Charles Ingersoll, April 8, 1825, Arents Letterbook; see also Richard Caton to Rembrandt Peale, November 12, 1830, Arents Letterbook.

Slavery Questions

245   *"behaved outrageously..."*: CCC to William Gibbons, February 14, 1823, Letterbook 1824–1829, Carroll Family Papers, Library of Congress.

245   *"for telling me..."*: CCC to William Gibbons, April 9, 1825, Letterbook 1824–1829, Carroll Family Papers, Library of Congress.

245   *without solid evidence*: see CCC to William Gibbons, March 15, 1823, Letterbook 1824–1829, Carroll Family Papers, Library of Congress.

245   *He promoted Moses*: CCC to William Gibbons, May 23, 1825, Letterbook 1824–1829, Carroll Family Papers, Library of Congress.

245   *"old and of...and to forgive"*: CCC to William Gibbons, May 19, 1827, Letterbook 1824–1829, Carroll Family Papers, Library of Congress.

245   *He forbade...attended them*: CCC to William Gibbons, March 23, 1825, Carroll Family papers, Library of Congress.

245   *appointed teachers..."for themselves"*: Richard Caton to the *National Gazette*, December 20, 1832, in Gurn, 269–270.

245   *Missouri kept...corruption in government*: CCC to Robert Harper, February 17–18, 1820, Hanley 1447.

245   *"Why keep alive...for ever"*: CCC to Robert Harper, April 22–23, 1820, Hanley 1451.

245   *Encouraged by Harper*: John H. B. Latrobe, "Scrapbook," MHS 523.

245   *Madison, James Monroe, and Henry Clay*: Burstein, 253–254.

245   *elected its president*: Rowland, II:362.

246   *"lauded beyond measure..."*: Gurn, 265.

246   *"I have injured..."*: CCC to William Gibbons, March 21, 1825, Carroll Family Papers, Library of Congress.

246   *When it came...memory*: Smith, 308.

246   *for removing a dead horse*: CCC to William Gibbons, December 11, 1826, Letterbook 1824–1829, Carroll Family Papers, Library of Congress.

246   *He remembered the debt...after the fact*: CCC to John H. B. Latrobe, May 29, 1828, Charles Carroll Personal Miscellaneous file, MHS.

246   *cider be bottled...in the northwest*: CCC to William Gibbons, April 27, 1822, MHS 4202, 2258.

246 *Hogs were not...of the moon*: CCC to William Gibbons, December 7, 1824, Letterbook 1824–1829, Carroll Family Papers, Library of Congress.
246 "*nox vomica*"...*kill pests*: CCC to William Gibbons, February 17, 1825, Letterbook 1824–1829, Carroll Family Papers, Library of Congress.
246 "*will be found some day...*": CCC to [Robert Oliver?], February 18, 1828, MHS 4204, 2660.

Manifest Destiny

246 "*A great deal...*": As observed in 1832 by "Mr. J. J.," who wrote a reminiscence of Carroll; Kwilecki, 54.
246 "*A railroad from*"...*along the Potomac*: CCC to Daniel Brent, January 24, 1828, Hanley 1736.
247 *he chaired...board of directors*: Leonard, 229.
247 "*one of the largest...*": CCC to Lady Stafford, February 26, 1828, in Field, 210–211.
247 "*fever of excitement...*": Latrobe, "Sundries of Many Sorts," 176, MHS 523.
247 *Two young men..."mutual affection"*: Gurn, 256–258.
247 *In 1822...schismatic Fr. Hogan*: ibid., 198.
247 *outlawed lay control of parishes*: Carey, 30.
248 "*to see that the Church...*": Gurn, 262–263.
248 "*It is again urged...Independence*": ibid., 233–234.
248 "*to obtain religious...every virtue*": CCC to Rev. John Sanford, October 9, 1827, in ibid., 253–254.
248 "*what I now...*": Pise, 23.
248 *He gave land...St. Mary's Church*: Rowland, II:328–329.
248 *significant contribution...Cathedral*: Spalding, *Premier*, 86.
248 *funded orphanages*: Peter Paul, 241–242.
248 *and contributed...poor children*: CCC to Rev. Eccleston, May 30, 1824, Hanley 1570.
248 *Harper asked...dowry land*: CCC to Robert Harper, November 17, 1813, Hanley 1299.

Family Tragedy and Triumph

248f. "*station in society*"..."*or too cold*": CCH to Robert Harper, December 5, 1821, MHS 1225.
249 "*Your Affectionate Father*": CCC to CCH, March 30, 1821, MHS 203, 166; April 6, 1821, MHS 203, 167.
249 "*He knows he...*": CCC to CCD, May 30, 1823, MHS 203, 173.
249 *ordered his steward*: CCC to William Gibbons, November 16–20, 1824, Hanley 1578.
249 "*I have lost...*": CCC to William Gibbons, January 15, 1825, Letterbook 1824–1829, Carroll Family Papers, Library of Congress.
249 *forcibly removed to Emmitsburg*: CCC to CCD, March 8, 1825, MHS 203, 178.
249 "*My Dear Harriet...*": CCC to Harriet Carroll, April 12, 1825, Arents Letterbook.

[328]

Notes

250 *not in the chapel...from Annapolis*: Elder in Van Devanter, 60.
250 *He continued to pay...annually*: CCC to Harriet Carroll, April 12, 1825, Arents Letterbook.
250 *Harriet offered...wished*: Harriet Carroll to CCC, April 15, 1825, Hanley 1612.
250 *Carroll recommended...good marriages*: CCC to Harriet Carroll, April 18, 1825, Hanley 1613.
250 *"that in this republic..."*: CCC to CCD, June 6, 1823, MHS 203, 174.
250 *"a want of steadiness..."*: CCC to CCD, October 19, 1826, MHS 203, 181.
250 *He put the heir..."I would not"*: CCC to CCD, October 19, 1826, MHS 203, 181.
250 *Back in 1807...opposition to Napoleon*: CCC to CCH, March 13, 1807, MHS 203, 82.
250 *"totally ruined...Napoleon's conqueror"*: Longford, 114.
250 *prenuptial agreement*: "Articles of Agreement between Marquis Wellesley and Mary Anne Patterson," October 28, 1825, Hanley 1621.
250f. *The Anglican primate...Roman Catholic ceremony*: *Freeman's Journal*, November 5, 1825, in Field, 201–204.
251 *"That house...not be heard"*: Longford, 121–122.
251 *The new Marchioness'..."reigns a queen"*: Field, 204.
251 *"The partiality...endeavour to gain"*: CCC to the Marquis of Wellesley, February 9, 1826, in Field, 197–199.
251 *"mixture of good"...money on his account*: CCC to Marchioness Wellesley, March 16, 1826, Arents Letterbook.
251 *made an exception...ten thousand dollars*: CCC to Marchioness Wellesley, September 12, 1830, in Field, 212.
251 *"a large portion..."*: CCC to Marchioness Wellesley, January 10, 1828, in ibid., 205–207.
251 *"the perverted policy..."*: Marquis Wellesley to CCC, February 20, 1829, Hanley 1851.

John H. B. Latrobe

252 *"I consider myself...will be appointed"*: CCC to CCD, March 8, 1825, MHS 203, 178.
252 *his other lawyer, Roger Taney*: see Roger Taney to John H. B. Latrobe, April 26, 1825, MHS 523; Semmes, 291.
252 *He gave the McTavishes..."a moment longer"*: Latrobe, "The Breaking of the Entail on Doughoregan Manor," in "Scrapbook," MHS 523.
253 *studied law...Harper's office*: Latrobe, "Sundries of Many Sorts," 171, MHS 523.
253 *"weak and emaciated...Charles Carroll of Carrollton"*: Semmes, 214–215.
253 *"partial friends...dim and dull"*: CCC to Marchioness Wellesley, January 10, 1828, in Field, 205–207.
253 *the old man sent...a few cents*: Semmes, 214–215.
253 *Codicil 3..."such a woman"*: ibid., 292.
254 *"Well, Mr. Latrobe..."*: Latrobe, penciled note dated April 24, 1856, in MHS copy of Latrobe, "Charles Carroll of Carrollton," 261.

Rehabilitation

254 *"little influence"*: CCC to Bishop Ambrose Maréchal, December 19, 1818, *American Catholic Historical Researches* XV, 77.

254 *"lost all relish..."*: CCC to William Murdoch, July 27, 1818, Arents Letterbook.

254 *The Signer was asked...in Baltimore*: Gurn, 217–218.

254 *"I regretted much..."*: John Quincy Adams, Journal, February 7, 1825, in Gurn, 226–227.

254 *spoken on Burr's behalf*: Fleming, 387.

255 *"I wish to God...of both"*: CCC to Judge Hanson, February 26, 1826, in Rowland, II:337.

255 *"sentiment and power...benevolent aggressiveness"*: Burstein, 289.

255 *"unleashed the power..."*: Alasdair MacIntyre, "The American Idea," in Doyle and Edwards, 60.

255 *"of course...the public good"*: *Niles' Weekly Register*, June 2, 1827, in Gurn, 254.

255 *"What government..."*: CCC to Richard Peters, June 28, 1824, *American Catholic Historical Researches* XIX, 56–57.

255f. *to recommend...farewell address*: CCC to Franklin Sturgis, August 2, 1828, Hanley 1797.

August 2, 1826

256 *The tent of Washington...fort to Baltimore*: Gurn, 223–224.

256 *"praised & dispraised...forgotten & forgiven"*: CCC to Charles Wharton, July 19, 1826, Theodorus Baily Myers Collection, 760, New York Public Library.

256f. *"As their lives...with new light"*: Daniel Webster, "Adams and Jefferson, August 2, 1826," in Charles M. Wiltse, ed. *The Papers of Daniel Webster, Speeches and Formal Writings, Vol. 1, 1800–1833* (Hanover, NH: University Press of New England, 1986), 240.

257f. *"for the blessings...family of man"*: Gurn, 242–3.

Democracy in America

258 *"every expression..."*: *National Journal*, July, 1826, in ibid., 246.

258 *"the schoolboy used..."*: Senator Hoar, January 31, 1903, in Gurn, 273.

258 *"that bright constellation..."*: Robert P. Hay, "Charles Carroll and the Passing of the Revolutionary Generation," MHM 67:1 (1972), 57.

258 *"His star continued..."*: Gurn, 246.

258 *"this very active patriarch...more this afternoon"*: Josiah Quincy, *Figures of the Past* (Boston: Little, Brown & Co., 1926; first ed., 1883), 246–247.

258 *"I shall never...ardent spirits"*: Gurn, 251–252.

259 *cold bath...secret of health*: *American Farmer*, September 22, 1826, in ibid., 247; ibid., 252, 264–265.

259 *especially Horace*: CCC to CCD, August 6, 1827, MHS 203, 183.

259 *Franklin's works*: CCC to William Gibbons, December 21, 1822, Hanley 1529.

259 *"friction wheel"*: Semmes, 388.

259 *chess-playing automaton*: Gurn, 253.

Notes

259   *New-York Historical Society*: CCC to New York Historical Society, January 19, 1829, Hanley 1844.
259   *"American Box"*: Mr. Waters to CCC, September 19, 1828, Hanley 1809.
259   *beaver hat*: *American Catholic Historical Researches* XXII, 313.
259   *"I am too..."*: CCC to Mary Caton, September 23, 1826, Hanley 1643.
259   *$50*: Rowland, II:351.
259   *Fourth of July ceremonies*: see CCC to Philip Thomas, June 27, 1828, Hanley 1780.
259f.   *"A mere Democracy...not yet see clearly"*: Alexis de Tocqueville, *Journey to America*, George Lawrence, trans. (New Haven, Conn.: Yale University Press, 1960), 85–86.

Last of the Romans

260   *It was as if...Carroll's death*: see Hay, 61; also, Daniel Brent to CCC, May 23, 1828, Hanley 1762.
260   *turned over his affairs*: Richard Caton to Virgil Maxcy, June 22, 1831, Arents Letterbook.
260   *"I should be afraid..."*: CCC to I.J. Cohen, Esq., February 20, 1832, in Rowland, II:365–366.
260   *The centennial procession...heads bared*: Hay, 56.
260   *"galaxy...on admiring millions"*: Gurn, 266–267.
260   *"You find me very"...to console them*: Pise, 22.
260of.   *Dr. Stewart...Carroll died*: Gurn, 276–278.
261   *convention wore mourning...only to Washington*: Rowland, II:367.
261   *could not attend the funeral*: Gurn, 280.
261   *"the last of the Romans"*: Hay, 59.
261   *But to those...the Catholic Signer's relics*: Carpenter, "Doughoregan Manor," September 12, 1874, 322.
261   *the tableau...was the cross*: Gurn, 283.

[331]

Works Cited.

Allison, Robert J., ed. *American Eras: Development of a Nation, 1783–1815.* Detroit: Gale, 1997.

American Catholic Historical Researches. Philadelphia: Published and edited by Martin I. J. Griffin, 1887–1911.

American Memory. http://memory.loc.gov.

Archives of Maryland. Baltimore: Maryland Historical Society, 1883–1972.

"At a full meeting of the inhabitants of Anne-Arundel County... on Monday the 16th day of January, 1775." Annapolis, Md.: Anne Catharine Green and Son, 1775, Evans 13817.

Balch, Thomas. *The French in America during the War of Independence of the United States, 1777–1783,* vol. 1. Boston: Gregg Press, 1972; reprint of Philadelphia: Porter & Coates, 1891–1895 edition.

Barker, Charles A. "Maryland before the Revolution." *American Historical Review* 46:1 (October 1940).

Baumgarth, William, and Richard Regan, eds. *St. Thomas Aquinas on Law, Morality, and Politics.* Indianapolis: Hackett Publishing, 1988.

Bedwell, C. E. A. "American Middle Templars." *American Historical Review* 25:4 (July, 1920).

Bellarmine, Robert. *De Laicis or the Treatise on Civil Government.* Edited by Kathleen Murphy. New York: Fordham University Press, 1928.

Black, J. William. "Maryland's Attitude in the Struggle for Canada." *Johns Hopkins University Studies in Historical and Political Science,* 10th series (July 1892).

Blassingame, John W. "American Nationalism and Other Loyalties in the Southern Colonies, 1763–1775." *Journal of Southern History* 34:1 (February, 1968).

Bobrick, Benson, *Angel in the Whirlwind.* New York: Penguin Books, 1998.

Bond, Beverly W. "State Government in Maryland, 1777–1781."

Johns Hopkins University Studies in Historical and Political Science, series 23, nos. 3–4 (March–April, 1905).

Brackett, Jeffrey R. "The Negro in Maryland." *Johns Hopkins University Studies in Historical and Political Science,* extra volume VI (1889).

Burstein, Andrew. *Sentimental Democracy.* New York: Hill & Wang, 1999.

"By the General Assembly of Maryland, a proclamation…" February 13, 1777. Early American Imprints, first series, 43273.

Callcott, Margaret Law, ed. *Mistress of Riversdale: The Plantation Letters of Rosalie Stier Calvert, 1795–1821.* Baltimore: Johns Hopkins University Press, 1991.

Care, Henry. *Draconia.* London: George Larkin, 1687.

Carey, Patrick W. *The Roman Catholics in America.* Westport, Conn.: Praeger, 1996.

Carpenter, John C. "Charles Carroll of Carrollton." *Magazine of American History with Notes and Queries* II. New York and Chicago: A. S. Barnes & Co., 1878.

Carroll Papers in *Maryland Historical Magazine.* Vols. 10–16 (1915–1921) and 32 (1937).

Cassell, Frank A. "The Great Baltimore Riot of 1812." *Maryland Historical Magazine* 70:3 (Fall, 1975).

Catalogue of the Library of Charles Carroll of Carrollton, Embracing Many Old, Curious and Rare books, to Be Sold at Auction, Commencing on Monday Evening, December 5, 1864. Baltimore: Gibson & Company, 1864.

Caton, Richard. "A Brief Statement of Facts in the Management of the Late Mr. Carroll of Carrollton's Moneyed Estate." December 11, 1832. Maryland Historical Society.

Cawley, William, *The Laws of Q. Elizabeth, K. James, and K. Charles the First &c.* London: John Wright and Richard Chiswell, 1680.

Chadwick, Hubert, S.J. *St Omers to Stonyhurst.* London: Burns & Oates, 1962.

Charles Carroll of Carrollton Biography from the New York "Truth Teller." 1827. Maryland Historical Society.

Charles Carroll of Carrollton Letterbook. Arents Tobacco Collection, S0767. New York Public Library.

Works Cited

"Charles Carroll's Plan of Government." Edited by Philip A. Crowl. *American Historical Review* 46:3 (April 1941).

Coad, Oral S. "A Signer Writes a Letter in Verse." *Journal of the Rutgers University Library* 32:1 (December 1968).

Colbourn, H. Trevor. *The Lamp of Experience*. Chapel Hill: University of North Carolina Press, 1965.

Cometti, Elizabeth. "Inflation in Revolutionary Maryland." *William and Mary Quarterly*, 3rd series, 8:2 (April, 1951).

Countryman. "To the People of Maryland." Baltimore: Mary Katherine Goddard, 1776, Evans 15111.

Crowl, Philip. "Maryland during and after the Revolution: A Political and Economic Study." *Johns Hopkins University Studies in Historical and Political Science*, Series LXI, no. 1 (1943).

Doyle, David Noel and Owen Dudley Edwards, eds. *America and Ireland, 1776–1976*. Westport, Conn.: Greenwood Press, 1980.

Dulany, Daniel. "Military and Political Affairs in the Middle Colonies in 1755." December 9, 1755. *Pennsylvania Magazine of History and Biography* III:1, 1879.

Dunlap's Maryland Gazette. Baltimore: 1775–1792.

Edwards, Owen Dudley. "The Writers of the American Revolution—Variations on a Theme by Auden" in Doyle and Edwards.

Elder III, William Voss. "The Carroll House in Annapolis and Doughoregan Manor." In Van Devanter.

Ellis, Joseph J. *American Sphinx: The Character of Thomas Jefferson*. New York: Knopf, 1997.

———. *Passionate Sage: The Character and Legacy of John Adams*. New York: W.W. Norton, 1993.

Ernst, Joseph A. "The Political Economy of the Chesapeake Colonies, 1760–1775." In *The Economy of Early America: The Revolutionary Period, 1763–1790*, edited by Ronald Hoffman et al. Charlottesville: University Press of Virginia, 1988.

Everest, Allan S., ed. *The Journal of Charles Carroll of Carrollton as One of the Congressional Commissioners to Canada in 1776*. Fort Ticonderoga, N.Y.: Champlain–Upper Hudson Bicentennial Committee, 1976.

EWTN Library. http://www.ewtn.com/library.

Farrand, Max, ed. *Records of the Federal Convention of 1787* III.

New Haven, Ct.: Yale University Press, 1911.
Field, Thomas Meagher, ed. *Unpublished Letters of Charles Carroll of Carrollton*. New York: United States Catholic Historical Society, 1902.
Fleming, Thomas. *Duel: Alexander Hamilton, Aaron Burr and the Future of America*. New York: Basic Books, 1999.
Force, Peter, ed. *American Archives*. Washington, 1837–1853, 4th–5th series.
Gilbert-Hamerling, Geoffrey. *Exitus Acta Probat: George Washington and the American Civil Religion*. Dissertation. University of California at Berkeley, 1993.
Graham, Michael, S.J. "Popish Plots: Protestant Fears in Early Colonial Maryland, 1676–1689." *Catholic Historical Review* 79:2 (April, 1993).
Greene, Evarts B. "Persistent Problems of Church and State." *American Historical Review* 36:2 (January 1931).
Griffin, Martin I. J. *Catholics and the American Revolution*. 3 vols. Philadelphia: published by the author, 1907–1911.
Guilday, Peter. *Life and Times of John Carroll*. New York: Encyclopedia Press, 1922.
Gurn, Joseph. *Charles Carroll of Carrollton, 1737–1832*. New York: P. J. Kenedy & Sons, 1932.
Hanley, Thomas O'Brien, S.J., ed. *Charles Carroll Papers*. Microfilmed, 1971.
———. *Charles Carroll of Carrollton: The Making of a Revolutionary Gentleman*. Washington, D.C.: Catholic University of America Press, 1970.
———, ed. *John Carroll Papers*. Notre Dame, Ind.: Notre Dame University Press, 1976.
———. *Revolutionary Statesman: Charles Carroll and the War*. Chicago: Loyola University Press, 1983.
———. "Young Mr. Carroll and Montesquieu." *Maryland Historical Magazine* 62:4 (December 1967).
Haw, James, et al. *Stormy Patriot: the Life of Samuel Chase*. Baltimore: Maryland Historical Society, 1980.
Hay, Robert P. "Charles Carroll and the Passing of the Revolutionary Generation." *Maryland Historical Magazine* 67:1 (1972).
Henle, R. J., ed. *Saint Thomas Aquinas, the Treatise on Law*. Notre

Dame, Ind.: University of Notre Dame Press, 1993.

Hennessey, James, "An American Roman Catholic Tradition of Religious Liberty." *Journal of Ecumenical Studies* 14 (Fall 1977).

Hoffman, Ronald. "Charles Carroll of Carrollton: Conservative Revolutionary, 1776–1781." In Van Devanter.

———. *Charles Carroll of Carrollton: the Formative Years, 1748–1764*. Working Paper Series 12:3 (Fall 1982).

———, et al., eds. *Dear Papa, Dear Charley: The Peregrinations of a Revolutionary Aristocrat, as Told by Charles Carroll of Carrollton & His Father, Charles Carroll of Annapolis, with Sundry Observations on Bastardy, Child-Rearing, Romance, Matrimony, Commerce, Tobacco, Slavery, & the Politics of Revolutionary America*. 3 vols. Chapel Hill: University of North Carolina Press, 2001.

———. "'Marylando-Hibernus': Charles Carroll the Settler, 1660–1720," *William and Mary Quarterly*, 3rd series, 45:2 (April 1988).

———, in collaboration with Sally D. Mason. *Princes of Ireland, Planters of Maryland*. Chapel Hill: University of North Carolina Press, 2000.

———. *A Spirit of Dissension*. Baltimore: Johns Hopkins University Press, 1973.

Hume, David. *The History of England, from the Invasion of Julius Caesar to the Revolution in 1688*. Edited by Rodney W. Kilcup. Chicago: University of Chicago Press, 1975.

Ives, J. Moss. *The Ark and the Dove*. London: Longmans, Green, 1936.

Johnson, Keach. "The Genesis of the Baltimore Iron Works." *Journal of Southern History* 19:2 (May 1953).

Jordan, David W. "'God's Candle' within Government." *William and Mary Quarterly*, 3rd series, 39:4 (October 1982).

"Journal of a French Traveller in the Colonies, 1765, II." *American Historical Review* 27:1 (October 1921).

Ketchum, Richard M. *Saratoga*. New York: Henry Holt & Co., 1997.

Kline, Mary Jo, and Joanne Wood Ryan, eds. *Political Correspondence and Public Papers of Aaron Burr*. Princeton, N.J.: Princeton University Press, 1983.

Kwilecki, Susan Eugenia. *Through the Needle's Eye.* Dissertation. Stanford University, 1982.

LaMonte, Ruth Bradbury. *Early Maryland Education.* Dissertation. Ohio State University, 1976.

Latrobe, John H. B. "Biographical Sketch of Daniel Dulany." *Pennsylvania Magazine of History and Biography* III:1 1879.

———. "Charles Carroll of Carrollton." In *Biography of the Signers to the Declaration of Independence.* Edited by John Sanderson. Philadelphia: R. W. Pomeroy, 1827.

Lee, Henry. *A Correct Account of the Conduct of the Baltimore Mob.* Winchester, Va.: John Heiskell, 1814.

Leonard, Lewis A. *Life of Charles Carroll of Carrollton.* New York: Moffat, Yard & Company, 1918.

Letterbook 1684–1771. Carroll Family Papers. Library of Congress.

Lewis, Jan. "Domestic Tranquillity and the Management of Emotion among the Gentry of Pre-Revolutionary Virginia." *William and Mary Quarterly*, 3rd series, 39:1 (January 1982).

Lewis, Ronald L. "Slavery on Chesapeake Iron Plantations before the American Revolution." *Journal of Negro History* 59:3 (July 1974).

Longford, Elizabeth. *Wellington: Pillar of State.* New York: Harper & Row, 1972.

MacIntyre, Alasdair, "The American Idea," in Doyle and Edwards.

McSherry, James. *History of Maryland: From Its First Settlement in 1634 to the Year 1848.* Baltimore: John Murphy, 1849.

Maryland Gazette (Annapolis: 1745–1839).

Mason, Sally D. "Charles Carroll of Carrollton and His Family, 1688–1832." In Van Devanter.

———. "Mama, Rachel, and Molly: Three Generations of Carroll Women." In *Women in the Age of the American Revolution.* Edited by Ronald Hoffman and Peter J. Albert. Charlottesville: University Press of Virginia, 1989.

Matson, Cathy, and Peter Onuf. "Toward a Republican Empire: Interest and Ideology in Revolutionary America." *American Quarterly* 37:4 (Autumn 1985).

May, Henry F. *The Enlightenment in America.* New York: Oxford University Press, 1976.

Works Cited

Mayer, Brantz, ed. *Journal of Charles Carroll of Carrollton during His Visit to Canada in 1776, as One of the Commissioners from Congress.* Baltimore: John Murphy for Maryland Historical Society, 1876; reprinted, New York: New York Times and Arno Press, 1969.

Milobar, David. "Quebec Reform, the British Constitution and the Atlantic Empire: 1774–1775." *Parliamentary History* 14:1 (1995).

Montesquieu, Charles Louis Joseph de Secondat, Baron de. *The Spirit of Laws.* Translated by Thomas Nugent. Edited by David Wallace Carrithers. Berkeley: University of California Press, 1977.

Mount, Charles M. *Gilbert Stuart.* New York: W. W. Norton, 1964.

Mullett, Charles F. *Fundamental Law and the American Revolution.* New York: Octagon Books, 1966; reprint of 1933 edition.

Mullett, Michael A. *Catholics in Britain and Ireland, 1558–1829.* Houndmills, Basingstoke, Hampshire: Macmillan Press Ltd., 1998.

Mundey, Paul Eston. *"Beware of False Allegiance": Origins of Civil Religion in the United States, 1776–1791.* Honors Thesis. Towson State College, 1973.

Nagel, Paul C. *Descent from Glory: Four Generations of the Adams Family.* New York: Oxford University Press, 1983.

O'Brien, Conor Cruise. *The Long Affair: Thomas Jefferson and the French Revolution, 1785–1800.* Chicago: University of Chicago Press, 1996.

Officer, Lawrence H., and Samuel H. Williamson. *Measuring Worth.* https://www.measuringworth.com. Accessed November 30, 2017.

Onuf, Peter S., ed. *Maryland and the Empire, 1773.* Baltimore: Johns Hopkins University Press, 1974.

Papenfuse, Edward C. "Charles Carroll of Carrollton: English Aristocrat in an American Setting." In VanDevanter.

———, ed. "An Undelivered Defense of a Winning Cause." *Maryland Historical Magazine* 71:2 (Summer 1976).

The Papers of Benjamin Franklin. 37 vols. New Haven, Conn.: Yale University Press, 1959–1999.

Paul, J. Gilman D'Arcy. *The History of Homewood*. Baltimore: Johns Hopkins University, October 1939.

Paul, Peter Joseph. *The Social Philosophy of Charles Carroll of Carrollton*. Dissertation. University of Chicago, March 1947.

Pauley, William Everett. *Religion and the American Revolution in the South: 1760–1781*. Dissertation. Emory University, 1974.

Perkins, Edwin J. *The Economy of Colonial America*. New York: Columbia University Press, 1988.

Petrie, George. "Church and State in Early Maryland." *Johns Hopkins University Studies in Historical and Political Science*, tenth series (April 1892).

Pise, Charles Constantine. "Oration in Honor of the Late Charles Carroll of Carrollton." Georgetown: Joshua N. Rind, 1832.

Proceedings of the Conventions of the Province of Maryland, Held at the City of Annapolis, in 1774, 1775, & 1776 (Baltimore: J. Lucas & E. K. Deaver; Annapolis, Md.: J. Green, 1836).

Quincy, Josiah. *Figures of the Past*. Boston: Little, Brown & Co., 1926; reprint of 1883 edition.

Randall, Willard Sterne. *Benedict Arnold: Patriot and Traitor*. New York: William Morrow & Co., 1990.

Ridgely, David, ed. *Annals of Annapolis*. Baltimore: Cushing and Brother, 1841.

Riley, Elihu S. *"The Ancient City": A History of Annapolis, in Maryland, 1649–1887*. Annapolis, Md., 1887; reprinted, Baltimore: Genealogical Publishing Company, Inc., 1995.

Rosenfeld, Richard N. *American Aurora: A Democratic-Republican Returns*. New York: St. Martin's Press, 1997.

Rowland, Kate Mason. *The Life of Charles Carroll of Carrollton, 1737–1832*. 2 vols. New York: G. P. Putnam's Sons, 1898.

Rutland, Robert A., et al., eds. *Papers of James Madison* 11. Charlottesville: University Press of Virginia, 1977.

Scharf, J. Thomas. *History of Maryland from the Earliest Period to the Present Day* II. Baltimore: John B. Piet, 1879.

Semmes, John E. *John H. B. Latrobe and His Times, 1803–1891*. Baltimore: Norman, Remington, 1917.

Silver, John Archer. "The Provisional Government of Maryland

(1774–1777)." *Johns Hopkins University Studies in Historical and Political Science*, 13th series, no. x (October 1895).

Skaggs, David Curtis. "Maryland's Impulse toward Social Revolution: 1750–1776." *Journal of American History* 54:4 (March 1968).

Smith, Ellen Hart. *Charles Carroll of Carrollton*. Cambridge, Mass.: Harvard University Press, 1942.

Spalding, Thomas W. *The Premier See: A History of the Archdiocese of Baltimore, 1789–1994*. Baltimore: Johns Hopkins University Press, 1989.

———. "'A Revolution More Extraordinary': Bishop John Carroll and the Birth of American Catholicism." *Maryland Historical Magazine* 84:3 (Fall 1989).

Sparks, Francis Edgar. "Causes of the Maryland Revolution of 1689." *Johns Hopkins University Studies in Historical and Political Science*, 14th series (Nov.–Dec. 1896).

Steiner, Bernard C. *Life and Correspondence of James McHenry*. Cleveland: Burrows Brothers, 1907.

———. *Roger Brooke Taney, Chief Justice of the United States Supreme Court*. Westport, Conn.: Greenwood Press, 1970, reprint of Baltimore: Williams & Wilkins, 1922.

Syrett, Harold C., ed. *The Papers of Alexander Hamilton*. 26 vols. New York: Columbia University Press, 1961–1987.

Terrar, Edward. "Was There a Separation between Church and State in Mid-17th Century England and Colonial Maryland?" *Journal of Church and State* 35:1 (Winter 1993).

Tierney, Brian. *The Idea of Natural Rights*. Atlanta: Scholars Press, 1997.

———. *Religion, Law, and the Growth of Constitutional Thought, 1150-1650*. Cambridge, Mass: Cambridge University Press, 1982.

Tocqueville, Alexis de. *Journey to America*. Translated by George Lawrence. New Haven, Conn.: Yale University Press, 1960.

Twohig, Dorothy, ed. *George Washington's Diaries: An Abridgment*. Charlottesville: University Press of Virginia, 1999.

Van Devanter, Ann C. *"Anywhere So Long As There Be Freedom"*. Baltimore: Baltimore Museum of Art, 1975.

Votes and Proceedings of the House of Delegates of the State of Mary-

land. Annapolis, Md.: 1777–1819.

Votes and Proceedings of the Senate of the State of Maryland. Annapolis, Md.: 1777–1819.

Wegemer, Gerard B. *Thomas More: A Portrait of Courage.* Princeton, N.J.: Scepter, 1995.

Wilson, James. "Introductory Lecture of the Study of the Law in the United States." In *Selected Political Essays of James Wilson.* Edited by Randolph G. Adams. New York: Knopf, 1930.

Wiltse, Charles M., ed. *The Papers of Daniel Webster, Speeches and Formal Writings,* Vol. 1, *1800–1833.* Hanover, N.H.: University Press of New England, 1986.

Index.

Index Note to Readers

To locate Saints in the index, look under either their given or family name: e.g. **Aquinas, St. Thomas** or **Thomas Aquinas, St**. Places can be located based on the use of either St. or Ste. as they are presented in the book. Entries are listed letter by letter, and readers should continue down the S- section so as not to miss any entries.

abatis, 136, 140
Abbé de l'Isle-Dieu, 47, 48
abolition, 245
   See also African-Americans; black people; Carroll, Charles, of Carrollton; negroes; slavery; slaves
Acadians, 34
Acts. See individual names of Acts
Act to Prevent the Growth of Popery (1704), 30
Adams, John, 45, 51, 69–70, 123, 141
   alcoholic sons, 223
   in the American constellation, 257
   on Carrollton, 131
   and Congress friends, 163
   on Congressional Board of War and Ordnance, 160
   death of, 256
   on debt, 94–95
   dislike of France, 167
   on government, 72
   on John Jay, 128
   on Mayhew, 71–72
   praise for Carrollton's risk, 145
Adams, John Quincy, 120, 145, 254, 258
Adams, Samuel, 127
Adelaide, Queen, 251
Adirondacks, 175
Africa, 76, 245
African-Americans, 185, 213, 234
   See also black people; colonization; negroes; slavery; slaves
Albany, 134

Alcock, Mr., 48
Alien and Sedition Acts (1798), 215
Allen, Ethan, 129
Alps, 130
America, 72, 75, 90, 96, 111, 133, 140, 167–68, 231, 256–59
   See also Constitution; Declaration of Independence; Founding Fathers; liberty
"American Box," 259
American Colonization Society, 245
American Independence, 143–44
   See also Declaration of Independence; Fourth of July; individual names
American Revolution, 22, 24, 66, 70, 75, 119, 190
   See also Declaration of Independence; Lexington and Concord
American Society for Promoting and Propagating Useful Knowledge, 121
American spirit, 78
Anabaptists, 23
anarchy, 100, 118, 230
Anas (Jefferson)
André, John, 168, 183, 220
Angelic Doctor, 72
   See also Aquinas, St. Thomas
Anglicans, 20, 22, 26, 96, 126, 250
   See also Church of England; Episcopal Church
Annapolis, 26, 28, 36, 66, 67, 149
   arrival at by *Peggy Stewart*, 112

Carrollton's absence, 88
  lore, 113, 115
  mock funeral in, 106
  Sons of Liberty in, 78, 79
  standards for voting, 150
Anne, Queen, 30
Anne Arundel Committee of Correspondence, 112–13
Anne Arundel County, 83, 110, 131, 141, 149–50, 151, 154
Anti-Federalists, 201, 203, 204, 210, 215, 217, 255
  See also Federalists
antilon, 99
"Antilon," 99–108, 188
  See also "First Citizen"; "Second Citizen"
Antinomians, 23
anti-papists, 169
  See also Papists
anti-popery, 126, 169
  See also Popists
Antony (slave), 84
apathy, 155
apologetic works (*apologia*), 91, 219
"Apostle of Maryland," 24
  See also White, Fr. Andrew
"Apostles of Confusion," 139
Appalachians, 126, 173, 236
Aquinas, St. Thomas, 18, 19, 42, 44, 70, 72
Arbuthnot, Marriot, 186
Archimedes, 107
Arfvedson, C.D., 258
Arkansas, 46
armaments, 117
  See also munitions
army, 129, 133, 149, 155
  British, 130, 141, 160–61, 184
  commanders, 137, 139, 149
  conditions, 138, 154
  Continental, 122, 124, 130, 131, 138, 159–66, 180–89
  See also military; militia; privateers; soldiers
Arnold, Benedict, 112, 129, 130, 136–38, 163, 182–83
arrests, 35, 36, 51

Articles of Confederation, 173–74, 199
"A Sentry," 178
Asia, 76
  See also colonialism; colonies; colonization
"Association of the Freemen of Maryland," 116–17
Augustine, St., 248
Avalon, 21–23

back lands, 174, 178
"Bacon Face," 98
  See also Chase, Samuel
Baker, Louisa, 64–66, 85, 87
Baltimore, Lord, 49, 52, 80, 87, 140, 248
  See also Calvert, Cecilius; Calvert, Charles; Calvert, Sir George
Baltimore, Lord Cecilius, 22, 27
Baltimore, Lord Charles, 25, 26
Baltimore, Lord George, 21, 22
Baltimore American, 261
Baltimore and Ohio Railroad (B&O Railroad), 244, 247
Baltimore Cathedral, 248
  See also Basilica of the Assumption; Cathedral of the Assumption
Baltimore City, 17, 78, 94, 98, 148, 149
  activism, 113
  and architecture, 221, 252–53
  as center of commerce, 241
  creation of, 34
  riots, 236
  scandal, 233
  Sons of Liberty in, 78, 79
  See also "CX"; *Dunlap's Maryland Gazette*
Baltimore Committee of Observation, 118
Baltimore Company, 230
  See also Baltimore Iron Works
Baltimore County, 83
Baltimore Iron Works, 36, 49, 84, 120, 209, 230
  Dulany share of, 188
  expansion of, 119

Index

history, 35
Baltimore Museum, 244
Baltimore/Washington International Airport, 17
Baltimore Whig Club, 117
Bank of Maryland, 236
Bank of New York, 209
Bank of the United States, 235, 241, 255
Barrowists, 23
barter economy, 170
Basilica of the Assumption, 252–53
  See also Baltimore Cathedral; Cathedral of the Assumption
Bath (England), 65, 66
Bath County (Virginia), 166, 170, 175
battalions, 160
Battle of Camden, 181
Battle of Cowpens, 184
Battle of Eutaw Springs, 185
Battle of Long Island, 146
Battle of the Boyne, 29
Battle of Waterloo, 242
Battle of Waxhaw, 180
bayonets, 184–85
Beaumarchais, 167
Belgium, 33
Bellarmine, St. Robert, 20, 21, 37, 43
Ben (slave), 245
Bill of Rights, 30, 178
biographies, 108, 167, 189, 253–54
Bird, Christopher, 90
bishops, 42, 91
  See also Carroll, Rev. John; individual clerical names
black people, 46, 184, 185, 186, 218, 185, 186 See also African-Americans; negroes; slavery; slaves
Blackstone, Sir William, 68–69
Bladen, Governor, 54, 55
Bland, Richard, 71
"Blue Book," 164
Board of War, 182
Bohemia Manor, 36–37
Boleyn, Anne, 19
Bonaparte, Madame Jerome, 233, 242, 250
  See also Napoleon; Patterson, Betsy

Bonaparte, Napoleon. See Napoleon
Bonham, Dr., 68
books, 43, 48, 144, 196, 222
  See also libraries; literacy
Boston, 82, 94, 112, 124, 126, 132, 211, 256
Bostonnais, 129
Boston Port Act (1774), 110
Boston Tea Party, 110
Boucher, Jonathan, 89, 106, 148
bounties, 160, 165
Bourbons, 51, 243
Bourg, Baron du, 186
Bourges, 48–49
Bowie, John, 177
Bowling Green, Manhattan, 143
boycotts, 77, 78, 94, 95, 197
  See also embargoes; trade
Brandywine Creek, 162
Brents, 37
Briand, Jean Olivier, 129–30, 139
bribery, 75, 95, 152, 171
British Crown, 18, 23, 30, 100, 102, 111, 126, 143, 161
  See also British Empire; England; Great Britain; loyalists; individual rulers
British Empire, 17, 64, 111, 133
  See also British Crown; England; Great Britain; mother country
British Navy stock, 235, 241
Brooke, Clement, 84
Brooke, Elizabeth, 17, 18, 40, 41, 239
  See also Carroll, Elizabeth (mother)
Brooke, Rachel, 87, 90–91
Brookes, 37
"Broomstick and Quoad," 109
Brown, Mr., 177
Browne, Fr. Levinas, 39
Brownists, 23
Bunker Hill, 124
bureaucracies, 172, 247
Burgess (slave owner), 234
Burgoyne, John, 162–63
Burke, Edmund, 55
Burr, Aaron, 129, 210, 217, 228–30, 254
Burstein, Andrew, 255

Calvert, Benedict, 31, 76–77
Calvert, Cecilius, 26, 52, 146, 248
  See also Baltimore, Lord Cecilius
Calvert, Charles, 31
  See also Baltimore, Lord Charles
Calvert, Rosalie Stier, 17, 239
Calvert, Sir George, 21
Calverts, 26, 51–53, 87
Calvinists, 23, 71
Cambridge, 122, 124, 129
Camden, 180–81
Campion, Edmund, 37
Canada, 127–40, 131, 134, 136, 146, 162, 237
  See also Montreal; Quebec; War of 1812; York
Canadian campaign, 128–31, 137–39
Canadian Whigs, 140
canals, 246
capitalism, 85, 225, 255
Caribbean, 119
caricatures, 100
Carleton, General (Governor), 128, 130
Carlos III, 176
Carolinas, 181
  See also South Carolina
Caroline County, 154
Carroll, Anne Brooke (daughter), 175
Carroll, Anthony, 29, 37, 40
Carroll, Benjamin Chew, 232
Carroll, Catherine (daughter), 221, 226, 233
  as "Kitty," 191 See also Harper, Kitty
Carroll, Charles (cousin), 35–36, 95
Carroll, Charles, of Annapolis (father), 34, 37, 51, 58, 170
  on Antilon contest, 102–3
  arrests, 35, 36, 105
  and Baltimore Iron Works, 35
  character, 34, 222
  character of, 18
  clandestine marriage, 41, 42
  concern for estate, 63, 65, 66
  as Councillor, 155–56
  death, 103–4, 191
  debate with Daniel Dulany, 96
  defamation, 92–93
  direction of Carrollton, 54–56, 59, 64, 74, 82–83, 91, 99
  education, 33
  emigration plan, 47, 49, 53
  and France, 47, 48, 61
  and honor, 157
  Irish identity, 47
  on Jesuit obedience, 50
  law vocation, 33–34, 58
  letters, 40, 113, 120
  management of business, 174
  marriage, 17, 40–42, 61
  as Marylando-Hibernus, 29
  recognition of Carrollton, 41
  relationship with Carrollton, 104, 108, 159, 174, 176
  relationship with grandchildren, 120–21
  relationship with Molly Darnall, 88–89, 120, 174–75, 189
  and slavery, 18, 49, 83–84
  sued by kinsman, 95–96
  tolerance of religious enthusiasts, 115
  treatment of chattel, 84
  vocation to priesthood, 33
  See also relationship with Carrollton, above; slaves
Carroll, Charles, of Carrollton, 101, 177
  alienation from political life, 145
  as ambassador to Spain, 176
  and the American constellation, 260
  announcement of victory, 190
  appearance, 56, 102, 104, 105, 241, 253
  biographers, 108, 253–54
  birth, 17
  and Canada, 133, 136, 139
  celebrity, 253–54, 256
  character, 40, 41, 53–55, 63, 81, 91, 175–76, 229, 251
  courtship of Louisa Baker, 64–66
  as "CX," 125
  death, 260–61
  decision to stay in Maryland, 236
  "Declaration of the Delegates of

Index

Maryland," 141–43
defamation, 92–93
departure from Congress, 176
depression, 65, 86
on discipline, 164
early life, 17
education, 36–43, 46, 48–49, 53, 58–60, 81
election, 151
engagements, 86, 87
English correspondents, 74, 77, 82, 89–90, 110, 120
and family business, 58, 63
grave, 261
grief, 191
hatred of Napoleon, 231
and heavy taxes, 169–70, 177
illegitimacy, 17, 39, 40, 239
influence of Enlightenment, 50
influence on Declaration of Rights, 151
interests, 59–60, 176, 259
intimacy with others, 53–54, 82, 176
investments, 174, 241, 244, 246
journals, 134
knowledge of history, 38, 42, 43, 48, 60, 136, 152
last days, 188
as leader, 98, 101, 106, 108, 119, 148–49
letters, 39, 167, 176 *See also* English correspondents, above
lobby against Stamp Act, 74
loss of friendships, 89–91
and loyal Catholics, 167
marriage, 61, 64, 65, 86, 87, 88
and memory, 246, 252
on Molly's support, 160
on morality, 255–56
named to Canadian commission, 131
name for Jefferson, 228
nicknames, 55, 63
in Paris, 48
personal habits, 258–59
piety, 111, 220
plantation management, 244–46
as planter, 98, 213
portrait, 56, 102, 253 *See also* biographies
potential for presidency, 176
predictions about America, 65
as President of American Colonization Society, 245
as President of Senate, 192
relationships
  with daughters, 233, 240
  with family, 159, 249
  with father, 40, 132, 133
  with grandchildren, 227, 233, 241–44, 251, 252
  with Homewood, 223, 232–33, 238, 239, 249–50
  with Molly, 175–76
  with mother, 59, 61, 62, 86
  with parents, 61–63, 66, 104
and religion, 56, 219, 226–28, 232
See also Catholics; Declaration of Rights
residence at Carrollton, 82
return to America, 66, 67
and romance, 48, 54, 85–86
as Senator, 169–218
shrewdness in business, 82, 85, 244, 246
signature, 145, 148, 247, 253, 257
and slaves, 185–86, 234–35, 244–46
smallpox, 56
and Sons of Liberty, 78, 79
on spirit, 78, 84–85, 133–34, 158, 165, 167, 209, 229 *See also* spirit
as symbol of national unity, 260
as "the last of the Romans," 261
as "the Signer" *See* the Signer
and Washington's strategy, 163
on wilderness, 135–36
will, 252, 253
in York, 166
See also Catholics; Declaration of Independence; Founding Fathers
Carroll, Charles, of Doughoregan, 224, 227, 233, 240, 243–44, 260
Carroll, Charles, of Homewood (son)
alcoholism, 220, 223, 232, 237–40, 243, 249

birth, 120–21
business difficulties, 233–34, 238
character, 220, 224–25, 249–50
death, 248–49, 250
early life, 191, 223, 224
education, 195–96, 211
plantation management, 225
relationship with family, 232, 233, 239
and slaves, 225
Carroll, Charles, the Barrister, 95–97, 113, 151
Carroll, Charles, the Settler (grandfather), 27–37, 51–52, 58, 157
Carroll, Charles, the Surgeon, 35–36, 95
Carroll, Daniel, 37, 181, 196, 197, 200, 201, 207, 208
Carroll, Elizabeth (mother), 41, 67, 87
  Carroll's relationship with, 59, 61–63, 86, 87
  death, 60–61, 62
Carroll, Harriet, 220, 222, 224, 232, 237–40, 250, 252
Carroll, Henry, 37
Carroll, James, 35, 37
Carroll, Louisa Rachel, 120
Carroll, Mary (daughter), 89, 120, 190, 191, 221, 233
Carroll, Molly (wife), 93
  addiction, 120–21, 175–76, 186, 223
  death, 191
  declining health, 165–66
  and her mother, 188–89
  letters to the Squire, 174–75, 190–91
  and politics, 156, 166, 182, 186
  portrait, 120
  See also Darnall, Mary ("Molly")
Carroll, Rev. John, 40, 131–32, 188, 197, 233
  as archbishop, 37, 137, 140, 238, 239
  arrest, 51
  as bishop, 208, 219, 221, 229, 233
  founding of Georgetown University, 229
  as "Jacky," 37

Carroll, Samuel S., 243
Carroll, Thomas, 29
"Carroll dissenting," 191
Carrolls, 112, 169
  and American Catholicism, 221
  confederacy with Independent Whigs, 103
  dispute with Hammonds, 110
  domestic history, 42
  estate of, 65, 66, 81, 115, 186 *See also* individual names of holdings
  feud with Dulanys, 92–94, 97
  graveyard, 250
  interest in Canadian events, 131
  lawsuits against, 233
  List of Assets, 85
  management disagreements, 83–85
  and money lending, 31, 209, 230, 244
  motto, 27
  and prenuptial agreements, 87, 250
  quarrels, 252
  reactions to Poplar Island, 186
  rents, 170
  and slaves, 83–84, 115, 121, 187, 222, 224
  social status, 239, 242
  transfer of custom, 120
  upbringing of children, 120–21
Carrolltonian, 259
Carrollton Manor, 82, 170, 187, 217–18, 238, 239, 249, 261
"Carrollton March," 247
Cathedral of the Assumption, 261
  See also Baltimore Cathedral; Basilica of the Assumption
Catholic Church, 20, 24, 35, 50, 57, 68, 69, 107, 221
  and American politics, 193, 207, 247–48
  in Canada, 126, 127–28, 130
  dogmatism, 69
  embodiment theory, 70–71
  and England, 19, 21, 143, 251
  on marriage, 41–42, 145
  orthodoxy, 91, 247
  relics, 257
  See also Communion; Mass; rites;

sacraments; Saints; Vatican; individual names
Catholics, 33
  in America, 132
  in Canada, 127
  disenfranchisement, 32
  exclusion from public office, 81
  Irish, 18, 19, 49, 161, 164, 190
  in Maryland, 17, 28, 52–53, 106, 145, 148
  and penal laws, 30, 47, 49
  perceived menace, 127
  persecution, 19, 20
  and public office, 81, 131, 183
  and Puritans, 21, 22, 26
  refuge, 21, 46
  See also Carroll, Charles, of Carrollton; Catholic Church; individual names
Caton, Betsy, 242
Caton, Emily, 227–28, 241
  See also McTavish, Emily
Caton, Louisa, 227, 242
Caton, Mary (daughter), 224, 225, 238, 239, 259, 261
Caton, Mary Ann (granddaughter), 211, 227, 233, 242
Caton, Richard, 225, 227, 232, 238, 240, 245, 260
Cavaliers, 25
"Censor," 188
censorship, 156
Chambly (Fort), 136
Chancery Court, 31
Chanche, John M., 260
Charity (slave), 234
Charles County, 190
Charles I, 19, 21, 22, 25, 28, 100
Charles II, 25, 26
45 Charles Street, 235
Charleston, 180, 185
Charlotte, 181
Chase, Rev. Thomas, 46
Chase, Samuel, 46, 89, 97, 101, 109, 110, 113, 135, 172
  acquittal of, 229
  as "Censor," 188
  debt, 98

named to Canadian commission, 131
  seats won, 151
  in Sons of Liberty, 78, 79
Chatham, Lord, 73
Chesapeake Bay, 22, 36, 161, 181, 189
Chesapeake & Ohio Canal Company, 246
Chester, 189
Chew, Benjamin, 220, 232
Chew, Benjamin, Jr., 237
Chew, Harriet, 220
Chew, John, 222
Chew, Peggy, 220
  See also Howard, Peggy Chew
Chew, Sophia, 237
Chews, 221
chi, 125
  See also Greek
Christianity, 69
  See also Catholic Church; Catholics; individual names of institutions and groups
Christie, Robert, 117
Christopher (slave), 225
Churchill, Winston, 231
Church of England, 21, 26, 29, 31, 32, 91, 100
  See also Anglicans; Episcopal Church
Church of Rome, 91
  See also Catholic Church; Church of England; Vatican; individual names
cider, 246
citizen-soldiers, 123, 147
  See also militia
civil war, 120, 122, 154, 157, 230
Civil War, English, 25
Claiborne, Captain, 25
classics, 37–39, 229, 259
Clay, Henry, 245, 254, 260
Clement XIV, 51
climacterics, 64
Clinton, Sir Henry, 161, 162–63, 180, 183
code duello, 93
  See also duels

Coke, Sir Edward, 68–69, 107
College of Louis-le-Grand, 43, 49
College of Paris, 243
colonialism, 76
colonies, 33, 36, 57, 71, 141–42, 144
   and Britain, 76, 80, 99, 110–11, 125
   and Canada, 126–27
   smuggling, 76
   Spanish, 230, 231
   and taxes, 77, 80, 95 *See also* taxes
   and unity, 133
   and war, 119, 123, 131, 138
   See also individual names of colonies and planters
colonists, 51, 73, 126, 127, 133, 144
   loyalty to mother country, 75–76, 111
   population, 73–74
   and rights, 29, 30, 70
   and taxes, 76, 78, 80, 109 *See also* taxes
colonization, 245
commercialism, 224
Commissioners' Point, 135
common good, 18, 101, 244, 247
   after pursuit of happiness, 255
   and Carrollton's politics, 157, 172
   and the individual, 42–43, 75
   and mixed constitution, 79
   and natural law, 70
common law, 58–60, 100, 107
   and compound interest, 85
   views on, 68, 70, 100
"Common Sense" (Paine), 122
Common Sense theory, 121–22
commonwealth, 70
Communion, 38, 91
   See also Catholic Church; Mass; sacraments
"Complaint from Heaven with a Hue and Cry," 27
Concord. *See* Lexington and Concord
Confession, 91, 109
   See also Catholic Church; rites; sacraments
confiscations, 138
   of Tory property, 176–80, 187, 188, 212

Congregational Church, 71
Congress. *See* individual names of congressmen
Congressional Board of War and Ordnance, 160, 163
Connecticut, 80, 139
consanguinity, 86, 87
conservatives, 100, 111, 140, 158
"Considerations on the Propriety of Imposing Taxes in the British Colonies" (Dulany), 99, 100–101
"Consistent Protestant," 109
constellation metaphor, 256–59
   See also Adams, John; Carroll, Charles, of Carrollton; Jefferson, Thomas
Constitution, 13, 45, 68, 80, 151, 153, 200–202, 214, 219, 259
   changes to, 125, 142, 155, 214, 228, 229, 255
   guardianship, 219
   and liberty, 255
   See also Declaration of Independence; Declaration of Rights; Founding Fathers
Constitutional Convention, 37, 196–201
constitutionalism, 107, 143
Continental Army, 122, 160, 189
   See also army; Washington, George
Continental Congress, 127, 128, 131, 133–40
contraband, 116
   See also smuggling
conversions, 30, 91, 181
   See also Jesuits, evangelism of Native Americans
convicts, 20, 84, 87, 160, 185
   See also arrests; black people; negroes; slavery; white indentured servants
Conway, Thomas, 166
Conwell, Bishop, 247
Cooke, Rachel, 86
Cooke, William, 86
Copley, Fr., 22
Copley, Governor Lionel, 30
Cornwallis, Lord, 146, 154, 180–81,

184, 187, 189–90
corporal punishment, 36, 83–84
  See also black people; negroes; slavery; slaves
corpus mysticum reipublicae, 70–71
Cortelyou House, 146
Council of Safety, 117–19, 146
Council of Trent, 41
"Countryman," 125
credit, 137, 157, 169–71, 183
creditors, 244
Cromwell, Oliver, 25
Crookshanks, Alexander, 64
cross, 69, 261
  See also crucifix
Crown Point, 134
crucifix, 111, 260, 261
  See also cross
currency, 95, 169, 171, 179, 187
  change as, 184
  continental money, 185
  in inspectors' certificates, 98
  modern equivalencies, 81, 152
  paper, 77, 82, 157
  paper at face value, 170–71
  See also paper money; printed money; specie
Currency Act (1764), 77
Custis, 192
"CX," 125
  See also Carroll, Charles, of Carrollton

Danbury, Connecticut, 139
Daniel (slave), 234
Daniel, Major, 104
Darnall, Henry, 31
Darnall, Henry III, 52, 87
Darnall, Henry IV, 87
Darnall, Mary ("Molly"), 31, 87–89
  See also Carroll, Molly (wife)
Darnall, Nancy, 191
Darnall, Rachel Brooke, 188
Darnalls, 37
Darne, William, 244
dauphin, 51
Deards, William, 92, 93
debt, 75, 157, 179, 183

British, 76, 180
collections, 116, 150
colonial, 77, 94–95
discharge of, 244
national, 180, 230
payment forms, 77, 170–71
debtors, 34, 150, 159, 174
DeButte, Mr., 99
Declaration of Independence, 20, 141–43, 248
  copies of, 145, 247, 254
  language of, 127
  signing of, 145, 256
  as "the Great Charter of Mankind," 258
  See also Carroll, Charles, of Carrollton; individual names of agents
Declaration of Rights, 151–52, 153, 156
"Declaration of the Delegates of Maryland" (Carrollton), 141
Declaratory Act (1766), 80
Deists, 92
Delaware
democracy, 44, 126, 151, 202, 237, 255, 258–60
democrats, 13, 100, 110, 113, 116, 125, 149, 150, 154, 204, 219, 230, 260
Deschambault, 138
despotism, 43, 80, 127, 154, 248
d'Estaing, Admiral, 77, 181
Deux-Ponts, Guillaume de, 189
the Devil, 230
  See also Satan ("Old Nick")
Dickinson, John, 57, 111, 122, 127–28, 132
Digges, Ignatius, 95–96
Digges, Mary, 96
diplomacy, 21, 133, 176
discipline, 38, 50, 107, 121, 162, 164, 224, 244–45, 249
  military, 123–24, 138, 146, 162, 164, 180, 237
  See also slavery; slaves, and punishment; St. Omers
disease, 58, 186, 187, 190, 223
  See also Carroll, Charles, of Home-

wood; Carroll, Molly; inoculations; jaundice; smallpox
District of Columbia, 205
divine law, 19, 20
divine right, 19, 20–21, 25, 26, 57, 67, 71, 102
dominion, 111, 228, 231
Don Quixote, 159
Dorchester county, 154
Dorsey, Thomas, 119
double tax, 47, 52, 157
Doughoregan Manor, 17, 82, 87, 88, 91
  battalion, 160
  chapel, 188
  General Lee's visit to, 182
  library at, 219
  resting place of Carrollton, 261
  See also Carroll, Charles, of Carrollton
dowries, 65, 248, 252
Duché, Jacob, 169
duels, 93–94, 188, 229
Dugnani, Cardinal, 208
Duke of Gloucester Street, 35
Dulany, Daniel Jr., 36, 87, 92, 99, 104–5, 108, 112, 156, 188
  poem on Carrollton's marriage, 87–88
  rivalry with Carrollton, 57–58
  See also "Antilon"; "First Citizen"; "Second Citizen"
Dulany, Daniel Sr., 35, 96, 104
Dulany, Lloyd, 57, 89, 92–93, 115
Dulany, Walter, 97
Dulany, Walter, Mrs., 192
Dulany-Carroll quarrel, 92–94, 97
Dunlap's Maryland Gazette, 125
  See also Baltimore City
Dunmore, Governor, 118
Dutch, 27, 109
duties. See taxes; individual names of Acts and countries

East India Company, 109
Eddis, William, 89, 98, 154, 155, 160
Eden, Governor Robert, 89, 96–100, 104, 108, 109, 117–18, 155

education, 33, 37, 46, 248
  and women, 226–28
Edward I, 71
Edward III, 117
Edwards, Owen Dudley, 141
Edward VI, 18
effigies, 78–79, 124
elections, 24, 67, 89, 143, 150–51, 200–202, 215
  See also property qualifications; rights; voting; individual names of politicians
electoral college, 45, 119, 152–53, 200, 230
electricity, 193
  See also Franklin, Benjamin, kite of; hydropower
Elizabeth I, 19, 20, 68
Elk Ridge, 17, 66, 78–79, 96, 186
Ellicott City, 82
Ely, 18
embargoes, 74, 110, 172, 230–35
  See also boycotts; trade
Emmitsburg, 241, 249
England, 25, 34, 57
  code of honor, 100, 136, 164–65, 182–83
  Constitution of, 43, 69–70, 76, 100, 105, 107, 111, 122, 143, 231
  politics of honor, 74–76, 81, 93, 100
  Reformation, 18–21, 37, 46, 69, 107
  See also British Crown; British Empire; Great Britain; London; mother country
England, John, 248
Enlightenment, 43, 50, 224
enlistments, 123, 130, 137, 160, 185
  See also army; military; militia; soldiers, recruitment
Episcopal Church, 206, 207, 221
  See also Anglicans; Catholic Church; Church of England; Henry VIII
"Era of Good Feeling," 241
executions, 87, 183, 236
  See also Guy Fawkes' Day
Exodus, 72
ex post facto laws, 178

Falmouth, 124
"False Frenchmen," 127
famine, 187
Faneuil Hall, 256
feast days, 38
Federalist Papers, 45
Federalists, 219, 228, 230, 235–36, 254, 299
   See also Anti-Federalists
Federal Republican, 235
fiat, 233
fiat of Mary, 71
the '15 (Jacobite Rebellion), 31
First Amendment, 153, 206, 207
"First Citizen," 99–109, 125, 178
   See also "Antilon"; "Second Citizen"
First Continental Congress, 110–12, 128
   See also Continental Congress
Fitzgerald, John, 164, 166
Fitzherbert, Maria, 251
Fitzhugh, William, 149, 151
Fitzredmond, William, 32
Fitzsimons, Thomas, 194
Flanders, 33, 37, 51
Flavia (slave), 234
flotilla, 181
Folly Farm, 225, 238, 252
   See also Carroll, Charles, of Carrollton, relationships, with Homewood
Fort Edward, 162
Fort George, 139
Fort McHenry, 256
Fort Ticonderoga, 129, 136, 162
Fort Washington, 147
Founding Fathers, 45, 70, 73, 121, 144, 153
   See also individual names of Founding Fathers
Fourth of July, 143–44, 247, 256, 259
   See also Declaration of Independence
France, 24, 29, 33, 57, 164, 167
   See also French alliance; French America; French and Indian War; French Revolution; Paris
Franklin, Benjamin, 33, 73, 142, 162

   and Canadian campaign, 131, 134, 137
   and the Great Seal, 72
   kite of, 193
   letters, 119, 135, 167
   "Plain Truth," 132
   quip on rhyme, 144
   relationship with Carrolls, 132
   as sage of Philadelphia, 121, 193
   works of, 259
Freemasons, 50, 194
   See also Masonic rituals
freemen, 24, 116–17, 149–52
French alliance, 128, 140, 166–68, 181, 188, 194, 204
French America, 47, 53
French and Indian War, 46, 76, 136
French diarist, 17, 18, 34, 73, 161
French Revolution, 204, 210
funerals, 106, 183, 188, 261
   See also Catholic Church; rites; sacraments

Gage, General, 124
Gallatin, Albert, 235
Gallicans, 50
Galloway, James, 160
Galloway, Joseph, 111
Garrison, William Lloyd, 246
Gates, Horatio, 140, 147, 163, 166, 180–81, 184, 196
The Genuine Principles of the Ancient Saxon, or English Constitution, 143
George I, 30, 31, 32
George III, 67, 111, 126, 130, 141–43, 167
George IV, 220, 251
Georgetown University, 229–30
   See also Carroll, Rev. John
Gerard, Ambassador, 176, 189
Gerard, Thomas, 22–23
Germain, Lord George, 160
Germans, 161
Germantown, 162, 220
Gibbon, Edward, 43
Gibson, John, 41
Girard, Stephen, 246
Glasgow, 82

[353]

Glorious Revolution, 27–30, 68, 105, 125, 143, 149
Godwin, William, 43
gold, 77, 137, 187, 241
  See also currency; silver; specie
"Golden Thighs," 129
Gordon, Lord George, 126
Gothic tribes, 69
Grace (slave), 84
Gracie, Archibald, 244
Gracie Mansion, 244
Grasse, Comte de, 189, 190
Graves, William, 74, 90, 91, 120
Great Britain, 18, 31, 112, 125, 128, 154, 203, 231, 235
  rapprochement with, 194–96
  See also British Crown; British Empire; England; mother country
Great Depression, 224
"Great Legislator of the Universe," 69
Great Seal of the United States, 72, 194
Greek, 38, 125
  See also Latin
Greene, Nathaniel, 184, 185, 191
Grey, General, 162
Grotius, Hugo, 27
gunpowder, 46, 118, 124, 137
Gunpowder Plot, 32, 91
Guy Fawkes' Day, 90–91, 124

habeas corpus, 126
habitants, 130, 138
Halifax, Marquis of, 34
Hall, Basil, 241
Hall, John, 110, 150, 151
Hamilton, Alexander, 79, 144, 153, 163–65, 171, 193, 229
Hammond, John, 57, 150
Hammond, Matthias, 106, 110
Hammond, Nicholas, 213
Hancock, John, 118, 134, 137, 145, 146
Hannibal, 130
Hanson, Alexander Contee, 235
Hanson, John, 181–82
Harding, Mr., 253

Harlem Heights, 147
Harper, Charles Carroll, 232, 243, 253
Harper, Charlotte, 253
Harper, Kitty, 233, 240, 244
  See also Carroll, Catherine (daughter)
Harper, Mary Diana, 241
Harper, Robert Goodloe, 226, 228–29, 232, 233, 240, 244, 248, 249, 253
Harriet (slave), 225
Harry (carpenter slave), 234
Harry Browne (slave), 83–84
Hart, Governor John, 32
Harvard, 33, 243, 244
Hay, P. C., 258
Head of Elk, 161
Henrietta Maria, Queen, 21, 22
Henry (slave), 83
Henry, John
Henry, Patrick, 73
Henry VIII, 19, 71, 90, 117, 143
  See also Catholic Church; Church of England; England, Reformation
heretics, 23, 24, 215
Hervey, Louisa Caton, 242
  See also Caton, Louisa
Hervey, Sir Felton Bathurst, 242
hierarchy, 44, 45, 70, 72, 129, 139, 153, 207, 247
Hindman, William, 216
History of England (Hume), 28
Hockley Mills, 209
Hoffman, Ronald, 42
Hogan, Fr., 247
Hollyday, James, 36
Hollyoke, Ann, 244
Holy Roman Empire, 42
  See also Catholic Church
Homewood House, 111, 221–26, 234, 240
Homony Club, 78, 89, 110
honor, 157, 164–65
  See also code duello; England, code of honor
Hood, Zachariah, 78–79
Hook, Paulus, 180

Horace, 48, 259
horse, 246
Hot Springs, 166
House of Commons, 55, 75
House of Delegates, 26, 35, 81, 97, 101, 109, 158, 171–79, 195, 197, 206, 213, 252
   See also individual names of delegates
Howard, John Eager, 184, 220, 236, 238–39, 249, 256
Howard, Peggy Chew, 236
   See also Chew, Peggy
Howe, General, 146–47, 159–62, 168
Hudson-Champlain waterway, 127, 134, 140, 146
Hudson Cliffs, Manhattan, 147
Hudson River, 134, 135, 162, 163
   See also Hudson-Champlain waterway
human law, 20, 68
Hume, David, 19, 28, 43, 68, 69, 74, 105, 125
Hussites, 24
hydropower, 246
   See also electricity; Franklin, Benjamin, kite of

idolatry, 23, 46, 61
Ignatius Loyola, St., 38, 39
   See also Jesuits; Society of Jesus
Illinois-Wabash, 174
indentured servants, 35, 36, 83, 84, 94, 118, 160–61, 185
   See also black people; negroes; slavery; slaves
independence, 14, 65, 73, 125, 172
   See also American Revolution; Declaration of Independence; individual names of agents
Independent Whigs, 97, 99, 100, 103, 109, 141
   See also Popular Party; Whigs
Index of Forbidden Books, 43
Indiana, 174
   St. François, 127
individualism, 18–19, 27, 43, 70, 145
inflation, 152, 157, 170, 174, 177

Ingle, Richard, 25
Inner Harbor, 188
Inner Temple, London, 27, 58–60
inoculations, 138–39, 186
   See also disease; smallpox
Inquisition, 127
Institutes (Justinian), 48
interest, 31, 234
   compound, 85
   payments, 169, 230
   private vs. public, 171–73
   rates, 77, 209, 230
the Irish, 28, 29, 69, 78, 159–61, 215, 218
   in army, 160–61, 164, 189–90
   Catholics, 18, 19, 49, 161, 164, 190
   identity, 29, 47, 251
   indentured servants, 84
   in Pennsylvania, 189–90
   Protestants, 32
Iron Works. See Baltimore Iron Works
Isle aux Noix, 135
Italians, 56
   See also Rome; Vatican
ius naturale, 18
   See also natural law
Izadod (slave), 224

Jackson, Andrew, 254, 255
Jacobite Rebellion, 31
Jacobites, 28, 29, 57, 105, 210n3
James I, 19, 20, 21, 37
   See also British Crown; England; Gunpowder Plot; Guy Fawkes Day; Jacobites; Scotland
James II, 19, 27, 28, 105, 126
   See also British Crown; England; Glorious Revolution; Scotland
Jansenists, 50
jaundice, 190
   See also Carroll, Charles, of Homewood; disease
Jay, John, 73, 128, 132, 167, 176
Jay Treaty, 213, 214
Jefferson, Thomas, 69–70, 121, 145, 173, 190, 230, 231
   in the American constellation, 257

death of, 256
and Declaration of Independence, 141–43, 144, 256
and the Great Seal, 72
as president, 228–31
and revolution, 216–18
as Secretary of State, 205, 215
Jemima (slave), 187
Jenifer, Daniel of St. Thomas, 104, 112, 141, 157
  chosen as president, 155
  defection, 117
  gunpowder requested of, 118
  on Maryland, 148
Jenison, John, 41, 54
Jennings, Edmund, 90
Jennings, Thomas, 110
Jersey, 236
Jesuits, 21, 22, 41, 50, 64, 149
  dissolution, 51, 53
  and education, 36, 37, 40
  evangelism of Native Americans, 23
  expulsion, 50, 51, 79
  influence, 43, 50
  in Maryland, 23, 92, 131
  ratio studiorum, 38
  See also Society of Jesus; St. Omers; individual names
Jews, 24, 73
John (slave), 234
Johns Hopkins University, 111, 221
Johnson, Joshua, 95, 109, 120, 191
Johnson, Louisa Catherine, 120
Johnson, Thomas, 95–96, 97, 110, 149, 161
  as governor, 155
  praised by Carrollton, 178
  request from Carrollton, 167
  on vigilante justice, 156
John the Baptist, 46
  allusion to, 231
judicial review, 152, 219
juries, 24, 27, 68, 92, 155, 195, 229
jurymen, 155
Justinian, 48

Kalb, Baron de, 167, 181
Kennebec River, 129
Kent Island, 25
Ketchum, Richard, 134
"King in Parliament," 67
Kings Mountain, 184

labor, 36, 83–84
  See also black people; negroes; slavery; slaves
Lac du Saint Sacrement, 135
  See also Lake George
"Ladies' Light Infantry," 146, 147
Lafayette, Marquis de, 181, 187, 256
Lake Champlain, 129, 135, 162
  See also Hudson-Champlain waterway
Lake George, 134, 139
  See also Lac du Saint Sacrement
Lancaster, 162
"the last of the Romans," 261
Latin, 38, 39, 86
  See also Greek; mottoes, in Latin
Latin America, 231
Latrobe, Benjamin Henry, 98, 145, 252–53
Latrobe, John H. B., 98, 99, 113, 220, 247
  as lawyer, 252–53
  relationship with the Carrolls, 252–54
laudanum, 175, 223
  See also Carroll, Molly, addiction; disease; opium
Laurens, John, 57
laws
  ex post facto, 178
  penal, 30, 46, 47, 49, 157
  Roman and civil, 48, 59
  tax, 191
  tender, 156–59, 171–72, 174–75, 179, 194
  See also common law; divine law; lawsuits; natural law; individual names of Acts
lawsuits, 59, 204, 233, 244
  Carrolls and, 58, 65, 82, 95–96, 209, 244
  by servants, 22
Lee, Arthur, 57, 161, 176

Lee, Charles, 119, 147, 182
Lee, Henry "Light-Horse Harry," 180, 235
Lee, Richard Henry, 118
Lee, Robert E., 235
Lee, Thomas Sim, 189, 190
Lee, William, 126
Leeds, Duke of, 242
"Legion," 117
Le Havre, 243
Lent, 91
Leonard, Lewis, 108, 189
Leo XIII, 44
Lewis, William, 22
Lexington and Concord, 117, 119, 135
libel, 93–94
liberty, 45, 47, 50–51, 80, 90, 97, 100–103, 106, 122, 145, 152, 215
  in America, 145, 147, 217, 229, 255, 257
  civil, 53, 248
  empire of, 75, 96, 193
  enemies of, 156
  in England, 68, 69
  land of, 117
  public, 75, 152
  right of, 142, 153, 180
  spirit of, 78–80
  See also American Revolution; Declaration of Independence; Declaration of Rights; rights
libraries, 43, 144, 209, 219
  See also books
Liège, 195–96, 211
Lingan, James Maccubin, 236
literacy, 144
  See also books
Liverpool, 243
Locke, John, 43, 120, 121, 152
Lombard Street, 188, 241, 258, 259, 260
London, 27, 33, 49, 54, 55, 80, 194, 243
  and Carrollton, 89, 90
  merchant wealth, 82
  See also England
London Magazine, 194

Long Island, 146
Louisiana, 46, 47, 127, 228
Louis XV, 46, 47, 50
Louis XVI, 140, 167, 168, 189
  See also Marie-Antoinette, Queen
Louvain, Sack of, 39
Low, Isaac, 126
Lower House, 126
loyalists, 108, 117, 118, 149, 154, 177, 220
  aristocrats, 156
  army of, 184
  exiled, 160
  See also British Crown; England; mother country
Loyola, St. Ignatius, 38, 39, 109
  See also Jesuits; Society of Jesus
Lumbrozo, Jacob, 24
Lutherans, 23
luxuries, 221–22
"Lycurgus," 199

macaroni, 146
  See also Yankees
MacIntyre, Alasdair, 255
Maclay, William, 203
Macready, William, 258
Madewell, Mr., 233
Madison, James, 201, 205, 215, 230, 235, 237, 245
Magdalen, 83–84
Magee, Alexander, 149
Magna Carta, 68, 69, 71
Magotty, 238
Maine, 124, 127, 129
maior et sanior pars, 71, 142
Manhattan, 143, 147
manifest destiny, 246–48
Mariana, 50
Marie-Antoinette, Queen, 51
  See also Louis XVI
Marie-Thérèse, Empress, 51
Marshall, John, 200–201, 213–14, 219, 255
Martin, Luther, 201
martyrs, 37, 94
Mary, Mother of God, 71
Mary II, 28

See also William and Mary
Maryland, 18, 26, 34, 66, 102, 147
  Assembly, 109
  attacked, 25
  battalion desertions, 160
  under Carrollton's leadership, 119
  Catholic population, 148
  Catholics in, 17, 34, 47, 57, 89, 91, 106, 143, 145, 146
  charters, 22, 23, 30, 47, 57, 173
  Constitution, 150–54, 179
  contributions to war effort, 148
  currency, 77
  early legislation, 24, 29–30
  elites and power, 148, 192, 229, 239
  founding of government, 22, 148, 158
  independence, 140–43
  navy, 181
  politics in, 99, 104, 106, 108, 110
  preparation for invasion, 186
  regiments, 184
  and religion, 24, 33, 153
  society, 17–18, 26, 32–34, 49, 54, 57, 89, 94, 98
  sources of troops, 160
  and taxes, 177
  voting, 150
Maryland Committee of Correspondence, 110, 115–16
Maryland Constitution, 150–54, 165, 171–73, 178, 179
Maryland Convention, 115, 117, 119, 140, 141, 147, 148
Maryland Council, 28
Maryland Gazette, 67, 88, 97, 99–108, 178, 187, 188
Maryland Line, 146–48, 180, 236
"Marylando-Hibernus," 29
  See also Carroll, Charles, of Annapolis (father)
Mason, Sally, 42
Masonic rituals, 247
  See also Freemasons
Mass, 36, 139, 183, 190, 230, 249, 251
  daily, 38
  prohibition of, 20, 30
  and tolerance, 26

See also Catholic Church; Communion; rites; sacraments
Massachusetts, 25, 71, 72, 80, 107, 122, 123, 193
Massachusetts Bay, 24, 25, 123
Massachusetts Convention, 127
Mathews, Dr., 234
Matson, Cathy, 75
Mayhew, Jonathan, 71, 72
McCulloch vs. Maryland, 201
McHenry, James, 236
McKean, Thomas, 57
McTavish, Emily, 227, 252
  See also Caton, Emily
McTavish, John, 252, 260
Meara, 184
mechanical company, 78
Meminimus, et ignoscimus, 106
mercantilism, 75–78
Mercer, John Francis, 201, 202, 230
Mercury, 247
Meschianza ball, 168
metaphor, of starlight, 261
  See also Adams, John; Carroll, Charles, of Carrollton; constellation metaphor; Jefferson, Thomas
Middle Ages, 18
Middle Temple, 57
military, 124, 146, 160, 164, 165, 189, 237
  See also army; discipline, military; soldiers; troops; individual names of leaders
militia, 118, 147, 149–50, 153, 154, 163, 165, 189, 238
  Catholics barred, 47
  private, 117, 235
  republican, 123
  and Sons of Liberty, 78
  See also army; soldiers; troops; individual names of leaders
Miralles, Juan de, 183
Missouri Compromise, 245
mixed constitution, 18, 28, 44, 67, 79
mixed government, 28, 44, 45, 72, 101, 103, 106, 107, 143, 151
mobs, 13, 53, 78–79, 94, 116–17, 126,

143, 156, 159, 173, 181, 235, 259
  See also vigilantes
Mohawk, 127
  See also Native Americans
Molasses Act (1733), 76
Molly (slave), 83
monarchies, 19, 43–45, 72, 111, 126, 141, 201, 251
  code of honor, 165
  constitutional, 259
  and Parliament, 28
  and revolutions, 243
  and Washington, 96
monasteries, 18, 57, 65
monks, 248
Monroe, James, 245
Montcalm, General, 53
  See also Canada; Quebec City; Seven Years' War
Montesquieu, Baron de, 43, 72, 74, 79, 119
  on liberty, 45, 103
  on natural law, 43–44
  on republics, 228
  on the Senate, 153
  on subsidiarity, 44–45
Montgomery, Richard, 130, 136
Monticello, 214
Montreal, 128–30, 136–37
  See also Canada; Quebec
moral sense, 71, 121–22, 129, 133, 164, 193, 228, 247, 255, 256
More, St. Thomas, 71
Morris, Gouverneur, 169
Morris, John B., 247
Moses, 22, 72
Moses (slave), 245
mother country, 144
  loyalty to, 75–76, 111
  protest against, 76
  and trade, 77, 95, 110
  See also British Crown; British Empire; England; Great Britain
mottoes, in Latin, 27, 37, 38, 39, 56, 106, 192, 194
Moylan, Stephen, 123, 141
munitions, 119, 169
  See also armaments

murders, 50, 128, 183, 225
Murdoch, William, 231
Murray, Dr., 251
mutinies, 189

Nanny (slave), 83
Napoleon, 230, 231, 233, 237, 241, 250
  See also Bonaparte, Madame Jerome
narcissism, 121, 224–25
National Journal, 258
National Republican party, 260
Native Americans, 23, 28, 46, 127, 129, 133, 139, 204, 210, 255
  Abenaki (of Maine), 127;
  and Jesuits, 23
  Mohawk, 127;
  St. François tribe, 127
natural law, 27, 30, 42–43, 67–70, 100
  and conscience, 71
  distortion by Jefferson, 145
  as foundation for government, 142–43
  individualistic take on, 255
Neales, 37
negroes, 47, 224, 261
  See also African-Americans; black people; Carrolls, and slaves; slavery; slaves; individual names
Neill, William, 119
Nelly (slave), 234
New England, 123, 129, 131, 134–35, 146–47, 180
  See also colonies; colonists; individual states
Newfoundland, 21
New Jersey, 154, 162, 182, 189, 229
New Light theology, 71, 129, 256
Newman, John Henry, 107
Newmarket races, 55
Newport, 24, 72–73, 181
New York City, 77, 94, 132, 134, 141, 235
  British in, 146
  consequences of loss, 147
  exposed to attack, 162–63
  martial spirit in, 133
New-York Historical Society, 259

New York State, 81
Nicholas of Cusa, 71
Nicholson (town major), 139
Niles' Weekly Register, 255
noblesse oblige, 74
non-associators, 116–17
nonexportation, 112
nonimportation, 77, 94–96, 110, 112, 116
non-popery, 181
Normans, 69
Northern army, 123–24, 139, 187
Northwest annexation, 127
Northwest Ordinance (1787), 207
Nova Scotia, 34, 195
nox vomica, 246
nuns, 194

Oates, Titus, 25–26, 27
oaths, 24
O'Carroll, Tiege, 18
O'Carrolls, chiefs of Ely, 18, 19
   See also individual Carroll names
Ockham, William of, 18–19, 42
officers' fees, 97, 101, 107
   See also army; military; soldiers; troops
Ogle, Henrietta Hill, 191
Ohio River, 126, 246
Old Hickory, 254, 255
"Old Nick" (Satan), 79
   See also the Devil
oligarchy, 96
Oliver, Robert, 240
Onuf, Peter, 75
opium, 49, 89, 120–21, 175
   See also Carroll, Molly, addiction; disease; laudanum
Otis, James, 72
Otter, 119

Paca, William, 57, 79, 89, 97, 101, 106, 109, 110
Pacas, 112
Paine, Thomas, 122
Paoli ambush, 162
paper money, 77, 82, 157, 169, 170, 194, 197, 198
   for confiscated property, 177
   as legal tender, 179
   payments to Carrollton, 174
   See also currency; printed money
papists, 21–24, 32, 35, 46, 90–91, 96, 149, 166, 183
   See also anti-papists; anti-popery; popists
pardons, 185
Paris, 43, 46–48, 64, 167, 208, 243
   See also College of Paris; France; Treaty of Paris
parlements, 50–51
Parliamentary Register, 194
Patience (slave), 245
Patriot, 231
patriotism, 75, 90, 101, 164, 166
patriot party, 96, 97
patriots, 99, 101, 106, 110, 117, 118
   and bribery, 95
   Carrollton as, 90, 104, 116, 131, 148, 246, 257
   increase to militia, 124, 163
   in Maryland, 104, 115, 148
   optimism of, 132
   spirits of, 154
   See also America; Declaration of Independence; loyalists; individual names
patronage, 101, 155
Patterson, Betsy, 233, 242
   See also Bonaparte, Madame Jerome
Patterson, Mary Ann, 242
   marriage to Marquis of Wellesley, 250–51
   See Caton, Mary Ann (granddaughter)
Patterson, Robert, 233
Paulding, James K., 241
Peale, Charles Willson, 89, 120
Peale, Rembrandt, 244
peerage, 21
Peggy Stewart, 112–13, 115, 116
penal laws, 30, 46, 47, 49, 157
   See also laws
Penn, William, 24
Pennsylvania, 24, 81, 122, 148, 189, 194, 199, 203, 220

Catholic rights in, 208
government, 150, 204, 205
Irish in, 161, 190
and troops, 147, 161
pensioners, 193
persecution, 112, 128, 156
  of Catholics, 17, 19, 46–49, 52, 106
  religious, 22, 27, 53, 91, 99
"personal attachment," 100
Persons, Fr. Robert, 37
petitions, 174, 177
Petyt, William, 69
Philadelphia, 77, 94, 110–11, 133, 138, 141, 146, 189, 247
  boycotts, 78, 94
  and Britain, 154, 168
  and Carrolls, 88, 119, 132, 141, 161, 236, 259
  fall of, 162
  financiers of, 82
  and Harriet Carroll, 220, 221, 238, 240, 250
  the sage of, 121, 193 *See also* Franklin, Benjamin
Philadelphia Convention, 197, 201
philosophes, 50
physiognomy, 102
Pickering, Judge, 228
The Pillars of Priestcraft and Orthodoxy Shaken, 72
Pinckney, Charles Cotesworth, 216
Pinckney, Thomas, 215
Pise, Charles C., 240–41, 248, 260
Pitt, William, 55, 76
Pius V, 20
Pius VI, 130
Pius XI, 200
placemen, 81, 92, 97, 100
"Plain Truth" (Franklin), 132
Plan of Union, 111
plantation management, 83, 120, 244, 246
  See also Carrolls, and slaves; slavery; slaves
planters, 47, 73, 98, 101
  debt, 94–95
  and finances, 226
  in Maryland, 29, 34, 35, 77, 226

vs. populists, 148–50
Princes of Ireland, Planters of Maryland (Hoffman and Mason), 42
  and slaves, 213, 214
  Southern, 59, 259
"plundering time," 25
plutocracy, 171
Plymouth Colony, 22
poetry, 236, 247
  by Broomstick and Quoad, 109
  by Dulany, Jr., 87–88
  by Franklin, 135
  See also rhymes
politics of interest, 165, 172, 188, 193
politics of will, 19, 28, 179, 225, 230, 259
poll tax, 150
  See also taxes
Pompadour, Madame de, 50
popists, 22–27, 30, 127, 132, 167
  See also anti-papists; anti-popery; papists
Poplar Island incident, 186, 187
Popular Party, 97–98
popular sovereignty, 21, 27, 43, 70, 142, 151, 200
popular will, 80, 119, 142, 148, 151, 254, 255
population, 81, 126–27, 147, 148, 193, 251
populists, 148–50, 254
portraits, 56, 102, 192, 220, 253
Portugal, 50
Potomac Company, 81, 246
Potomac River, 81, 187, 246
Powis, Lord, 27
prenuptial agreements, 87, 250
  See also Carroll, Charles, of Carrollton; Patterson, Mary Ann
Prerogative Court, 31
Presbyterians, 23, 129, 164, 190
Princes of Ireland, Planters of Maryland (Hoffman and Mason), 42
Princeton University, 129, 154
print, 43, 48, 144, 196, 222
printed money, 183–84
  See also currency; paper money
privateers, 167, 211

[361]

See also citizen-soldiers; military; militia; soldiers
Proclamation of 1763, 173
Proctor's Pennsylvania Artillery, 161
Prometheus, 193
promissory notes, 130, 138
    See also credit; currency; debt; specie
propaganda, 122, 133
Propaganda Fide, 207, 208
    See also Catholic Church; Vatican
property qualifications, 150–51, 152, 171, 187, 219
prostitutes, 124, 137
"Protestant Declaration," 25
"Protestant Planter," 109
Protestant Revolution, 29
Provincial Council of Baltimore, 247
Pufendorf, Samuel von, 27
Pulaski's Legion, 148
punishment, 164, 219
    of deserters, 236–37
    of slaves, 224–25
    See also discipline, military; slaves, and punishment
purgatory, 183
Puritans, 21–26, 44
"pursuit of happiness" (Jefferson), 142, 198, 255
    See also Declaration of Rights; Jefferson, Thomas; rights
pursuivants, 19, 78
Purviance, Samuel, 118, 119

Quadragesimo anno (Pius XI)
Quakers, 24
quarantine, 139
Quebec, 53, 126, 134, 136–38
Quebec Act (1774), 126–28, 130, 173
Quebec City, 129–34
    See also Canada; Montcalm, General; Seven Years' War
Quincy, Josiah, 99, 135, 258
quitrents, 35, 81
quotas, 146, 160, 185

Racine, Jean, 48
railroads, 244, 246, 247
    See also Baltimore and Ohio Railroad
Rapin, Paul de, 43, 69
Razolini, Onorio, 40
recruits. See also enlistments; military; soldiers, recruitment; troops
recusancy, 20, 21, 156
redcoats, 189
    See also American Revolution; army; England; loyalists; patriots; soldiers
Reed, Governor, 148
Reformation. See under England
refugees, 179, 236
Regnans in Excelsis (Pius V), 20
relics, 257, 261
    See also Carroll, Charles, of Carrollton; Catholic Church
religion. See Carroll, Charles of Carrollton, and religion; Catholic Church; Catholics
religious tolerance, 22–25, 105, 140, 145–46, 153, 207, 208
Religious Toleration Act (1649), 22, 23, 25, 47
Republican Advocate, 217
Republican Empire, 73–75, 193, 257
republicanism, 123, 193, 198
Republicans, 235–36, 260
    See also individual names of Republicans
republican virtue, 44, 51, 98, 100, 138, 165
republics, 43–45, 70, 153
    See also Republican Empire
Restoration, 26, 69
Reynolds, Sir Joshua, 56
Rezin (slave), 234
Rheims, 43
Rhode Island, 24, 72–73, 80
rhymes, 144
    See also poetry
Richelieu River, 134, 135
Ridgely, Charles, 113
Ridout, Horatio, 230
Ridouts, 156
Riedesel, Frederika von, 175
rights, 142

to bear arms, 185
Catholic civil, 106, 208
and common law, 70
jurying, 24 *See also* juries
liberty, 180
natural, 14, 70, 71, 122, 142, 144, 174
property, 178–80, 185–86
pursuit of happiness, 142, 198, 255
resistance to tyranny, 50, 71
trial by jury, 69, 126
voting, 14, 30–32, 47, 67, 150
See also Declaration of Independence; Declaration of Rights; liberty
rites, 22, 183
last, 260–61
See also Catholic Church; Communion; funerals; Mass; sacraments
Robert Bellarmine, St., 20, 21, 37, 43
Rochambeau, General, 181, 186, 191
Roman Empire, 69, 193
See also Holy Roman Empire; "the last of the Romans"; individual names
Rome, 69, 91, 205, 207–8
See also Catholic Church; Italians; Vatican
Roosevelt, Theodore, 133
Roundheads, 23
Rousseau, Jean-Jacques, 43
Roziers, 37
Russia, 237
Rutledge, John, 217

Sack of Louvain, 39
sacraments, 129–30, 249
See also Catholic Church; Communion; funerals; Mass; rites
Saints, 249
See also Catholic Church; names of individuals and institutions; relics
salt, 119, 154, 170
saltpeter, 119
See also armaments; munitions
salvation, 33, 84, 220
Sanderson's, 253–54
Sandwich, Earl of, 135

Saratoga, 161–63, 166, 175
Saratoga (Ketchum), 134
Satan ("Old Nick"), 79
See also the Devil
Savannah, 180, 185
Saxon myth, 69–70, 143
schism, 23, 100, 247
See also Catholic Church; Holy Roman Empire
Schuyler, Philip, 129, 130, 134, 140, 163
Scotch Peggy, 113
Scotland, 121
the Scots, 84, 95, 121, 156, 160–61, 190, 199
Scott, Dr., 223
Scotus, John Duns, 19
Sears (slave overseer), 234–35
Sears, James, 187
"Second Citizen," 99–100
See also "Antilon"; "First Citizen"
secularism, 43
seigneurial system, 127
seigneurs, 138
seminaries, 102, 229, 230
"A Senator," 178
senators
See also individual names of senators
sensus fidei, 179
Separatists, 23
Seven Years' War, 68
See also Canada; Montcalm, General; Quebec City
Sewalls, 37
Shaftesbury, Lord, 121
Sharpe, Governor, 35, 46–47, 51–53, 77, 79
Shipley, George, 115
Sidney, Algernon, 69
the Signer, 102, 143–46, 220–24, 227, 232, 238, 241, 247, 252–58, 261
See also Carroll, Charles, of Carrollton
"Silk Stocking Infantry," 146
silver, 77, 137
See also currency; gold; specie
slavery, 18, 49, 245
See also African-Americans; black

people; Carrolls, slaves; negroes; slaves; white indentured servants
slaves, 127
  and Baltimore Iron Works, 36
  compensation for, 185–86
  education of, 245
  enlistment, 185–86
  field vs. house, 83
  Guinea, 161
  indentured servants, 36, 84, 94
  and Jesuits, 23
  manumission, 213, 245
  overseers, 246
  owners, 185
  and punishment, 83–84, 118, 224–25, 244–46
  social cohesion, 186
  threat of rebellion, 118
  used to spread infection, 124
  West Indian, 118
  See also Carrolls, and slaves; individual names of owners and slaves
smallpox, 124, 137–39
  See also disease; inoculations
Smallwood, William, 123–24, 146–47, 156, 161–62
Smithfield fires, 46
smuggling, 37, 51, 76, 94, 109
Society of Jesus, 23, 37, 50, 51
  See also Catholic Church; Jesuits; St. Omers; individual names
soldiers, 124, 147, 189, 193
  American, 152, 160, 161, 190
  bounties, 160, 165
  British, 124, 160–61
  Catholic, 124
  conditions, 137–38, 164, 181–82, 185, 186
  European, 164
  French, 181
  hardships, 137, 138, 164
  plundering, 182, 187, 237
  Quebecois, 130
  recruitment, 130, 154, 161, 185
  See also enlistment; military; militia; troops; individual unit and leader names
Somerset County, 154, 156

Sons of Liberty, 78, 79, 108
Sorel River, 136
the South, 73, 123, 147, 180, 184, 187, 259
South Carolina, 180, 181, 260, 261
sovereignty, 19, 27–28, 70–72, 142
Spa Creek, 17, 34, 89, 187, 191, 192, 221
the Spanish, 21, 42, 56, 127, 176, 183, 231
  See also colonialism; colonies; colonization
Spanish Doctor, 42
  See also Suarez, Francisco
Spartanism, 222
specie, 77, 130, 169 194, 170, 185
  See also currency; gold; silver
speculators, 173, 177
spirit, 49–50, 77–78, 91–92, 107, 111, 121–23, 133–34, 147, 154, 164, 202, 255
  of liberty, 78–80
  See also Carroll, Charles, of Carrollton, spirit
The Spirit of Laws (Montesquieu), 45
Squiers (servant), 84
"Squire Carroll," 34
  See also Carroll, Charles, of Annapolis (father)
Squire Carroll's Point, 192
Stafford, Lady, 242
  See also Caton, Betsy
Stamp Act (1765), 67, 73–78, 80–81, 89, 94
stamp agents, 78
stamped paper, 78, 79
St. Andrew's University, 121
Star Chamber, 150
St. Charles' Seminary, 230
St. Elizabeth Seton's school, 241
St. John 136, 138
Ste.-Marie (Quebec) 130
sterling, 179
  See also currency; gold; silver; specie
Sterling, Rev. James, 46
Sterne, Laurence, 121
Steuart, Richard, 98
Steuben, Baron von, 164

Stevenson, Dr., 156
Stewart, Anthony, 112–13
Stewart, Peggy, 113
St. François tribe, 127
Stirling, General, 146
St. John's College, 229
St. Lawrence River, 130
St. Mary's Church, 248
St. Mary's City, 28
stock, 187, 195, 209, 229, 235, 241
Stoicism, 18, 19, 62, 63, 121
St. Omers, 31, 33, 37–39, 41, 43, 51, 102
  See also Carroll, Charles, of Carrollton; education; Jesuits; seminaries
Stone, Governor William, 25
Stone, Thomas, 141
Stonyhurst, 51
Stony Point, 180
St. Patrick's Day, 124, 126
  See also Boston; Washington, George
St. Paul's Cathedral, 55
Stuart, Gilbert, 220
Stuarts, 21, 26, 28, 29, 51, 57, 72, 102
the Pretender, 32
  See also British Crown; individual names of rulers
Suarez, Francisco, 42–44, 50
subsidiarity, 44, 70, 72, 153, 200
Suffolk Resolves, 128
suffrage, 150, 198, 218, 229
  See also elections; rights; voting
Sugar Act (1764), 76
Sully, Thomas, 102
surrender and regrant policy, 19–20
"Suspending Act," 30
Susquehanna Canal Company, 230

Tacitus, 69, 96, 100
Tametsi, 41
Taney, Roger, 252
tariffs. *See* taxes; individual names of Acts and countries
Tarleton, Banastre, 180, 185
taxes, 23, 29, 71, 98–99, 103, 169, 173, 177, 191
  coach excise, 241

  collection in kind, 170
  on colonies, 77, 80, 94–95, 109, 151, 152, 197
  double, 47, 52, 157
  high, 26, 45, 77, 169, 177, 241
  laws on, 191
  molasses, 76
  poll, 150
  tea, 109, 112, 115
  tobacco, 29
  triple, 177
  unconstitutional, 110
  See also individual names of Acts
tea, 86, 175, 211
  Dutch, 109
  on Peggy Stewart, 112–13
  tax, 94, 112
  untaxed, 115
  See also Boston Tea Party; Tea Act
Tea Act (1773), 108–10
temperance, 34, 75, 232, 258
"Temple of Virtue," 192
tender law, 156–59, 171–72, 174–75, 179, 194
  See also laws
Teutons, 69
Thomas, General, 137, 138, 139
Thomas Aquinas, St., 18, 19, 42, 44, 70, 72
Thomas More, St., 71
"Three American Graces," 240–42, 252
Ticknor, George, 241
Tilghman, Edward, 57
Tilghman, Matthew, 177
Tilghman, Richard, 57
Tilghman, Tench, 147, 190
Tilghmans, 67, 169
tobacco, 22, 33, 101, 109, 170, 173
  market, 83, 95, 98, 119
  nonexportation, 112
  tax, 29
Tocqueville, Alexis de, 259
Todd, Mr., 185
Toleration Act (1674), 25
  See also Religious Toleration Act (1649)
Tom (slave), 245

Tories, 57, 80, 102, 117, 140, 149, 156, 166, 178, 181, 191, 194
   See also confiscations, of Tory property; individual names of Tories
Toronto, 237
   See also Canada; Canadian campaign; War of 1812; York
"To the Public," 178
Tower of London, 27
Townshend, Charles, 94
Townshend Acts (1767), 81, 94–96
   duties from, 81
trade, 169, 178, 194, 212
   boycotts, 77, 78, 94, 95, 197
   embargoes, 74, 110 172, 230–35
   with Native Americans, 133 See also colonies; currency; mother country; names of individual Acts; taxes
   with West Indies, 214
Trajan, 96
Trappists, 248
Treatise on Education (Locke), 120
   See also education; Locke, John
Treaty of Alliance with France (1778), 168, 169
Treaty of Ghent, 237
Treaty of Paris (1783), 192, 194
Trenton, 154
trial by jury, 69, 126
   See also juries; jurymen; rights
triple tax, 177
troops, 80
   American, 124, 147–48, 156, 160–64, 180, 185
   British, 108, 137–38, 141, 147
   in Canada, 146
   Catholics in, 189–90
   conditions of, 186
   French, 181
   Northern, 124, 187
   Southern, 147
   See also army; enlistment; military; militia; soldiers
Trumbull, John, 192
Truth Teller, 98
Tudors, 19
   See also British Crown; individual names of rulers
Turks, 73
Tyndale, William, 19
tyranny, 20, 30, 43, 51, 53, 67–69, 117, 126, 136, 141, 158
   See also Declaration of Independence; despotism; liberty; rights
the "Tyrant," 141

uniforms, 146, 169, 187, 192
   See also army, conditions; redcoats; soldiers, conditions
United States Capitol Rotunda, 192
Universal History (Voltaire), 43
"Unlimited Submission" (Mayhew), 71
Upper House, 125–26
Upper Marlborough, 186

Valley Forge, 163–66, 180
Vandalia, 174
Vatican, 130
   See also Catholic Church; Rome; individual clerical and papal names
Vergil, 48
Versailles, 136
vigilantes, 116, 156, 236
   See also mobs
Virginia, 22, 67, 71, 118, 166, 170, 175, 184
   and Catholics, 73, 208
   claims, 173, 174
   and Constitution, 214
   and Maryland, 197, 202
   massacre, 180
   minister's lobbying, 33
   planters, 34
   and Potomac Company, 196
   royalists, 25
   troops, 147
"Virginius," 127
Voltaire, 43
"Voter," 109
voting, 147, 151, 191, 218
   privilege of, 31, 32, 47
   viva voce, 150, 152, 204
   See also elections; property qualifications; rights; suffrage

Index

Wallace (Tory), 156
Wallace and Company, 110, 120
War of 1812, 235–37, 241
   See also America; Canada; Canadian campaign; Toronto; York
Washington (city), 237
Washington, George, 96, 159–61, 220
   in the American constellation, 257
   and arrival of French fleet, 189
   and Canada, 124, 129
   Carrollton's view of, 122
   centennial of birth, 260
   character, 163
   on citizen-soldiers, 123
   entry into Boston, 124
   esteem of army, 180
   farewell address, 255–56
   investments, 173
   leadership of, 166–67
   and Maryland Line, 146
   and Masonic ornaments, 194
   motto, 192
   and Moylan, 141
   on patriotism, 164
   plan to block, 162–63
   portrait, 192
   request for reinforcements, 163
   resignation, 192
   retreat, 154
   signature, 153
   size of army, 160
   war tactics, 154
   withdrawal from New York, 147
Washington, Martha, 192
Washington College, 229
Washington Monument, 241, 254
Watson, Elkanah, 194
Waxhaw, Battle of, 180
Webster, Daniel, 256–58
Weehawken, 229
Weems, John, 244
Wellesley, Lady, 251
Wellesley, Marchioness of, 251
Wellesley, Marquis of, 250, 251
Wellington, Duke of, 242, 250–52
Westminster Bridge, 55
Westphalia, King of, 233

West Point, 182–83
Whig Club, 118, 156
Whigs, 80, 97, 100, 102, 107, 109, 116, 140, 149, 150
White, Fr. Andrew, 24, 37
White House, 228
white indentured servants, 36, 83–84, 94
   See also negroes; slavery; slaves
White Plains, 147
Will (slave), 84
William and Mary, 28
William and Mary (College of), 33
William III, 28, 29, 33
William IV, 242
William of Ockham, 18–19
Williams, Otho, 184, 185
Williams, Roger, 24, 28
Willoughby, Mr., 48
Wilmington, 185
Wilson, James, 72, 150
witenagemot, 69
women, 124, 137, 146, 167, 175, 227, 234, 253
   and education, 226–28
   See also Carroll, Charles, of Carrollton; dowries; prostitutes; individual names
Wooster, David, 130–31, 136, 137, 139
Worcester county, 154, 156
World War I, 39
World War II, 224, 231
writing, 43, 48, 144, 196, 222
   See also books; libraries; literacy; poetry; rhymes

Yale, 33
Yankees, 123, 135, 147
   See also macaroni
Yeo, Rev., 26
York, 162, 166, 168, 190, 237
   See also Canada; Toronto; War of 1812
York, Duke of, 26, 27
Yorktown, 188–90, 224
Youngs, 37